Cambridge South Asian Studies

CLASSICAL POLITICAL ECONOMY AND BRITISH POLICY IN INDIA

CAMBRIDGE SOUTH ASIAN STUDIES

These monographs are published by the Syndics of Cambridge Univeristy Press in association with the Cambridge University Centre for South Asian Studies. The following books have been published in this series:

CLASSICAL
POLITICAL ECONOMY AND
BRITISH POLICY IN INDIA

S. AMBIRAJAN
ASSOCIATE PROFESSOR OF ECONOMIC HISTORY
UNIVERSITY OF NEW SOUTH WALES

CAMBRIDGE UNIVERSITY PRESS
CAMBRIDGE
LONDON · NEW YORK · MELBOURNE

Published by the Syndics of the Cambridge University Press
The Pitt Building, Trumpington Street, Cambridge CB2 1RP
Bentley House, 200 Euston Road, London NW1 2DB
32 East 57th Street, New York, NY 10022, USA
296 Beaconsfield Parade, Middle Park, Melbourne 3206, Australia

© Cambridge University Press 1978

First published 1978

Photoset and printed in Malta by
Interprint (Malta) Ltd

Library of Congress Cataloguing in Publication Data
Ambirajan, S.
Classical political economy and British policy in India.
(Cambridge South Asian studies; no. 21)
Bibliography: p.
1. India – Economic policy. 2. Great Britain
– Colonies – India – Economic policy. 3. Economics
– History – To 1800. 4. Economics – History – 19th
century. I. Title. II. Series.
HC435.A629 330.9′54′03 76-21020
ISBN 0 521 21415 7

CONTENTS

For
Prabha, Amrit and Neela

ACKNOWLEDGMENTS

It is a pleasure to acknowledge the debts I owe to various individuals and institutions for the assistance they provided during the writing of this book. I have profited enormously from discussions with my colleagues and ex-colleagues at the Universities of Manchester and New South Wales; in particular I would like to thank Professor Bruce Williams, Professor Werner Stark and Mr Philip Leeson of Manchester, and Professor Gordon Rimmer and Dr Igor Gordijew of New South Wales for reading and criticising various chapters of an earlier version of the work. My thanks are also due to Professor Dharma Kumar and Dr W. J. Macpherson for invaluable comments on the final draft. My greatest debt is to Professor A. W. Coats who not only read the entire work and made many suggestions for improvement, but also gave generously his advice and encouragement. The encouragement and help received from my father, Professor K. R. Srinivasa Iyengar, at every stage of the preparation of this book is incalculable. I am greatly indebted to Stephen and Joan Bach for making my stay in England pleasant and fruitful while I was collecting material for writing this book. However I am alone responsible for errors and shortcomings that remain.

I wish to thank the Librarians of the India Office Library, British Library, London University Library, London School of Economics Library, Manchester University Library, John Rylands Library, Cambridge University Library, Bodleian Library, Library of Christchurch College, Nottingham University Library, National Archives of India, Bombay Secretariat Library, Tamilnadu Archives, Fisher Library, Public Library of New South Wales, University of New South Wales Library, Victorian State Library and National Library of Australia for providing much efficient helpfulness. I would like to thank in particular Mr Martin Moir of the India Office Library for giving valuable bibliographic assistance.

Thanks are due to the Houblon-Norman Fund, British Council, the University of Manchester and the University of New South Wales for financial assistance they provided at various times.

Finally, I must thank my wife, Prabha, for the many ways in which she has contributed to this work.

I

INTRODUCTION

Of all the instruction which the servants of the Honourable East India Company have ever brought with them from their parent land to India, that which they derived from the lectures of that truly amiable man Dr Malthus, on Political Economy, has been, perhaps, the most substantially useful to the country. Of the Civil Servants scarcely one can have discharged his duties for many years in any part of India without having often found the welfare and happiness of thousands placed in dependence upon his knowledge of the great principles of this science, and upon that feeling of assurance in the truth of its conclusions which will make him risk his reputation, and all that he holds most dear, in the enforcement of the measures which these conclusions prescribe.

> Sir William Sleeman
> (Officer in the Military and Civil Service of the
> Honourable East India Company)

ECONOMISTS AND INDIA

It is possible that the influence of economic events on the formation of economic theory has lessened as a consequence of the professionalisation of the discipline of economics in the past hundred years; but it has not disappeared altogether. Whether as explanation of certain economic phenomena or as prescription to cure certain economic ills, economists do take into account the hard realities, not just build theoretical structures. Whoever it may be – from Josiah Child to Joan Robinson – an economist's theoretical writings, reflect at some point the problems faced by contemporary policy makers. It could be said that economic doctrines respond to the challenge of social problems, and one can plausibly argue that the history of economic thought is the history of such intellectual responses to the social and economic problems faced from time to time.

But what of the influence of economic ideas on events? It is a palpable fact that economists – of past times as well as of the present – take themselves seriously and consider the offering of gratuitous advice to policy makers as a major role of their profession. Not only is such advice proffered, but it is also frequently claimed that economics is indispensable to the making of economic policy. Policy by definition is a particular course of action planned and carried out. The course of action is directed towards certain basic objectives, and it is to achieve these that the course of action is planned. These objectives, in their turn, spring out of human needs, aspirations and interests which call for equally varied courses of action. The function of the policy maker, is to decide which of these objectives to choose and how to achieve them. Economists usually claim with some justification that their ideas play a significant part in this process of decision making. That 'theory' should play a large part in policy formation is natural for theory is only observed actuality in some spheres of life reduced to logic. Thus theory enables us to foresee what would be the consequences of certain actions. But few policy makers are capable of creating economic ideas; they have necessarily to work on the basis of the currently dominant economic thought. Policy makers themselves have perceived this, as Pierre Mendes-France (a former French Prime Minister) and Gabriel Ardant (the General Commissioner for Productivity in France) said, 'The interaction of economic theories and policies is seen all through modern history.'[1]

For a student interested in the interaction of economic ideas and policies, India should prove rewarding because India has long been of interest to academic economists, particularly of Britain. In the early days of the East India Company, the Directors were forced to act as economic theorists in order to defend the very existence of the Company. The writings of the employees of the Company defending its commercial activities and by the critics of the Company attacking its trading operations both contributed to the development of English economic thought in the seventeenth century. Later, in 1771, when the currency situation in the Indian possessions of the East India Company became chaotic, the officials prudently referred the matter to the then leading economist, Sir James Steuart. After examining the problem he wrote the interesting pamphlet, *The Principles of Money Applied to the Present State of Coin in Bengal*. Adam Smith, of course, is well known for his strictures on the East India Company's monopoly, but the Court of Directors of the Company, in spite of his attacks on them, actually wanted to include him in a Board of Commissioners which they were planning to send to India to investigate existing administrative malpractices; although Smith was prepared to go, the Board was never in fact sent.[2] Ricardo was a shareholder of the Company and used to attend the General Court of Proprietors, and there were occasions when he addressed the General Court on economic problems. Thomas Robert Malthus and Richard Jones were two important economists who were employed by the East India Company to teach their young civil servants at the East India College

---

[1] *Economics and Action* (London, 1955), p. 13.
[2] See John Rae, *Life of Adam Smith* (London, 1895), p. 254.

established at Haileybury. James Mill made his name with a massive history of India, and later joined the East India Company as an examiner. John Stuart Mill also joined the Company as a writer and finally rose to the position of chief examiner. Francis Horner served on the Carnatic Commission from 1806 to 1809. Herman Merivale and William Thornton had both spent many years at the India Office in London as senior civil servants. James Wilson, the founder of the London *Economist* was India's first minister of finance. Besides these, Jean Baptiste Say, Robert Torrens, John Ramsay McCulloch and Karl Marx also wrote about India. Henry Fawcett, the blind Professor of Political Economy at Cambridge, wrote on Indian finance and for many years upheld Indian interests in Parliament with such zeal and knowledge that he became known as the 'Member for India'. Stanley Jevons, H. D. McLeod, Alfred Marshall and John Maynard Keynes were also concerned about Indian economic problems and all of them had at different occasions given evidence before parliamentary commissions on various aspects of the Indian economy.

Thus there was a significant body of thought (composed variously of monographic writings and policy documents as well as formal and informal discussions with policy makers and would-be civil servants) developed by generations of British economists relating to Indian economic problems. To this should be added their contributions to the theory of economic policy providing general guidance for the policy maker. The question immediately arises as to the extent of the impact of these efforts of the economists on the actual policies pursued in India. The possibilities of British economic ideas being applied to concrete Indian economic policies were considerable particularly in the hundred years after the publication of the *Wealth of Nations*, in view of the unusual circumstances in which India and its rulers were placed. The four most relevant aspects of this milieu were: (1) British attitudes towards India; (2) Structure of Indian administration; (3) Intellectual equipment of the rulers of India; and (4) Nature of British economic thought.

BRITISH ATTITUDES TOWARDS INDIA

The establishment of British rule was a novel phenomenon for India. Not that India had never been invaded before, but all the previous invaders had accepted India as their home, and had become a part of her life. The invaders had accepted the prevailing social and economic condition of the country and tried to fit themselves into it. But with the arrival of the British, India found herself placed in an entirely new political situation, with the 'centre of gravity' located outside her land, and in this way she was subjected to a class of rulers who were 'permanently alien in origin and character'.[3] Even in social and cultural life the new rulers remained foreign. The settlers adopted 'English rather than Indian standards of living and amusement'; and 'making every English settlement an exact replica, as far as possible, of an English town' was the aim.[4] This was perhaps due to what the Oxford historian Sir John Seeley has described as a clash of two cultures. The previous invaders found in India a superior culture and were, as time went on, culturally assimilated. The British, on the other hand, finding an old-established culture, were at first amazed (see, for instance, the works of Warren Hastings, William Jones, William Robertson and other early Indologists); but later, once the initial enthusiasm had cooled down, they found Indian society barbaric and set about 'civilising' it.

Till the death of Edmund Burke, the idea that India should be made a replica of England found little favour with the ruling classes. A conservative and a believer in the Natural order, Burke felt that British institutions were out of place in India. The Burkean conservative ideal was one of Imperial trusteeship. In other words, he believed that India should be allowed to develop according to her own experience and tradition, and thus Indian society should be insulated from the incursion of Western institutions, practices and prejudices. While developing according to their own cultural patterns, the people of India must nevertheless be given an opportunity to appreciate the European concept of liberty. For Burke, reform meant the expansion of existing values rather than the realisation of Utopian dreams. This conservative philosophy that the stronger country and society had a moral obligation to preserve the weaker lost its vogue after Burke. Jeremy Bentham, the utilitarian philosopher-jurist, on the other hand, thought it essential to carry out fundamental changes in Indian institutions.[5]

But it was left to his disciple James Mill to successfully introduce a certain amount of political and economic messianism into British attitudes towards India. It was James Mill who in his *History of India* made for the first time a savage frontal attack on Indian culture and Hindu civilisation and branded the whole system as barbaric and despotic. What he wanted was the transfer of Western civilisation and culture to India, and thus to impart a dynamic element into what he believed to be a stagnant society. His son John Stuart Mill also justified British rule in India in these terms and pointed out that only

---

[3]   K. S. Shelvankar, *The Problem of India* (Harmondsworth, 1940), p. 18. See also for a contemporary comment, Mrs Julia Thomas, *Letters from Madras During the Years 1836–1839* (London, 1846), p. 44.

[4]   T. G. P. Spear, *The Nabobs* (Oxford, 1963), p. 34.

[5]   See S. G. Vesey-Fitzgerald, 'Bentham and the Indian Codes' in George Keeton and Georg Schwarzenberger (eds.), *Jeremy Bentham and the Law: A Symposium* (London, 1948), p. 222.

this form of control 'which in the existing state of civilisation of the subject people, most facilitates their transition to a higher stage of improvement'.[6]

This idea that Britain's moral, intellectual and political power should be used to transform India continued to dominate British attitudes throughout the nineteenth century. Indeed many Englishmen believed that they had been chosen by Providence for the task of civilising India and that they should carry out the duties properly. F. C. Hodgson, for example, in his Le Bas Prize Essay for 1862, declared solemnly: 'We shall work out faithfully in common the task that Heaven has set us to do.'[7] Even critics of the British Empire such as Robert Knight thought that Britain should perform its duties towards India with a sense of responsibility in view of the fact that 'the all-wise Ruler of the World should have prepared the English people . . . for the guardianship and rule of nearly 200 000 000 of the human race'.[8] The British intelligentsia who ultimately provided the Indian administrators were thus taught to believe that it was the responsibility of Britain to emancipate India from the despotisms of the East by training India 'to English institutions'.[9] It is therefore hardly surprising to see reflected so many British ruling ideas in the actual governance of India.

STRUCTURE OF INDIAN ADMINISTRATION

Apart from this general attitude, the structure of Indian administration itself was such that Indian problems were always viewed in the light of English

[6] *Considerations on Representative Government* (London, 1861, reprint 1910), p. 134. Mill applied the same considerations to Ireland. Writing to Prof. John Nichol, he said: 'I myself have always been for a good stout despotism – for governing Ireland like India. But it cannot be done. The spirit of Democracy has got too much head there, too prematurely.' 'Unpublished Letters from John Stuart Mill', *Fortnightly Review* (January–June 1897), LXVII, 675. On the whole British economists seem to have reserved self-rule for white colonies only, whereas for the non-white countries, they urged Britain to provide a benevolent but authoritarian rule. See for example the views of Adam Smith in E. A. Benians, 'Adam Smith's Project of an Empire', *The Cambridge Historical Journal*, 1 (1926), 251–6. James Mill also visualised independence for only the white colonies. In spite of the economic burden, he was against freedom for West Indies because of the white population 'with half a million of slaves at their throats' See the *Parliamentary History and Review* (1825), pp. 639 *et seq.*

[7] *British Influence in India* (London, 1863), p. 98. See also *Destiny of the British Empire as Revealed in the Scriptures* (London, 1865).

[8] *The Indian Empire and Our Financial Relations Therewith* (London, 1866), p. 4.

[9] Many distinguished writers in the late nineteenth and early twentieth centuries including the historians Sir John Seeley and James Anthony Froude, jurists like Lord James Bryce and Sir James Stephen and politicians like Lord Curzon and Earl of Cromer compared the British Empire in India to the Roman Empire of early Britain as the harbinger of civilisation to a place where only barbarism prevailed. See R. F. Betts, 'The Allusion to Rome in British Imperialist Thought', *Victorian Studies* (December 1971), XV, no. 2, pp. 149–59.

ideas and notions. India was being ruled from London as well as Calcutta and other local capitals. Normally it is the responsible administrators on the spot who decide policy. But during the late eighteenth and nineteenth centuries, the Home authorities had a major voice in the formation of policies. In the initial stages, of course, most of the power was concentrated at the head office in London. But with the passage of time and the growing need to take prompt action, the power of policy making was gradually delegated to the man on the spot.

The administration was managed by a Court of Directors elected by the share-holders of the East India Company. These directors were divided into various committees for different subjects. After discussing the many administrative problems of their Indian possessions, the committees put their recommendations before the Court for its final decision. The Court of Directors was itself responsible to the Board of Control, the body set up by the government in 1784 to supervise the Indian administration. The Court of Directors conducted Indian administration by replying to queries from India and communicating the policies to be implemented. The Board of Control could only examine and review the orders of the Court of Directors, but not initiate them; on the other hand, the Court had no certainty that its orders would be approved by the Board of Control.[10] This delicate balance was perhaps responsible for the close cooperation between these two bodies over the long period of their currency. Much of the business appears to have been transacted in informal meetings between the Chairman of the Court of Directors and the President of the Board of Control.[11] When in 1858 the Crown took over the Indian territories from the Company, both the Court and the Board were abolished; and a secretary of state with an advisory council was installed to advise and supervise the Indian government.

However, with the Secretary of State becoming the supreme master of the Government of India, English politics began more and more to influence Indian administration. While the East India Company was primarily interested in the Indian territories as such, the Secretary of State was interested in India as a political weapon in the armoury of his party and his policy had

[10] The mechanism of this system is described in a Memorandum by Broughton. See Report of the Select Committee on Indian Territories, *Parl. Papers*. H.C. 533, vol. X of Session 1852. See also 'Chairs' (Abbreviation for the Chairman and Deputy Chairman) to Ellenborough, 27 August 1829, *Letters to the Board*, India Office Records, vol. IX.

[11] Joseph Farington, a contemporary diarist recorded: 'Mr Majoribanks, being Deputy Chairman of the East India Company, told me that the Chairman and Deputy Chairman for the time being have a *weekly meeting* with the President of the Board of Control (now Mr Canning) at which they make their respective reports and amicably arrange matters.' *The Farington Diary* edited by James Greig (London, 1922), VIII, 205.

to trim its sails according to the shifting breezes in Parliament. Thus the periodical adjustments in the balance of power between various parliamentary groups introduced an unstable element in Indian policies too. This was in marked contrast with the state of affairs during the East India Company's regime. The Court of Directors was usually able to resist the play of British politics in Indian affairs, and sometimes even went against the wishes of the government – in the words of a former member of the Indian civil service, acting as an effective barrier between 'the interests of the people of India and the powerful classes in England'.[12]

The Court of Directors first prepared the drafts in answer to queries from India. The Directors' chief adviser in all matters affecting the administration of India was the Examiner of Indian correspondence, and it was in his department that the bulk of the Company's despatches to the various Governments in India were prepared. Until 1804 one man alone had to study and pass all the despatches from India and also to prepare the replies of the Directors relating to political, revenue, judicial and military affairs. It was the Auditor of Indian accounts who looked after the financial despatches, but in 1804 the military despatches were also entrusted to the Auditor. Two new assistant secretaries were appointed in 1809 to look after the judicial and revenue sides respectively under the direct supervision of the Chief Examiner, and an assistant examiner to deal with the miscellaneous subjects labelled as 'public'.[13] These were the examiners who composed the drafts and converted the vague suggestions of the Directors into workable orders. The examiners ordinarily received little help from the Directors, and they first prepared the drafts and then received the Directors' approval. About half of these drafts returned from the Board of Control without any alterations,[14] and such of the changes – often merely verbal – that were made, were usually in the political department. Less than one per cent of these drafts underwent 'alteration in principle and substance by the Board of Control'.[15]

[12] A. J. Arbuthnot, *Memories of Rugby and India* (London, 1910), p. 221.
[13] See the chapter 'The Examiners Department' in William Foster, *The East India House* (London, 1924).
[14] J. C. Melvill's evidence on 5 May 1852 to the House of Lords Select Committe, III Report, *Parl. Papers*, H.C. 20 III, vol. XXX of Session 1852–3, Q. 269.
[15] John Stuart Mill's evidence on 22 June 1852, *ibid*, Q. 3038. The situation was not different even during the present century. See for the experience of Keynes in the India Office in R. F. Harrod, *The Life of John Maynard Keynes* (London, 1951), p. 143. See for a caustic comment on the power wielded by the India Office bureaucrats: Lord Dalhousie to Sir George Couper dated 8 December 1851 in A. C. Banerjee (ed.) *Indian Constitutional Documents* (Calcutta, 1948), I, 287.

Not only was the power of the Home authorities over the Government of India complete on paper, the Government of India was required to administer the Indian territories under the 'direction and authority' of the East India Company, and was subject to the superintendence of the Board of Control (after 1858 of the Secretary of State for India). In other words, the decisive policies were laid down in London, and the Government in India had merely to execute them. With every added means of communication, this legal power over the Indian Government enabled the Court of Directors (or the Secretary of State) to strengthen their control over India. In spite of this, in practice, much of the administrative work was done without any serious interference from the Home authorities. The various Governments in India proceeded each 'to act upon its own decision', assuming that their actions would be approved at home as soon as information was received. The Indian authorities had in many cases to take the necessary decisions themselves, because despatches took four to six months to reach India, which meant eight months to a year to get instructions from home. But as 'the despatches from the India House have in many cases tended greatly to form the opinions of Indian politicians in India',[16] there was little fear of Indian policies being radically different from what the Court of Directors were likely to prescribe. Hence considerable tolerance was shown to the actions of the Indian Government.

On the other hand, for all the leeway that was given to the Indian administrators, there was always a threat hanging over their heads, for laws passed by the Government, although they could have immediate effect, were liable to be rescinded later on by the Home Government. It was little wonder the Governor-General and all concerned in the administration of India were generally content to carry out faithfully the wishes of the Court of Directors and its successors.

When the Crown assumed the responsibility for the Government of India, the influence of the Home Government became more pronounced still. This curtailed the power of the local authorities even in minor details, and they naturally resented such interference.[17] That the Indian officials resented political interference in Indian policy was a source of great irritation to the officials of the India Office. Indeed it was felt in some official quarters that the obstinate and insolent Indian bureaucracy should be firmly kept in check.[18]

[16] John Stuart Mill's evidence, *op. cit.*, Q. 2990.
[17] See for example the views of Sir John Strachey: Strachey to Lytton, 6 August 1878 (Lytton Papers, India Office Library).
[18] Mallet to Ripon, 28 January 1881 (Ripon Papers, British Museum).

In the Indian sphere, the Governor-General was the supreme authority. There were two bases to his power. Apart from the constitutional position, it always happened that most of the Governor-Generals and Viceroys were distinguished figures in English politics and consequently commanded much respect in Britain as well as India. It was the Governor-General (or the Viceroy as he was called after the Crown takeover) who took the final decisions, and his Council was nothing more than a panel of advisers 'offering opinions on the cases put before them, but exercising no individual responsibility'.[19] The Council had no power to alter, but only the privilege to record its views in case of any differences of opinion.

THE INTELLECTUAL BACKGROUND

The above is a brief description of the institutional aspect of policy making in nineteenth-century India. What of the intellectual side in the formation of economic policies? This would naturally depend on the individual thinking of the policy makers as it was conditioned by prevailing ideas and current conceptions of problems. Consequently the intellectual content can be ascertained only by a study of the policy makers themselves and the factors that conditioned their mental attitudes towards various economic problems.

An important factor which conditioned the mental attitudes of those involved in formulating and executing economic policies in India in the nineteenth century was the acceptance of the British public of the value of political economy as an aid to policy making. Although Adam Smith was not the originator of most of the concepts and arguments to be found in the *Wealth of Nations*, he undoubtedly gave political economy its distinct form by his coherent synthesis of the contributions of his predecessors. Within a short time of its publication, the work became indispensable reading for most politicians, and the new discipline acquired a reputation of usefulness.[20] In a modern commentator's words, many of the educated class in nineteenth-century Britain had great faith in the principles of political economy as 'truths to be explained and accepted, not hypotheses to be debated'.[21] Early in the century, the Utilitarian aim of diffusing useful knowledge found much favour. Political economy as founded by Adam

---

[19] George Chesney, *Indian Polity* (London, 1868), p. 122.

[20] See for example Edmund Burke's forthright views: C. R. Fay, *Burke and Adam Smith* (Belfast, 1956), p. 14.

[21] J. F. C. Harrison, *Learning and Living 1790–1960: A Study in the History of the English Adult Education Movement* (London, 1961), p. 81. See also R. K. Webb, *The British Working Class Reader 1790–1848 Literacy and Social Tension* (London, 1955), pp. 97 *et seq.*

Smith and developed by the Classical School of Economists was deemed part of this useful knowledge.[22] It was the view of David Ricardo that 'By an adherence to these (Principles of Political Economy), Governments cannot fail to promote the welfare of the people.'[23] Indeed the official Utilitarian organ, the *Westminster Review*, went even further and declared that 'The application of a wise system of political economy' was absolutely essential 'to prevent waste, and to diffuse enjoyment' in India.[24] Envious foreign observers even claimed that 'England is indebted for the gigantic increase and flourishing state of most of her colonies, [to] a policy built on the soundest principles of political economy.'[25]

Throughout the century, attempts were made to educate the public at large – especially schoolchildren and the working classes – to appreciate the truths of this new science. Many popular expositions of political economy were published to spread the message. The teaching of political economy in the schools was encouraged and suitable extracts from the writings of eminent economists were made readily and widely available to schoolchildren.[26] The British adult education movement, which was mainly founded by middle-class intellectuals, stressed the spread of the principles of political economy among the working classes. So did the many institutions (e.g. Birkbeck Schools) that mushroomed to educate the children of the poor. Young or old, rich or poor, man or woman, very few in the nineteenth century could have escaped the predisposition of opinion in favour of learning political economy.

Indian administration from the beginning was largely in the hands of people who had grown up in such an atmosphere and thus had been inculcated in their formative years with a belief in the virtues of political economy. Further, many of the key individuals in the policy making apparatus were trained economists. There were directors of the East India Company like David Scott, Francis Baring, Charles Grant, Randle Jackson, Henry St George Tucker and R. D. Mangles who had acquired an understanding of the then current principles of political economy; and in the background there were the examiners who wrote the despatches and did what present-

[22] See Richard D. Altick, *The English Common Reader: A Social History of the Mass Reading Public 1800–1900* (Chicago, 1957), chapter VI.

[23] Ricardo to Malthus, 4 September 1820: P. Sraffa (ed.), *Works and Correspondence of David Ricardo*, VIII (Cambridge, 1951), 228.

[24] Issue dated October 1825, p. 266.

[25] Count Bjornstjerna, *The British Empire in the East* (London, 1840), pp. 176–7.

[26] See J. M. Goldstrom, 'Richard Whately and Political Economy in School Books' *Irish Historical Studies*, XV (September 1966), 140 *et seq.* See also R. Gilmour, 'The Gradgrind School: Political Economy in the Classroom', *Victorian Studies* (December 1967), XI, no. 2, pp. 212–19.

day economic advisers are expected to do. They supplied ideas for new policies and justified old policies, and in general provided technical knowledge and doctrinal support. While converting the vague suggestions of the Court into compact orders, these economists also interpolated some theoretical arguments in justification of their standpoint. Similarly after 1858, the successive Secretaries of State for India also exhibited knowledge of political economy, and many of them counted as intimate friends the leading contemporary economists whose advice they sought often in matters of economic policy. The 'Examiners' were replaced by permanent under secretaries equally well-versed in the principles of political economy. Political economy thus was part of the *psyche* of those who were ruling India from England. However in some respects the individuals who conducted the on-the-spot administration in India were even more imbued with the economic ideas prevalent in Britain.

Most of the important administrators in India, including the Governor-Generals and Viceroys, had a knowledge of at least Adam Smith and, in the latter part of the nineteenth century, of John Stuart Mill as well. In their letters (both official and private) and in their memoranda, minutes and despatches, the names of economists appeared frequently. Statesmen and rulers like Bentinck, Elphinstone, Ellenborough, Northbrook, Lytton, Ripon and many others gave evidence in their correspondence of their having read Smith, Mill or Ricardo. There were, besides, servants of the East India Company who wrote tracts on economic subjects: for example Sir Thomas Munro and Sir William Sleeman both had deeply studied the writings of Ricardo to the extent of publishing critical comments on them.

Apart from the senior statesmen, even the ordinary civil servant who came in search of a career to India was likewise armed with a knowledge of political economy. Considering the favourable climate towards political economy as an essential prerequisite for policy making, it is hardly surprising that the Court of Directors decided to add a study of these 'immutable laws of society and economy' to the syllabus for the training of officials who were to rule India. The East India Company decided to start its own training centre for civil servants because, first, it was found increasingly difficult to recruit properly trained candidates through open competition;[27] and secondly, owing to the 'crass ignorance and gross apathy about Indian subjects at the Universities'.[28] Future civil servants were required to spend two

---

[27] Thomas Robert Malthus, *A Letter to the Rt. Hon. Lord Grenville occasioned by some Observations of His Lordship on the East India Company's Establishment for the Education of their Civil Servants* (London, 1813), p. 4.

[28] 'Reminiscences' by M. Monier Williams in F. C. Danvers et al. (eds.), *Memorials of Old Haileybury College* (Westminister, 1894), p. 33.

years at the East India College, which was established at Haileybury in Hertfordshire in 1805. The study of law and political economy was to form an essential part of the education provided at this institution, and the Company appointed no less an economist than the Reverend Thomas Robert Malthus as the first incumbent of the Chair of Political Economy.[29] When Malthus died in 1834, Richard Jones, another famous economist, was appointed in his place. Jones taught till 1855, and was succeeded by Sir James Stephen, but the college itself was abolished in 1858. Political economy, however, was retained as a compulsory subject for the candidates of the covenanted Indian civil service selected through open competition. After 1892, it became an optional subject but two thirds of the candidates took the option of political economy.[30]

When the establishment of the Haileybury College was being discussed the Court of Directors desired a course of lectures on 'statistics and political economy' be delivered by the Professor, with particular attention 'given to the explanation of the political and commercial relations subsisting between India and Great Britain'.[31] As it turned out, the lectures at Haileybury were mainly based on Adam Smith, the students being given an elementary course on the production, distribution and exchange of wealth. They were also introduced to 'the different systems of taxation which have prevailed or do prevail, in the World; to the connection of these with modes of occupying in the soil; to the reaction of these systems on the wealth and mechanism of nations, especially Asiatic nations' and, finally, to barter, exchange, money and credit.[32] After 1858, when the selection of the civil servants was thrown open to competition, the selected candidates had to take an examination in political economy among other subjects at the end of their probation. The Civil Service Commissioners of 1854 specified that every

probationer ought to prepare himself for the discharge of his duties by paying some attention to financial and commercial science. He should understand the mode of keeping and checking accounts, the principles of banking, the laws which regulate

---

[29] The professorship was for 'General History, Politics, Commerce, and Finance'. See Malthus to Charles Grant, 10 July 1805, *Writers' Petitions*, India Office Records, No. J/1/19, pp. 468–9.

[30] See A. Lawrence Lowell, *Colonial Civil Service, the Selection and Training of Colonial Officials in England, Holland and France* (New York, 1900), p. 36.

[31] 'A Preliminary View of the Establishment of the Honourable East India Company in Hertfordshire for the Education of young persons appointed to the Civil Service in India'. *Writers' Petitions*, India Office Records, *op. cit.*, pp. 451–7.

[32] See evidence of Rev. H. Melville, Principal of the Haileybury College on 28 April 1853 to the Select Committee of the House of Lords, *Parl. Papers*, H.C. 627, vol. XXXI of Session 1852–3, Q. 4839, 4840.

the exchanges, the nature of public debts, funded and unfunded, and the effect produced by different systems of taxation on the prosperity of nations.[33]

This time the Civil Service Commissioners unlike the Court of Directors, in framing the syllabus, recognised legitimate areas of disagreement: 'We would by no means require him to subscribe any article of faith touching any controverted point in the science of political economy; but it is not too much to expect that he will make himself acquainted with those treatises on political economy which have become standard works.'[34] For a number of years the recommended books on political economy were McCulloch's edition of *Wealth of Nations*, Ricardo's *Principles of Political Economy* and John Stuart Mill's *Principles of Political Economy*. Viscount Goschen's *Foreign Exchanges* and Sir Stafford Northcote's *Twenty Years of Financial Policy* were added to this list later.

On the whole the instruction in political economy to the Indian civil servants was welcomed. Economists in the nineteenth century had by and large subscribed to the view that the virtue in political economy lay in its applicability to practical matters. Malthus had always stressed that it was not a mere gymnastic exercise for the mind but a science capable of positive application.[35] Richard Jones also held similar views.[36] Civil servants themselves believed that political economy formed part of their essential intellectual equipment, and in their quest for answers to specific administrative problems they found economic theory to be of considerable help. An anonymous civil servant with Indian experience pointed out in 1823 that 'In India, the grossest errors in policy, arising from a want of knowledge of the former science [political economy], have notoriously prevailed in times past, and should, therefore, be guarded against for the future.'[37] John Cosmo Melvill, a senior official of the India Office claimed in 1853 that 'Law and Political Economy are the most important subjects of instruction for persons destined for the civil service of India.'[38] Indeed there were many civilians who claimed that insufficient attention had been paid to political economy at Haileybury.[39]

[33] *Parl. Papers*, Cmd. 1446, vol. LV of Session 1876, p. 304.
[34] *Ibid.*
[35] See my *Malthus and Classical Economics* (Bombay, 1959), chapter VI.
[36] See his *Literary Remains Consisting of Lectures and Tracts in Political Economy* (London, 1859), p. 575.
[37] *A Letter to the Chairman, Deputy Chairman and Court of Directors of the East India Company on the subject of their College at Haileybury*, by a Civilian (London, 1823), pp. 6–7.
[38] Evidence before House of Lords Select Committee on 6 May 1852. *Parl. Papers*, H.C. 20 III, vol. XXX of Session 1852–3, Q. 418.
[39] See for example the evidence of L. R. Reid of the Bombay Civil Service, *Parl. Papers*, H.C. 41

In spite of a slight stammer, Malthus was a persuasive speaker who compelled attention. As for the qualities of Richard Jones as a teacher, according to one of his old students, Monier Williams, 'it was difficult not to listen to every word he said'.[40] With such eminent teachers and impressionable trainees, a considerable portion of the material presented in the lectures must have been retained by the listeners. When it was pointed out that as the trainees entered the college at a comparatively young age of seventeen and hence were not capable of understanding the involved and abstract arguments of political economy, Malthus replied:

I confess that I once thought so myself. But the particular examples, which I have witnessed, of distinguished progress in this study at the East India College, and the numerous instances of very fair progress, enable me to say, with confidence, that a youth of seventeen (and this is the most usual age at which the study is begun, as it is generally confined to the last year or year and a half), with a good understanding, is fully able to comprehend the principles of political economy, and is rarely inclined to think them either too difficult or too dull to engage his attention.'[41]

The five lectures a week delivered by him were usually 'given in a manner to make previous preparation necessary, and to encourage most effectually habits of industry and application'.[42] A former student of Richard Jones writing in the *Calcutta Review* in 1845 said that 'The lectures of the present able professor are attended with less reluctance by the students than those of any other branch, and it is here that we generally see at the close of every term the fairest average of merit distributed amongst the greatest number.'[43]

Not only did the futuve civil servants receive sound coaching in political economy, but they were also able, while in India, to keep themselves informed of the latest developments in the discipline. In the capital cities such as Calcutta, Bombay and Madras, literary associations were formed, libraries were established and journals were run by enthusiastic civil servants. In the interior, they were well served by the regimental book clubs maintained by the residents which procured the latest books from Britain as well as maintaining subscriptions to all the leading journals. As W. H. Spry of the Bengal Medical Corps wrote in 1837, 'long before a book has got into general

---

Footnote 39 continued

vol. XXX of Session 1852–3, Q. 2514. See also Sir William Sleeman's exasperation with certain 'European gentlemen' in the service of the Company 'exhibiting the most lamentable ignorance of Political Economy'. *Rambles and Recollections*, I (London, 1844), 191.

[40] *Memorials of Old Haileybury College, op. cit.*, p. 70. See for Sir George Campbell's opinion of Jones's teaching, *Memoirs of My Indian Career* (London, 1894), I, 9.

[41] *A Letter to the Rt. Hon. Lord Grenville* (London, 1813), p. 14.

[42] *Ibid.*, p. 13. See also *Asiatic Journal*, May 1824.

[43] 'The East India College: Haileybury'. *The Calcutta Review*, vol. IV, no. VII (1848), 12.

circulation in England, it has been received in Calcutta, read by all the societies in Hindostan, and thrown aside'.[44]

An important reason why the Indian civil servants took so eagerly to political economy is to be seen in their social origin. The Indian civil service in the nineteenth century almost entirely originated in the British middle class. Looking at the professions of the fathers of Indian civil servants from 1860 to 1874 (see Table I), we find less than 5 per cent belonging to the category 'Clerks, butchers and bakers etc.'. Another ten per cent is accounted for by the Aristocracy. For the rest the parents were all in solid middle-class professions. When this is related to the researches of Professor R. K. Webb indicating that in the nineteenth century political economy spread rapidly 'as a cardinal article of middle class faith'[45] and that the middle-class were making efforts to spread the faith to other classes, we can see why political economy should have held a powerful hold over the Indian civil service mind. In addition the East India College at Haileybury which was in existence for half a century was fashioned like the typical middle-class institution, the public school. These public schools enabled middle-class values to be passed on to future generations and at these schools 'a boy's steps were set on the first part of that steady and inevitable progress

TABLE I *Professions of fathers of civil servants 1860–1874*[46]

Profession	% of total
Aristocracy	10.0
Army, civil service	9.8
Religion	27.5
Indian Civil Service and Indian planters	8.5
Law	7.4
Medicine	9.7
Merchants	7.2
Engineers	1.7
Education	4.0
Accountant, Librarian, etc.	3.0
Farmer and Rural origin	4.2
Clerks, butchers, bakers, etc.	4.9
Unspecified	2.1
	100.0

[44] Henry H. Spry, *Modern India; with Illustrations of the Resources and Capabilities of Hindusthan* (London, 1837), II, 86. Apart from Book Societies, the itinerant book seller who frequented the district headquarters was a source of diffusion of knowledge. See Colonel W.F.B. Laurie, *Sketches of Some Distinguished Anglo-Indians* (London, 1887), p. 334.

[45] *The British Working Class Reader 1790–1848* p. 97.

[46] Source: *Parl. Papers*, Cmd. 1446, vol. LV of Session 1876, p. 311.

towards positions of command over the majority ... The emotional attachment to the ideas inculcated at such schools lasted a man all his life.'[47]

It was in 1807 that the first batch of candidates from Haileybury were
placed in the Presidency of Fort St George. From 1809 onwards, batches of
old Haileyburians found their way to important administrative jobs all over
the British possessions in India. Influenced by the ideals of the French
Revolution and the prevailing romanticism, these young administrators
repaired to their posts to rule over the 'natives' with an almost missionary
fervour. As they had been recruited young and taught to believe themselves
specially fortunate, they took great pride in their services,[48] and they aimed to
be impartial and objective in their dealings. No doubt, they had ordinarily to
use their commonsense and presence of mind to solve the problems as they
arose, for most of the situations in which these young officials found themselves were new and had no British precedents which could be followed. On
these occasions they did not fail to handle the tools given to them by Malthus
or Jones at Haileybury. Even administrators who came to India without having gone to Haileybury acquired their knowledge of political economy
through assiduous self-study, and found that theory facilitated policy formulation. For example, Alexander Read, an army Major who was given the task
of revenue settlement in some newly conquered districts in the last decade
of the eighteenth century, remarked: 'My main design is to demonstrate, by
a reference to facts and experience, those principles in economics, which I
conceive are essential to the prosperity of a country and by means of which
alone one so dificient [sic] in arts and trade as these districts can be brought
to a state of improvement.'[49] Even much later in the next century, when a
novel problem presented itself, the civil servant was apt to go to first principles to help him out of his difficulties. R. B. Chapman, for example, was a
student at Haileybury, and yet when confronted with the deteriorating
currency situation, 'studied or re-studied' the works of Adam Smith, Nassau
Senior, J. R. McCulloch, J. S. Mill and others to write an official memorandum preparatory to policy formation.[50] This accounts for the presence of
lengthy abstract discussions – deemed by some economic historians to be
rather irritating[51] – in the official writings of the Indian civil servants.

---

[47] A. P. Thornton, *The Imperial Idea and Its Enemies: A Study in British Power* (London, 1959),
pp. 90–2.
[48] For example see Sir George Campbell's *Memoirs, op. cit.,* I, 8. See also the opinion of S. S.
Brown of the Bengal Civil Service in *Home Letters Written from India* (London, 1878), p. 36.
[49] Read to Lord Hobart, 10 February 1796, *Baramahal Records,* vol. XXI, p. 95.
[50] Note dated 13 July 1876, *Financial Department Consultations,* India Office Records, no.
L/F/5/19.
[51] For instance, Mrs Sarada Raju in her *Economic Conditions in the Madras Presidency: 1800–
1850* (Madras, 1941), complains of the 'elaborate and often verbose exposition of theory',

Primarily, as Marx sneeringly said, the Indian Government was 'one immense writing machine'.[52] Whatever the local governments did had to be communicated to the Home authorities. Every one of their policies had to be justified; and in order to persuade the Home authorities to take certain desirable courses of action, detailed information had to be given. 'By the very nature of circumstances,' said Sir George Campbell who as an administrator was aware of the circumstances, 'the British administrators had to put on record their most secret designs and inmost thoughts, desires, and motives, which ordinarily are never known to outsiders.'[53] Obviously 'political economy' was very much part of these 'inmost thoughts', for the members of the local governments frequently used phrases like 'founded upon those just principles' or 'upon the true principles of political economy', often buttressed by arguments derived from conventional economic theory.

The development of political economy as a useful discipline, the acceptance of it by the middle classes of Britain, the middle-class origin of the Indian civil service, the presence of trained economists in the highest policy-making organs, the systematic instruction of the subject at an impressionable age, the 'missionary' zeal of the civil servants to be objective and impartial and the lack of precedents all indicate the enormous scope that was available for political economy to influence the economic policies pursued in India.

ORIGIN AND FORMATION OF POLICIES

As will be seen in later chapters, in virtually every policy measure that had anything to do with 'economics', references had been made to economists and their arguments utilised. If the names and arguments did not figure, at least a reference to the 'principles of political economy' or *laissez-faire* was made. If this is related to the intellectual background of the Indian administration, it would appear that 'political economy' was almost the only factor in the formation of economic policies. Straightforward as this all seems, it can however be wrong and misleading to conclude from this that, because economic ideas were referred to, they were alone decisive or that the influence of economic ideas was uniformly felt in all areas of policy formation.

The evidence we have is still not quite conclusive enough, because we are

Footnote 51 continued
p. xix. Even administrators like Sir Thomas Munro found such excursions into the realms of economic theorising very irritating. See Munro to George Canning, 1 May 1823, Gleig, *Life of Sir Thomas Munro* (London, 1830), II, 66.
[52] 'Government of India', *New York Daily Tribune*, 20 July 1853, reprinted in Marx and Engels, *On Colonialism* (Moscow, n.d.) p. 62.
[53] *Memoirs, op. cit.* II, 865.

dealing with the inner mind of administrators and statesmen who usually take decisions as a matter of daily routine. The temperament and zeal of individuals varied and so did their actions. Not all economists in the service were able or determined to translate their ideas into practice. For example, if John Stuart Mill's economic ideas had any influence at all in the formation of economic policies, it was entirely through the influence his writings had in shaping the discipline in the mid-nineteenth century, and not through his own presence as an examiner in the office of the East India Company. Indeed he never had much to do with the shaping of economic policies because he wrote mostly political despatches.[54] He lacked his father's aggressive intolerance towards Indian institutions and keenness to 'civilise' India; as Abram Harris says, his 'approach to India was more tolerant than his father's and was devoid of the latter's dogmatism and chauvinism'.[55] India seems to have been nothing more to him than an opportunity to earn his livelihood; as he frankly wrote to John Nichol: 'shall go to the India House tomorrow to *resume my drudgery*'.[56] For a long time, in fact, not everyone at the India office accepted Mill as a great practical economist.[57]

The temperament and zeal of the policy makers apart, there are other important aspects of the realities of decision making that deserve close consideration. Why was a certain policy pursued? Was it because of the intellectual training the policy maker had had? One could certainly assert that a knowledge of political economy equipped policy makers with a better understanding of the structure and operation of the economic organisation than if they were unlettered in political economy. On the other hand, it is extremely difficult to determine whether the arguments based on economic ideas were aids to reach a particular decision or were mere ancillary arguments used to buttress policies already adopted as a result of other non-doctrinal reasons. The administrators respected political economy, no doubt, but they were also susceptible to divers influences – ideological, practical and sectional; and account must be taken of their conception of

---

[54] Out of 1686 despatches that he wrote, not one was on revenue or a financial topic. See *Home Miscellaneous Series*, India Office Records, no. 832.

[55] 'John Stuart Mill: Servant of the East India Company', *Canadian Journal of Economics and Political Science*, XXX, no. 2 (May 1964), p. 186.

[56] Mill to Nichol, 29 June 1837 in F. Mineka (ed.), *The Earlier Letters of John Stuart Mill* (Toronto, 1963), XII, 323 (italics mine). It would appear that India had little to interest him. 'One might read Mill's *Principles* twice through,' says C. R. Fay, 'without suspecting that he spent his working life in the India Office.' *Imperial Economy and its Place in the Formation of Economic Doctrine* (Oxford, 1934), p. 73. It is also not a little surprising to see that out of the 32 questions he set for discussion at the Political Economy Club, not one was on India. See Political Economy Club, *Minutes of Proceedings etc. 1821–1882* (London, 1882).

[57] See Lord George Hamilton, *Parliamentary Reminiscences and Reflections: 1865–85* (London, 1917), pp. 101–2.

interests, which also could be individual, sectional and social. All this could affect their attitudes towards the particular theory and the policy emanating from it. In other words, apart from economic theory, factors such as strongly held (and sometimes irrational) beliefs, precedents, absence of policy alternatives and external pressure also could (and in India they did) influence the formation of economic policy.

It is not necessary to labour the point how strongly held ideological positions can inhibit a purely rational approach to arriving at conclusions. But theology and ideology were strong in influencing the British in India. Conservatism, utilitarianism, romanticism, platonism, paternalism and evangelical Christianity were all strongly held by various people at various times,[58] and they naturally coloured their thinking on many sometimes even purely economic issues.

In large organisations decision making means, as James March and Herbert Simon point out, the selection through certain well-defined processes of one method of doing something from among the many such methods the organisation has experience of.[59] The Government of India was not only a large organisation but it was also bureaucratic. As Robert Merton has observed, an effective bureaucracy 'demands reliability of response and strict devotion to regulations'. Hence the bureaucratic structure strives constantly to make the individual bureaucrats to be 'methodical, prudent, disciplined'. If it is to function successfully, 'it must attain a high degree of reliability of behaviour, an unusual degree of conformity with prescribed pattern of action'.[60] That is why the administrative mind, if we can conceptualise it, has an understandable preference for past experience in the form of precedents and conventions as reliable guides to action. This was so in India and it became rather pronounced in the second half of the nineteenth century for three reasons. First, the administration as a whole gained experience; it was hence natural that references should be made to previous occasions when similar problems had been encountered. Secondly, the Home authorities were becoming increasingly involved with the formation of economic policies in India, and it was accordingly easier to cite precedents than to enter into discussions of doctrine for justifying any particular action. And, finally, what was most important was the development of regional attitudes towards problems; thus, in the history of Indian economic policies, one comes across the various 'schools' of administrative thinking, the Bengal

---

[58] See E. T. Stokes, *The English Utilitarians and India* (Oxford, 1959), part I; and Raghavan Iyer, 'Utilitarianism and All that (The Political Theory of British Imperialism in India) in *South Asian Affairs Number One* (St Antony's Papers Number 8), pp. 9–71.
[59] J. G. March and H. Simon, *Organisations* (New York, 1958), pp. 191 *passim*.
[60] *Social Theory and Social Structure* (Glencoe, 1968), pp. 151–60.

School, the Punjab School and the Madras School, associated with the names
of Lord Cornwallis, Sir John Lawrence, Alexander Read and Sir Thomas
Munro. While theoretical ideas played a part in forming the attitudes of these
men, their individual personalities made their mark too on the administrative mores of the regions in which they served. Young civil servants fresh
from Britain were naturally amenable to these influences and soon became
converts. Sir George Campbell, himself a distinguished member of the
Indian civil service, thought that this was due to geographical separation![61]
The regional attitudes developed thus by geographical factors tended to
become rigid and intolerant of alternative opinions. Believers used every
available means to enforce conformity from their subordinates. Thus a
civil servant speaking from personal experience wrote in an anonymous
article that promotions were based on the willingness to accept the views of
the superior officers.[62]

Decision necessarily involves choice. However it is not always that the
policy makers are presented with numerous alternatives to make their
choice. Immediate economic circumstances which require urgent attention
could have a profound influence on the administrators with a limited range
of policy alternatives. If the current responsibilities of the policy maker
coincide with the long term interests of the country, then theory might
facilitate the search for an appropriate economic policy. Were it not so,
theory must give way to other considerations. For example, a senior civil
servant countered the proposal to abolish indirect taxes because of their
allocational effects by simply affirming: 'Four millions sterling are too much
to be sacrificed to a Principle of Political Economy.'[63] It is often the case that
the short-run outcome seems more relevant to the average administrator.
Because of his small time horizon, he is likely to be more exercised about
finding a solution for the problem before him rather than be neutral towards
short- and long-run issues and look for an ideal policy.

The last of the four major non-doctrinal influences on policy is the
existence of pressure groups. If a policy happened to anger special interests
and if these were sufficiently organised, then they would try to exert direct
or indirect pressure to amend or cancel that policy. At other times the
concerned interests could also put pressure on the authorities to make them
decide upon any desired policy. While by careful examination of the decision-
making processes it is thus possible to ascertain the existence of pressures, it
is nevertheless doubtful whether any precise quantification of the pressures
is possible. Sometimes, as indeed it happened in India, the pressure groups

[61] *System of Land Tenure in various countries* (London, 1870), p. 256.
[62] See *The Calcutta Review*, vol. XLII, no. LXXXIV (1866), p. 372.
[63] H. T. Prinsep, *The India Question in 1853* (London, 1853), p. 42.

may be active in order to uphold the application of a particular type of economic theory. This could not, however, be construed as a case of theory directly influencing a policy, because it does not involve the conscious utilisation of theoretical abstractions to reach a policy conclusion.

Pressure groups are the logical outcome of monolithic government structures; they are inevitable in any democratic system of government, and once the entire pressure group system is organised, it could produce 'if not "optimal", at least "satisfactory" results'.[64] The authoritarian nature of the Indian government made it difficult for any but the very few pressure groups to have any say in the formation of policy, but the British Parliamentary system allowed much greater scope for pressure groups based in England to influence policies at the London end of the Indian government. Many pressure groups with Indian interests operated in England such as the ship-building interest, Lancashire cotton industries, Cheshire salt manufacturers, and Dundee jute manufacturers. As for the presence of Indian pressure groups (confined mainly to the British trading interests and the Indian landowning aristocracy), no less a person than Sir Richard Temple had acknowledged 'that the Chambers of Commerce in Calcutta, and of Bombay especially, exercise a great influence in British India, that they render great assistance to the Government, that they represent all the best phases of public opinion, and of many of the most influential classes of the community'.[65] Even so Indian pressure groups like the British planters of indigo in India, British traders in India and the Indian landowners thought it useful to operate from London as well, in addition to their Indian operations. The influence of these various groups waxed and waned in accordance with the political climate and the shifts in the administrative set-up. On the whole the administrators acknowledged the power possessed by the pressure groups and tried to accommodate them by making them part of the decision-making apparatus through giving representation to Lancashire interests in the Secretary of State's Council[66] and to the British traders in the various legislative councils in India.

In addition to the factors that influence policy makers' attitudes, there is also the question of time. Decisions were sometimes taken by forceful

---

[64] James Buchanan & Gordon Tullock, *The Calculus of Consent: Logical Foundations of Constitutional Democracy* (Ann Arbor, 1962), p. 288. See chapter 19 for a theoretical analysis of pressure groups in the pure theory of governmental decision making.

[65] *Conditions and Prospects of British India*, address delivered to Manchester Chamber of Commerce on 15 March 1881.

[66] The idea of the introduction of commercial representation into the India Council was originated by Lord Salisbury himself when he visited the Manchester Chamber of Commerce. See Edmund Ashworth (of the Manchester Chamber of Commerce) to Lord Mayo, 5 February 1869 (Mayo Papers at the Cambridge University Library).

individuals, but usually policies were not made overnight. Sometimes years could pass before the final outcome was known. For example on a question relating to the canal rates in North-Western Provinces it took nearly seven years for the government of India to reach a decision.[67] Policies as they finally emerge are the result of considerable discussion, mutual give and take and resort to compromise. The question therefore arises as to where exactly political economy stands in this tortuous process of decision making.

CLASSICAL POLITICAL ECONOMY AND ECONOMIC OPINION

In order to assess the role of political economy in the complex task of policy formation, it is necessary to start with some standard by which to judge the strength of the various factors. This is where difficulties arise in any evaluation of the relationship between economic ideas and policy formation. It is impossible to assign relative weights to the various non-doctrinal influences on policy makers that would always hold good because the theory–policy relationship is not a constant force but a continuously fluctuating one. While the nature of the problem is too thickly shrouded in the mist of historical processes and personal idiosyncrasies to be amenable for solution within a simple, deductive and analytical schema, yet it is essential to have a framework to reduce the complexities and understand the process of theory–policy interaction.

Economic policy involves choice relating both to objectives and the means of achieving those objectives. The theory of economic policy provides a system to guide the selection of these goals and the methods to fulfil them. Whereas ends and means could be identified as two separate entities, it is in practice difficult to do so because the means themselves might in certain cases be the objectives of particular economic policies. It would be useful here to distinguish between different types of economic policy objectives. T. W. Hutchison refers to the German practice of conveniently distinguishing between *Ordnungspolitik* and *Prozesspolitik*, meaning 'policies concerned with the economic order or constitutional framework, and policies concerned with economic processes'.[68] *Ordnungspolitik* refers to the provision of an appropriate institutional order in which the economic processes will automatically specify relevant objectives and achieve them. *Prozesspolitik*, on the other hand, refers to objectives that have to be achieved by the direct and deliberate manipulation of policy instruments available to the policy maker. Various theories of economic policy have specified the ideal

[67] See B. B. Misra, *The Administrative History of India 1834–1947* (London, 1970), pp. 137–8.
[68] *'Positive' Economics and Policy Objectives* (London, 1964), p. 125.

combination of means and ends. Some have been concerned with only one of the categories in the above classification while others have not limited themselves to any one type of policy objectives. These systems of economic policy are essentially dependent upon theoretical investigations into economic phenomena, because without an adequate knowledge of the logic of internal relationships the system builder would have little idea of consequences to be expected from any suggested policy.

The theory of economic policy is a fusion of experience or knowledge of real economic phenomena with theoretical constructions; thus the formulations are built not in a socioeconomic vacuum in which the problems faced by the real world would be entirely obliterated. Further, the theory of economic policy looks at the whole economic problem faced by the economy because of the essential interdependence between most economic phenomena. Hence it is conceived always in broad and comprehensive terms.[69]

The theorists in their private welfare functions cannot avoid introducing their own conceptions of what economic equity and efficiency are, and they have their own visions as to how policies should be formulated and executed. In this way the selection of objectives and of the instruments of policy is influenced by the political and philosophical beliefs of economic theorists. That is the reason why economists who profess the same discipline arrive at different theories of economic policy depending upon their particular perceptions of socioeconomic problems. Thus the theory of economic policy is an 'ideal' in the sense that if followed it would be fully satisfactory because the policy is visualised by its architect as a perfect specimen of its kind.

The two important conditions that are necessary for 'theory' to have an impact on policy are, first, the emergence of problems which have no actual precedents, and secondly, full freedom for policy makers to act. If problems are quite novel and the social and sectional interests of the administrators are not immediately affected, they will naturally seek enlightenment and guidance from 'theory', that is to say, from typical or ideal economic relationships, organisations and sequences. These might enable them to predict possible future outcomes by appropriately comparing the components of the 'ideal' system of the economists with the very obvious limitations of actuality. Although the formation of economic policies can be explicitly or implicitly guided by one or other of the alternative theories of economic policy, they must nevertheless take into account all the complex political, social and economic institutions, procedures, practices etc. that are part of the real world. A policy being a course of action to be followed, it should have

---

[69] See Jan Tinbergen, *Economic Policy: Principles and Design* (Amsterdam, 1956), pp. 7–18 *passim*.

an objective as well as a mechanism to achieve the objective in a given institutional setting. Thus it has an 'ideal' element as well as a 'practical' element which takes into account the difficulties of achieving those ideals. If we can thus see the structure of policies in terms of their two constituents, the ideal and the practical, it may become somewhat easier to evaluate the influence of economic ideas on policy formation. In other words, we should start with a study of the political processes, to find out how the 'ideal' was conceived and how much of the 'ideal' was able to survive after the 'practical' aspects had distorted it.

It is very rare for a policy maker to get the opportunity to plan the transformation of an entire economy at a stroke. The formation of economic policy is the work of many individuals and each has to chip away at different places before the final figure is sculpted. Each individual would most certainly possess an ideal structure in his mind, but his own responsibility would be limited. If all the policy makers responsible for the policy have the same overall policy framework or ideal structure, the end product will not be different from the objectives of that theory of economic policy. If however policy makers, operating as they do in different times and places, have different ideal structures their individual efforts will not add up to any one recognisable shape. Hence the test is to see whether the objectives of the dominant theory of economic policy bear any resemblance to the mosaic of various economic policy objectives formulated and executed by the policy makers in particular situations.

This raises the question of the 'dominant' theory of economic policy. Earlier it was observed that political economy emerged in the nineteenth century (which we characterise as Classical Political Economy) as the fervently accepted creed of the British middle classes. Political economy as understood in the nineteenth century was an amalgam of the three technically separate branches of economics, namely economic analysis, applied economics and economic policy. Hence the term political economy meant many things to many people, and unanimity of opinion was conspicuous by its absence whatever conception of it was adopted. If by the term was meant theoretical constructions, there were wide areas of disagreement among the leading economists of the day, and no set of theories commanded a large following for any length of time. For example, within two decades of its emergence the dominant school of political economy in the first half of the nineteenth century, viz., Ricardian economics, ceased to be 'a living force'.[70] Similarly differences of opinion prevailed even more among the practitioners of that discipline, when by political economy was meant economic policies.

[70] J. A. Schumpeter, *History of Economic Analysis* (New York, 1954), p. 478.

However these disagreements and differences of opinion should not be overemphasised because there were considerable areas where most economists agreed, and it must be remembered that the fountainhead of many of their ideas and techniques was the encyclopaedic *Wealth of Nations* to which all economists of the post-1776 period paid reverential attention. In the area of the theory of economic policy, Classical Political Economists, that is to say Adam Smith and his followers, had unanimously advocated the establishment and maintenance of 'a constitutional framework in accordance with the competitive market mechanism, that is with "rules" or with "Ordnungspolitik"'.[71] It is true that Smith's successors (notably David Ricardo under the Benthamite influence of James Mill) paid some attention to the *Prozespolitik*, but this never replaced their main policy objective of establishing an appropriate socioeconomic framework for the correct functioning of the capitalist economy. In other words, they sought the establishment of what Adam Smith called the System of Natural Liberty. The main idea behind this system is that government interference would retard the full development of human beings. Prudence and initiative are the two most important virtues which man, a social animal, should possess. Man can be happy and enter a prosperous and virtuous state of life only if he is endowed with these qualities. The function of government should therefore be to encourage these two qualities in man and enable mankind to evolve the good and prosperous life. The government should never – consciously or unconsciously – do anything that will impair these virtues of prudence and individual initiative. Rather the regulations of the government should help to promote these qualities in the people. But, then, these qualities could be developed only under a good government which preserves social stability and organises and maintains good political and social institutions. Thus, in their view, the role of state in economic matters was minimal but not nonexistent; and the theory of economic policy in which unanimity was observed could be reduced to three cardinal points. *Firstly*: Free trade. Internal and external trading ought to be allowed to function without tariffs and other irksome indirect taxation. Purely economic factors alone should have say in the allocation of resources. *Secondly*: The provision of infrastructure. The intervention of government could be resorted to in areas where (*a*) the market mechanism failed; and (*b*) they are necessary for the successful functioning of the private enterprises. Public works, law and order, and education were all legitimate areas of state activity. However it was agreed upon that in pursuing these activities the government should not encroach unduly (e.g. through taxation) on the resources available to the private sector. And *thirdly*: Non-legal forces of social control. It was essential to retain certain institutions such as custom,

[71] T. W. Hutchison, *'Positive' Economics and Policy Objectives*, p. 126.

morals and religion because they exercise a check on social behaviour. They are as much necessary for the smooth functioning of the competitive economy as legal institutions (e.g. the law of contract) and economic infrastructure.[72]

In any case, by the time the policy prescriptions of the economists percolated down to the interested layman and civil servants, the doctrinal differences became blurred and what was apparent was the broad similarity of the conclusions respecting the ideal economic policy. It seemed to them that the economists have 'provided, if not all the answers at least the categories and the methods by which the right answers could be reached'.[73] The guarded statements, the logical subtleties, warnings, explicit and implicit assumptions, qualifications, exceptions and similar safeguards that surrounded the various elements of the Classical theory of economic policy as expounded by Adam Smith and his successors were quickly forgotten, and in the perception of the nineteenth century students of political economy it was in most cases a set of clear-cut principles that seemed to have universal applicability.[74] These were the ideals and worth bringing them to the concrete reality of the world.

Were these ideals brought to India by its British rulers in the nineteenth century? Was there any correspondence between the Classical theory of ecomic policy and the actions of the Indian government? If so, how far this similarity due to the general acceptance of the Classical political economy? We shall venture to make an attempt to answer these questions in the following chapters.

[72] See Robbins, *The Theory of Economic Policy* (London, 1953), lectures 1 & 2; W. J. Samuels, *The Classical Theory of Economic Policy* (New York, 1966), chapter 2; and Coats (ed.), *The Classical Economists and Economic Policy* (London, 1971), Editor's Introduction, pp. 1–32.

[73] R. K. Webb, *Harriet Martineau: A Radical Victorian* (London, 1960), p. 100.

[74] As A. W. Coats points out, A. V. Dicey was one of the several distinguished and influential late nineteenth-century scholars 'who erroneously attributed to the classical economists a simplistic conception of laissez-faire which contrasts sharply with their often cautious and moderate attitude toward state intervention', 'Editor's Introduction' *op. cit.* footnote, p. 11. He is referring to Dicey's *Lectures on the Relation Between Law and Public Opinion in England During the Nineteenth Century* (London, 1905). If people like Dicey could understand the theory of Classical economic policy in this manner, need we be surprised at the ordinary civil servants' perception of political economy also in these simplistic terms?

2

ECONOMIC IDEAS AND BRITISH POLICY TOWARDS INDIA

The question may be asked, 'What have we done for India? India has been the nursery of great soldiers, administrators, financiers, statesmen; yet even to this hour she has hardly been governed with higher aims than as a field in which cadets of English families may push their fortunes, or as a market in which English merchants may with advantage sell their wares.

Bishop of Manchester
(in a sermon given at the Manchester
Cathedral on 29 March 1874)

THE STATE AND THE COMPANY'S EMPIRE

As we are dealing with the formation of economic policies in India by individuals who owed their origin, allegiance and interests to Britain, it would be unreal to deal with the making of policies for India by itself without taking into account the policy adopted by the dominating towards the dominated country. It has already been observed that policies in India were affected by the modes of British thought, and in this chapter we propose to examine how the ideas of economists and others who were in a position to form public opinion influenced the attitudes and policy towards India as a subordinate country. How did the economists elucidate the relations between Britain on the one hand and the colonies on the other, through the application of economic theory to the subject of colonial trade and occupation? Did these conclusions have any impact on the policies pursued towards India?

Ever since Britain started acquiring an empire, discussions regarding its value and the usefulness of colonial trade were frequent. Until the last quarter of the eighteenth century the most prevalent view among the colonial theorists was that the value of colonies depended on their commercial possibilities. Colonial policy was to them but an aspect of the larger goals of the nations, for whom economic objectives were mainly the growth of trade and increase in national power. Colonial policy, then, has to ensure that the colonies made the fruition of the national economic goals possible. Colonies were not coveted just for the love of possession, nor were they desired as an outlet for the surplus population. Their functions were to supply certain goods and receive certain other goods. In other words, the colonies were conceived as

subordinate spheres of development for the mother country.[1] In the seventeenth century the colonies were envisaged as a 'self-sufficing economic
empire' where goods not producible in Britain could be produced, such
as tobacco in Virginia and sugar in the West Indies. But in the eighteenth
century, the changing industrial character of Britain necessitated the import
of raw materials such as cotton, dyes and raw silk in addition to the original
imports, spices, sugar and tobacco. Thus the supposed role of the colonies
was to specialise in the manufacture of raw materials and other goods that
would not compete with the mother country. The main issue was trade,
preferably without colonisation, but colonisation and aggression would not
be avoided if found necessary for the pursuit of trade. This attitude fitted
also with Adam Smith's conception of colonies: 'Some particular branches
of commerce, which are carried on with barbarous and uncivilized nations,
require extraordinary protection. An ordinary store or counting-house could
give little security to the goods of the merchants . . . To defend them from the
barbarous natives, it is necessary that the place where they are deposited,
should be, in some measure, fortified.[2] It is not very surprising to see Adam
Smith advocating this method, for he had nothing against foreign trade, and
colonies as he visualised were a great help; colonies would be small yet armed
trading posts, more a protective shield than mere possession. As far as India
was concerned, Adam Smith had no objection to the methods adopted by the
East India Company in acquiring colonies. We must remember that he wrote
in the 1770s when the Company had few territorial possessions. If the
Company did not do it, it would have to be done by the State, and 'the extraordinary expense, which the protection of any particular branch of commerce
may occasion, should be defrayed by a moderate tax upon that branch'.[3] Smith's
objection was to the East India Company itself, as we shall see presently.

It is possible to argue that the vicissitudes of the East India Company's
policy in India followed the prescriptions of the colonial economic theorists.
'Empire' in any real sense of the term began in India only after 1765, the
attitude of the Headquarters at London earlier being one of great caution.
The company was only a trading body, and meddling in local politics by their
officers was not tolerated. In the early years, the East India Company had no
Indian territory of their own except Bombay, and they occupied other territories only as tenants of local powers. These small settlements consisted of
a few acres of ground in which were constructed warehouses and lodgings.
As the English Company did not enjoy the active support of their Govern-

[1] See Klaus Knorr, *British Colonial Theories 1570–1850* (Toronto, 1944) Chapter IV.
[2] *Wealth of Nations* (London, 1776: Modern Library Edition), p. 690.
[3] *Ibid.*, p. 691.

ment as did the Dutch, French or Portuguese Companies, the East India Company were compelled to carry on their trading activities with the help and protection provided by the Mughal emperors. But in extending their trade, the English traders gradually went more and more beyond the sphere of Mughal protection. The trading posts like Madras, Bombay, Calcutta and Surat were far away from the centre of Mughal power. It was also significant that the Mughal power itself was crumbling. The Company realised by the beginning of the eighteenth century that they could consolidate their trading position in India only on the basis of territorial sovereignty, and accordingly approved of their servants in India combining trade with warfare, fortification, military prudence and political government. Anglo-French rivalries in Europe had their repercussions in India and this provided yet another reason why territories had to be acquired in India. The Company thus thought that the chaotic situation in India was itself a field of opportunities to the trader who had also the abilities of soldier, statesman and administrator. Besides, the authorities had no illusions about the nature of the protection they were receiving from the ruling monarchs, for the Company had ultimately to rely on their own strength. A typical instruction from the Court of Directors to the President and Council at Fort William reads: 'We can only for the present, recommend it to you to be on your guard to defend, according to the best of your ability, our trade and settlements.'[4] But political conquests and colonising were strictly for advancing trade only, as a letter of the Court of Directors affirms: 'Our business is trade, it is not politic for us to be encumbered with much territory.'[5] Thus whatever territories Britain acquired in India in the eighteenth century were for the most part due to the presence of her European rivals.[6]

Although the territories acquired in India were in this sence incidental, it was thought by many that the colonies could be a good source of income to Britain. In fact, as P. J. Marshall points out, for more than two decades after the decisive battle of Plassey the British Parliament and public were hoping to acquire large tributes from their Indian possessions.[7] As it was realised that good governance was essential to draw the tribute from India, the nationalisation of the East India Company was frequently suggested.[8] Al-

---

[4] Letter dated 11 November 1757, H. N. Sinha (ed.), *Fort William – India House Correspondence* (Vol. II of Indian Record Series: Public), p. 45.

[5] Quoted by Peter Auber, *Rise and Progress of the British Power in India* (London, 1837), vol. I, p. 24.

[6] See Harlow and Madden (eds.), *British Colonial Developments: 1774–1834* (Oxford, 1953), p. 47.

[7] *Problems of Empire Britain and India 1757–1813* (London, 1968), pp. 58–9.

[8] See for example Clive to Chatham, 7 January 1759, John Malcolm, *Life of Lord Clive* (London, 1836), vol. II, p. 119.

ready we have seen that Adam Smith saw the necessity of raising fortifications
to protect colonies, and colonial trade. He went a step further with reference
to India. One of his most important arguments for the nationalisation of
the East India Company was that it would contribute materially to the
revenue of the government.[9]

But complete nationalisation was too drastic a measure to find universal
acceptance in the 1770s. The East India Company was not prepared to
surrender without a fight and its directors used contemporary ideas to good
advantage. They claimed that the rights of long established institutions
should not be lightly interfered with. Besides, the self-interest of the
Company was thought sufficient to induce the Company to secure the full
benefits of the colonies to Great Britain. It is interesting to see very Mande-
villian arguments used by Governor George Johnstone, who played a large
part in the Company's confrontation with the Government in the 1770s,
in opposing nationalisation: 'Avarice, again, may be compared to dung in
agriculture, disgusting in itself, and hateful in every operation; but at the
same time, it is a passion more essential to society than any other, and whose
fermentation puts the whole in motion.'[10] Apart from the Company's resistance, there were other reasons the most important being the fear of corruption induced by the sudden acquisition of enormous revenue and patronage
by the British government.[11] The East India Company had also the backing
of a section of the British Parliament. Throughout the history of the Company, this element tempered the government's policy towards the Company.[12]

To these reasons must be added the 'Mercantilist' views held by some
key officials at the Whitehall. Mercantilist economic policy, as Eli
Heckscher has shown, had a tendency 'to employ private interests as the
best implements of its policy'.[13] Inadequate financial and administrative
resources encouraged the policy makers to create joint-stock companies
to exercise certain functions which according to Classical economists,
should be in the public domain. As against this, Adam Smith in 1776
advocated the nationalisation of the East India Company, because a
company of merchants are 'incapable of considering themselves as sovereigns, even after they have become such ... As sovereigns, their interest is
exactly the same with that of the country which they govern. As merchants,
their interest is directly opposite to that interest.'[14] Hence Heckscher's

[9] *Wealth of Nations*, p. 898. Similar views were expressed by others. See the anonymous
     pamphlet, *The Present State of the British Interest in India* (London, 1773), pp. 13–14.
[10] *Thoughts on Our Acquisition in the East Indies*, (London, 1771), p. 7.
[11] P. J. Marshall, *op. cit.* pp. 23–4.
[12] See C. H. Philips, *The East India Company: 1784–1834* (Manchester, 1940), p. 299.
[13] *Mercantilism* (Translated by Mendel Shapiro) (London, 1955), vol. 1, p. 455.
[14] *Wealth of Nations*, pp. 602–3.

judgement that 'Mercantilism from one particular angle was more individualistic than *laissez-faire*', has considerable merit.[15] Any policy of non-interference before the full flowering of Classical liberalism could also have derived theoretical support from economists such as Dudley North. Hence when Smith demanded the Company to be stripped of its territorial possessions, he was asking for a revolutionary shift in economic policy.

In the 1770s and 1780s, Indian affairs were largely managed at the Whitehall by Charles Jenkinson, known first as Lord Hawkesbury and later Lord Liverpool, and John Robinson. Both of them belonged to the old school and in particular Jenkinson 'regarded theorists such as Adam Smith and Richard Price as dangerous heretics who, if allowed to have their way, could irremediably weaken the nation in relation to rival Powers'.[16] They were worried that the Younger Pitt and his ministerial colleagues were all 'too evidently infected with these new-fangled doctrines' and they did their best to curb the attempts to change the established economic policy drastically. They too believed like Adam Smith that the Indian possessions were most fertile sources of wealth but were not convinced that direct government rule would enable Britain to enjoy the benefits of India.[17] Their view was that the government was not likely to rule the Indian possessions in any way better than the Company and so the Company should retain the territories subject to sharing the dividends with the State and giving substantial loans to the government from time to time.[18]

William Pitt, as Prime Minister, although a disciple of Adam Smith, could not implement Smith's economic policy towards the East India Company. Circumscribed by political pressures, the views of the permanent civil servants and fears of corruption and nepotism, he did his best to control the Company through his lieutenant, Henry Dundas. Dundas too had great admiration for Smith's economic ideas and he found that administration by a commercial body 'strikes every one as a Solecism', yet he consoled himself that the system inaugurated by Pitt's India Bill of 1784 had a practical base, for 'it is at all times much wiser to found upon the basis of old and Established Systems, than to substitute in their room, the most plausible untried theories'.[19]

---

[15] *Op. cit.*, vol. I, p. 455.

[16] Vincent Harlow, *The Founding of the Second British Empire 1763–1793* (London, 1952), vol. II, p. 252.

[17] See Lucy Sutherland, *The East India Company in Eighteenth Century Politics* (Oxford, 1952), p. 354.

[18] See John Robinson's Policy memorandum quoted extensively in *Ibid.*, pp. 338–9.

[19] Memorandum to F. Russell, *Charters and Treaties*, India Office Records, vol. IIA, ff. 184, 185; 186. On the whole Dundas was sceptical of the theoretical arguments used by free-traders and frequently stated that the free traders are apt to be misled by 'general theories, without attending to the peculiar circumstances of the trade they are treating of'. See

THE END OF MONOPOLY

The core of British policy towards India at the time of the passing of the Pitt's India Act consisted of two elements: firstly, that the territories acquired in India should be under the control of the East India Company; and secondly that the Company should be the sole agency in Britain to trade with India. Though as we have seen, Smith's advocacy of the national-isation of the East India Company's Indian territories to increase the public revenue was not accepted, there were other elements of his policy towards the empire that were immensely influential in shaping policy.

Smith was one of the most vehement critics of any policy that reserved the trade of the colonies exclusively to the mother country. It was his opinion that colonial trade breeds a certain fatal smugness and is liable to serious disorders at the slightest injury.[20] As the manufacturers became confident of safe colonial markets complacency and inefficiency set in, and Britain thus ran the risk of losing its competitive position in the world. However the future prospects of the Indo-British trade had been made even more precarious by vesting this monopoly in one single firm. Thus it was argued that for the future wellbeing of British industry, it was vital to put an end to the monopoly of the Asian trade being enjoyed by the East India Company.

Opposition to the East India Company had existed ever since its in-ception. There had always been some who disliked the Company. Sometimes it was a liberal who opposed the Company for its monopoly. Many found fault with its practice of exporting precious metals to the East. British producers always opposed the Company for bringing in cheap Eastern com-modities and thus destroying home industry.[21] But the Company survived it all. However, in the last quarter of the eighteenth century, there were many developments that strengthened the Company's opposition. The Company's political functions had increased and the British government found it necessary to exercise a more positive control over the affairs of the Company. The British economy itself was experiencing the beneficial effects of the Industrial Revolution, and various inventions had made British industry very efficient and capable of underselling its powerful Indian rivals. As P. J. Marshall has pointed out, the element of risk in-

Footnote 19 continued
> *Letters from the Right Honourable Henry Dundas to the Chairman of the Court of Directors* (London, 1813), p. 5.

[20] *Wealth of Nations*, p. 571.

[21] See P. J. Thomas, *Mercantilism and the East India Trade* (London, 1926), Chapters II & III. See also Michael Edwards, *The Growth of the British Cotton Trade 1780–1815* (Manchester, 1967), p. 42.

volved in the Indian trade had lessened considerably after the War of American Independence.[22] Above all, the Company lacked an apologia (or an apologist) as they had in the days of Child, Papillon and Mun. By hitting out against monopoly, Adam Smith's *Wealth of Nations* actually served the cause of the anti-Company elements by providing theoretical backing to their opposition.

Adam Smith had demonstrated that monopoly as practised by the East India Company was not only against good political economy but also against *national prosperity*. He was no internationalist,[23] and it is his distinct nationalism draped in the diaphanous veil of political economy that made the *Wealth of Nations* immediately very popular and led to its being used as a weapon to attack the privileges of the East India Company.

Although the break up of the Company's monopoly of trade with India started in 1793, it was not until the 1813 Charter that the monopoly was removed and only in 1833 that the commercial functions of the Company ceased. In 1793, the situation was far too difficult for the entire confiscation of the monopolistic privileges being enjoyed by the Company. In the 1790s the arguments expressed against the Company were uncertain, and the demands of the anti-East India Company lobby were contradictory.[24] For example, in spite of the enormous increase in the efficiency of the British textile industry, the Manchester merchants were still apprehensive of Indian competition. They petitioned for a reduction in the Company's imports of cotton goods, while their Glasgow counterparts petitioned for the prohibition of the importation of textiles and of exporting textile machinery.[25] Various business groups in Britain like the Cornish tin miners and Exeter woollen manufacturers either demanded exclusive supply contracts or participation in the Company's exclusive privileges. All in all, one does not find much evidence of the spirit of Adam Smith in its larger setting, although his works remained the essential belief of the small group clamouring for free trade between India and Britain. These free traders saw evil in the East India Company's monopoly because they anticipated good profits by importing from India. Thus the interests of

[22] *Op. cit.*, p. 95.
[23] See *The Theory of Moral Sentiments* (London, 1774), Part IV, Section II, Chapter II. In fact all Classical economists were essentially concerned with the well-being of only Britain and their main aim was the enrichment of their own nation-state. See Robbins, *The Theory of Economic Policy in English Classical Political Economy*, pp. 9–11.
[24] See Amales Tripathi, *Trade and Finance in the Bengal Presidency 1793–1833* (Bombay, 1956), p. 25.
[25] For the activities of Manchester and other British merchants, see Arthur Redford, *Manchester Merchants and Foreign Trade* (Manchester, 1934), vol. I, pp. 108–9. See also *Charters and Treaties*, Volumes 10 and 11, India Office Records.

the traders were opposed to the interests of the manufacturers. Dundas was particularly anxious to help the British manufacturers but he could not countenance the complete prohibition of imports in view of the advice he received from David Scott who pointed out to him the dangers of the clandestine trade that was going on. Owing to the lack of proper remittance facilities, this form of illegal trade was found useful by the British residents in India; and owing to the restrictive export policies of European nations, this trade was found equally useful by the continental traders.[26] Nor could he open up the Indian trade completely because as he suggested 'National interests are at stake as those connected with the subject of India.' It would be 'madness in the extreme not to give due weight to the reasonings of those whose opinions are derived from local knowledge'.[27] Naturally, local officials like Lord Cornwallis were very much against free trade, since it was bound up with the question of colonisation. The Company itself with monotonous regularity continued to stress that monopoly was a 'material and necessary instrument towards the safety and preservation of the Empire'. According to the Court of Directors, the Empire would not survive the separation of political and commercial functions.[28]

Pitt and Dundas, disciples as they were of Adam Smith, nevertheless visualised an imperial role for India. Throughout the Napoleonic wars, British politicians aimed at political domination in the adjoining French colonial possessions throughout the world.[29] Viewed in this context India was of crucial importance. The question was how to make the possession of India bring about increased power and increased profit for Britain, without at the same time disappointing the various groups that were exerting pressure to alter the policy towards the Company's monopoly. Dundas saw the solution in terms of the Indian trade being controlled entirely by the British.[30] His knowledge of political economy probably

---

[26] See Scott's letter to Dundas, 3 April 1787 in *Home Misc.* No. 404, pp. 61–7 *et seq.* India Office Records.

[27] Memo from Dundas to F. Russell, *Charters and Treaties*, vol . IIA, p. 182, *et seq.* India Office Records.

[28] Baring to Dundas, 1 June 1793, *Charters and Treaties*, vol. 10, India Office Records.

[29] Helen Taft Manning, *British Colonial Government after the American Revolution 1782–1820* (New Haven, 1933), p. 293.

[30] Dundas to John Perry, 1 July 1797, Martin (ed.), *Wellesley's Despatches* (London, 1836), vol. V, pp. 117–8. Most directors of the Company maintained similar views. For example, Jacob Bosanquet who became a director of the Company in 1782 and was very influential asserted that the most desirable policy was 'to bring to Great Britain the largest possible share of the Indian trade, consistent with the safety of the Empire established there, and in the mode most conducive to the strength and welfare of the Mother Country', 'Cursory Remarks Respecting India' No. 927 (R 81525) Item 80. Melville Papers at John Rylands Library. See also Henry Dundas's speech in the House of Commons, 20 December 1796. He remarked that the policy of the British was 'to bring the Riches of the Ganges and of Canton to the Thames.' *East India Budget Speeches*, vol. II, p. 38.

bothered him a little as he said, 'I should on commercial principle be obliged to say that the produce and trade of India should be brought home in that species of shipping which can be got at the cheapest rate.' He did not, however, let this trouble him too much because there were 'grounds of great and essential national importance which stand in the way of that general proposition'. Hence it is hardly surprising to find Dundas opting for what he terms 'Regulated monopoly' and seeking to satisfy all sections of Indian trade. On the one hand the monopoly was left intact with the Company, and on the other an opening was provided for the merchants and manufacturers who clamoured for a share in the Indian trade.[31] He also instructed the Company to adjust its trade in such a way that it would complement rather than compete with British industry.[32]

The 1793 Charter was not an unmitigated defeat for the free traders. Indeed, within a decade of the passing of the Charter, anti-monopoly forces grew so strong that the *Edinburgh Review* wrote that the wisdom of allowing free trade to India had been generally accepted ever since Adam Smith formulated it.[33] With the changing structure of the British economy, there was growing too an unanimity in the opinions of both the trading and the manufacturing sectors of British industry and commerce. The manufacturing interests were not now afraid of Indian competition as they had been in 1793. Although there was a section of the British industry which wanted the monopoly to continue, the majority wanted the trade to be thrown open to all. The clamour that resulted from the union of these two strands of thought was responsible to a large extent for the removal of the East India trading monopoly in 1813.

ECONOMIC IDEAS IN THE CHARTER DEBATES

The critics of the Company's monopoly gave many reasons why the trade should be opened to private traders. First, they felt confident of selling more in India than the Company could because they claimed to have superior inventive skill and abundant surplus capital to do extensive trading in the East.[34] Secondly, free trade was expected to increase Britain's trade and also reduce the trade of the rivals. The free traders of Britain were particularly jealous of the American traders who were conducting business in India under the umbrella of protection provided by the Royal Navy and with

---

[31] Dundas to Baring, 16 February 1793, *Charters and Treaties*, India Office Records, vol. IIA, pp. 349–65.
[32] Memo to F. Russell, *ibid.*, p. 206.
[33] July 1804, p. 308.
[34] *Parliamentary Debates*, 7 April 1812. See also 'Ignotus', *Letters on the East India Monopoly* (Glasgow, 1812), p. 120.

clandestine English capital.[35] Thirdly, Napoleon's Berlin and Milan Decrees, his supremacy in Europe and effective measures of blockade had succeeded in curtailing British exports to the Continent. Thus a 'large quantity of British disposable produce is scotched in the hands of the English merchants or manufacturers'.[36] Fourthly, the Company was evidently unable to expand its trade or conduct it profitably and thus by its dog-in-the-manger policy of not allowing others to do profitable trading was actually standing in the way of the enrichment of the nation.[37]

The most important reason given for abolishing the Company's monopoly was that contemporary economic theory supported a policy of free trade. No pamphlet or essay or speech that was written or spoken against the East India Company's privileges was complete without a reference to Adam Smith and political economy. Whether to attack the Company or to defend a cause from the counter-attacks of the Company, Adam Smith was found indispensable. Smith had categorically stated: 'exclusive companies, therefore, are nuisances in every respect; always more or less inconvenient to the countries in which they are established, and destructive to those which have the misfortune to fall under their government'.[38] This sentence was quoted with great approval in almost all the pamphlets written by the free traders, and Smith's arguments were freely used – sometimes with and sometimes without acknowledgment. An Edinburgh author – typical of the free trade writers – forcefully contended that Smith's doctrines were applicable to India as much as they were to Britain. Consequently monopoly was thought incompatible with the 'most liberal and enlightened views of political economy, and equally prejudicial to the interests of the mother country and the colonies'.[39] The opponents of the Company argued that freedom of commerce and the right to trade were the birthright of the British people, and by stifling competition the East India Company was obstructing not only increased trade but also cheaper prices for consumers. Some argued that monopoly was effective and 'politic' only in the early stages when capital was scarce and people had to combine

---

[35] See W. Lester, *The Happy Era to One Hundred Millions of the Human Race* (London, 1813), p. 41.

[36] *A Demonstration of the Necessity and Advantages of a Free-trade to the East Indies and of a Termination to the Present Monopoly of the East India Company* (London, 1807), p. 32.

[37] See for example, David Laurie, *Hints Regarding the East India Monopoly Respectfully submitted to the British Legislature* (Glasgow, 1813), pp. 32–3.

[38] *Wealth of Nations*, p. 606. It is interesting, but not surprising, to see a private merchant in 1803 naming his ship *Adam Smith*. See *Asiatic Annual Register*, 1803, p. 166.

[39] *The Question as to the Renewal of the East India Company Monopoly* (Edinburgh, 1812), pp. 4, 8.

to do trading. But the changing circumstances necessitated competition because of the abundance of capital.[40] Another line of attack flowed from Smith's attitude towards the state—people relationship. The function of the state is to look after the interests of the people it governed. The interests of the people were concentrated in maximising consumption. Such being the situation, how could a company interested in only its own profits, be expected to show consideration for others? On the one hand, by stifling competition from Britain it sells to India at the highest price, and on the other, by being the only buyer of Indian goods for the British market, the Company is able to impose its own price.[41] This argument was also used by the East India Company to put forward its own case why the monopoly should not be given up. The Company was afraid that the removal of restrictions would end in a mad rush with the result Britain would be overstocked with Indian goods and prices would consequently fall.[42] In an unsigned article in *The Edinburgh Review* James Mill castigated the Company's argument as 'blind and deceitful', and argued that monopoly did not reduce prices in India but actually stood in the way of reduction because 'it prevents all that encouragement to, the manufacturer which competition would afford; and of which the inseparable consequences would be, those improvements in the productive powers of labour, by which prices are, to an infinite extent reduced'.[43]

It would appear that in the first decade of the nineteenth century very few would have supported a policy of continuing the Company's monopoly. The pamphlets were only reflecting this general acceptance of free trade ideas because the policy makers had made up their minds long before many of these pamphlets were published.[44]

The East India Company now realised the way the wind was blowing. Consequently they decided to combat the ideas on which their exclusive monopoly was being attacked. The Company's defenders even as early as the Seventeenth Century had used theoretic generalities in addition to more

[40] See for instance, Thomas Lee, *The Right of Every British Merchant to Trade Within the Geographical Limits Defined by the Charter of the East India Company* (London, 1812), p. 2.

[41] James Mill, *History of British India* (London, 1820), 2nd edn, Vol. II, pp. 39–41.

[42] Chairs to Robert Dundas, 13 January 1809, *Charters and Treaties*, India Office Records, Vol. 14, pp. 18–39.

[43] Issue of April 1810, p. 130 (Authorship determined by F. W. Fetter in 'The Authorship of Economic Articles in the Edinburgh Review' in *Journal of Political Economy*, Vol. 61, June 1953). See also Thomas Lee, *op. cit.*, pp. 16–17, where he uses typical Smithian arguments.

[44] See the views of Robert Dundas, President of Board of Control: Dundas to Chairs, 28 December 1808, *Charters and Treaties*, India Office Records, Vol. 14, pp. 15–16.

specific arguments and certainly they knew the advantages of detached reason as the only method of making a case which would at the same time enable them to avoid the stigma of self interest.[45]

By that time, Adam Smith's ideas had acquired a reputation which made the Company and its defenders reluctant to attack them directly. Instead the Court of Directors argued against the working of the rules of political economy in practice while refraining from attacking the basic principles of political economy. The opponents used Smith because they thought Smith had completely unravelled the mystery of political economy. The Court of Directors, on the other hand, argued thus:

The just application of general principles, even where they were well understood, is known to be a matter of difficulty. That science, which is itself very much built on fact and experience, may be supposed yet capable of improvement by further knowledge; and the constitution and the system of the Company, instead of being judged by principles adopted before any sufficient experience was acquired of the effects of such a constitution and system may afford new and useful data for enlarging the boundaries of the science.[46]

Instead of using this argument to enlarge upon the inadequacy and *ad hoc* nature of the principles of political economy, the supporters accepted the validity of the theories of political economy, confining themselves only to a criticism of the application to the Indian case. Almost all the pro-East India Company pamphlets paid tributes to the learning and scholarship of Adam Smith and the usefulness of the principles of political economy. If at all they had reservations about anything in Adam Smith, it was his 'practical knowledge'. For instance, defending the East India Company 'Fabius' said, 'Dr Adam Smith, whose opinions on the subject of monopoly, will always, theoretically speaking, carry great weight, but when reduced to practice will lose much of their convincing powers. He continually sets up *Theory* against *experience*, and *possibilities* against *facts*.'[47] As against the speculative theories, facts indicated that free traders would be disillusioned if they thought that the abolition of the monopoly would solve all their problems.[48] They conceded that Adam Smith was a great authority, but even he was by no means infallible.[49]

---

[45] There is a document in the India Office Library, which says 'Extracts from Authors Lawyers etc. to Serve as materials for the Defence of the East India Company'. The extracts include pieces from Abbe Raynal, Adam Smith, Michle's Lusiad, and Governor Johnstone. *Charters and Treaties*, India Office Records, Vol. 9.

[46] Court of Directors to Bombay Government, 22 February 1811, *Parliamentary Papers*, H.C. 306, Vol. X of Session 1812–13.

[47] *A Letter to the Rt. Honble. The Earl of Buckinghamshire* (London, 1813), p. 23.

[48] *The Quarterly Review*, December 1812, p. 241.

[49] *Considerations on the Policy of Renewing the Exclusive Privileges of the East India Company*

Other economists were brought to oppose Smith's views. In his defence of the Company against the attack from arguments derived from Smith's writings David Macpherson used a quotation from Abbe Raynal, and 'Fabius' used Lord Kames to make the point: 'A noble author writing on the subject of Political Oeconomy observes, that commerce pushed to the extent to which the spirit of speculation would induce individuals to carry it, would involve not only themselves but their country in inevitable ruin.'[50]

Many pro-Company pamphlets objected to using the word 'Monopoly' for the exclusive privileges of the Company. John Bruce, for instance, contended that the East India Company should not be classified 'under that unpopular denomination' (monopoly) because 'the strong feature which pervades monopolies generally, disfiguring and rendering them repulsive, is not to be found on the face of the Company's qualified monopoly'.[51] The chief shortcoming of a monopoly is to act on a purely selfish principle. As for the Company, not one of its ships had traversed the Indian seas but some price had been paid 'either in the shape of compulsory exports, or stipulated returns, or in hard gold, for the license or privilege of sailing'.[52] 'Verax' argued that a real monopoly implies not only 'an exclusive *right* to buy, but to *sell* also, and upon the monopolists' own terms'.[53] This he said the Company did not have.

Even if the Company possessed a pure monopoly, some argued, it did not mean the result would be oppressive. Although in abstract theory monopoly is an evil, there are always exceptions. Not all monopolies need be pernicious or evil. Already the Bank of England was accepted as an established institution. Monopolies should be tolerated if they are beneficial to the society in supplying goods cheaply. Did not Adam Smith himself support the monopoly of the Post Office? Every trade has its monopolistic elements; so it would be wrong to single out one instance alone for criticism, overlooking the various benefits accrued by having the East Indian monopoly.[54]

In their anxiety to counter the forcefully varied pleas of the free traders,

---

Footnote 49 continued

(London, 1812), p. 6. See also for an extreme view on Adam Smith, Robert Grant, *The Expediency Maintained of Continuing the System by which the Trade and Government of India are now Regulated* (London, 1813), pp. xii–xiii.

[50] Fabius, *A Letter to the Rt. Honble. The Earl of Buckinghamshire*, pp. 25–6, David Macpherson, *The History of the European Commerce With India* (London, 1812), quoted on p. 349.

[51] *Substance of a Speech in the Committee of the House of Commons* (London, 1813), p. 4.

[52] *Observations on the Territorial Rights and Commercial Privileges of the East India Company* (London, 1813), p. 27.

[53] *East India Question* (London, 1813), p. 12.

[54] *Considerations on the Policy of Renewing the Exclusive Privileges of East India Company*, p. 6.

the supporters of the Company used every effort to produce theoretical and pseudo-theoretical arguments. One pamphleteer even suggested that if 'Adam Smith were now alive he would probably have changed many of his opinions.'[55] Since Adam Smith had been wrong in many prophecies, he should not be taken too literally and restraint was not always bad! After the French Revolution, 'every restraint was done away, but instead of things improving thereby, they grew visibly worse'. 'Probus' charged Smith with ignorance of the Portuguese experiment of free trade in India, which was 'a disgrace to commerce, was ruinous in every principle'. He accordingly concluded that the 'grand machine' of British commerce should not be 'sacrificed to the dreams and dotage of theory'.[56]

There were some writers who referred to the works of 'Mercantilists' like Malachy Postlethwayt and Thomas Mun to show the beneficial effects of the East Indian trade and the Company's monopoly. It was argued that the legal rights of the Company should not be tampered with because 'security of property and rights of every kind' were the roots of commerce.[57] In the same vein, an 'Impartial Observer' gave the reason why the demand for British goods had declined in India; it was simply 'the lamentable result of the culpable infatuation which has promoted, in the districts of Hindusthan, the manufacturing arts of Europe. This evil, so destructive of the prosperity of Great Britain, has increased in the enlargement of our settlements.'[58]

For all that has been said of the arguments that were used to defend the Company's monopoly, it had little to counter the ever increasing acceptance of free trade ideas based on Smithian economics. Indeed opinions differed even within the Company, and influential directors like David Scott and Francis Baring opposed the views of Charles Grant who believed in the Company's monopoly and the rigorous exclusion of foreign merchants in Indian trade. Baring for example said that the attacks on free trade and free ports by the 'Chairs' originated in 'a narrow confined view of the subject' and he was pleased that politicians and statesmen were not so narrow minded.[59] Joseph Hume, the radical, himself a shareholder of the East India Company, actually moved a motion against the monopoly in the General Court of Proprietors a few months prior to the Parliamentary discussion. Although the motion was defeated, it shows how the new liberal ideas had penetrated into the organisation. This becomes especially clear

[55] 'Commonsense' in *Free-Trade with India*, 3rd Edn. (London, 1813), p. 4.
[56] *Letters on the East India Question*, (London, 1813), pp. 32, 36–7.
[57] D. Hughson, *The East India Question* (London, 1813), p. 11.
[58] *Considerations on Colonial Policy with Relation to the Renewal of the East India Company's Charter* (London, 1813), pp. 62–3.
[59] Letter 16 December 1807, *Home Misc.* India Office Records, No. 494, f. 157.

when one observes a respect for received doctrine in the policy statements of the 'Chairs' intended for the guidance of Indian administrators. It is made clear that policies 'so diametrically at variance with the admitted maxims of political economy' should not be entertained.[60]

What has been observed so far indicates, first, that the newly emerging discipline came as a useful weapon for the anti-Company propagandists; and secondly that political economy had gained such a measure of acceptance that even within the East India Company it did not encounter unqualified condemnation. It must be admitted that the adherence to the new ideas very often cut across party lines. Not all politicians were concerned solely with the short term interests of their party. At the turn of 1812, the Whigs were about to go over to the Company's side simply to oppose the government. But Lord Grenville, an influential member of the Whig party, was against such shortsightedness and appreciated the correct doctrines of his political opponents. In a letter to Lord Temple he said,

We shall view the question on something of a more enlarged scale, and on principles a little higher than the temporary object of party politics, and I am confident that in this view there never was a measure less suited to the real interests of a country than would be the renewal, at this moment, of the Company's monopolies ... the claims of the Company and City to a continuance of a commercial monopoly, is inconsistent with every principle of political economy, with justice to the people of England, and with good faith to Ireland.[61]

Again Lord Liverpool, the Prime Minister in 1813, had been influenced in his early life by the 'Mercantilist' ideas of his father Charles Jenkinson (later Lord Hawkesbury) and had retained a few of them for a long time. However by the time he became the Prime Minister in 1812, he was like most educated people in early nineteenth century Britain a convert to the economic ideas of Adam Smith and a convinced free trader. Throughout his prime ministership he pursued free trade policies wherever he could, and if he had to deviate from the path of free trade he made it clear that as a general principle 'the thing must be left to right itself'.[62]

The two decades after 1813 saw a movement for the abolition of the last surviving privilege of the East India Company, the monopoly of the China trade. By 1833 British government had become increasingly receptive to *laissez-faire* economic policy, and the demolition of the China trade

[60] Court of Directors to the Government of Madras, 24 April 1811 (Revenue) *Despatches to Madras*, India Office Records, Vol. 47, E/4/907, Para. 92, pp. 243–4.
[61] Grenville to Temple, 10 January 1813, Duke of Buckingham and Chandos, *Memoirs of the Court of England During the Regency* (London, 1856) Vol. II, pp. 15–16.
[62] Quoted in W. R. Brock, *Lord Liverpool and Liberal Toryism 1820 to 1827* (Cambridge, 1941), pp. 43–44.

monopoly was relatively easy. It is hardly surprising to see the Company and its supporters, in defending themselves, never once whispering anything against the validity of received doctrine. Henry St George Tucker, a Director of the East India Company, provided some interesting arguments regarding the need of certain preconditions and limitations upon free trade with distant countries. He did not ask the government to 'abandon the doctrine of free trade as an abstract proposition', but urged that 'it cannot be received for practical purposes as a rule of commercial policy without certain conditions and limitations'.[63] Tucker argued that in order to reap the maximum benefits from a policy of free trade, it should be practised by both the trading partners, in this case Britain and China. If a trading partner does not reciprocate, not only the total trade is reduced but also the terms of trade goes unfavourable with all its consequences to the country with no tariff. Tucker was certain that China was not likely to free its trade from tariffs. He also argued that a free trade policy implicitly assumes very little unemployment. During times of high unemployment, an increase of imports will by increasing the domestic consumption of foreign goods aggravate the unemployment problem. Another argument he used related to the distance between the markets. Market variations are not known in good time which makes trading with China hazardous. Tucker's thesis was that the successful use of the Classical theory of international trade depended on certain preconditions. As these were not present the policy was inapplicable. In the same vein R. Montgomery Martin took McCulloch to task for opposing the Company's tea monopoly while treating the Bank of England with 'candour' in his *Commercial Dictionary*.[64] A few defenders of the East India Company accepted the idea that restrictions on trade were unjust. But the privileges of the Company had been long enjoyed, and the empire had been built so that 'the opinions, habits, manners and prejudices of a vast population have been formed under, and are adapted to, this system'. Under these circumstances, it was doubtful 'whether, for the sake of conformity to theoretical principles, we should, by resorting to a different mode of policy, endanger a dominion built, more than any other, upon the slightest foundation of opinion'.[65]

The East India Company received relatively less support this time, as it was obviously fighting a losing battle, and unlike the earlier generation of civil servants like Munro or Hastings, the new civilians like Holt Mackenzie and Sir Charles Metcalfe enthusiastically supported the cause of abolishing the Company's monopoly of China trade. In Britain the economists had made

---

[63] Minute dated 11 June 1833, *Charters and Treaties*, India Office Records, Vol. 19, f. 219.
[64] *The Past and Present State of the Tea Trade of England* (London, 1832), p. 136.
[65] *The Asiatic Journal*, December, 1821, p. 523.

it clear long before that the ideal economic system should be based on free trade. When this was comprehended by the politicians and bureaucrats, the general policy began to move towards the ideal of free trade from the 1820s onwards.[66] The government's task became considerably easier with the decline of the East India Company's lobby in Parliament. After 1832, the most powerful section in the House of Commons was the pro-free traders. With Huskisson and Peel in the Government, a wider programme of freedom was envisaged and many steps were taken in that direction long before the Great Reform Bill of 1832.[67] In that age of free trade, the Company had really no chance of retaining its China trade monopoly.

Even granting that leaders of Whigs (e.g. Lord Grenville) and leaders of Tories (e.g. Lord Liverpool) were converted to political economy, we cannot argue that the acceptance of the new principles of political economy alone was responsible for the abolition of the Company's monopoly. There were other valid reasons that made the end of the monopoly inevitable. The influence of free trade concepts in this particular policy should not lead to uncalled-for generalisation about the spread of *laissez-faire*, because simultaneously with the removal of the East India Company's monopoly we also notice sharp increases in import duties on Indian textiles and the imposition of extra duties on goods imported into India from countries other than Britain.[68] However because a quantitative evaluation of the influence of ideas is not possible, they are often underestimated. Nevertheless, it is clear enough that in this case economic ideas (as distinct from a particular school of thought) *were* used in the arguments – both for or against. The profusion of theoretical arguments employed in the discussion shows that the participants believed in economic theory as an important ingredient for the making of policies.

INDIA AS A COLONY, ECONOMIC IDEAS AND POLICY

Free trade without free mobility of resources was meaningless, and hence far more than the question of the Company's monopoly controversy during the period centred on the question of colonisation and the acquisition of landed property in India by Britishers. Throughout its history, the East India Company zealously enforced the powers granted to it by Parliament to prevent individuals from Britain from settling down and

[66] See Peter Mathias, *The First Industrial Nation* (London, 1969), p. 294.
[67] See C. R. Fay, 'The Movement towards Free-Trade 1820–1853' in *Cambridge History of the British Empire*, Vol. II, p. 388 *et seq.*
[68] See C. J. Hamilton, *The Trade Relations Between England and India* (Calcutta, 1919), p. 160 *et seq.*

acquiring property in India. Hence alongside the agitation for removing the Company's monopoly, a campaign to permit colonisation in India was also carried on by the free traders from the 1780s. However, after the American War of Independence the British government had become very sensitive to any attempts at colonisation. There was also the fear of depopulation in Britain, for as Charles Grant said in 1792, 'Multitudes of the needy and the idle, allured by the fame of that country, and eager to seize novel privileges, would flock thither at once. Britain would, in a short space, be thinned of inhabitants and those eastern provinces filled with a new race of adventurers, many of them low and licentious.'[69] Moreover, it was stressed by Sir Philip Francis among others that the Indian soil belonged to the Indians and 'to alienate them in favor of strangers, may be found a dangerous as well as an unjust measure'.[70]

But all these considerations gave way to new ideas in the first decade of the nineteenth century. Although it was seldom suggested that India could really relieve Britain of her surplus population, a favourable climate had nevertheless been created for this agitation to permit colonisation in India by the appearance of Malthus's *Essay*, the 1801 Census, and a general fear of being overpopulated. The defenders of the Company's positions presently gave up raising the bogey of depopulation, although the dangers of raising a mongrel race that would be difficult to control were stressed.

According to the new Charter issued to the Company in 1813 colonisation was not permitted, but the agitation favouring British colonisation in India continued however. It was suggested that nothing but the 'pernicious tendency and spirit of the Government' could explain why the automatic 'transfusion of the arts, the example, the skill, the intelligence, the capital, and industry of the superior country and race into the inferior'[71] should be prevented. This campaign for the removal of obstacles to free mobility of resources between England and India was successful. By 1829, Lord Ellenborough, the Secretary of State, was able to report to Lord Bentinck, the Governor-General in India, how the 'tide of public feeling had gone strongly in favour of what is called colonization'.[72] One important reason for this changed attitude towards colonisation was the increasing attention it received from the economists. By 1830 many leading economists considered

---

[69] *Observations on the State of Society Among the Asiatic Subjects of Great Britain*, Reprinted in *Parl. Papers*, H. L. Paper, Vol. XXXII of 1852–3, p. 73.

[70] Minute dated 12 May 1775, *Bengal Revenue Consultations*, India Office Records, Range 49, Vol. 52, f. 706.

[71] *An Appeal to England Against the New Indian Stamp Act* (London, 1828) p. 22.

[72] Ellenborough to Bentinck, 15 June 1829 (*Bentinck Papers*, Nottingham University Library).

the colonies to be useful outlets for the surplus population of Britain.[73] To give an example, in 1790 Jeremy Bentham opposed colonisation, whereas by 1831 his opinions changed to such an extent that he drew up a scheme for Wakefield for the formation of a joint-stock colonisation society.[74] There was the nagging suspicion in the minds of economists and politicians that there was a surplus of capital in the economy and competition was reducing profit to a low level. Hence it was urged in the Parliament that a 'larger field for the employment of capital, a greater vent for our manufacturers, a wider range for our shipping, are the objects we should aim at'.[75] The opinion of the Wakefield school of thought was that the emigration of labour and capital from England would reduce the competition and raise the productivity of industry. Colonies would also be able to buy English manufactures in return for a steady and cheap supply of corn and cotton. This school of thought regarding overseas investment had the support of the philosophical radicals, J. S. Mill, Grote, Buller and others.[76] British business interests too had similar views. For example, a Mr Fortune, representing many Lombard street merchants petitioned to Lord Melville that from the overpopulation of Britain, 'thousands of well-educated and intelligent persons are compelled to seek employ in foreign climates ... An immense surplus capital, finding no employment at home, is adventured upon rash and ruinous schemes ... This, if allowed a vent in India ... would find ample employment, and would ensure innumerable benefits to the mother country.'[77] Thus a combination of national interest and political economy prompted the agitation for colonisation in India, although these advocates were not blind to realities. They knew that 'the redundant *labouring* population of England or Ireland could find [no] relief by emigrating to India',[78] as they would in Canada or the Cape of Good Hope. The sort of

---

[73] See for quotations illustrating this point from the writings of classical economists: Donald O. Wagner, 'British Economists and the Empire' in *Political Science Quarterly*, June 1931, Donald Winch, *Classical Political Economy and Colonies* (London, 1965), Chapters V and VI, and Edward R. Kittrell, 'The Development of the Theory of Colonization in English Classical Political Economy' in *The Southern Economic Journal*, Vol. 31, January 1965.

[74] See Edward Kittrell, 'Bentham and Wakefield' in *The Western Economic Journal*, Vol. IV, No. 1, Fall 1965. And R. N. Ghosh, 'Bentham on Colonies and Colonization' in *Indian Economic Review*, Vol. VI, No. 4, August 1963, pp. 78–80.

[75] W. W. Whitmore in the House of Commons, 14 May 1829, *Substance of a Speech on the Subject of the Trade with the East Indies and China* (London 1829), p. 3.

[76] See Bernard Semmel, 'The Philosophical Radicals and Colonization' in *Journal of Economic History*, Vol. 21, December 1961, pp. 513–25 and *The Rise of Free Trade Imperialism* (London, 1970), Chapter 4.

[77] Fortune to Melville, 9 July 1828, Manuscript 523 (R 68275) *Papers on the Tea Trade*, f. 45. (Melville Papers at the John Rylands Library).

[78] Gavin Young, *A Further Inquiry into the Expediency of Applying the Principles of Colonial Policy* (London, 1828), p. xi.

people who were required in India were 'British landlords, farmers, traders and artisans, of every description'. These people 'would rapidly and indefinitely advance the agricultural and commercial interests of India', thus giving stability and infusing vigour into the government.[79] It was anticipated that the settlers 'would form a nucleus of intelligence and industry' exerting a favourable influence on the wants and industry of the Indian population.[80]

This new attitude is seen to be complete when we set side by side the opinion of the Governor General in 1794 and in 1829. In 1794, Lord Cornwallis wrote that, 'It will be of essential importance to the interests of Britain, that Europeans should be discouraged and prevented as much as possible from colonising and settling in our possessions in India ... It should be a fundamental principle in the New system.'[81] On the contrary, Sir Charles Metcalfe said in 19 February 1829, 'I have long lamented that our countrymen in India are excluded from the possession of land, and other ordinary rights of peaceable subjects ... I am further convinced that our possession of India must always be precarious, unless we take root by having an influential portion of the population attached to our Government by common interests and sympathies.'[82] The unspecified economic reasoning behind Metcalfe's argument was very different from those of the British economists like Wakefield, Bentham and Malthus. Bentinck, Metcalfe and others in India, following implicitly the Classical theory of economic development, saw in colonisation a way to infuse capital and technical expertise to a backward socioeconomic structure like that in India. India's balance of payments could not be perpetually balanced by a flow of precious metals from India, and the inevitable shortage must lead to a depression. Again, the influx of British skill and capital would increase agricultural productivity, resulting in the increased production of raw materials for British industries. The socioeconomic conditions of India were such that what happened in America in 1776 would not be repeated in India. Metcalfe realised that the restrictions had outlived their usefulness because the British were securely entrenched by 1830, and the main concern was the increasing overseas competition in the indigo trade. The best way to ensure the indigo market, therefore, was to cut down the cost of production through increased efficiency which could be brought about through colonisation. Even if some over-production occurred in the beginning the prospect

[79] *Ibid.*
[80] *Reflections on the Present State of British India* (London, 1829), p. 197.
[81] Letter dated 7 November 1794, *Personal Records*, India Office Records, Vol. IV, p. 261.
[82] *Parl. Papers*, Vol. VIII of Session 1831–2, HC 734, p. 274. This was approved by Bentinck in his Minute of 30 May 1829, *Ibid.*

was not viewed with anxiety for that 'may be left to work its own cure'. The more dangerous thing was to let the market go out of the hand of India.[83] In a sense colonisation *was* necessary. By the 1830s the British rulers realised that a prosperous India could be a benefit to Britain. Since their doctrinal predilections and financial difficulties did not enable them to launch a massive programme of economic development, private enterprise was the only available alternative. They also found that the *zemindars* of Bengal did not innovate and promote economic development as was expected of them. Thus there was no other way except to attract colonisers who would infuse 'energy and intelligence' into the 'torpid population' of India.[84]

Consequent on the change in intellectual climate, the resistance to colonisation in the 1830s was very meagre. Even the Chairman of the Court of Directors of the East India Company said that he had always 'been friendly to the measure of permitting respectable Europeans under certain restrictions to resort to India, being satisfied that their skill, enterprise and industry would facilitate and expedite the development of the resources of that country'.[85] John Ravenshaw, a former civil servant and a friend of Bentinck, while opposing colonisation as a general policy, nevertheless agreed that the skill and enterprise of immigrants would be useful to India.[86] But even these few critics argued that already facilities had been given to the colonisers; in May 1824, for example, the Court of Directors had allowed Europeans to hold land under a 99-year lease to grow coffee and cotton. The objection was only to certain types of colonisers, as the following preference list indicates:[87]

Missionaries & Schoolmasters	Favourable
Barristers & Attorneys	Tolerated
Clerks to Attorneys	Against
Capitalists	Favourable
Shipwrights, Coachmakers or other Mechanics	Limited to 'what may be sufficient for the instruction and improvement of the natives in the useful arts'.
Commercial Speculators & Menial Servants	Against

---

[83] Governor General in Council to Court of Directors, 1 January 1830, *Parl. Papers*, Appendix, Vol. VIII of Session 1831–2, *Ibid.*, p. 280.

[84] Bentinck's Minute dated 1 July 1829 (*Bentinck Papers*, Nottingham University Library).

[85] Robert Campbell to Bentinck 27 May 1830 (*Bentink Papers*, Nottingham University Library).

[86] Ravenshaw to Bentinck, 3 May 1830 (*Bentinck Papers*, Nottingham University Library).

[87] John Jebb and James Pattison of the East India Company to George Canning, 27 February 1818, *Parl. Papers*, Appendix, Vol. VIII of Session 1831–2, *op. cit.*, p. 253.

This was the crude basis by which the prospective colonisers in India were screened by the Court of Directors. If Europeans were allowed to colonise India without any restriction, they might compete and reduce the value of the 'produce of whatever kind destined for exportation'. In such an event, those who had 'left their own country in the expectation of turning their skill and industry to profitable account' would suffer considerably.[88]

ANTI-IMPERIALISM, IMPERIALISM AND INDIA

The passing of the Charter Act in 1833 finally established a system assuring free mobility of resources between Britain and India. This victory for free trade ideas was succeeded by the abolition of corn laws and the removal of navigation acts, and by the middle of the nineteenth century, British people enjoyed free trade and free economic relations with their colonies. However, certain developments in the British economy necessitated a rethinking of the *political* relations between Britain and its overseas territorial possessions. If untrammelled economic relations between Britain and colonies could guarantee maximum benefit to the British people and the inhabitants of the colonies, what was the sense in holding on to the colonies and in the process increasing British public expenditure for the purpose? In other words the question was: Are the colonies in any way 'beneficial' to the mother country and if so, was it because of the political connection?

Earlier economists like Jeremy Bentham, David Ricardo, James Mill, J. B. Say and J. R. McCulloch thought that labour and capital could never simultaneously be over-abundant. But in the 1830s, the Wakefieldian School supported by economists like Robert Torrens and Charles Buller contested the idea that capital gets employed automatically. Production is limited not only by capital and labour but also by the 'field of employment' or investment opportunities which meant lack of adequate land for cultivating food. This point was later endorsed by John Stuart Mill and J. E. Cairnes. These three problems – want of food, surplus population and surplus capital – had two remedies.[89] Either free trade had to be pursued and/or the nation should engage actively in colonisation. Free traders like Sir Henry Parnell thought that with the abolition of the corn laws coupled with further division of labour and free mobility of capital this problem would cease.[90] The advocates for colonisation were not optimistic about the success of free trade or the possibility of its ever becoming popular abroad.

[88] Campbell to Bentinck, 27 May 1830 (*Bentinck Papers*, Nottingham University Library).
[89] See Klaus Knorr, *British Colonial Theories 1570-1850*, p. 301.
[90] See Parnell's *On Financial Reform* (London, 1830), pp. 239–40, 251–2.

Even the *Edinburgh Review,* considered to be an opponent of the Wakefieldian thesis, pointed out that colonies ought to be retained because once they are set free they promptly erect tariff barriers.[91] In any case they thought, in the words of John Stuart Mill, that 'there needs be no hesitation in affirming that colonization, in the present state of the world is the best affair of business, in which the capital of an old and wealthy country can engage'.[92] Mill obviously felt that there was much surplus capital about and that colonies would not be entirely useless. However, the free traders had the dominant voice, and the Manchester School led by Richard Cobden and John Bright was vociferous throughout the twenty or more years up to the mid-1860s. Using arguments not unlike those of Adam Smith's, they argued that imperial connections were an unjust burden on Britain, and so the best policy would be to terminate them. Such anti-imperial ideas were entertained by many British thinkers according to whom free trade should lead to 'prosperity, peace and progress', instead of to 'protectionism, militarism and imperialism'.[93] Recent researches however indicate that these anti-imperial ideas were neither as influential as claimed nor were they as widely held by the British public as had been suggested by earlier scholars.[94]

Whatever the British attitudes towards other colonies might be, there was hardly any change in the thinking of British statesmen and intellectuals towards India, as India was always treated as a special case. It is true that one can observe a few discordant views, particularly after the traumatic happenings of the 1857–8 cataclysm. Some like the 'Plain Speaker' bluntly pointed out that India was of no value economically to Britain.[95] Cobden thought that India was even useless politically, for, as he wrote to J. B. Smith of Manchester, 'from a politico-economic view, *as a Nation,* we could have no advantages from our territorial aggrandizement in India.'.[96] James

---

91 'Shall we Retain the Colonies?' in *The Edinburgh Review,* April 1851, pp. 494–7.
92 *Principles of Political Economy,* (London, 1848: Ashley Edition), p. 971.
93 See C. A. Bodelsen, *Studies in Mid-Victorian Imperialism* (London, 1924), pp. 32, *et seq.* See also R. L. Schuyler, 'The Climax of Anti-Imperialism in England' in *Political Science Quarterly,* December 1921, pp. 544 *et seq.* Arnold Haultain (Ed.), *Goldwin Smith's Reminiscences* (New York, 1910), p. 169. H. J. Habbakuk, 'Free trade and Commonwealth Expansion' in *Cambridge History of British Empire,* vol. II, p. 751.
94 The debate relating to the Imperialism of Free Trade began with Messrs. Gallagher and Robinson's important paper 'The Imperialism of Free Trade' in the *Economic History Review,* Vol. VI, No. 1, 1953. Contributions were made by Professors McDonagh, Platt and Fieldhouse subsequently. For summaries of the controversy see A. G. L. Shaw (Ed.) *Great Britain and the Colonies 1815–1865* (London, 1970), pp. 1–26; B. Semmel, *The Rise of Free Trade Imperialism,* Chapters 7, 8 & 9; and B. A. Knox, 'Re-considering Mid-Victorian Imperialism', *The Journal of Imperial and Commonwealth History,* Vol. 1, No. 2, January 1973.
95 *Justice for India* (London, 1858), pp. 5, 8.
96 *Letters from Cobden* (Letter dated 12 August 1857), Vol. XIV, p. 62. (J. B. Smith Papers

Geddes, who belonged to the Indian civil service, went further. He held that retention of India was detrimental to the British workmen. English people would 'be better off if the English capital, which in enormous sums every year is drained away to India ... were applied reproductively in this country'.[97] One of these very rare members of the Manchester School who advocated freedom and representative government for India was William Stokes. With a barrage of statistics he showed that free countries like the United States, Australia and Tasmania consumed more British manufactured goods than a dependent India. And from this he deduced that an independent India would be more valuable to Britain.[98] Such rarities apart, even the most ardent anti-imperial member of the Manchester School did not envisage India as an independent country on a par with former colonies like Australia or Canada. In fact, by employing their characteristic political pressure technique, the followers of Cobden 'contributed to the strength and endurance of Britain's imperial connection with India'.[99]

It must be stressed here that even if the anti-imperial 'Little Englanders' desired the separation of India from Britain, it could not have taken place because of the opposition of powerful forces whose economic position would have been threatened. The enormous Indian bureaucracy would most certainly have resisted any such attempts, and the colonial bureaucracy has always wielded a key influence on the formation of the metropolitan policy towards the colonies.[100] They influenced policy not only by the most common technique of *fait accompli*, but also by exerting group pressure on the British policy forming apparatus. The non-official Europeans in India – most of whom were in business – had too much at stake in the British presence of India to entertain any anti-imperial sentiments. There were large groups of people in Britain who also would have viewed any move to free India with great alarm.

If India were to be treated as a special case, what arguments were advanced in favour of this policy? In 1858, the *London Quarterly Review* asked the question, 'What is the value of India to England?', and listed the

Footnote 96 continued

    at the Central Library, Manchester) Underscoring in the original. See also J. M. McLean, *The Indian Deficit and the Income Tax* (London, 1871), p. 14. McLean served the *Manchester Guardian* before 1859 and edited the *Bombay Gazette* from 1859 to 1879. In the 1880s he represented Oldham in the British Parliament.

[97] *The Logic of Indian Deficit* (London, 1871), p. x.

[98] *India Reform Bills* (London, 1858), pp. 23–48. See also Richard Congreve, *India* (1858), pp. 15–16, who had similar opinions.

[99] R. J. Moore, 'Imperialism and Free Trade Policy in India, 1853–54' in *Economic History Review*, Vol. XVII, No. 1, August 1964, p. 145. See also P. Harnetty, *Imperialism and Free Trade* (Manchester, 1972), pp. 1–6, 123–6.

[100] See W. David McIntyre, *The Imperial Frontier in the Tropics 1865–1875*, (London, 1968), pp. 42–5.

four most commonly given answers: (i) moral obligation to hold India for its benefit; (ii) an outlet for our young men; (iii) to provide for Britain 'weight and dignity in the Council of European nations'; and (iv) the commerce of India has raised 'whatever country has for the time possessed it'. The conclusion was that 'Any one of these answers is sufficient to show that India is at least worth the trouble we take in retaining it.'[101] Whereas the reasons (i) and (iii) could be construed as emotive, the other two reasons are basically economic as also was the often mentioned advantage of India as a suitable outlet for the surplus capital available in England.

Edward Thornton stated as early as 1835: 'England is saturated with the capital of which India stands in need',[102] and this has been confirmed by modern scholars.[103] Queen Victoria's reign saw Britain accumulate vast quantities of capital to such an extent that not all of it could be profitably utilised at home. An India with its amazing potentialities of raw materials, cheap labour and so forth ruled benevolently but firmly by the Birtish seemed an obvious outlet for this surplus capital.

Once economists of the standing as John Stuart Mill and Robert Torrens gave their *imprimatur* to the idea that capital could be over-abundant, it was almost bound to become part of the prevailing economic opinion. As the tendency of profits was to fall, anything that could be done to arrest it – that is by exporting capital – should be welcomed. Even the orthodox *Economist* came to the conclusion in 1881 that the colonial possessions were a 'first rate field, if properly cultivated, for the utilisation of British surplus capital and population'.[104] In the 1830s and 1840s 'India's requirement of British surplus capital' was the main theme of contemporary discussion, presumably because of the other investment outlets available throughout the world, but the theme changed to 'British surplus capital's requirement of India' in the 1870s and 1880s owing to certain developments (e.g. the Great Depression) in the British economy itself. When the export of British capital goods fell owing to the industrialisation of the United States and Western European countries, investment in Britain was diverted to home industry and the public sector. When this phase was over in about 1879, Britain was once again in troubled waters.[105] The period from 1873 onwards witnessed

---

[101] 'Crisis of the Sepoy Rebellion' in *London Quarterly Review*, 1858, p. 530.

[102] *India Its State and Prospects* (London, 1835), p. 65. See also John Crawfurd, *A Sketch of the Commercial Resources and Monetary and Mercantile System of British India* (London, 1837), Chapter VII.

[103] See William Ashworth, *An Economic History of England 1870–1939* (London, 1960), p. 7. See also S. G. Checkland, *The Rise of Industrial Society in England* (London, 1964), pp. 189, 412.

[104] *The Economist*, 27 August 1881, Vol. XXXIX, No. 1983, p. 1074.

[105] See W. W. Rostow, *British Economy of the Nineteenth Century* (Oxford, 1948), pp. 179 *et seq.*

a favourable shift in the terms of trade, a fall in the interest rate, equity prices, profit margins and commodity prices. Thus the easier flow of savings tended to seek safer avenues of investment even at somewhat reduced rates of interest.[106] The quest for safe outlets for British investments was also somewhat due to the full *exposé* by a Select Committee of the British Parliament in 1875 of the shady side of the foreign loans.[107] In the meantime, both American and European financial groups had been showing their capacity to compete with the British in foreign countries, and hence the British investor was looking towards the Empire for investment opportunities.[108]

It was firmly held that India had ample opportunities for profitable investments for both joint stock companies and emigrants with capital, and employment for enterprising and intelligent men. India had a stable and secure administrative structure and millions of acres of fertile and uncultivated land ready to produce all the food and raw material requirements of the mother country. Considering all this, an observer said in 1857, India 'is of infinitely more importance to Great Britain than all its other possessions of the Globe'.[109] Similarly influential politicians like Sir Charles Dilke specifically mentioned that without India Britain would be injured 'commercially'.[110]

The availability of employment opportunities – particularly for middle-class youths – was the greatest attraction of the Indian empire. Again and again when the value of India was discussed, this advantage was stressed. Considerable expansion took place in middle-class education from the 1830s to the end of the century which had not been matched by the expansion of middle-class employment.[111] This was a source of great middle-class anxiety, as can be seen in the blunt statement of T. H. S. Escott, 'Among the chief wants of domestic England is that of careers and professions for her sons.'[112] Archibald Graham, using typical Malthusian–Wakefieldian arguments, suggested that increasing population, gluts, lack of foreign demand and disastrous mercan-

---

[106] See for a statement by Viscount Goschen, *Ibid*, pp. 69–70. See also A. K. Cairncross, *Home and Foreign Investment* (Cambridge, 1953), pp. 266–31.

[107] See for an extract from the *Report from the Select Committee on Loans to Foreign States* 1875, *Parl. Papers*, H. C. 367, Vol. XI in W. H. B. Court (Ed.), *British Economic History 1870–1914* (Cambridge, 1965), pp. 216–18.

[108] See C. K. Hobson, *The Export of Capital* (London, 1914), p. 81.

[109] Edward West, *Emigration to British India* (London, 1857), p. 143. See also Robert Knight, *The Indian Empire and our Financial Relations Therewith*, p. 10. Knight also pointed out the advantages of the 'invisible' income from India (e.g. Pensions, dividends on the India stock, capital transfer, expenditure in England for the education of the British children etc.) that enter into the British balance of payments accounts.

[110] *Greater Britain* (London, 1868), Part IV, Chapter 20.

[111] See F. Musgrove, 'Middle-Class Education and Employment in the Nineteenth Century' in *Economic History Review*, 2nd Series, Vol. XII, No. 1, 1959, pp. 99–111.

[112] *England, Its People, Polity and Pursuits* (London, 1879), Vol. II, p. 482.

tile crises had made it necessary to expand employment opportunities for British youth. The solution obviously lay in the British empire.[113]

The Indian empire had always taken a sizeable number of the British seeking employment. For instance, a typical nineteenth-century English public school like Marlborough College typically sent about 11.5 to 17.5 percent of its students to various civil and military offices in India. This figure would be considerably greater if we add the non-official employment provided in India.[114] Not only did the Indian empire provide employment to many but also it was felt that it had great potentialities as a source of employment.[115]

The third economic argument that was given for maintaining and indeed strengthening the political control of India was the growing interdependence between the Indian and British economies. The main burden of Classical economics was to expound and argue for an international economy without taking into account the national differences or the political relationships between different economies. This was fundamentally opposed to 'Mercantilist' economics which believed in building powerful national economies on the basis of extensive colonial possessions. British attitudes towards India in the Victorian era alternated between the Classical view and a crude neo-Mercantilist view which desired the colonies to perform a complementary if not subordinate role to the strong and stable British economy. Englishmen, in spite of holding such contrary opinions about the way India should be linked to Britain, nevertheless expected that India would emerge as an excellent source of raw materials and a never-failing market for the finished products of English factories. In all seriousness, they considered this to be the ideal economic policy for Britain to pursue in India. This feeling was further strengthened by the precariousness of the raw materials supply in the mid-Victorian era. John Bright, for example, who along with Cobden repeatedly emphasised the purely 'moral' duty towards India, nevertheless

---

[113] Archibald Graham, *The Industrial Improvement by European Settlers of the Resources of India* (London, 1868), p. 16, *et seq*. See also H. J. S. Cotton, *England and India* (London, 1883), p. 20 'Have we a Colonial Policy?' in *The National Review*, September 1883, pp. 13–14. See also David Wedderburn, M.P. 'Modern Imperialism in India', Speech at the East India Association, 26 June 1879.

[114] See F. Musgrove, 'Middle-Class Education and Employment in the Nineteenth Century: A Rejoinder' in *Economic History Review*, 2nd Series, Vol. XIV, No. 2, 1961, pp. 325–6.

[115] 'The Government of India: its Liabilities and Resources', *The Westminster Review*, July–October 1859, New Series, Vol. XVI, No. 1, p. 116. *The Calcutta Review* in a critical review of Goldwin Smith's attack on the Indian empire said 'It is no small matter that the official and non official element in India is mainly recruited from the youth of the middle-class in England ... (they) at once meet with better salaries and occupy a better position that they could have dared to hope for at the same age at home.' 'The Connection of India with England' Vol. XLI, No. LXXXI, p. 79.

stressed the need to develop public works in India which would enable her to increase her output of cotton. It is no less interesting to see the actual policy of an economist who belonged to the Cobden school of 'anti-imperialism'. When James Wilson went to India in 1859 as the first finance member of the Viceroy's Council, he set himself five tasks: (i) to extend a 'system of sound taxation to the great trading classes who hitherto have been exempted, though chiefly benefited by our enormously increased civil expenditure'; (ii) to establish a paper currency; (iii) to remodel the financial system with an effective credit; (iv) to form a great police system of semi-military organisation but usually of purely civil application; and (v) to promote 'Public works and roads, with a view to increase production of cotton, flax, wool and European raw materials'.[116] As can easily be seen, only one of these objectives was concerned with positively promoting economic development, but even that was intended to support the British industrial economy.

On the whole in the 1850s and 1860s British theory and policy towards India conformed to the Classical theory of international trade. In this period, British industry was supreme in the world markets in spite of the growing tariff walls and the industrial revolutions in rival countries. India needed only stable political conditions as economic development could take care of itself. If left to itself, India was expected to develop those resources for which it had the comparative advantage – in this case food and raw materials. In other words, British rule was essential to develop Indian resources not for Britain's own sake but for the sake of enriching the world, including of course, Britain. During the 1870s, British industry began increasingly to feel the chill blasts of international competition from the rapidly industrialising countries of Europe and America, and in the succeeding decade Britain ceased to be the prime industrial nation. This declining importance relative to other countries gave rise to two phenomena. One was the mounting strength of the 'fair trade' movement which aimed at preserving the British market for local industries through retaliatory tariffs.[117] The second phenomenon was the rise and popularity of the so-called 'new imperialism'. In fact, the slowing down of the growth of British exports, its impact on the British economy in general and the consequent emergence of 'doubts, self-questioning and disenchantment' (to use the words of Peter Mathias[118]) were responsible to a great extent for the rise of the 'new imperialist' school of

[116] Wilson to Bagehot, 4 July 1860, Quoted in 'Memoir of the Rt. Hon. James Wilson', in Mrs Russell Barrington (Ed.), *The Works and Life of Walter Bagehot* (London, 1915), Vol. III, pp. 341–2.

[117] See for a full account of this phase of British reaction to foreign industrialism, Benjamin Brown, *The Tariff Reform Movement in Great Britain 1881–1895* (New York, 1943), Chapter V, and Sydney Zebel, 'Fair Trade: An English Reaction to the Breakdown of the Cobden Treaty System in *Journal of Modern History*, June 1940, Vol. XII, No. 2.

[118] *The First Industrial Nation*, p. 397.

thought which aimed at securing at least the colonial markets exclusively for British industries through imperial federation, imperial preferences and similar methods.

When the old confidence in dominating world markets declined, British industrialists realised how valuable the colonial markets had been all along. No doubt the empire was taking only 25 to 35 per cent of Britain's total exports, but it had the advantage of stability unlike the intake of the other foreign markets – a point that was stressed particularly in discussions of India's position in the empire.[119] A particularly common theme to be found in the contemporary writings on the subject was that 'in the open race we are no longer alone', but Britain has enormous advantages over other countries 'in the value of our Indian dependency and in the enormous area of our Colonial Empire'.[120]

A significant aspect of the arguments in favour of retaining the empire is that many of them run counter to the spirit of Classical political economy in matters such as free trade and internationalisation of the division of labour. This raises an interesting question concerning the relationship of the rise of 'the new imperialism' and the growth of disenchantment towards certain features of English political economy and the theory of economic policy. Imperialism involved mainly safeguarding British political and economic supremacy which meant that Britain should follow a policy advantageous to itself even if harmful to other countries. The policy in this case need not be justified purely in terms of received economic theory.[121] A policy such as protection, for example, although it violated the Classical theory of international trade policy, would nevertheless be acceptable provided it satisfied the 'national' requirement. Again if the full benefit of the colonial possessions could not be secured by a non-interventionist policy, state intervention in its economic sphere would have to be resorted to although that might militate against the orthodox theory of economic policy. Thus the theory of economic policy of imperialism had a different set of norms from the norm of the

---

[119] See George R. Parkin, *Imperial Federation and the Problem of National Unity* (London, 1892), p. 246. See also C. W. Dilke, *Greater Britain*, Vol. II, pp. 2–4.

[120] See Daniel Grant, *Home Politics or the Growth of Trade Considered in its Relation to Labour Pauperism and Emigration* (London, 1870), pp. 167, 184–5. See also William Birkmyre, *The Revival of Trade by the Development of India* (Glasgow, 1886), p. 9.

[121] Extreme versions of Imperialism went to the extent of suggesting that adherence to political economy was responsible for the British government's unwillingness to expand its empire. For example Thorburn reacted to the Colonial secretary's statement of 1874 which said that Britain will not embark on territorial possessions, thus: 'It was hardly possible to believe that he had become a pervert to the Manchester School of Radicals. When cheap John comes forward to peddle his bits of Brummagem Political economy, no one expects anything but nastiness puffed with vehement shallowness.' He regrets that national honour has been sacrificed at 'the altar of the great god *laissez-faire*'. *The Great Game: A plea for a British Imperial Policy* (London, 1875), pp. 1–3.

'ideal allocation of resources to maximise welfare' adopted by the Classical economists.

That the British government did not fundamentally depart from a free trade economic policy (especially regarding tariffs) in the nineteenth century was not due to lack of support for ideas opposed to the Classical political economy. Nor would it mean that 'imperialism' was without influence. Indeed the growth of a critical approach to the entrenched orthodoxy provided a milieu for the development of the economic basis of the 'new imperialism'. Throughout the Victorian era we could see a strand of thought that persistently refused to accept many cherished themes of Ricardian economics. We have seen how in the issue of colonisation, Gilbert Wakefield, Robert Torrens and John Stuart Mill made fundamental departures from the orthodox doctrine. By the mid-century, under the influence of writers such as Frederick List, Alexander Hamilton and H. C. Carey, there was in England what Bernard Semmel calls a 'Mercantilist Revival'.[122] In fact as early as 1844 Robert Torrens had formulated a programme of neo-mercantile imperialism and he even suggested an 'imperial Zollverein'.[123] The concepts of free trade and *laissez-faire* in all their forms had taken many knocks from economists. Already in the 1850s a Drummond Professor of Political Economy at Oxford who was also for some time a Member of Parliament, Charles Neate, had contested the validity of free trade on purely methodological grounds. Economic theorists of repute like J. E. Cairnes and Henry Sidgwick had criticised the view that political economy was merely 'a scientific development of *laissez-faire*'.[124] Other influential economists of the period like Leonard Courtenay, Arnold Toynbee and David Syme had ventured into areas considered taboo by the orthodox political economy. William Cunningham gave a far brighter picture of English mercantilism and corrected in England the previously held view based on what Schumpeter called Adam Smith's 'unintelligent criticism'.[125] Thus in the second half of the nineteenth century in Britain – and especially after 1870 – it was not possible to gain acceptance of free trade or any other aspect of Classical economics merely by referring to an 'authority'.[126] Those who had doubts about the suitability of free trade for Britain thus had alternative sources of theoretical inspiration. To give an example, Sampson Samuel Lloyd who

[122] *The Rise of Free Trade Imperialism*, Chapter 8.
[123] See Lionel Robbins, *Robert Torrens and the Evolution of Classical Economics* (London, 1958), pp. 225–31, 254–7.
[124] See T. W. Hutchison, *A Review of Economic Doctrines 1870–1929* (Oxford, 1953), p. 10.
[125] *History of Economic Analysis*, p. 361. J. R. Seeley, the publication of whose book *The Expansion of England* in 1883 was called by Richard Koebner as 'the most influential factor in the development of Empire awareness' (*Imperialism: The Story and Significance of a Political Word*, Cambridge, 1964 p. 173), particularly acknowledged the help received from W. Cunningham in the preface.
[126] See A. W. Coats, 'The Historist Reaction in English Political Economy, 1870–1890' in

was one of the founders of the Birmingham Chamber of Commerce and a leading figure in the 'fair trade' movement had translated List's *National System of Political Economy* in 1885.

While the mid-Victorian 'anti-imperialism' had no perceptible effect in loosening the hold of the Indian empire, the 'new imperialism' did have an impact on Indian policy. As has already been said, the economic advantages of the possession of India were fully recognised, and from 1869 onwards until the end of Lord Curzon's Viceroyalty British policy towards India was one of active involvement in administration and of making India serve as an instrument in retaining British political and economic supremacy in the world. This 'new imperialism' did not manifest in the deliberate acquisition of large territorial possessions. Such of the additions made to the empire (e.g. in Africa) and the aggressive military campaigns (e.g. the Afghan wars) seem to have been done for the sake of maintaining India firmly under the control of Britain. As Lord Mayo, the Viceroy appointed by Benjamin Disraeli, said, 'we are determined as long as the sun shines in heaven to hold India. Our national character, our commerce, demand it; and we have, one way or another, two hundred and fifty millions of English capital fixed in the country.'[127]

Imperial economic policy showed itself on three specific grounds. The adherence or non-adherence to Classical theory of economic policy depended on whether a particular policy suited the economic interests of Britain. *First*, there was great concern about the repeated famines that were devastating India. As will be seen in another chapter, when Indian officials adopted rigid policies based on received economic theory they were criticised because it was not in the interests of Britain to have a weak and vulnerable Indian economy. *Secondly*, India was considered a great market for British manufactures and anything that would go against it was to be prevented. In this case Indian officials were often given lectures on orthodox economic theory whenever India imposed taxes on British imports for purely financial reasons. And *thirdly*, the prime requirement of India was considered to be the build-up of infrastructure through massive injection of British capital as well as heavy public investment. Government was to intervene actively to enable the Indian economy to develop its resources fully so that India could play a significant role in the British economy.

Through these policies that aimed at developing India and linking its economy with that of Britain, Britain hoped to reduce its own economic

Footnote 126 continued

    Economica, New Series, Vol. 21, May 1954, pp. 143–4. See also A. W. Coats, 'The Role of Authority in the Development of British Economics' in *The Journal of Law and Economics*, Vol. 7, October 1964, p. 96.

[127] Lord Mayo to Sir A. Buchanan, 26 September 1869, quoted in S. Gopal, *British Policy in India 1858–1905* (Cambridge, 1966), pp. 120–121.

dependence on other countries. It was because in the last quarter of the nineteenth century Britain felt rightly or wrongly it was being threatened politically and economically that British policy took its inspiration at least partly from the theory of economic policy prevalent in the seventeenth and eighteenth centuries.

CONCLUSION

Stated in terms of wide generality, two broad issues were debated over the century and a quarter concerning the economic consequences to Britain as a result of its political domination of India. Firstly: what was the economic advantage of keeping India; and secondly: how should the political domination be arranged in terms of an economic relationship that would be to the maximum advantage for Britain. As has been seen, both these general issues were relevant to particular policy decisions, and hence were argued about continuously during the period. Economists and economic ideas naturally played their role in these discussions.

A remarkable fact that emerges from the foregoing discussion is that no economist of standing had urged the political separation of India from Britain. Economists were on the whole rational in the sense that they juxtaposed the costs of holding India with the benefits accruing from this political relationship. Naturally, the definition of costs and benefits changed from time to time in response to the then prevalent economic conceptions. Whereas the benefits of the empire to Adam Smith were essentially 'widening of the market', they included 'vent for surplus capital' to John Stuart Mill. Certainly nothing that economists said had any arguments to throw doubts on the value of India for Britain. If anything, arguments from economic treatises helped to justify the stand taken by those who wanted India to be a fixed part of the British empire.

It is admittedly difficult to say what impact economic ideas had on this because every other consideration (political, emotional etc.) also favoured the retention of India within the Empire. However the role of economic thinking can be charted with greater certainty when the discussions centred around particular policy measures for organising the economic relationship of Britain and India. In this category come policies regarding the role of the East India Company, the colonisation controversy, and the nature of Indo-British trade organisation. As we have seen, in all these controversies the ideas of economists played an important part. Whatever obvious political pressures might have decided the policies, it cannot be denied that economic ideas played a significant if indirect role in identifying the problems and analysing their implications.

3

ECONOMIC IDEAS AND FAMINE POLICY

... no one has a right to bring creatures into life, to be supported by other people ...

John Stuart Mill

POLITICAL ECONOMY AND FAMINES

From whichever side we may look at the Classical model of economics the same policy conclusion will emerge with regard to the question of the alleviation of 'distress'. The economics of Adam Smith and his disciples stressed the economic development of nations, and their hero was the strong and self-reliant individual. He it was who made a nation rich. Anything therefore that undermined this crucial variable of economic development by weakening its strength and self-reliance had to be avoided. The main reason why a majority of the Classical economists objected to the poor laws was that they tended to encourage paupers to depend upon state charity. Poor laws, moreover, had to be financed by taxing the 'haves', which added one more burden to the hard working and prudent sections of society.

On the other hand, if we consider the Classical economists to have been solely concerned with the 'allocative' problem, the policy must be that the state should not interfere with the proper functioning of the market. According to them, the market was an efficient instrument for distributing goods. Hence any distribution of resources in favour of the 'have-nots' and against the 'haves' through state action would induce an element of inefficiency and result in reduced social welfare. In other words, if individuals were allowed to look after their own interests, society's well-being (or, in the language of the Philosophic radicals, 'the greatest good of the greatest number') would automatically be looked after. It is true that the classical position regarding the superiority of the free market as an allocative mechanism was compatible with state grants to the poor. But there was the other powerful argument which supported this negative attitude towards the alleviation of distress. The population theory and its implications as taught by the Malthusians emphasised the futility of doing anything to prevent distress. After all, left to itself, population has a tendency to rise; and distress, dispelled once, is bound to recur again. Why, then, bother about an evil that cannot be permanently alleviated. In the very nature of things, there was some sort of equation between population pressure and distress on the one hand and the subsistence level on the other.

These concepts were based on a belief in certain inevitable tendencies: free trade, on an optimistic view of a system of economic harmonies, and population theory, on the supposition that Nature had bestowed on mankind an instinct which, if unchecked properly, would result in starvation and misery. If mankind (or at least a portion of it) suffered through privation, there was nothing to do but endure it. And free trade and the population theory combined indicated a competitive struggle for existence and the consequent survival of only the fittest.

Such were the general ideas that contributed not a little towards the formation of an 'economic opinion' and the evolution of a policy for alleviating distress. We are not concerned here so much with the historical and institutional reasons that encouraged the growth of these ideas in Britain and elsewhere, but rather with the effects of the application of such ideas to alien conditions. The problem of alleviation of distress arises when positive action is needed to reduce the mental or physical anguish caused by a sudden and unexpected misfortune. Sometimes action is also necessary to correct a system that has acquired a propensity to cause such mental and/or physical anguish. In the Indian context, an example of the first source of distress would be the misery caused by a failure of the seasonal rains; and the system of rural money-lending would be a typical case of the second. In this chapter, we shall consider a few of these sources of distress and the influence of economic ideas on the formation of an effective economic opinion and policy.

A 'free market' meant that, even in the face of famine, the state would not interfere in the free market processes by price control, financial encouragement to import, or prohibition of the export, of foodstuffs; and the correct price level would always be reached through the forces of supply and demand. It was not that the economists who advocated such measures were unaware of famine-time misery, but they thought in all honesty that non-interference was in the best interests of the people. In the short run, the free market would regulate all available grain according to the demand of the population, and in the long run, it would regulate the population to the level of the available means of subsistence. Government interference during a famine was not only not beneficial but would actually result in aggravating the distress.[1] The corn dealers who put up their prices in anti-

---

[1] See Adam Smith, *The Wealth of Nations*, p. 493.

cipation of a dearth actually prevented the people 'feeling them [the prices] afterwards so severely as they certainly would do, if the cheapness of price encouraged them to consume faster than suited the real scarcity of the season'.[2] In other words, while it is no doubt true that a free market would lead to higher prices during famines, that very increase in prices must assure a maximum of supply and a minimum of demand of foodstuffs. The interests of the corn dealers were not against the interests of the public because they performed the inestimable service to the community of keeping consumption adjusted properly to 'the supply of the season'. The corn dealer could not raise the price of corn as he pleased because thereby he would only be injuring himself without hurting the consumers. Hence adequate protection should be given to this trade because 'no trade requires it so much; because no trade is so much exposed to popular odium'.[3]

These ideas became well known both with the policy makers and other theorists soon after the *Wealth of Nations* was published. Like Adam Smith, Malthus also considered the middlemen to be benefactors of society because it was they who maintained through careful speculation the 'supplies of a large nation, whether plentiful or scanty'. 'Most happily for society,' said Malthus, 'Individual interest is, in these cases, so closely and intimately interwoven with the public interest, that one cannot gain or lose without a gain or loss to the other.'[4] Writing in 1800, Malthus felt sure that Britain's inability to support the population was not due to the middleman's rapacity, but rather the high birth rate, as stated clearly in his *Essay on Population* published two years earlier. Another distinguished follower of Adam Smith in this matter was Edmund Burke who said that it was not in the government's power to provide food and other necessities for the people,[5] indeed, it would be 'a vain presumption in Statesmen' to think they could provide all the wants of people, because it was the people who maintained the administrators and not the other way about.[6]

When we turn from the opinions of the economists to the actual policy of the British government, we can at once see how interventionist it was in the last decade of the eighteenth century. Certainly its spirit was not Smithian free trade. Until 1795, the British government directly imported foodgrains from overseas. After 1796, however, direct government trading in foodgrains was abandoned as it was found that there was hardly any import by the private traders when the government also involved itself in the import

[2] *Ibid.*, p. 500.
[3] *Ibid.*, p. 493.
[4] *An Investigation of the Causes of the Present High Price of Provisions* (London, 1800), p. 13.
[5] Published posthumously as *Thoughts and Details on Scarcity* in 1800.
[6] *Ibid.*, p. 2.

trade. Government policy henceforth was to provide cash bounties and other help for importation of food by private importers. Not only were the private traders thus subsidised, but prices were also interfered with following the rather ancient method, 'Assize of Bread'.[7]

The extreme doctrinal support for the interventionist attitude was surprisingly enough provided by Jeremy Bentham who, while agreeing with Smith that 'the interest of the vendor of corn is always the same as that of the public', qualified it by saying that it was only during a 'time of moderate plenty' and during 'the time of a light degree of scarcity'. During 'a time of extraordinary scarcity', on the other hand, the interests of the corn dealers and the public at large diverged,[8] calling for active intervention by the state.

It must be pointed out that the objective of both these views – free trade and interventionist – was the same. Prices of foodgrains should be such as to ration the available supplies as well as prevent undue suffering by the poor. The free traders thought that a policy based on the open market would lead to a greater inflow of foodgrains with a consequent reduction in prices. On the other hand, interventionists wanted a direct tampering with these processes so as to keep the prices down. In the economic thinking of the time, we find free traders making more converts and the Smithian tradition getting entrenched at the turn of the century. The classical economists accepted Smith's ideas completely, and their policy prescription during famines was to use the necessarily limited available quantity of grain in the best possible way. Government rationing could not do this as effectively as the automatic mechanism of a free and unfettered market. Prices would necessarily rise, but this would have the advantage of inducing a greater inflow of food grains – provided the state did not intervene and prevent corn dealers from importing because of the possibility of rationing by government.

These ideas were never to be absent from the corpus of the Classical political economy. Even as late as 1871, John Stuart Mill emphasised the futility of government intervention, for he was afraid that private merchants would not 'venture to compete with the government; and though a government can do more than any one merchant, it cannot do nearly as much as all merchants'.[9] These ideas on the inadvisability of tampering with the market[10]

---

[7] For a detailed study of the British policy towards the 1795–6 wheat scarcity, see Walter Stern, 'The Bread Crisis in Britain, 1795–6' *Economica*, vol. XXXI, no. 122, May 1964.

[8] 'Defence of a Maximum' in Werner Stark (Ed.), *Jeremy Bentham's Economic Writings* (London, 1954), vol. III, pp. 255, 257–8.

[9] *Principles of Political Economy*, p. 931.

[10] It is interesting to note that a very widely used modern text-book of elementary economics echoes these sentiments. In the form of a loaded parable, Samuelson compares the famine

were impressed on the administrators by the teachers at the East India Company's College at Haileybury, and they formed part of their 'economic opinion'. It is, then, hardly surprising that they were incorporated in the famine policies of India throughout the nineteenth century.

EARLY POLICY TOWARDS FAMINES

Indian history provides numerous instances of famine, but the pre-British monarchs almost always interfered with the free market processes. In medieval India, the Hindu or Buddhist king considered himself to be the protector of his subjects, and so he accepted his responsibility for providing relief during natural calamities.[11] In later times, during the period of the Islamic imperialism in India, the Muslim kings made attempts to mitigate the effects of famine through active intervention.[12] Importation of food, fixation of maximum prices and punishment and/or torture of offending grain dealers were the usual methods employed in fighting famines.[13] Even during the British period, areas under Indian administration had a positive famine policy. For example, considerable relief measures were undertaken by the Mahratta rulers in western India during the 1791–2 famine.[14] The Poligars, who reigned in South India, only the year before they were conquered by the British, took active steps to fight famines, and James Mill records how through heavy importation they induced the profiteering merchants to restore the normal prices.[15]

The advent of British rule, however, resulted in the gradual abrogation of this policy of active intervention. The formation of ideas is one thing and their application another; thus it took some time to get used to new ways of thought, and even more to utilise the new ideas in policy formation. Although British administrators in India were perhaps the earliest to take note of Adam Smith, it was not until after the turn of the century that the Smithian ideas seeped into the famine policies of the various governments in India.

Footnote 10 continued
policy of two mythical kingdoms and by many unstated but important assumptions shows that whereas under a regime of free market people survive a famine, under rationing they do not. It would be interesting to speculate on the effect of this on the formation of current 'economic opinion'! See *Economics: An Introductory Analysis*, 7th Edition, p. 45.

[11] Lallanji Gopal, *The Economic Life of Northern India: 700–1200* (Delhi, 1965), p. 249.

[12] See R. P. Tripathi, *Some Aspects of Muslim Administration in India* (Allahabad, 1936), pp. 277–8. See also W. H. Moreland, *The Agrarian System of Moslem India* (Cambridge, 1929), p. 36.

[13] See A. Appadorai, *Economic Conditions in Southern India 1000–1500* (Madras, 1936), vol. II. pp. 745, 751.

[14] A. T. Etheridge, *Report on the Past Famines in the Bombay Presidency* (Bombay, 1868), p. 87.

[15] *History of British India*, vol. IV, fn. p. 42.

The period between 1770 and 1800 witnessed some of the worst famines in the history of India. But although rare, government intervention was at least timely. During the 1770 Bengal famine there was, in the words of Sir George Campbell, 'some interference with freedom of trade contrary to modern economical laws, but not to a very injurious extent'.[16] The authorities imported foodgrains on their own account from outlying provinces to sell at subsidised prices, and this was done in spite of many of the Company's servants being engaged in private trade.[17] Again, during the 1780s, both in Madras and Bengal, government intervened on a large scale to alleviate distress. When Warren Hastings was at Madras, William Webb made a proposal to establish a Superintendent of Police who would periodically inspect the market and regulate prices. The Madras government approved the proposal and wrote to the Court of Directors: 'we judged his Plan might be beneficial to the Public at this time of Scarcity. We appointed him to that Employ.'[18] Another method adopted in 1783 was state-aided migration from famine stricken areas. In two months nearly 9000 starving people were sent to relatively more prosperous districts of the Northern Circars.[19] The experience gained at Madras enabled Warren Hastings to cope with a much bigger famine in Bengal in 1783–4. According to him, a 'well regulated State' could suffer from no famines. During the period of near-famine conditions in England in 1800, Hastings must have been concerned about the free trade views propounded by leading politicians. In anguish he wrote to Lord Liverpool (who, he thought, was close to Dundas) enclosing a list of proposals to fight the English scarcity based on his Indian experience. In this *Memo* we find also a description of his own active interventionist famine prevention policy as pursued in the Bengal famine of 1783–4.[20]

During the 1787–8 famine in Bengal and Bihar, the government actively interfered with the price mechanism by preventing the export of foodgrains. Similar and even more drastic methods were used to bring down food prices and reduce the sufferings caused by the 1790–2 famine in the Andhra districts. All import and transit duties were repealed to encourage food imports. Foodgrain prices were fixed by the authorities and free food was given to the destitutes. When parts of the present-day eastern Uttar Pradesh

[16] 'Memoir on the Famines which affected Bengal in the Last Century' in J. C. Geddes (Ed.), *Administrative Experience Recorded in Former Famines*, (Calcutta, 1874), p. 421.

[17] See N. K. Sinha, *The Economic History of Bengal* (Calcutta, 1970), vol. II, pp. 56–9.

[18] Public letter to the Court of Directors, 9 January 1781. Q.n. H. D. Love (Ed.), *Vestiges of Old Madras* (London, 1913), vol. III, p. 309.

[19] R. A. Dalyell, *Memorandum on the Madras Famine of 1866* (Madras, 1966), p. 14.

[20] See Warren Hastings to Lord Liverpool, 24 April 1800 (Liverpool Papers at the British Museum. Add. Mss. 38, 191, pp. 90–1). For a full account of this famine, see C. E. R. Girdlestone, *Report on Past Famines in the North-Western Provinces* (1868), pp. 8–11.

(including the cities of Banaras, Allahabad, Kanpur and Futtehgarh) were hit by a severe scarcity in 1803, the government intervened with subsidies for food imports.[21] When administering the 1802–4 famine, Governor Jonathan Duncan of Bombay prevented exports of foodgrain and caused considerable quantities to be sold by government agencies. Unlike Adam Smith, Duncan did not idolise the grain dealer as a saviour, but rather looked down upon him contemptuously and declared it as his duty to save people from the grain dealer.[22] This seems to have been the last big famine in which the government interfered with the foodgrain market to bring down prices. From that time till practically the end of the century, the various governments in India showed considerable reluctance to take a more active role in tackling the famine problem through price control, rationing and similar measures.

SIGNS OF CHANGE IN FAMINE POLICY

Already during the famine of 1806–7 in Madras, there were contradictory opinions as to the policies to be pursued. The Board of Trade desired deliberate state intervention in the economy to increase the food supply, but the Board of Revenue preferred a non-interventionist policy. The monsoon failed in 1806 (from August to November) in the Madras Presidency. This meant an impending scarcity, if not famine; hence the Governor, Lord William Bentinck, thought cautiously that it would be quite 'proper to hold out every practicable encouragement' for the importation of foodgrains from Bengal.[23] The Board of Trade followed this suggestion by formulating a vigorous programme of government intervention to increase foodgrain supplies and enforce proper distribution to alleviate distress, and thought that the 'pressure of our wants' was sufficient justification for its 'recommendation founded upon humanity and policy'.[24]

As against the Board of Trade, the Board of Revenue formulated a pure Smithian policy to deal with scarcities and bluntly told the Governor that no good could come from active intervention. In fact, one can observe a close similarity between the following sentences from the letter from the Board of Revenue to the Governor and the quotation from the *Wealth of Nations* (p. 413) referred to earlier:

[21] *Ibid*, pp. 12–13. See also Baird-Smith Report, *Parl. Papers*, H.C. No. 29, vol. XL of Session 1862, pp. 55–6.

[22] Duncan's Minute, 10 June 1805, Etheridge, *op. cit.*, pp. XXXIX, XII.

[23] G. Buchan (Chief Secretary, Government of Madras) to W. Ramsey (Secretary, East India Company), 9 January 1807, *Madras Public Diaries and Consultations*, India Office Records, January – February 1807, Range 243, vol. 15, p. 95.

[24] Board of Trade to Governor, 10 January 1807, *Madras Public Diaries and Consultations*, January–February 1807, pp. 121, *loc. cit.*

Convinced by observation and experience of the impolicy of the measures usually resorted to on the occurrence of the calamity of dearth, or famine and that any restrictions on the freedom of the grain market, whether by enforcing the sale, limiting the price, or other direct interference with the speculations of private grain dealers are more calculated to aggravate than to diminish the sufferings of the people ... The inconvenience of a scarcity of grain though not always capable of being removed may by proper precautions, be considerably alleviated ... In seasons of dearth, it is for the benefit of the people that the general consumption should be regulated with exact reference to the general stock and as it is for the interest of the grain dealer to adapt his price in a just Ratio to the existing necessity or demand, so he procures the best information on this point, and that information renders him the best judge if he sell too high he discourages consumption makes the people frugal, and may ultimately disappoint himself. If too low he needlessly foregoes a possible profit, may induce an improvident expenditure, and to the calamity of a dearth may superadd the miseries of a famine but this last circumstance is not likely to happen, as it is not likely he should so much disregard his individual interest – The grain dealer without contemplating the interest of the People, necessarily provides for it, in providing his own – For the people, by feeling the inconveniencies of scarcity by his means sooner perhaps than they otherwise would, feel them ultimately less severely than they otherwise might. It is for their benefit, that these inconveniencies by divided – that they be felt gradually and not suddenly. This operation can be performed by none so exactly as by the grain dealer – for, as no other person can have either the same interest, the same knowledge, or the same abilities duly to perform it, so it is the best policy that the grain market be left entirely to him – that is that it be left entirely free.

The Board of Revenue was equally against any artificial prevention of the export of foodstuffs because 'it is a restriction on natural liberty ... an infraction of public justice'. As for the general concept of government interference, the Board of Revenue considered it with horror exactly as Adam Smith had done some decades earlier. Here again, the affinity between the *Wealth of Nations* and the proceedings of the Board of Revenue can be perceived clearly:

Whenever the officers of Government, influenced by a humane desire of obviating the inconveniencies of scarcity, imprudently direct that private grain be sold in the public market at a fixed price, or injudiciously send grain themselves into the market for that purpose, they either prevent dealers from bringing their grain thither, which sometimes increases the dangers of a famine, or they encourage the people to consume it so fast, as must necessarily, in the end produce such a calamity. The unrestrained freedom of the Grain market, is at the same time the best preventative of famines and the best palliative of dearth.[25]

The Board of Revenue had the support of some of the district collectors, many of whom had lately been influenced by the economics of Adam Smith in

[25] Board of Revenue to the Governor, 29 November 1806, *Madras Board of Revenue Proceedings*, India Office Records, December 1806, Range 288, vol. 47, pp. 7222–6. See also *General Report of the Board of Revenue to the Court of Directors*, India Office Records, vol. 12, p. 195.

their approach towards the famine problem. The collector of Tanjore, F. Hodgeson, complained in 1807 that 'the grain market has never been free for many years. The *Sircar* has always had grain of its own in the store and constrained the market.'[26] Thomas Munro like many other fellow district officials felt that the severity is not felt at any one time. In this process not only is the severity evened out, but because of the numerous grain dealers in India the foodgrain price also is kept 'as low as it ought to be, by rendering combinations for raising it impracticable'.[27] Hence he concluded that the government should not interfere with the workings of the grain market as that would only 'deter many of the persons who usually carry on this trade from prosecuting it'.[28] Following the teachings of Adam Smith to the letter, Munro said: 'The scarcity which arises from the seasons is converted into a famine in the territories of the native powers by war ... by absurd, though well-meant, regulations for keeping down the price and supplying the great towns.'[29]

This heavy dose of Adam Smith administered to him by the Board of Revenue as well as the admonitions he had received from the Court of Directors regarding the Government Bank made Bentinck very cautious. He firmly refused to accept the suggestion regarding the use of the Company's 'Investment' ships for importing grain. There was also the other proposal made by the Board of Trade to guarantee foodgrain prices and this was defended on the ground that the price so fixed would not entail any expense on the part of the government because the market price would not fall below it. But William Petrie, a member of the Board of Revenue, and the Governor himself argued that encouragement in any form to stimulate the supplies of foodgrain involved tampering with the market. They were afraid that such encouragement would result in too large an import and a consequent fall in the prices which would in its turn mean heavy public expenditure.[30] In spite of the misgivings of Bentinck and Petrie, the Board of Trade's proposals not only regarding the price guarantee but also regarding shipments were accepted and neutral vessels (especially American) were permitted. The Board had also suggested that foodgrain shipments from Canara district should be diverted to the other famine-stricken districts of the Madras Presidency through deliberately planned discriminatory export duties. But this idea was defeated mainly because of the views of Thomas Munro who opined that deliberate

[26] Quoted in A. Sarada Raju, *Economic Conditions in Madras Presidency*, p. 248.
[27] Minute dated 9 February 1807. A. J. Arbuthnot (Ed.), *Major General Sir Thomas Munro: Selections from his Minutes* (Madras, 1886), vol. II, p. 227.
[28] Minute dated 11 January 1805, *Ibid.*, p. 216.
[29] *Ibid.*, p. 218.
[30] See Bentinck's Minute dated 15 January 1807, *Madras Public Diaries and Consultations*, India Office Records, January–February 1807, Range 243, vol. 15, p. 218.

prohibition of grain exports should never be resorted to 'without the strongest necessity' because it hinders 'the farmers from making up for the loss of
almost the whole of their crop by the high price of the remainder'.[31] The
Madras government was able within two months to report of the success of
the proposal of price guarantee. A 'very extensive shipment of rice' was
brought to the Madras Presidency. A committee was also appointed to supervise the marketing of the grain, but with elaborate instructions for the
'necessity of giving every practicable encouragement and protection to the
importers of grain and of avoiding any interference with the retail of the
public market, as such interference by discouraging the operations of the
Trade must be obviously productive of permanent injury'.[32] Altogether
5211 *garce* of grain were imported at the guaranteed price. The Madras
government was happy to note that no material loss was sustained compared
to the 'incalculable benefit which has resulted to the community'.[33]

It was the Governor, Lord William Bentinck, who prevented the policy of
the Madras government from entirely being based on *laissez-faire*. While
believing in the principles of free trade he was by no means dogmatic, and
he imparted a humanitarian interpretation to the Court of Directors'
platitudes on the necessity of looking after the well-being of the people.[34]
Bentinck justified his partly activist famine policy on the ground that the
primary care of the government was the preservation of the 'real resources
and riches of the country and of the state'. It was necessary to preserve the
lives of people in the interest of long-run economic development, because
'agricultural improvement' depended upon the assured supply of labour.[35]
Hence he gave his wholehearted support to the provision of public works to
employ the unemployed penurious population, which he thought was a
'beneficial mode of combining objects of charity, with the public interests'.

When the Court of Directors learnt of the cautious policy pursued at
Madras, they gave their full approval to the adopted measures.[36] The Court's
appreciation of such partial intervention came because they believed the
'peculiar traits in the native character' made it essential for the state to take
active steps to mitigate the rigours of famine. This does not mean that the

---

[31] Munro's Minute 9 February 1807, *Arbuthnot, op. cit.* p. 222.
[32] Government of Madras to the Court of Directors (Public) 6 March 1807. *Letters from Madras*,
India Office Records, E/4/335, para. 92.
[33] *Ibid.*, dated 2 May 1807, para. 13.
[34] See Bentinck's Minute dated 20 January 1807, *Madras Revenue Consultations*, India Office
Records, 22 January 1807. Range 276, vol. 12, p. 259.
[35] Bentinck to Board of Revenue, 26 January 1807, *Ibid.*, p. 267.
[36] Court of Directors to Madras, 7 September 1808 (Public), *Public Letters to Madras*,
India Office Records, L/PJ/3/1312, pp. 291–7. See also R. A. Dalyell, *Memorandum on the
Madras Famine of 1866*, p. 25.

Court of Directors were altogether immune to the all-pervading influence of the economics of Adam Smith! To give an example of the Court's attitude, we may examine their view of a proposal to buy cattle in the government account to help the impoverished agriculturists:

We are pleased to find that the measure originally in contemplation of purchasing cattle on the Government account was abandoned ... upon the general principle that a sudden and unexpected interference on the part of Government in the public markets generally has the effect of deranging them sometimes in retarding the supply of the article in demand and almost always in unnecessarily increasing its price.[37]

The attitude of the Court to the new economic thinking shows how powerful ideas could be. We find the Court in the first decade of the nineteenth century fighting a desperate battle against the Smithian views on the discontinuation of its trading monopoly; and yet were simultaneously espousing the truth of the allocative problem as presented by Adam Smith!

FAMINE POLICY AND FREE TRADE

Shortly after the 1806–7 Madras famine, the opposition to the free trade theorists of economic policy came to an end. One could see very clearly the pervading influence of the new economic ideas in the many official communications on famine. For example, anticipating famine conditions, H. Fraser, the military officer commanding Pondicherry wrote to the Governor of Madras begging him to 'direct the merchants at Madras to send a supply of Bengal rice' or adopt some measures that would save the public from misery and exploitation.[38] The new Governor, Sir George Barlow, was a non-interventionist in the economic sphere, just as he was in the political arena. His views are reflected in the reply to Fraser's requests, drafted by D. Hill, secretary to the Madras government. After expatiating on the merits of free trade, Hill pointed out that 'in the case of a partial scarcity ... the most effectual means of supplying the market is to leave it entirely free to those whose business it usually is to supply it and who are more interested in supplying it during a scarcity than at any other period'. Fraser was firmly told that the most certain method of increasing the evil was to destroy the 'freedom of the market'. There was no need to worry about the possibility of a price increase consequent on the impending scarcity, because that

is fortunately not only the natural consequence of a scarcity, but also the natural

---

[37] Court of Directors to Madras Government (Revenue) 24 April 1811, *Madras Despatches*, India Office Records, vol. 47, no. E/4/907, pp. 305–6, para. 122.

[38] Letter dated 24 December 1811, *Madras Public Consultations*, India Office Records, 27 December 1811, Range 244, vol. 7, pp. 6388–9.

remedy for that evil. It is a remedy which cannot altogether fail, while those, by whom it is to be administered, entertain a confidence that its operation will not be interrupted by the officers of Government and (short of gratuitous relief to all who stand in need of it) is the only remedy of which the evil admits.

It was pointed out that as this policy was based both on 'established principles and an invariable experience', the authorities at Pondicherry should 'scrupulously abstain and cause others to abstain from interfering with the natural course of the market'. Fraser was also cautioned against encouraging the suspicion of the trading community by indiscreet utterances.[39]

This sudden change in the policies at Madras in the first decade of the nineteenth century could have also been due to the shortage of financial resources. In 1782–3, the English possessions were not numerous, and by that time the British had recovered from their wars with the French in India. But by 1805, the British had become the undisputed masters of South India, although much weakened by the last struggle with Tipu Sultan as well as the suppression of the Poligar rebellions in the Tinnevelly and Madurai districts. However, this cannot provide a full explanation, for if the government had been unduly troubled by financial stringency, they would not have made a proposal for the establishment of public granaries to stock a sizeable quantity of grain at all times. The government's free trade bias surfaced immediately after making this proposal, and they declared that the granaries were not for

underselling private merchants and defeating speculations which in the fair course of trade they may carry on but to prevent them from combining (contrary in most instances to their own interest) to sell no grain whatever or not to sell so much as is wanted for immediate consumption, till the inhabitants are reduced to extreme distress.[40]

One is thus forced to the conclusion that the prevailing economic opinion had a lot to do with the formation of famine policy in India. The Madras government was emphatic that it was 'evident that if the general principle on which this doctrine is founded be sound, it is the duty of everyman when the emergency occurs to promote its practice, and the greater the emergency ... the more necessary it is to adhere to principle'.[41] In fact, until the third quarter of the nineteenth century, famine policies all over India were not a little influenced by the views on the subject expressed by Adam Smith in his *Wealth of Nations*.

[39] D. Hill to H. Fraser, 27 December 1811, *Ibid.*, pp. 6389–91. Almost identical answers (based on Smith's *Wealth of Nations*) were given to the collector of Nellore who reported collusion among grain dealers on the approach of a scarcity. Board of Revenue to the Collector of Nellore, 30 December 1811. R. A. Dalyell (Ed.), *The Standing Orders of the Board of Revenue 1820–1865* (Madras, 1866), pp. 447–8.

[40] Madras to the Court of Directors (Public), 5 March 1813, *Madras Letters Received*, India Office Records, E/4/342, Para. 55.

[41] Board of Revenue to the Collector of Nellore, 30 December 1811, *op. cit.*, pp. 447–8.

The prevailing economic opinion, increasingly influenced by the principles of political economy, was strongly in favour of a non-interventionist famine policy. In 1812, there was a famine in western India, particularly in Gujarat, Kaira, Surat and Broach, but the government did not 'think it expedient to take any measures that might tend to interfere with the ordinary course of trade'.[42] Having witnessed the misery generated by famines, the Judge–Magistrate of Kaira suggested the construction of public works to provide employment as well as the importation of grain on the government account to sell to the retailer on a cost-plus-moderate profit basis. However, while accepting the proposal of constructing public works such as irrigational dams, the Governor of Bombay flatly rejected the proposal to tamper with the freedom of market.

The Right Honourable the Governor in Council is disposed to think, from all the information before the Board, that those approved and recognised prinicples, founded as they have been on the experience . . . which prescribe an entire and unrestrained freedom in the grain trade, as best adapted to the relief of any existing scarcity and to the prevention of famine, are particularly applicable to the dealers in grain in the province of Goozerat . . . The digression of the celebrated author of the *Wealth of Nations* concerning the Corn-trade . . . and particularly as far as respects the *inland Trader*, is forcibly and irresistibly applicable to every state of society where merchants, or dealers in grain may be established.[43]

The next major famine was during 1823–4 when both the Madras and Bombay Presidencies were hit by the scourge. Like the Judge–Magistrate of Kaira, the Commercial resident at Masulipatam also saw the impending famine and immediately proceeded to fix prices and compel merchants to sell their stocks of grain, and also wrote to Bengal to send a consignment of grain on government account. At this the Government of Madras was scandalised, and Sir Thomas Munro, the Governor, felt compelled to write: 'The interference of Government on such occasion as is the present is often very prejudicial.'[44] The Resident was asked to withdraw all his interventionist measures, and the Bengal rice order was cancelled. Nevertheless one could not charge the Governor with having been callous, judging from the *indirect* measures his government took to 'alleviate the evils of scarcity'. As he was doubtful about the probable outcome of any policy of price control, he decided to give a bounty of Rs30 per *garce* (3s 8d per quarter) on imported grain.[45]

But the Bombay government did not go even as far as this because it did not have the 'slightest confidence in the efficiency of the propsed bounty . . . it

[42] Etheridge, *op. cit.*, p. 125.
[43] *Ibid.*, p. 128
[44] Minute dated 12 December 1823, Arbuthnot, *op. cit.*, p. 228.
[45] Minute dated 23 April 1824, *Madras Public Proceedings*, India Office Records, April 1824, Range 245, vol. 53, p. 1415.

will not lead to the importation of a single bag, or a single robin of rice beyond what we shall receive from the powerful encouragement naturally arising out of a scarcity price.'[46] The Governor of Bombay, Mountstuart Elphinstone, was at first in favour of a subsidy, but changed his opinion on an 'examination of the subject on general principles'.[47] Once again, he gave his warm support to the starting of public works such as building roads, desilting irrigation tanks and digging wells to provide employment.

Much the same policy was pursued during the notorious Guntur famine. When matters had become so bad that the local authorities appealed to the Government of Madras to import on government account a quantity of Tanjore rice at the ruling Guntur price, even then the Government at Madras refused on 'general principles'!

Thus every time there was a famine and an appeal was made to introduce measures such as price control and so on, the principles of political economy were cited to justify a policy of non-interference. To prevent arbitrary action by subordinate officials, such policies were also enshrined in general directions. To give an instance, a circular order of the Madras government categorically stated that high prices constituted the best security against a famine. 'The interference of Government in such emergencies . . . disturbs the natural current (by which, where trade is free, the demand of any commodity is sure to meet, as far as circumstances will allow, with a corresponding supply), and has a tendency to convert a season of scarcity into one of absolute famine.'[48] When junior civil servants questioned the wisdom of the Classical famine policy, the policy makers at the top firmly rebuffed such heresies. In 1839, when J. F. Thomas and John Sullivan (whose criticism of the famine policy will be referred to presently) raised doubts as to the utility of the Classical famine policy, the Governor Lord Elphinstone merely said: 'The remarks of Adam Smith appear to me to bear with such force upon this argument that I shall make no apology for introducing them.'[49] Elphinstone confirmed his belief in the Classical theory by not only stating that 'no theory can be more comprehensive' but also suggesting that the inconveniences of a real scarcity could not be remedied, they could 'only be palliated'. According to Elphinstone, free trade and employment provision in public works (but at

---

[46] Minute by Warden, Etheridge, *op. cit.*, p. 134.

[47] *Ibid.*, p. 135.

[48] Order dated 30 January 1833, Quoted in J. F. Thomas, 'Notes on Ryotwar' in *Madras Journal of Literature and Science*, No. 22, January 1839, p. 72.

[49] Lord Elphinstone's Minute, 17 February 1839. In this he cited from Edmund Burke to show that 'My business is against an overdoing of any sort of administration and more especially against this most momentous of all meddling on the part of authority, the meddling with the subsistence of the people.' Revenue and Agricultural Department Proceedings, 11 November 1839, no. 8, para. 34 (National Archives of India).

money wages) were the only two remedies that would mitigate the effects of severe famines.

It was sincerely believed that government action could do nothing to mitigate the sufferings of the public and it was very often claimed that the doctrine of the policy of non-interference actually brought good to the public. Colonel William Sleeman is a case in point. When he was the Magistrate administering Sagar (in the present-day Madhya Pradesh), he found signs of an approaching famine in the district, with people clamouring for the government to compel the merchants to sell foodgrains at a low price. But to do so would be betraying the first principles of political economy; and Sleeman thought it lamentable that 'European gentlemen of otherwise first-rate eduction and abilities', being ignorant of those principles, should by adopting measures 'arising out of such ignorance, aggravate the evils of dearth'.[50] But Sleeman supported a policy of absolute non-interference, and, as the *Dictionary Of National Biography* says of him, 'he displayed commendable firmness during a time of scarcity, refusing, though urged to do so by the military authorities, to put any limit on the market price of grain'.

The effect of this policy was such that an Indian soldier told him in amazement that 'every shop had become full of grain as if by supernatural agency' and remarked '*Kālē ādmi ki akal kahān talak chalégi?*' Sleeman very modestly ascribed this marvel not to the pigment of his skin, but to the wisdom of political economy! Defending his policy, he pointed out that the grain dealers and a free market were very vital for a proper distribution of foodgrains in all economies and more so in India where the major portion of its population depended upon agriculture for its livelihood, and agriculture was subject to the vagaries of the monsoon. Whereas in Europe, alternative employment opportunities in trade and manufactures existed for the unemployed rural population, in India it was necessary to distribute the available food evenly between good and bad seasons.[51]

The firm advocacy of such views really meant that the administrators were directed not to involve themselves in the actual market. On the other hand, local administrators could not completely shut their eyes to the suffering around them. Moved by their humanitarianism, they tried – funds permitting – to relieve the extreme misery. Some did this by providing bounties to encourage grain imports, and others believed in distributing free food and provision of employment in public works: Munro's subsidies for grain imports in 1825–6 cost the Madras exchequer about Rs4 lakhs and the assistance provided by the various local officials in Bengal during the 1838 famine

---

[50] *Rambles and Recollections of an Indian Official*, vol. I, p. 191.
[51] 'Letter to the Editor' in *Alexander's East India and Colonial Magazine*, vol. XVII, no. 99, February 1839, p. 160.

was about Rs 44,000.[52] The public works initiated by the local officials after the famine had struck to provide employment to the victims were conceived in haste and without any regular plan. Sir Arthur Cotton among others had suggested from time to time that the public works be put in a regular scheme of famine relief. His policy would have involved action in *anticipation* of a famine but not after the famine had occurred. He suggested that when a famine was anticipated, authorities should plan for specific projects and collect foodgrains by entering the market. With the onset of the famine, the government would be ready to employ the poor labourers in return for food and shelter. But given the climate of opinion these policies had no chance of being accepted.[53]

Classical political economy continued to play a significant part in the formation of famine policy even after the Indian administration was taken over by the British government. Between 1860 and 1880, there were many major famines involving untold misery, degradation and death, and because of these, there developed a questioning attitude towards the orthodox policy based on the economics of Adam Smith.

The first major famine to strike India after the British government nationalised the East India Company hit the North Western Provinces in 1860. Free trade, as usual, determined government action in the face of the famine. But mortality was not particularly high because of employment opportunities, not only in the neighbouring areas, but also in the military barracks being constructed as a result of the post-mutiny military expansion.[54] Colonel Baird-Smith, who was asked by the Government of India to report on the famine, put to good use his knowledge of political economy and the writings of Malthus in his diagnosis of the Indian famines and proposals for improving the situation. He correctly interpreted the recurrent famines in the light of the general Indian economic conditions. According to him they were caused by the already existing high number of paupers, which meant that in India it was employment and not food supply that was deficient. Hence any slight depression in the economy caused by a failure of seasonal rains increased unemployment. Even the slightest derangement swelled the unemployed labour force and there was consequent misery due to their incapacity to buy food. The remedy was not an interference with the processes of the market place but one of improving the economic position of the masses through measures such as permanent settlement, increased irrigation works and

[52] Government of Madras to Board of Revenue, 17 December 1832, *Board of Revenue Consultations* (Tamilnadu Archives), 16 December 1846, and H. J. Rainey, 'Famines in Bengal' in *Calcutta Review*, vol. LIX, no. 118, f. 1874, p. 334.
[53] Dalyell, *Memorandum on the Madras Famine*, p. 147.
[54] Bhatia, *Famines in India* (Bombay, 1963), p. 62.

expansion of communications. Baird-Smith believed that on the whole well-meaning administrators, without realising that famines were a natural dispensation, blundered into policies that aggravated the difficulties. It is no doubt true that the grain dealers during times of severe shortages increased their prices, but that 'process is a natural one, and if honestly and fairly pursued, not merely a legitimate but a desirable one'.

Considering the tenacity with which Indian administrators pursued for many decades a famine policy based on Smithian economics, it is surprising to hear from Baird-Smith that freedom of the market as 'the best and surest aids against famines,' is 'scarcely yet recognised universally among ourselves'. Attributing to Warren Hastings an ignorance of the principles of political economy, Baird-Smith said that Hastings was responsible for aggravating the famine in 1783. However the fault was not entirely that of Hastings! Because the 1783 famine of Bengal:

followed only by a few years, the first dawn of the revolution of thought on such questions produced ultimately by the publication of Adam Smith's *Wealth of Nations* in 1776, it could scarcely have been expected that those who had to meet it, even though Warren Hastings himself were among them, should do so on principles far in advance of contemporary opinion and experience.[55]

Baird-Smith reserved a word of praise for John Strachey, the Magistrate of Moradabad, for directing famine relief, and the chief 'native' judge, Syed Ahmad Khan ('a gentleman whose devotion to this work has been admirable, and whose knowledge of the political economy of famines was singularly exact and sound'), for the practical working-out of the whole scheme of relief.

Strachey certainly did not believe in entering the grain market. Like Sleeman, he too said that during times of scarcity every magistrate was urged 'both by Englishmen and by natives to interfere, in some way or other, for the purpose of cheapening food'. His advice was much the same as Sleeman's – with the exception of the provision of public works. Even here he was conscious of the need to remember the received doctrine. The famous Moradabad famine relief consisted of providing employment for the able-bodied unemployed on subsistence wages. Strachey declared that it was 'not possible to look upon human suffering from an economical point of view alone'. The problem was how to make people self-reliant during a famine. Making a comparison with the English poor laws, he said:

The problem as Mr J. S. Mill says regarding poor laws, 'is how to give the greatest amount of needful help with the smallest encouragement to undue reliance on it'.

[55] Report of Col. Baird-Smith to William Grey, Secretary, Home Department, Government of India, 14 August 1861. *Parl. Papers*, H.C. 29, vol. XL of Session 1862.

Whether relief be given in the shape of simple charity, or in return for labour performed upon public works ... the relief must be no greater than can be helped ... it
is better, ... that we should give somewhat too little than too much.[56]

Strachey's views on how to deal with Indian famines had very considerable
influence on the British Indian administration for the next two decades, and it
was in spite of the devastating famines that in the next two decades swept
over almost all parts of British India.

The famine that ravaged Orissa during 1865 and 1866 was one of the most
severe of the century and once again we find a firm adherence to free trade
principles in the administration of famine policy. The total mortality has
been estimated to be 1 364 529 which in some districts meant one fourth
of the population.[57] Ravenshaw, the Commissioner of the Cuttack division,
not only underestimated the symptoms, but also expected that grain would
pour into Orissa as soon as prices rose to an appreciable extent. But he agreed
later that he was disappointed, having not taken any action because

under all ordinary rules of political economy the urgent demand for grain in the
Cuttack division ought to have created a supply from other and more favoured parts,
and that, unless under the most exceptional circumstances, any interference on the
part of the Government with local trade was a measure fraught with danger and
opposed to all rule or precedent.[58]

It has been suggested that, during the Orissa famine, the deaths and
misery were not due to non-intervention on the part of the government as
such, but due to the difficulties of transportation: firstly there were no good
roads to move foodgrains from adjoining areas, and secondly the heavy monsoon that came so soon after the severe famine prevented even the use of sea-
transport.[59] There were practical difficulties, no doubt, and the odds against
which the officials had to contend were enormous. Sir Bartle Frere was probably right when he said, 'Let any one read the records of the Irish famine,
multiply every difficulty he reads by five, and he will have a very imperfect
idea of what, in the lowest computation, has to be done in Bengal.'[60] It is true
that local officers might have been negligent in anticipating the impending
famine,[61] and it is equally true that communications were poor. But after

[56] Geddes, *op. cit.*, p. 17.
[57] See appendix 11. *Parl. Papers*, H.C. 363, vol. VIII of Session 1871.
[58] Annual Report of the Commissioner of Cuttack, no. 313, dated 16 July 1866. *Parl. Papers*,
     H.C. 335, vol. LI of Session 1867, pp. 58–9.
[59] See William Digby, *The Famine Campaign in Southern India* (London, 1878), vol. II, p. 275.
     John Beames a Bengal civilian also attributed the sufferings to the absence of proper landing
     place in Orissa. See his *Memoirs of a Bengal Civilian* (London, 1961), p. 248. Beames was not
     in Orissa during the famine and it is likely that he swallowed the pretexts given by the fellow
     civil servants.
[60] *On the Impending Bengal Famine* (London, 1874), p. 45.
[61] It is possible that Ravenshaw was a victim of circumstances because his assessment of the

reading the mass of correspondence and official papers of the period, one cannot resist the conclusion that the officials as a class swore by the principles of non-interference in the grain market. Those who had studied at the East India College, Haileybury, were also firm believers in the principles of political economy. When it was difficult for intelligent academicians to repudiate the accepted doctrines in favour of radically different ones, how much more difficult was it for Indian civil servants of average ability.[62] This aspect is well illustrated by an ex-civil servant of the East India Company, W. H. Leslie Melville, who remarked 'I remember to have seen an order issued by an Indian Magistrate, fixing a maximum on the price of grain in a particular town; and I was immediately satisfied (as was the fact), that the authority who issued it, could never have attended, however negligently, the lectures of Mr Malthus.'[63] Even the Indian subordinate servants who had not gone to Haileybury often accepted the current orthodoxy in economics.[64]

When by October 1865 there were clear symptoms of famine, it was the decision of both the Commissioner of Cuttack and the Government of Bengal not to convert the scarcity into famine by the 'impolitic' action of the state. In other words, even if Ravenshaw and other local officers were willing to purchase grain from other areas and distribute to the starving population, they could not have done so. Their immediately higher authority, the Board of Revenue at Calcutta, provided very clear and explicit instructions. When the Commissioner reported to the Board of Revenue that the public works started by him had been at a standstill for want of rice and asked for permission to import rice to distribute to the workers in lieu of wages, the

Footnote 61 continued
   situation in Orissa was based on price statistics collected mostly by subordinate ranks of the police force. Very often the prices given were what the shopkeepers and other informants thought the prices should be and not at which the commodities were available in the market; the prices were almost mere wishful thinking. It is also possible that the grain dealers wouldn't charge the maximum prices to the government officials and especially the police force. All this could have misled the local officers into thinking that food was cheap and so available in plenty. See the Orissa Famine Enquiry Commission Report, *Parl. Papers*, H.C. 335, vol. LI of Session 1867. Paragraphs 121–5. It must also be pointed out that such discrepancies between the official price statistics and the real prices in the local markets were not uncommon. See for instance Bourdillon's remarks on the price data relating to the Madras Presidency. Minute dated 11 June 1855, *Madras Revenue Consultations* (Tamilnadu Archives), vol. 835.
62 There is, perhaps, an element of truth in what Sir James Fitzjames Stephen said: 'It is a melancholy truth and a glaring illustration of what I have told you is in my judgement the great feature of Indian Government, the necessity of doing first rate work with fourth rate instruments. You must never forget that nineteen civilians in twenty are the most commonplace and the least dignified of second or third class Englishmen.' Stephen to Lytton, 7 May 1876 (Stephen Papers at the Cambridge University Library), p. 11.
63 *Remarks on the East India Bill* (London, 1833), p. 26.
64 See Syed Mohammed Ulli Khan, *On the Origin of the Famine and Subsequent Pestilence in the Cuttack Division* (Calcutta, n.d.), p. 16.

Board of Revenue bluntly told the Commissioner 'The Government declines to import rice into Puri. If the market favours, rice will find its way into Puri without Government interference, which can only do harm. All payments for labour employed to relieve the present distress are to be in cash.'[65]

The members of the Board of Revenue were in the words of a very close observer, Sir George Campbell, 'not unduly sanguine or inclined to make light of threatened evil,' but they 'held by the most rigid rules of the driest political economy, and had the most unwavering faith in the "demand and supply" theory'.[66] Hence it is not very surprising that the Board told its subordinates that a strict non-interference 'would ensure the applications of the ordinary laws of political economy, which could alone, in a case of so-widespread scarcity afford real relief'.[67] In its view all the government could do was to disseminate information about price levels, encourage local private charity and provide employment for the poor in public works. It was also suggested that liberal expenditure on public works and similar methods be utilised to induce the landlords also to follow this example. Actually the policy would be to do nothing, as the following instruction will illustrate: 'All that the Government can do is to encourage and facilitate their [principles of political economy] operation. There can be no doubt that it is altogether beyond the power of Government to mend matters by any extraordinary operation in contravention of those laws.'[68] This shows that the Board of Revenue of Bengal could offer very little elbow-room for their district officers, and even if the Board of Revenue at Calcutta relaxed its rigid famine policy, there were strict regulations from the Government of India. For example,

Strict injuctions should be given to all local officers to abstain from any interference with the ordinary course of trade in the buying and selling of grain. Under no pretext whatever can anyone be held to be justified in bringing pressure to bear on the dealers, however serious may be the want of food, or however high may be prices

---

[65] Cited in *Famine Commission Report, Parl. Papers*, Cmd. 3086, Vol. LXXI of Session 1881, p. 46.

[66] *Memoirs of My Indian Career*, vol. 1, p. 156.

[67] *Parl. Papers*, vol. LI of Session 1867, para. 106. Apart from this general circular, the Government of Bengal in a specific communication asked the Commissioner of Cuttack not to interfere with the private trade. See Bengal to Commissioner of Cuttack, 23 October 1865, no. 5969, cited by Dharm Pal, *Administration of Sir John Lawrence in India* (Simla, 1952), pp. 77.

[68] *Ibid.*, Para. 106. See for similar statements by R. B. Chapman a member of the Board of Revenue, 'Principles, after all, though they may be sneered at, and even broadly denied, cannot be overcome. The state cannot successfully convert itself into a wholesale dealer in grain, and any attempt that it may make to do so is almost sure to end in widespread disappointment and failure' (1867). 'Efficient or not, we *must* rely upon this law alone, and whatever is done should be done carefully, with a view to encourage, and to avoid discouraging, the natural working of the Law' (1865). *Famine Commission Report, Parl. Papers*, Cmd. 3086, vol. LXXI of Session 1881, pp. 50, 51.

demanded ... without special authority, the purchase of grain by public officers, otherwise than for distribution to persons receiving relief, is prohibited.[69]

The Government of Bengal told its Board of Revenue that the price of government rice should not fall much below the market rate, and should the market rise the government prices should follow.[70] The Secretary of State, in his turn, approved these statements of policy as 'more likely to afford the necessary relief'.[71] The local officers were also able to point to the Irish famine policy to justify their own actions. According to a senior member of the Bengal Board of Revenue, its policy was certainly not original, and he cited C. E. Trevelyan's article on the Irish famine in 1846 in the *Edinburgh Review*, saying, 'it will explain and justify our hesitation to recommend a departure from rules and principles which para 8 of the Secretary of State's Despatch admits should not be lightly interfered with'. The problem of the Orissa famine was not unlike 'the question which so anxiously occupied the Home Government in 1846, and which was finally dealt with by adopting measures confining their interference in Ireland to minimum.'[72] Naturally this minimum interference would mean a reluctance on the part of the government to cause any difficulty to the private sector whether the private sector did its duty or not. Even when the government imported rice on its account in the later stages of the famine, it believed in not upsetting the market processes. This is particularly noticed in the *market-plus* rates charged for government sales of foodgrains.[73]

The British administration, although restrained by its doctrinal predilections from interfering with the market process, felt throughout the period under consideration that the provision of employment through public works was a suitable famine policy. The alternative would have been simple charity. But British thought since Malthus had never really come to approve of public charity because of the fears of increasing pauperisation and in-

[69] 'Memorandum of Measures approved by the Government of India for adoption in time of famine' Geddes, *op. cit.*, pp. 3–4. See also the letter from Government of India to the Government of Bengal in *Parl. Papers*, H.C. 335, vol. LI of Session 1867, p. 190.

[70] *Ibid.*, p. 172.

[71] Secretary of State to Governor General in Council, 2 May 1867, No. 41 (Public) *Ibid.*, p. 196. This was in spite of what the Secretary of State had privately written to the Viceroy condemning Chapman and Ravenshaw for their 'ill regulated enthusiasm for the doctrines of political economy'. Cranborne to Lawrence, 2 October 1866 (Salisbury Papers).

[72] See Grote's Minute 6 May 1867. Campbell Commission Report Part II. *Parl. Papers*, H.C. 335–1, vol. LI of Session 1867, p. 234. It would be difficult to conclude that Trevelyan's Irish Famine policy alone decided the Orissa Famine policy. But that was certainly an important factor. While Trevelyan's famine policy did not endear him to the Irish people, he was nevertheless a very respected member of the Indian civil service and as such his views had considerable influence in India.

[73] See Schalch to Beadon, 16 March 1867 (*Additional Manuscript* 50023, at the British Museum) p. 32.

efficiency.[74] As we have seen, even the most doctrinaire administrator did not feel that providing public works occasionally constituted a threat. However, caution was expressed against large-scale projects of the type persistently advocated by Sir Arthur Cotton among others.[75]

Those who approved public works as a sound method of reducing the rigours of famine nevertheless opposed the payment of wages in kind: partly because this would involve price fixation through the back door, but mainly since this would be turning backwards in the path of history. Instead of going forward to a 'commercial civilization' (to use a phrase from the *Wealth of Nations*), payment of wages in kind would lead back to barter!

Such, then, was the famine policy that was approved and used in the 1866 famine. But when the human misery reached gigantic proportions, even these dogmatic beliefs had to be relaxed. Finding the famine situation deteriorating, the Government of India gave instructions to the Government of Bengal to send a certain amount of foodgrain to Orissa, but asked that if possible 'sales are made at such prices as may not discourage private traders from importing grain'.[76] However, these tardy orders could not prevent the tragedy that claimed nearly one fourth of the total population of Orissa.

THE CLASSICAL FAMINE POLICY QUESTIONED

The significant aspect from our point of view in the Orissa famine was the first expression of doubt regarding the effectiveness of the Classical theory of economic policy at the highest echelons of policy making. The new Secretary of State, Viscount Cranborne, was troubled by the harrowing details that were being published in the British press of the mortality of the Orissa famine, and wondered why in spite of the applications of the principles of political economy, people were dying in thousands when famines occurred. Cranborne was unable to reject entirely the *laissez-faire* beliefs because there were hardly any alternatives available. This difficulty in reconciling the theoretical convictions and the practical policies made him effect a compromise. Thus we see him favouring active help by the state only on humanitarian grounds. He was not prepared to shed his beliefs in the freedom of market, but threw the blame not on the principles of political economy but on the systematic misuse of them by unintelligent officials. Cranborne realised that there were situations when laws of political economy should not be

---

[74] See J. S. Mill, *Principles of Political Economy*, Bk. II, Chap. XII, Sec. 2.

[75] Geddes, *op. cit.*, p. 19. Even the provision of public works for employment was fully recognised only in the 1837–9 N.W.P. famine as a duty of the Government. See *Famine Commission Report*, Parl. Papers, C. 3086, vol. LXXI of Session 1881, p. 22.

[76] Proceedings of the Government of India (Home Dept.), 20 June 1866. *Parl. Papers*, H.C. 335, vol. LI of Session 1867, p. 19.

mechnically followed,[77] but at the same time he also officially told the Viceroy of India:

That the rules and principles of economical science should not be lightly interfered with, and that the supply and the distribution throughout the country of the means of subsistence should, except under extraordinary circumstances, be left to the operation of the law of 'demand and supply', there can be no question at all. But there can be as little doubt that the rules of political economy, however valuable under ordinary circumstances, ought to give way whenever the lives or the health of the people would be seriously endangered by a pertinacious adherence to them.[78]

This eclectic approach to Classical famine policy had already been arrived at by many Indian civil servants. There had always been some administrators who were shocked by the destitution, sufferings and mortality they saw and had tried to question the validity of using economic ideas for policy making. An anonymous contributor to the *Calcutta Review* pointed out, after citing Nassau Senior, that the job of the political economists was not policy making, and even went so far as to blame J. S. Mill and other 'popular expounders of political economy' for considering it is 'an applied science'. This was the reason why it gave a feeling of confidence that the study of political economy was capable of solving all problems.[79] As early as 1839 when most people accepted the truth of Classical economics, a Madras civil servant asked why 'tens and even hundreds of thousands have perished by actual starvation under British rule, while it is certain, that there has been no tampering on the part of Government with the grain trade of the country, and the people have been left to the freest use of their own resources'.[80] Discussing the past famines of Bombay and Madras respectively, both Etheridge and Dalyell found that the effect of the famine policy derived from the prevailing economic ideas 'cannot be said to have been altogether satisfactory'.[81] Girdlestone, after investigating the history of famine in the North Western Provinces, concluded that 'the principle of political economy must be borne in mind, but not slavishly followed'.[82]

---

[77] Cranborne's speech in the House of Commons, 2 August 1867, *Hansard*, vol. CLXXXIX, p. 809.

[78] Secretary of State to the Governor General in Council, 9 October 1866, No. 85 (Public). *Public Despatches to India 1866*, India Office Records, L/PJ/3/1043, p. 327.

[79] 'The Operation of the Laissez-faire Principles', (1867), vol. XLVI, No. XCI, pp. 102 *et seq.*

[80] J. F. Thomas, 'Notes on the Duty of Government in Periods of Famine' in *Madras Journal of Literature and Science*, April 1839, p. 211. John Sullivan, another Madras civil servant was also prompted by similar doubts when he asked: 'In spite of what Adam Smith says famines do occur periodically in India without any blame being imputable to the regulations of government and in spite of what other great men say the markets are so inadequately supplied when left to private enterprise.' Minute dated 8 March 1839, *Revenue and Agricultural Proceedings*, 11 November 1839, no. 8 (National Archives of India).

[81] Dalyell, *Memorandum*, p. 153; Etheridge, *op. cit.*, p. 4.

[82] Girdlestone, C. E. R. *Report on Past Famines in the North Western Provinces*, p. 23.

It was accepted that trade should increase if the scarcity induced a price increase. But this seldom happened in India. Thomas showed how rice was cheap in the adjoining districts while famine raged in some districts, but still cheap grains did not flow from the abundant to the famine districts through the medium of private trade. It was equally clear to Dalyell that on those occasions when effective help was needed 'these so-called rules of political economy, were found to be ineffectual for the purpose intended ... though prices were enormously high, it was found that the natural course of trade did not supply the locality suffering from scarcity, with sufficient expedition'.[83]

What, then, had gone wrong? Having been serious students of political economy, these critics could not fly in the face of the doctrines of Smith. J. F. Thomas, who had been a student of Malthus at Haileybury, argued that while Adam Smith's ideas were perfectly correct for temperate climates and advanced civilisations, 'much of the reasoning of Smith appears to me inapplicable to this, or to any tropical country in an early stage of civilization'.[84] While in the West it was correct to say that the 'fault of the season alone' never caused a scarcity, in India bad seasons always resulted in famines. Certainly, according to Thomas, Smith never visualised a 'people in the fearful state of destitution'. India was the exceptional case. 'There is nothing parallel,' said Thomas, 'in the case under review of Smith, Chalmers, and other political economists of Europe, to the circumstances before us in India: I would rest my first objection to the unlimited application of the principle of non-interference ... on the manifest dissimilarity between the circumstances of dearth in the two countries.'[85]

India presented many unusual features according to these critics for the Classical famine policy to be effective. The unsettled conditions in many parts of India aggravated by famines always spelled insecurity for trade. There was also the problem of the high mortality of draught cattle during periods of famine. In areas not served by either railway lines or canals, this caused severe shortages of transport facilities. There was the equally important factor of the lack of adequate capital to embark on a vast scale of trading during famine periods. Traders in India, as noted by Thomas in particular, were operating with small quantities of capital, and this restricted them in using the opportunites provided by famines. However, above all, there were special institutional obstacles that were peculiar to India alone. It was pointed out very correctly that caste, custom and usage acted as effective

[83] Dalyell, *op. cit.*, pp. 155, 158.

[84] Thomas, *loc. cit.*, p. 209.

[85] *Ibid.*, p. 212 The same point was made in more general terms by an author in *Alexander's East India and Colonial Magazine*, vol. XVI, no. 96, November 1838, pp. 461 *et seq.* See also Dalyell, *op. cit.*, p. 156; Orissa Famine Commission Report, *loc. cit.*, para. 203, p. 265. See also the *Indian Economist*, 21 September 1871.

barriers to entry into the grain trading businesses. Whereas competition should in theory result in the lowest possible prices, in India this did not always happen because trading was a caste occupation which meant that only particular castes could enter the grain business. This made combination and collusion a lot easier and prevented competition.[86] The village grain dealer in ordinary times was not a channel of grain distribution. His primary function was to lend money and collect surplus grain to be sold in towns or exported. Lytton correctly said that the ordinary people

as a whole, *do not buy food*. They *sell it*: and, in the rural districts there is no natural self-acting agency for the sale of food on any large scale such as exists in the towns. In this fact lies the source of one of our greatest difficulties in times of famine. The people suddenly cease to be producers, and simultaneously become purchasers of food: and there is no pre-established agency for meeting their demand on a sufficiently large scale.[87]

Conditions in India, then, did not favour a vigorous pursuit of the grain trade. Institutional structure either prevented flourishing trade or, if allowed, the trade did not guarantee the beneficial allocational effects that political economy predicted. If so, what could be the alternative? Dalyell lamented that 'not one of the great masters of economic science have deliberately prescribed the course which a Government ought to follow, when its subjects are positively dying in huge numbers from starvation'. This led to the conclusion among many Indian administrators that the principles of non-interference should not be too rigidly adhered to especially by a 'Christian government'.[88] Thomas, on the contrary, derived support from Malthus's *Tract on the Corn Laws:* for his pleas for active participation:

Malthus and other writers, who have ranked high as followers of Smith, have maintained that the provisioning of the Country cannot always be safely relinquished to the operation of the ordinary Laws of supply and demand, which govern less necessary articles; and that there are considerations affecting the food of a people, which may take it out of the ordinary rules of Political Economy.[89]

Thomas, like many critics of the Classical famine policy, felt that the mere fact that sufficient foodgrains were available in the country would not be enough. If private trade failed to make the foodgrains available in the famine stricken areas, the government had no alternative but to interfere. Without

[86] Frequently one comes across references to the grain dealers stockpiling grain in the hope of price increases. See W. T. Munro's contributions to *Neilgherry Excelsior* (1864) reprinted in *Madrasiana* (Madras, 1889), pp. 233–41; Harvey Tuckett, *The Indian Revenue System as it is* (London, 1840), p. 148. John Sullivan of the Madras civil service wrote that in India 'we have much more to dread from combination, than to hope from competition'. Memorandum dated January 1839, *Revenue and Agriculture Department Proceedings*, National Archives of India, 11 November 1839, No. 8, para 7.

[87] Lytton to Caird, 1 March 1879, *Home. Misc.*, India Office Records, No. 796, p. 236.

[88] Dalyell, *op. cit.*, pp. 153, 210.

[89] Thomas, *op. cit.*, p. 213.

attempting to refute 'the truth of Dr Smith's general principle as respects trade in general . . . and even the grain trade in seasons of scarcity in Europe', Thomas presented a case for active state help to people in times of famine.[90] Similarly Dalyell and the Orissa Famine Commission did not try to question the validity of the economic ideas of Adam Smith. They argued the case for state interference on the basis of Sir Robert Peel's action in importing Indian corn during the notorious Irish famine of 1842–3. Dalyell, in particular, held that it was the duty of the government 'not to lay down fixed principles for its guidance, regardless of the varying circumstances of different localities, but to keep itself thoroughly acquainted with the food supply'. Should any variation of the season indicate an approaching famine, the government ought to be prepared 'to import food for the preservation of the lives of its people, on Government account or even establish depots for the sale of food'. He admitted that this policy was based on the 'general opinions given in the London journals' according to which 'there is a vast difference between acting in default of laws of political economy, and acting in contravention of them, and that when it was found that from natural or artificial causes, the demand for food was wholly unanswered, the Government was not only justified, but bound to provide for the exceptional necessity.'[91] Arguments were also proffered against the provision of money wages in the public works. By pumping more money into circulation money wages only increased food prices until 'the poorest competitors have no longer the means of competing'. Public works could be beneficial only if wages were paid in grain imported from elsewhere.[92]

It cannot be said, however, that the critics of Classical famine policy had lost all their faith in the principles of political economy. The Calcutta reviewer, for instance, found the arguments used by economists from Adam Smith to John Stuart Mill against price-fixing by government to be based on sound logic and hence valid.[93] Dalyell admitted that 'a return to a Government price for provisions could never be advocated'.[94]

---

[90] 'Notes on Ryotwar', *Madras Journal of Literature and Science*, January 1839, p. 75.

[91] *Loc. cit.*, pp. 160–2. John Sullivan of the Madras Civil Service made similar remarks.

[92] 'The Operation of the Laissez-faire Principles in Times of Scarcity' *loc. cit.*, p. 116. See also the statement of the acting sub-collector of Bellary made during the 1866 famine. *Parl. Papers*, H.C. 490 vol. LII of Session 1867, p. 73.

[93] 'The Operation of the Laissez-faire Principles in Times of Scarcity' *loc. cit.*, pp. 106 *et seq.*

[94] *Loc. cit.*, p. 153. Similarly another writer, while accepting government's duty to provide relief for the famine stricken population, nevertheless thought it absurd and wasteful to try to secure reduction in prices by either fixing prices or by entering the grain market itself. See Mentor, *The Political Economy of Indian Famines* (Bombay, 1877), pp. 20–4. The opinion of Thomas, the outspoken critic of the classical famine policy was the same. *Madras Journal of Literature and Science*, April 1839, p. 208. Once in a while critics of the Classical famine policy completely misunderstood the inner logic of that policy. See for instance the defence of price fixing provided in a contemporary pamphlet, *A White Pamphlet: Notes on the Indian Famine* (Calcutta, 1877), p. 18.

John Stuart Mill was aware of the difficulties of applying economic theory to concrete situations. Although he was quite certain of the ultimate benefits of a free and unfettered internal market, he was prepared to allow for exceptions. As he pointed out, 'Direct measures at the cost of the state, to procure food from a distance, are expedient when from peculiar reasons the thing is not likely to be done by private speculation. In any other case they are a great error.'[95] Anticipating this proposal, Thomas had said:

an importation of grain, through the means of Government capital, and possibly of Government Agency, from *foreign or distant markets*, where there is abundance; into districts suffering from dearth, may be under the existing circumstances of the country a measure of sound policy; and the best, if not the only practical method by which the distress ... can be greatly alleviated.[96]

Campbell's Orissa Famine Commission also quoted the sentence from John Stuart Mill cited earlier to advocate a similar policy for India in 1867.[97]

In this way we can see the formation of an opinion favourable to state intervention during famines. It also had considerable application during certain famines. When near-famine conditions prevailed in the North Western Provinces in 1869, the government announced 'its full responsibility for the really helpless irrespective of charitable institutions'.[98] One of the major characteristics of the famine policy of the North Western Provinces was for the government to import food grains on its own account to guard against an absolute shortage of food. Hunter reported in 1873 that a very general consensus among the district officers was achieved regarding imports of foodgrains during famines. The experience of Orissa obviously convinced many that the ordinary operation of trade 'breaks down during a famine, and that state interference in some form or other is necessary'. But, added Hunter, 'Different officers lay different degrees of stress upon state-interference.'[99]

Still it was a matter of policy that private enterprise should be allowed to function unmolested even during famines. Certain exceptions were made but these exceptional cases, in the words of Henvey, were 'only deviations from the general policy'.[100] Ultimately the policy pursued depended upon the particular officer or officers in charge of the famine area. Even the most interventionist officer could do little. At the most, he could import enough food on the government account to stabilise the price level until the private traders replenished their stock by importing from distant provinces. There was the constant worry for the district officers that they might be importing

[95] *Principles of Political Economy*, p. 931.
[96] *Madras Journal of Literature and Science*, January 1839, p. 76.
[97] *Parl. Papers*, H.C. 335, vol. LI of Session 1867, Para, 203.
[98] Henvey's Report on the Famine, see Geddes, *op. cit.*, p. 24.
[99] W. W. Hunter, *Famine Aspects of Bengal Districts* (Simla, 1873), p. XXVI.
[100] Geddes, *op. cit.*, p. 26.

too much, in which case, as the Collector of Rungpur put it, 'prices would fall, and the confidence of the merchants might be shaken, and private enterprise brought to a stop. Were there no importation at all, the scarcity might turn into famine even for the provident portion of the community, and irretrievable disaster might ensue.'[101] This fear as well as wrong assessment of the capacity of the private trade very often led to famines being administered on the basis of a policy of absolute non-interference even after serious doubts were cast on such attitudes.

Indeed, there was no uniform policy to tackle famines in the post-Orissa famine period until the early 1880s. This period saw the dethronement of the Classical famine policy, but not its annihilation. Successive administrators took decisions – sometimes on the basis of doctrine and sometimes on the basis of exigencies – but seldom making it clear why. Both interventionists (Sir George Campbell being a leading champion) and the non-interventionists (under Sir John Strachey) found inspiration from John Stuart Mill's *Principles of Political Economy*, although it is clear that both sides quoted Mill mechanically to prove their points. Ultimately the differences between these two sides boiled down to the existence of the preconditions for the successful application of the Classical famine policy.[102] Financial considerations and personality clashes also played their part in the formation of famine policies in the 1869–79 decade, as we shall see presently.

The famine that hit Bengal in 1873–4 presented a challenge to the new Viceroy, Lord Northbrook, as he was not only a confirmed believer in the *laissez-faire* orthodoxy but also a humanitarian liberal. Like Strachey, Northbrook was an admirer of the writings of John Stuart Mill. However, he not only comprehended the analytical core of Mill's economics, but was also aware of sociological realities. This fact more than anything else explains his administration of the 1873–4 famine. When as early as October 1873, he learnt that Bengal might be hit by a famine he decided at once what action would have to be taken. A Resolution was passed by the Government of India on 7 November 1873 indicating the main principles on which a famine policy would be based.[103] The Resolution stressed the following measures to fight famine: (1) construction of public works to provide employment; (2) payment of wages in grain; and (3)

---

[101] qn. W. W. Hunter, *op. cit.*, p. 89.

[102] Both Campbell and Strachey had not misunderstood the analytical part of Mill's economics. They differed only regarding the presence of the extraordinary conditions in India. According to Strachey, there was nothing special but for Campbell, India was the exceptional case. It is difficult to explain why they differed. Perhaps their political views coloured their assessment of the Indian actualities!

[103] *Proceedings of the Department of Agriculture*, India Office Records, Revenue and Commerce, 1873–4, vol. 685, pp. 9–14.

encouragement of emigration to places were food was available in plenty.

It is undeniable that Mill's influence was an important factor in the formulation of this policy.[104] One important thing to be noted here is that, for the first time, we do not come across a definite unalterable position with regard to the question of state interference. Northbrook certainly had great faith in the free processes of the grain market but he made it clear that he would avoid interferences such as the prohibition of exports, state assumption of wholesale and retail distribution of food grains and price control only 'so far or so long as they could possibly be avoided'. But this does not mean that the government intended to perform the functions of the private trader. Considerable unanimity of opinion could be observed among the important policy makers. Northbrook, Lord Argyll, the Secretary of State, and Sir George Campbell, the Lt. Governor of Bengal, all believed that the government should encourage the private market and let it distribute the available foodgrains except in isolated areas.[105] 'Commercial enterprise', said Argyll, was 'the most powerful agency in bringing the necessary supplies', and hence 'ought not to be unnecessarily discouraged or thwarted in its operations'. He was pleased that the Indian government will 'not supersede or interfere with the functions of the trader in grain as regards that part of the population, which is able to purchase'.[106] Campbell, who was critical of many aspects of Northbrook's famine policy, agreed with the view that private traders would need to ration the existing supplies.[107]

As we have already seen, by now it was accepted by most policy makers that the government was in duty bound to try to save people from distress in times of famine, and public works were the accepted mode of the provision of relief. The old doubts concerning wages in money did not trouble Northbrook, and he decided to remunerate the workers in the public works on what was 'most acceptable to them and most suitable to the surrounding circumstances'.[108] This was payment in kind, which meant foodgrains. In a

---

[104] Northbrook was not a doctrinaire believer in the principles of political economy and according to his biographer, Bernard Mallet, he 'was a Statesman, not a professor ... (was) inclined to take the political rather than the economic view of any particular case'. On the other hand, he was well aware of the writings of the economists. See B. Mallet, *Thomas George, Earl of Northbrook: A Memoir* (London, 1908), pp. 72–3.

[105] There were large areas where the dealers in grain were assisted in conducting their business. As Temple remarked: 'In fact, the Government had, for the time, to fulfil the functions of both wholesale and retail dealers'. See his *Reports on the Scarcity 1873–74*, *Parl. Papers*, H.C. 123, vol. LIV of Session 1875, p. 551.

[106] Secretary of State to the Viceroy, 1 December 1873, *Parl. Papers*, Cmd. 933, vol. L of Session 1874, p. 51.

[107] Note dated 6 February 1874, *Parl. Papers*, Cmd. 955, vol. L of Session 1874, p. 305. See also J. W. Furrell, 'Famines in India and the Duty of Government', *The Calcutta Review*, 1874, vol. LVIII, no. 115, pp. 153–6.

[108] Resolution, 7 November 1873, *op. cit.*

sense, this was the most logical policy because the idea was to save lives, which was no doubt conceived as a duty by the humanitarian policy makers, but at the same time it was expected to encourage people to be self-reliant. With grain wages, it is possible to give subsistence wages (i.e. physical subsistence enough to keep body and soul together) and at the same time prevent anybody other than the most needy from flocking to the public works. This policy coupled with the freedom given to private enterprise would most certainly prevent mortality, but would also require people to exert their utmost to stay alive. With a policy of grain wages for those employed in the famine public works, the government had the added task of increasing the available supplies of food which would naturally involve considerable state interference.[109]

Northbrook's government was not hamstrung by rigid orders from the Secretary of State. Instead Lord Argyll gave Northbrook a free hand.[110] On his part, Northbrook was cautious in his intervention, especially with regard to the augmentation of food supplies in the famine-stricken areas of Bengal. This caution could be observed in his policy towards the purchases of foodgrains for payment to those employed in public works as well as his refusal to ban export of foodgrains from Bengal. He believed (along with J. S. Mill) that government purchases of foodgrains should be made as far away from the famine areas as possible so as not to interfere in the local grain market operations.[111] Should government enter the market as a bulk buyer, the demand would be artificially increased without at the same time increasing the supply of available foodgrains. Hence his proposal to import rice from Madras and Burma rather than the adjoining provinces.

Although Bengal was hit by a famine in 1873–4, there was considerable export trade in foodgrains – 278 944 Mds. of rice were shipped from the port of Calcutta during October 1873 alone. This prompted many including the British–Indian Association, to request the government to ban such export of foodgrains until the famine ceased. But Northbrook was against any such move to disrupt foreign trade, even after Argyll gave support to the proposal on political grounds. According to the Secretary of State, prevention of export had 'one recommendation not unimportant – that it would satisfy a considerable amount of native opinion. I am far from undervaluing this inducement, and it is one which may well prevail in many cases where less serious con-

---

[109] One such interference was reduction in the railway rates for the carriage of foodgrains. The railway companies were paid the difference by the Government, thus providing an indirect subsidy for importation.
[110] Argyll to Viceroy, 1 December 1873, *Parl. Papers*, Cmd. 993, vol. L of Session 1874, p. 51.
[111] Resolution of 7 November 1873, *op. cit.*

siderations are involved.'[112] Northbrook felt that government action was quite unnecessary because the rise in prices as a result of famine scarcity would automatically reduce the quantity exported. If exports were prevented by the government, the overseas customers would consider Indian markets unreliable and turn to other countries. He was opposed to the prevention of exports from Burma (which was at that time part of British India), for that would 'inflict a fatal blow'. He was equally opposed to preventing exports from Madras, which were mainly going to Ceylon, on the ground that he could 'not look upon Ceylon, as a foreign country on account of the accident that it is under the Colonial office, and not under the Secretary of State for India'.[113] In his view the trade in foodgrains was mainly interregional, and only when the interregional trade were left absolutely free could the foodgrain prices in the region as a whole be stabilised. An export trade, irrespective of whether the trading partner belonged to a different nation or different region within the same nation, was vital to encourage the production of food surpluses. In times of famine, such surpluses provided a safe cushion against probable shortages. Hence nothing should be done to damage the foreign trade prospects of any country. 'Trade is very sensitive,' he wrote to Argyll:

Once lost it is with difficulty recovered. Our customers may submit to very high prices; but if they find that on the first signs of serious scarcity we close our ports, they will feel no security in the future and try other countries, where trade is governed by stable principles, and is not subject to the sudden interference of the Executive Government.[114]

Northbrook's concern was, not only for overseas customers, but also for the 'mercantile classes' whose confidence might be shaken. Prohibition of exports, Northbrook argued, could artificially reduce prices and thus 'by checking commercial operations cut off sources of supply from without which would naturally come to our aid in time of need'.[115] In this manner, Northbrook was prepared to commit the government to much greater trouble and expense for preserving the private trade in grain and what he considered good for India.[116]

---

[112] Secretary of State to the Viceroy, 23 January 1874, *Parl. Papers*, Cmd. 993, vol. L of Session 1874, p. 381. The Indian opinion was strongly in favour of the banning of food exports for the time being. See *Special Narratives of the Drought in Bengal and Behar 1873–74* (Calcutta, 1874), p. 13.

[113] *Ibid.*, p. 54.

[114] Northbrook to Argyll, (*Northbrook Papers*, India Office Library), 27 November 1873.

[115] Viceroy to the Secretary of State, 7 November 1872, *Proceedings: Department of Agriculture, Revenue and Commerce*, India Office Records, vol. 685, pp. 16–17.

[116] In a private communication, Northbrook wrote to Argyll: 'It seems to me that almost any sacrifice of money would be better for the permanent interests than to run the risk, for no

He had the support of such leading British–Indian administrators of the day as Bartle-Frere, Trevelyan, Auckland Colvin and William Tayler.[117] But his policy came in for heavy criticism from many. Sir George Campbell, Lt Governor of Bengal, was a leading protagonist for banning the export trade of grain. The *Indian Economist* which had supported the main features of Northbrook's famine policy, nevertheless attacked the reluctance to ban the export of precious foodgrains from the famine-stricken districts. Even the London *Times* advocated a ban on grain exports during the period of scarcity.[118] As early as 1867, the *Calcutta Review* had pointed out the unsoundness of the logical foundations of the policy of not banning food exports during famines. Such a policy was based on the assumption that prices in the partner countries were roughly equal. This premise was not valid as far as India's trading partners were concerned. Citing the example of England, it was said that, as the English price was habitually double the Indian average, Indian exporters could send grain to England during famines and still make a profit.[119] As for the other Asian rice-surplus countries, their trade had never been free:

Unfortunately for India, Political Economy is not much studied in those quarters. On the first symptoms of scarcity His Majesty of Burmah and his compeers stop exportation, and India cannot therefore count with certainty on relief in that direction. The upshot is that Mill's argument will not apply to this Country. Our virtue will most certainly not be its own reward.[120]

The *Indian Economist* queried the use of the extra food grown if during the scarcities it was 'held sacred for export'.[121] By not banning the export of foodgrains the urban population suffered most because in bad times little rice came from the villages to the towns and even that went to the export market. It was a 'purely chimerical fear' to think that the Indian ban on foodgrain exports during the famines would have disastrous consequences on the future trade, because foreign trade depends upon the comparative costs and not on irrational fears. 'So long as Bengal can grow the qualities of rice

---

Footnote 116 continued

   real advantage, excepting to please the public opinion of the hour, of striking a fatal blow at an export trade.' Northbrook to Argyll, (*Northbrook Papers*, India Office Library), 27 November 1873.

[117] See William Tayler, *Famines in India: Their Remedy and Prevention* (London, 1874), p. 9. See also J. W. Furrell, *op. cit.*, pp. 168–9; Colvin, 'Indian Famines and Press' in *The Fortnightly Review*, April 1874, p. 495.

[118] 27 November 1873.

[119] H.J.S. Cotton pointed out that the bulk of Bengal's rice exports went to Britain and France and not to colonies with Indian population as alleged. See 'Rice Trade of the World', *The Calcutta Review*, 1874, vol. LVII, No. 116, pp. 274–5.

[120] 'The Operation of the *Laissez-faire* Principles in Times of Scarcity' *op. cit.*, pp. 108.

[121] Issue 28 February 1874, pp. 173–4.

she now does at the existing price,' said the *Indian Economist*, 'there is not the remotest prospect of her being beaten out of the field by other lands.'[122] Campbell's criticism was directed not only at the refusal to ban exports but also at the policy of buying foodgrains for the government public works from distant markets. He argued that whereas the export trade was draining the existing food supplies, the government was importing from distant markets. This was 'reduction to the absurd' and most certainly not free trade, and the only effect of such a policy was increased public expenditure.[123] The policy was neither fully free trade, nor its opposite. He feared that 'to follow a middle course, neither leaving things to the laws of supply and demand on the one hand, nor stopping the export of food on the other, may lead to this, that one set of forces militate against and neutralize the other, and we gain nothing but may rather lose on the whole.'[124]

The *Indian Economist* in a series of articles attacked the idea 'that for the Government to prohibit the export of rice ... would be to contravene, and fly in the face of, well-established principles'. According to this journal, 'A more cruel application of the principles of this great science, a more complete perversion of them, were impossible.' Pointing out that political economy was not a set of axioms and rules to be 'applied without regard to times, places and circumstances', the author said that conditions were such that a prevention of export of foodgrains was absolutely necessary. Famine was a calamity like an all-out war, and during such emergencies every other consideration would have to be shelved except the sole object of saving lives. There was nothing absolute in political economy; it was simply a guide to 'men's judgement', and not to stand in the place of judgement.[125]

---

[122] *Ibid.*

[123] See *Parl. Papers*, Cmd. 955, vol. L of Session 1874, p. 204. Campbell citded a letter from the Bhaugulpore Collector: 'Cartmen were especially willing to carry Government grain to the distressed parts in the north of the district, because they expected to get return loads of grain to bring back from thence.' See also Campbell's *Memoirs of My Indian Career*, vol. II, pp. 324 *passim*, Bhatia, *op. cit*, pp. 109–10.

[124] *Ibid.*, Cmd. 955, p. 205.

[125] Issue dated 31 January 1874. The *Indian Economist* lamented that 'There is certainly no country in the world in which graver mistakes are made, from a dread of infringing what are supposed to be principles of political economy, than India.' p. 147. An Indian contemporary commentator, Dinshaw Ardeshir said in 1874, that 'the conventionalism which has disastrously misconceived genuine political economy' ought to be set aside. *British Policy Respecting Famines in India* (Bombay, 1874), p. 7. Sir George Campbell said that, because Northbrook was 'bred in the strictest sect of English free-traders,' he looked upon the proposal to stop grain exports 'as a sort of abominable heresy – was as much shocked as a bishop might be with a clergyman who denied all the thirty-nine articles'. *Memoirs*, vol. II, p. 323. In spite of these comments, Northbrook does not seem to have been a dogmatic believer in the prinicples of political economy, as he used to assert that there was more to practical economic problems than mere principles. In any case the 1873–4 famine administration was considerably more interventionist than the policies pursued in the previous famines.

None of the criticisms directed against the policy of letting food exports go unchecked had any effect on Northbrook. He was not prepared to budge an inch from his position. The famine ended without claiming as many lives as some of the famines of the previous decade, but this was possible only because of the large sums spent on the famine operations. Rs 675.9 lakhs were spent during this famine while only Rs 275.9 lakhs were spent on the three earlier famines together. Whereas the total population involved in the earlier famines was 112.0 million, only 21.4 million were involved in 1873–4.

The twin aspects of the famine policy, viz., the policy of saving people from starvation and the policy of guarded and indirect intervention in the grain trade, which elicited much praise, also came in for very severe criticism. The *Economist* pointed out that it was an English idea that 'it is the duty of the Government to keep them alive,' and 'in setting about this new duty,' the Government of India 'has scattered money which ought to have been saved'.[126] Alfred Lyall, a distinguished civil servant, was worried at the social and economic consequences of indiscriminate relief in India, and said, 'to say that a Government is responsible for the lives of all its subjects is pure Fourierism. We must now set up phalansteries and ateliers nationaux, or we must be placed in charge of the population department at both ends.'[127] Another civilian, R. H. Wilson, rebuked the Indian government for purchasing grain at all on the ground that men 'write of the laws of political economy as if they were moral precepts which it is possible to obey or disobey at pleasure, instead of as inexorable natural laws'.[128]

Apart from stray exceptions, the critics were from the Indian civil service. While there was perhaps some truth in Lord Salisbury's assertion that 'The Anglo-Indian criticisms are obviously based on an ineradicable feeling that it is a mistake to spend so much money to save a lot of black fellows,'[129] it was nevertheless insufficient by itself to explain the hostility of many. The enormous expenditure was ascribed to the inevitable consequences of interfering with the natural processes of the market, a fault which the authorities determined to avoid in future famines.

It was not long before another famine hit India. In December 1875 signs of an impending famine were perceived in the Madras Presidency. This became a certainty within the next three months, and the famine spread into the Bombay Presidency. In the meantime, owing to a change in the British

---

[126] 4 July 1874, vol. XXXII, p. 802.
[127] Lyall to W. W. Hunter, 2 March 1874. Quoted in F. H. Skrine, *Life of Hunter* (London, 1901) pp. 225–6. Many civilians including Sir William Muir and other very high officials held such opinions.
[128] Cited in *Indian Economist*, 28 February 1874, p. 189.
[129] Salisbury to Northbrook, (*Northbrook Papers*, India Office Library), 21 September 1874.

government, Northbrook was succeeded by Lytton as the new Vicery of India.

Unlike his predecessor's government, Lytton's policy did not countenance the responsibility for saving lives during a famine. As it bluntly maintained:

Even for an object of such paramount importance as the preservation of life, it is obvious that there are limits which are imposed upon us by the facts with which we have to deal ... we must plainly admit that the task of saving life, irrespective of the cost, is one which it is beyond our power to undertake.[130]

The cost and financial factor of saving lives came to occupy an important part – although by no means the entire part – in the formation of Lytton's famine policy. One important complaint of the majority of the civil service against Northbrook's policy was that it was extravagant and once the famine was over, people even suspected that the famine was perhaps no famine at all.[131] Hence the policy makers were all the time on guard against a recurrence of such 'extravagance'. Lytton's government had to incur considerable expenditure in putting into practice the forward policy of Lord Salisbury. Silver depreciation added to the financial difficulties. Above all, owing to pressure from British manufacturing interests, it was found necessary to repeal certain import duties which were bringing in considerable revenue. Against these pressures Lytton's government was not willing to shoulder the enormous responsibility of saving people from starvation deaths, as suggested by many British publicists. In a candid letter to Sir Louis Mallet of the India Office, Lytton wrote:

I anxiously hope you will not encourage any humanitarian hysterics in England about this famine. That is now our greatest danger. If the British public insists on keeping our ryots alive, 'regardless of expense', and imposes on us a 'life at any price' policy, the British public ought, in fairness, to find us the money (which we have not).[132]

Lytton's financial position was not good, and, further, the famine his administration faced was much worse than the earlier famines.[133] Lytton was from the beginning a believer in the freedom of trade and was surrounded by civilians like Chapman and Strachey who all held that a good famine policy as far as possible should not interfere with the ordinary market

---

[130] Instructions to Sir Richard Temple dated 16 January 1877. *Parl. Papers* Cmd. 1751, vol. LXV of Session 1877, p. 159. Temple vehemently denied this change in policy while giving evidence to the Famine Commission of 1880.

[131] Campbell, *op. cit*, vol. II, pp. 333 *passim.*

[132] Lytton to Mallet (Lytton Papers, India Office Library), 11 January 1877.

[133] See Bhatia, *op. cit.*, p. 89; and H. S. Srivastava, *The History of Indian Famines and Development of Famine Policy 1858–1918* (Agra, 1968), Chapter 5.

processes. It is quite possible that his financial difficulties encouraged Lytton to embrace the orthodox *laissez-faire* famine policy. When Lytton wrote to Sir James Caird that he was against 'any attempt on the part of the State to lay down a priori a complete body of hard and fast rules, or invariable principles for the organisation of famine relief', he meant the type of policy practised by Northbrook and Temple which insisted on saving lives from famine mortality through an organised relief system. Continuing, he declared: 'There are few practical subjects on which I more dread the influence of *Doctrinaires* – than the treatment of famines.'[134] Lytton's doctrinaire was not an advocate of 'no-state-interference-whatever-the-consequence' but 'save-famine-mortality-at-any-cost'.

As can easily be seen, in so far as the issue of free trade was concerned, there was little difference between Northbrook and Lytton. Both believed that private enterprise had the capacity for an optimal distribution of the available food grains. Whereas Northbrook's policy allowed for exceptions, Lytton applied the harshest Malthusian doctrine in its starkest form and enforced rigidly a policy of free market to the exclusion of all other considerations. Northbrook accepted not only the political economy, but also the humanitarianism of John Stuart Mill, but Lytton and his chief advisers knew only Mill's political economy.

The approaches of Bombay and Madras differed in their treatment of famines. Whereas the Government of Madras was anxious to adopt a policy similar to that of Northbrook's, the Government of Bombay chose to follow the Classical famine policy. The policy followed in Bombay consisted of providing employment to the unemployed in public works and the provision of a modicum of relief to the aged, infirm and women. There were differences of opinion with the supreme government concerning public works, Bombay preferring large works whereas the Government of India favoured small scattered works. Because the local authorities in Bombay had started the large works, the Government of India gave in finally. As far as the supply and distribution of foodgrains were concerned, the Government of Bombay was one with the Government of India: no importation on government account, and the market was to be entirely free to procure foodgrains for the population. It was also made clear that the government would only act through the private trade for procuring grains for its own relief centres. Occasionally, a local officer like the acting Collector of Satara, for instance, decided to interfere with the freedom of the market. He found that grain riots might ensue if he could not make some of the local hoarders release their stocks into the market. He therefore issued orders for the seizure of the stocks, which then he ordered to be sold at fair prices. Although this 'inter-

[134] Lytton to Caird, *Home Misc.* India Office Records, 1 March 1879, No. 796, pp. 193–5.

feres with the right in private property,' he still believed that 'the end justifies the means'. Such actions were viewed with alarm and were quickly withdrawn because they were 'interfering with the free action of the dealers'.[135] On the whole the Government of Bombay adhered to the free trade policy with 'entirely satisfactory results up to the present moment', as the Secretary of the Government of Bombay claimed.[136] Naturally the Government of India found this to be 'sound and excellent'.[137]

The Government of Madras – unlike the Bombay government – noticing the imminence of a severe famine, purchased 30 000 tons of rice at a cost of Rs 32 Lakhs. The core of their argument related to the time factor in supplying foodgrains to the local markets. 'The objection to interference with ordinary trade was not for a moment absent from the consideration of Government', declared the Chief Secretary of Madras, but 'could not wait for the restoration of a more normal condition of trade ... They had to secure the supply of food for vast numbers, daily increasing, who could not purchase grain.'[138] The prices in Madras in 1870s were being influenced by the telegraph, and

in the course of a single week, may be so equalized, relatively to the distance of the various markets from the chief seaports or other places of usual supply, that the transfer of stocks from one district to another which at the beginning of a week might have been highly remunerative and offered large profits, may suddenly cease to be so at its close, although the necessity for large transfers may be as urgent as ever.[139]

The government felt that, if the trade was unable to supply the necessary grain and if the 'Government can, they are then able to do more than all the trade put together, and their interference is perfectly justifiable'. The Madras government agreed that if time were given to the market, the necessary grain would eventually come, but time was what could not be given. As it was put in the official history of the famine of 1876, 'The laws of nature will not stand still to suit the grain trade.'[140] As far as the violation of the political economy was concerned, the government denied it; the Madras government was buying grain for consumption and was not 'interfering with the legitimate functions of the corn-dealers' who were buying only to sell.

This policy of government purchases involved arbitrary intervention in the grain market, and Lytton had grave objections. His aides like Norman,

---

[135] See *Parl. Papers*, Cmd. 1707, vol. LXV of Session 1877, pp. 41, 44.

[136] M. K. Kennedy's Note, *Parl. Papers*, Cmd. vol. LXV of Session 1877, p. 223.

[137] Secretary of Government of India (Rev.) to Government of Bombay (PWD), *Ibid.*, p. 227. Lytton was glad that Bombay 'managed its famine with great ability and on sound principles'. Lytton to Caird, 1 March 1879, *Home Misc.* India Office Records, no. 796, p. 217.

[138] *Ibid.*

[139] *Review of the Madras Famine 1876–78*, p. 16.

[140] *Ibid.*, p. 17.

Strachey and Chapman had told him that government buying of foodgrains would check the supply of private trade with disastrous consequences.[141] No wonder, then, that the Indian government was not satisfied with the answer of the Madras government. The authorities at Madras were accordingly prohibited from further action in this direction, and a complaint was made to the Secretary of State that the action 'is open to the grave prima facie objection that it may seriously interfere with the course of private trade'.[142]

In order to remedy the 'problem' created by the Government of Madras, Lytton decided to send Sir Richard Temple to Madras to supervise the famine administration. Temple had been carefully chosen. Earlier he had been accused of having been too extravagant. Hence he was 'burning to retrieve his reputation for extravagance in the last famine, by showing how efficiently he can work an economic policy; he carries with him great authority'. So Lytton thought that he could not have found 'a man more likely, or better able to help us to save money in famine management'.[143] Temple was able to enforce considerable economy in the Madras famine administration by some draconian measures which included the notorious 'Temple Ration' for workers in the public works. The result was that he was able to save nearly 2 million Rs. for the public fisc – a fact much appreciated by Lytton.[144]

Financial considerations were important no doubt, but they do not tell the entire story. Many of the civilians were confirmed free traders and they were even prepared to spend more on direct relief than on price stabilisation. When the Government of Madras pointed out that prices were rising and hence something ought to be done, the Government of India felt it was a fortunate consequence because high prices encouraged traders to import large quantities of food. This might increase the number of destitutes who would come to the government relief centres. But according to them that would be a far lesser evil.[145]

Lytton, as we have seen, had great faith in free trade. In a policy despatch to the Secretary of State, the Governor General said: 'absolute non-interference with the operations of private commercial enterprise must be the foundations of our famine policy'.[146] Importation of grain by the government

---

[141] Norman to Lytton, 11 November 1876 and 24 November 1876 (Lytton Papers, India Office Library). See Strachey's Minute in *The Indian Famine of 1877*, pp. 32–4.

[142] Governor General to Secretary of State, 17 November 1876, *Parl. Papers*, Cmd. 1707, vol. LXV of Session 1877, p. 81.

[143] Lytton to Mallet, 11 January 1877 (Lytton Papers, Indian Office Library).

[144] Lytton to Grant-Duff, 27 April 1877 (Lytton Papers, India Office Library).

[145] Additional Secretary of Government of India to Secretary of Government of Madras, 29 June 1877, *Parl. Papers*, Cmd. 1920, vol. LIX of Session 1878, p. 91.

[146] Governor-General to Secretary of State, 22 September 1877, *Parl. Papers* Cmd. 1920, vol. LIX of Session 1878, pp. 218–21.

would only discourage the private sector, and in any case he was 'convinced that far more food from abroad or elsewhere will reach Madras if we leave private enterprise to itself, and we should paralyse it by government competition. Free-trade cannot co-exist with government importation.'[147] But Lytton agreed that the government should provide information, additional facilities, the carrying power of the railways, removal of tolls and restraints, the improvement of roads and communications, the reduction of railway rates, and in general everything that would reduce obstacles, and promote a healthy functioning of internal trade.[148]

Lytton was convinced of the correctness of his beliefs and ascribed the continuing starvation deaths to the bad organisation of village relief which no government could prevent.[149] This shows clearly how blind Lytton was to certain sociological realities of the famine victims. Most of the victims were peasants and some were even small proprietors, and because of their attitudes and status in society they needed a humane treatment. This was why Northbrook's policy was successful. Lytton mistook Northbrook's attitude for a too liberal charity, and wanted stiffer tests to see whether the victims really needed help from the state.[150] In his anxiety to get the maximum return from public works, full work was extracted from the labourers in them. In spite of the absence of any trace of humanitarianism in his famine policy, Lytton nevertheless compared it to that of Turgot in France a hundred years earlier and eloquently suggested that he encountered the same problems and prejudices that Turgot had to face.[151]

Notwithstanding Lytton's self-satisfaction regarding his conduct of the famine administration, the famine of 1876–7 with its enormous mortality had such an impact on the official mind that it led to the appointment of the 1880 Famine Commission. A thorough investigation of the causes and remedies of famines was found imperative because of their recurrence and the

---

[147] Viceroy to Secretary of State, 15 August 1877, Telegram *Ibid*, p. 134.

[148] Lytton's Minute 12 August 1877, *Parl. Papers*, Cmd. 1920, vol. LIX of Session 1878, p. 128.

[149] Lytton to Salisbury, 10 May 1877, (Lytton Papers, India Office Library). Contemporary observers have felt otherwise. James Wilson of the *India Daily News* said 'It may be observed that these very men who professed to guide the famine policy have really been the occasion of the suffering. In the first place, their pretended axioms of political economy, misunderstood and misapplied, resulted in a policy that was fatal to a million people.' *The Government of India in Relation to Famines and Commerce* (Calcutta, 1877), p. 9.

[150] In his letter to Caird, Lytton wrote: 'It cannot, I think be assumed, that a man's life is more valuable to the State than it is to himself and that therefore the state is bound to preserve everyman's life for him on his own terms. The (proverb) which declares that Beggars cannot be choosers does not seem to me an unduly harsh expression of a universal experience – and the rule that 'If ye will not work, neither shall ye eat' a rule of life as old as the days of Adam.' Letter, 1 March 1879, *Home Misc*. India Office Records, no. 796, p. 216.

[151] Lytton's speech in the Legislative Council. Quoted in J. & R. Strachey, *The Finances and Public Works of India* (London, 1882), p. 184.

lack of a systematic policy to deal with them.[152] As we have repeatedly seen, the execution of policies depended on the officers in charge. It is true that, by and large, free-market-as-the-ideal-system was accepted by most of the civilians, but there were nevertheless many controversies arising out of the special stress laid by individual officers on particular aspects of policies. At times various governments were ranged on opposite camps. It was therefore logical to have the problems discussed and examined by an expert and impartial commission. Such an investigation, it was decided, would provide recommendations which then could be formulated into a uniform famine policy.

The Secretary of State was particularly anxious to have a settled policy concerning the supply and distribution of foodgrain during periods of famine. While giving his appreciation to the way Lytton applied the principle of free trade in India, he nevertheless thought it desirable 'for future guidance that the details of the process of supply should, as far as possible, be placed on record'. In other words, he wanted the Commission to inquire into the conditions under which the orthodox famine policy would work best.[153]

The Famine Commission came to the conclusion that the Classical famine policy was not wrong as regards free trade, the unwisdom of government purchases of grain and the policy of free grain exports during famines. The unanimity of opinion on these points among those who gave evidence before the Commission, was overwhelming. To the question, Can the government buy grain and sell cheaply below the market price to stabilise the price level, not one answer was in the affirmative. An Indian subordinate officer, Mr Hurry Row, went so far as to say, 'The system of purchasing grain and selling it at or below cost price is bad. It is wrong in theory and injurious to the people in practice . . . is interfering with the market in a most imprudent manner.'[154] The Report concluded that 'Opinion has more and more steadily settled down, as economical knowledge has advanced, to the conclusion that as a rule such intervention should be avoided, but that exceptional circumstances may justify or even require it.' But it cautioned that, when such intervention was resorted to, extreme care would be necessary 'in every case lest interference should aggravate the evil which it is designed to avert, and have the effect of preventing traders from entering the market while it is being operated upon by the Government'.[155]

While largely following the traditional principles of famine policy, the

---

[152] Secretary of State to the Governor General in Council, 10 January 1878, no. 2 (Revenue), Paragraph 5, *Parl. Papers*, Cmd. 1918, vol. LIX of Session 1878.

[153] *Ibid.*, paragraph 9.

[154] See *Parl. Papers*, Cmd. 3086–IV, vol. LXXI of Session 1881, pp. 288–93.

[155] *Famine Commission Report*, Part I, *Parl. Papers*, Cmd. 2591, vol. LII of Session 1880, para. 150, 159, pp.

Commission stressed the need to raise the general standard of living, which alone could prevent the extreme misery of the periodic famines. An increase in railway and other transport facilities, irrigation and the reduction of rural indebtedness, were other proposals that received attention. The Commission perceived that there was little that government could do to allocate the existing food grains (even to augment the supply) in the short run, but the government could do much to enable the economy to resist the rigours of the recurring famines. With the free trade convictions of most of the members of the Commission, this was the only solution they could offer.

The core of the recommendations of the Famine Commission comprised: (1) preparation of a uniform famine code; (2) provision of employment to the famine victims; (3) gratuitous relief and poor houses; (4) village inspection and control; (5) maintenance of 'a policy of non-interference with the ordinary operations of trade, unless in some very exceptional condition of affairs when there may be evidence that without such interference the supply of food will not be maintained'; (6) reduction of the impediments to trade; (7) grants-in-aid to land-owing classes; and (8) laying down precise limits of local responsibility.[156] These proposals were approved by the Government of India, and the basic principles on which the recommendations of the Commission were made, continued long to exercise their influence.

During the 1899–1900 famine, the government went further than during the previous calamities in putting into practice the new principle of governmental responsibility for safeguarding lives during periods of intense scarcity. The grip of Classical ideas had been so weakened that Sir George Forrest was able to declare: 'Famine, however, will not again be able to claim its victims owing to a blind following of the *laissez-faire* school.'[157]

CONCLUSION

Indian administrators viewed the problem of famines both in a long-run perspective as well as an immediate urgency. However the long-run perspective was not the same for everyone. Some held a strict Malthusian view of the Indian situation, being certain that the famines were inevitable given the population—resources ratio.[158] Others were not convinced that India had

---

[156] *Ibid* pp. 444–5 (Para. 112). The three cases when interference would be necessary were (a) provision of food required for relief works and free distribution; (b) when trade is 'sluggish'; and (c) when trade does not act or grain dealers refuse to sell at any price. Para 159.

[157] *The Famine in India* (London, 1900), p. 16.

[158] See for example, Lytton's speech in the Legislative Council: *Proceedings*, vol. XVI, 1877, p. 588; Sir George Couper's Confidential Memorandum on Famine expenses: dated 24 June 1881, (Ripon Papers, British Museum) Add. MSS 43, 615, pp. 27–31; See also the *Economist* 9 May 1874, vol. XXXII, p. 555.

already reached the Malthusian limit. Indeed, a large portion of official opinion thought that India had not yet realised its full productive potential. Hence we observe that most of the remedies suggested for preventing future occurrences of famines centred around measures to increase production – in other words, to achieve economic progress. Economic development involved diversification of employment opportunities, increasing productivity, provision of social overhead capital, a rational economic organisation and industrialisation. It was expected that the modernisation of economic and social life that would result from economic progress, would, in the long run, solve the major cause of poverty and famines, overpopulation itself.[159]

On the question of famines as an immediate problem opinion was remarkably unanimous. The unavoidable question was how to allocate the given amount of resources in the best possible manner. Received doctrine held that the answer was to be found in the maintenance of a free market. We have seen in the previous pages how generations of Indian administrators accepted this solution. The unmistakable conclusion is that in spite of the controversy that surrounded the policy in the last four decades of the nineteenth century, Classical conceptions of free trade played a considerable part in the formation of a policy of maintaining the unsullied freedom of the grain market. When virtually every document relating to the formulation and execution of famine policy over a century referred to the views of Adam Smith and/or John Stuart Mill, it becomes well nigh impossible to dismiss the role of Classical economic ideas in the formation of economic policy. Certainly the *ideal* economic policy continued to be an unfettered market system but the policy as practised in the last two decades increasingly became less rigid owing to other considerations. The policies pursued by successive governments were a composite of many things – Classical political economy, helplessness, frustration, humanitarianism, and even a certain callousness towards life. The reason why the economic ideas of Classical economists were so successful in shaping the *ideal* is very simple. There was really no serious or viable alternative to the free trade famine policy, for the problem of distribution could be ensured in no other way than the freedom of the market. Many administrators goaded by their humanitarianism in practice might have tried to break through the Classical net, but they had no answer to the remorseless logic of the Classical economists' thinking.

[159] 'Prudential checks will also assert themselves as education penetrates the masses.' See Hunter to Argyll, 12 April 1889, Skrine, *op. cit.*, p. 395. W. T. Thornton, a friend of John Stuart Mill and an India Office bureaucrat, pointed out in 1875, 'of all moral impediments to excessive multiplication of the species, there is none more so powerful as an elevated standard of material well-being'. *Indian Public Works* (London, 1875), p. 247.

4

ECONOMIC IDEAS
AND ECONOMIC RELATIONS

It appears to me that if the people of the Punjab do not understand that when they borrow money they must repay it, and that the whole of their property is liable for its repayment, they cannot be taught that lesson too soon or too emphatically. It appears to me to be one of the chief lessons which we are here to teach.

Sir James Fitzjames Stephen

You find your doctrinaire philosophers in London ride a hobby to death. But in London they are kept in order by checks and opposition in a thousand forms. Imagine how the same men would ride their hobbies, when invested with despotic power, over a million or two Indian peasants. It is such men who upset native tenures, turn society topsy-turvey, and with the best intentions drive a whole people in mad revolt.

Sir Henry Bartle-Frere

THE END OF USURY REGULATION

Distress caused by famine was due to man's uncertain relationship with Nature. There were other areas, however, where distress was the result of man's relationship with other men. As seen in the previous chapter, the policy of the government towards famine started as interventionist, then became inspired by free trade, and finally guardedly interventionist. British policy in the nineteenth century towards a number of economic relationships also underwent similar changes. We mean by economic relations the voluntary (or seemingly voluntary) arrangements that two parties come to in connection with either the allocation or production of resources. Such arrangements could be between a borrower and a lender who reach a contract as to how the funds would be repaid and the rate of interest charged. Landlords and tenants (and peasants) could similarly come to a mutual understanding; and the mutual relationship would ordinarily be determined by custom or usage. There is also the important relationship between capitalist and labourer who exchange wages and labour-power. In all these cases, relationships and mutual understanding are vitally necessary for the conduct of normal economic life. In so far as the above relations involve exchange, they are no different from the commonly observed relationship between the buyer and seller of any commodity. It is elementary economic knowledge that the market mechanism of the impersonal price system, where there are many buyers and many sellers, achieves an efficient allocation of resources. However, for its achievement, many conditions must be present, and the absence of any of them could lead to non-optimal situations and hence the exploitation of the weaker elements of society.

The relationships mentioned above operated in the Indian context without fulfilling all the requirements for the most efficient functioning of the economic market with a price system. The pattern of British policy towards these in the nineteenth century was the evolution towards a free trade ideal at first, and a gradual moving away once it was found that the conditions for a proper functioning of the market system were absent.

Of all these relationships, usury regulation is of particular importance. All traditional economic systems have condemned usury, but some systems, realising the necessity of credit for the functioning of the economy, merely regulated interest payments. The ancient Hindu system, while condemning material pursuits as an end, nevertheless reserved a place for interest, but its concept of interest was closely connected with a vague concept of just price. When chargeable interest rates were fixed, due attention was given to the qualitative differences among borrowers and lenders, and above all there was the determined legal maximum of the total interest payment. There was great variation between the different legal texts, religious and secular, and hence the actual practice depended on considerations such as the particular text the king or his advisers followed, the actual economic conditions, and so on. But most rulers seemed to prefer fixed rates of chargeable interest. Even as late as the 1770s, the powerful Maharashtra chief Nana Fadanavis of the only leading Indian kingdom other than the British fixed 10 per cent as the maximum chargeable rate of interest.[1]

Although Islam itself prohibited all interest as usury, usurious rates were common during the Muslim period of Indian history. It has been pointed out that the unwritten custom, rather than the laws of Islam, determined economic relations in medieval India. With the growth of the cash nexus, monetisation and the necessity of credit inevitably introduced usury, which presently flourished, as Irfan Habib points out, 'with the full sanction of the State'.[2] But both during the Hindu and Muslim periods, customary norms

---

[1] See R. D. Choksey, *Economic Life in the Bombay Deccan* (Bombay, 1955), p. 19.

[2] 'Usury in Medieval India' in *Comparative Studies in Society and History*, vol. VI, no. 4, 1963–4, p. 413. See also C. N. Cooke, *The Rise, Progress and Present Condition of Banking in India* (Calcutta, 1863), p. 22. It must be remembered that during the reigns of the more fanatical of the rulers (e.g. Aurangazeb) attempts were made to follow the Islamic law rigidly. See

were still largely followed in spite of the increasing complexity of economic life. The rates of interest were perhaps high but the interest was seldom allowed to accumulate beyond the value of the principal. The common law of rural India thus reduced the burden of the borrower while stressing the morality of debt repayment.[3] However, in the decades before the British were firmly established, the prevailing unsettled conditions were responsible for a considerable erosion of the common law with regard to interest rates.

When the British were firmly entrenched, in their anxiety to introduce legislation of the British type to control the current usurious interest rates, they promulgated the first usury regulation in India, the Bengal interest Regulation of 1793 (No. xv). Even before the promulgation of the usury regulation, the East India Company imposed restrictions on its servants from lending money at usurious rates of interest in India. Those who disobeyed these instructions were severely punished. For example, a Lieutenant Duncanson was tried and court-martialled for lending money at exorbitant rates to the Rajah of Cooch Behar.[4]

It may seem curious that a usury law was passed by the British rulers in India at the very time when there was raging a great controversy in Britain about the usury regulation. However, considering the financial situation of the government and the East India Company, it was hardly surprising. In the last quarter of the eighteenth century, while revenue was more or less fixed, expenditure was unstable owing to the recurrent wars. Balancing the budget thus became a difficult task. Very often governments had to resort to public borrowing, and several loans were floated in the period after 1780. High interest rates prevailed because of the scarcity of capital as well as competition among borrowers.[5] It was thus quite possible that the government at Fort William, worried by the high interest they had to pay, decided to reduce the permissible rate of interest to twelve per cent. The same was probably the case in Fort St George. At the turn of the century, the Madras administration was involved in the Mysore wars as well as with the Poligar rebellions, and its financial difficulties might well have prevented it from taking a critical look at the Bengal Regulation, which was the basis of the Regulation xxxiv of

---

Footnote 2 continued
M. L. Seth, 'Indian Money-Lender in pre-British Times' *Research Bulletin (Arts) of the University of Punjab*, 1955, p. 11.

[3] We could mention here the practice of *Dharna* to force repayment of debt. This is a form of moral persuasion abolished by the East India Company in 1810.

[4] See Despatches to Bengal, 6 May 1791, India Office Records, Vol. xxii, No. E/4/637, pp. 210–14.

[5] See Amales Tripathi, *Trade and Finance in the Bengal Presidency* (Bombay, 1956), for an argument that the Company servants were the gainers in the loan operations and hence they contrived to increase the government demand for loans by influencing its political policy.

1802. The Bombay government also fixed the maximum rate of interest at 12 per cent in 1814.

The motive for enacting usury laws has always been to protect the poor borrower against exploitation by the rich lender. But the seventeenth-century protagonists like Sir Thomas Culpeper (Sr), Sir Thomas Culpeper (Jr) and Sir Josiah Child also provided economic reasons for the usury laws.[6] They argued that low rates of interest explained the prosperity of Holland, and if rates of interest could be lowered in Britain, British prosperity too would increase. Such arguments, however, were seldom used by the Indian administrators. The British rulers had seen the usurious system develop alongside the growth of their power. It was the increasing monetisation of the economy without any corresponding increase in the money supply, coupled with the stable political conditions and the rule of law, that had contributed to the growth of interest rates. As R. D. Choksey suggests, with special reference to Konkan in western India, the system had arisen within twelve to fifteen years of the establishment of British rule.[7] It was from a humanitarian motive, then, in addition to the financial motive, that it was decided to introduce the usury laws. There were some sceptics, of course, who were not convinced of the beneficial results of these laws. For instance, Governor Clive of the Madras Presidency was warned that such regulations could not be useful as 'the interest of money is only increased by the disproportion between the stock in the market and the demands of the buyer or borrower'.[8] Clive ignored the warning.

The most celebrated discussion in opposition to the usury laws was Jeremy Bentham's *Defence of Usury* published in 1787.[9] Bentham opposed limitation of the rate of interest from an economic as well as a judicial point of view. Adam Smith had not been against the fixing of a rate of interest *per se*, but he insisted that it should be higher than the market rate to prevent 'projectors and prodigals' from misusing the national capital. If the rate of interest were lower than the market rate, the law would be evaded completely.[10]

Adam Smith was perhaps right as far as India was concerned. The legal maximum rate of interest was 12 per cent but the prevailing rate was a good deal higher. In his evidence before the Select Committee of the House of Commons, Sir Thomas Munro had said that the peasants paid often two to

---

[6] *A Tract against the High Rate of Usurie* (London, 1621), *A Discourse Showing the Many Advantages Which will Accrue to this Kingdom by the Abatement of Usury* (London, 1668). *A New Discourse of Trade* (London, 1688).

[7] *Economic Life in the Bombay Konkan* (Bombay, 1960), p. 157.

[8] From an unknown correspondent dated 9 December 1800. Excerpts from this letter is among the (*Bentinck Papers*, Nottingham University).

[9] Already Turgot in his *Sur La Formation et la Distribution des Riches* (1770) had advocated the abolition of interest regulations.

[10] *Wealth of Nations*, Book II, Chapter IV.

three per cent per month. But the interest rate among the 'substantial people' was about twelve per cent, slightly more or less depending upon the security offered.[11] In all three major Presidencies the effect of the legal limitation of interest was similar. C. E. Trevelyan, who had an intimate knowledge of the internal economy of northern India, reported in 1840 that whereas the lowest rate of interest was 24 per cent, ordinarily it was an *anna* (one sixteenth of a rupee) a month per rupee, or 75 per cent in the year.[12] R. D. Choksey's studies of Bombay Presidency have shown that the Regulation preventing usury in 1827 and its predecessor of 1814 were both quite inoperative. While the village *sowcar* thrived, the peasants wallowed in increased indebtedness.[13] As for the Madras Presidency, we have ample evidence to show that the law of usury was honoured more in the breach than in the observance. Every collector in charge of district administration affirmed that the usury laws were a dead letter, and rates ranged from twelve to thirty-six per cent in their districts.[14] It was shown that every type of malpractice was being resorted to for evading the Law.

The same was true in Bengal. Even the European agency houses were evading the anti-usury regulations, though legally; in addition to the twelve per cent, the agency houses often charged another one or two per cent on receipts and disbursements. Like the rest of the country, interest rates were registering a secular fall. With increasing monetisation and security of property, interest rates could no longer be as high as they were in the eighteenth century. But such a fall could be noticed only in the large cities where westernisation, monetisation and commercialisation had taken root. In the villages the position was different. Thus Holt Mackenzie was able to show that in Calcutta the market rate was below 12 per cent while the interest rate in rural Bengal was much higher.[15]

Usury regulation being thus largely inoperative, there was an internal agitation to remove the laws altogether. Firstly, it was argued that these

[11] *Parl. Papers*, H.C. 122, vol. VII of Session 1812–13. The Madras Board of Revenue wrote: 'It is notorious that 12 per cent is the rate of interest usually charged on loan transactions between Natives, and that in many cases a considerably higher rate is charged.' See *Madras Revenue Consultations*, 22 November 1833, India Office Records, Range 278, Vol. 86.

[12] Evidence before the East India Select Committee, *Parl. Papers*, H.C. 527, vol. VIII of Session 1840, Q. 1514.

[13] *Economic Life in the Bombay Deccan*, p. 19. See also G. Keatinge, *Rural Economy in the Bombay Deccan* (London, 1912), p. 83.

[14] *Madras Board of Revenue Proceedings* of the dates, 26 November, 29 November, 3 December, 6 December, 10 December, India Office Records, Range 296, vols. 40 and 41, *passim.*

[15] An undated Minute on Usury Laws. This was circulated in the Governor General's Council, (*Bentinck Papers*, Nottingham University).

regulations went against the accepted principles of political economy as ex-pounded by Bentham. Secondly, there was the conviction that the regulations were but aggravating the evils which they were supposed to eradicate.

The Madras collectors were emphatic and unanimous in their demand for the removal of the regulations.[16] Similar was the opinion of Bengal civilians; and according to one of them, Holt Mackenzie: 'It would be impertinent to enter on the general question, which as far as any moral or political truth admits of demonstration, may be considered to have been long ago, set at rest.'[17]

In general the arguments proffered against the usury laws were fitted into the Classical conception of economic growth. The rate of interest was thought to be determined by the rate of profit: India being an undeveloped country, profits were high; and interest on money would automatically fall when the economy reached the stationary state. It would be inefficient to stifle progress by artificially limiting the rate of profits. If the 'capitalist' knew that his borrower could make 30 or 40 or even 50 per cent profit, he would not naturally have any incentive to be satisfied with a mere 12 per cent. Being merely representative of other goods, money was subject to the ordinary laws of supply and demand. If by such regulations supply were to be curtailed, it could only increase the difficulty of securing capital for development.[18] It was also argued that the regulation limiting interest rates would prove in-effective. The usurer would demand more for taking the extra risk in lending money at illegal rates. As the demand for credit was more or less fixed because of the agricultural operations, few money lenders had the power to impose their own conditions. Not only were Indian rural money lenders charging usurious interest rates, but the European agency houses were equally guilty. The rate of interest charged seldom exceeded 12 per cent, but a sum called *munafa* was deducted from the principal at the time when the loan was advanced. All sorts of charges were levied for fictitious services, and some-times the agency houses insisted on conducting certain types of business through their own organs. The result was effective rates of interest in the

[16] The unanimous opinion was to remove usury regulation. But some argued that if at all the regulations were found necessary, the legal rate should be above the market rate. This division of opinion between the Benthamites and Smithians among the district collectors has been ably discussed by Dr B. Natarajan, 'Regulation of Interest in the Madras Presidency, 1800–1850' in *Indian Journal of Economics*, vol. 18, April 1938, pp. 581 *et seq.*

[17] Undated Minute, *loc. cit.* F. J. Shore who was for some time the Judge of the Civil Court and Criminal Sessions at Farrukhabad said in 1835 'the point has already been argued most conclusively to all unprejudiced minds by Bentham.' *Notes on Indian Affairs* (London, 1837), vol. II, p. 290.

[18] Harris (Collector of Cuddapah) to Board of Revenue, 20 November 1827, *loc. cit.*, India Office Records, Range 296, vol. 41, p. 14876.

18–20 per cent region.[19] It was also affirmed that usury regulations were training the Indian peasants to perjury.[20]

Some administrators stressed the 'demand' for loans rather than the lack of security as the reason for the rate of interest being so high.[21] But Mackenzie, Munro and many others emphasised the lack of security. Whatever the reason, it was generally acknowledged that rural peasant borrowers had to borrow in any case, usually in order to pay their land revenue. The assessment was always timed just before the harvest, with the result that the penurious farmers had to borrow to pay the land tax.[22] This seems to have been the case with both the major systems of land taxation.[23]

Although in mitigation of this situation an adjustment in the rent-collecting procedure was advocated, the abolition of the usury law was urged even more strongly. Harris, the collector of Cuddapah, suggested that the government should settle tax collection in such a way that taxes might become due after the sale of the produce, so that the poor peasants 'enjoy the benefit of equitable and open commerce'.[24] Mackenzie was also very optimistic about the beneficial results that would follow from abolition and thought that such freedom would bring about the best possible allocation of resources. 'Few things,' he said, 'would do greater good to a greater number than the recission of the Regulation in question.' Left to themselves, through the operation of their respective self-interest both the capitalist and the farmer would make the rate of interest socially beneficial. Mackenzie was not unaware of the possibility of increased interest rates but he was sure that a rise would not be permanent. The causes of high interest rates were the poverty and bad faith of the ryots, the general scarcity of capital, defects in law and inefficient administration. Mackenzie the Utilitarian thought that these causes would soon be eradicated by good administration.[25]

[19] See F. J. Shore, *op. cit.*, vol. II, p. 292.

[20] *Ibid.*, p. 295.

[21] John Orr to Board of Revenue, 28 November 1827, *loc. cit.*

[22] A contemporary observer, Benjamin Heyne, found this to be the bane of cultivation. As no 'Zemindar, renter, or cultivator has money to advance, he is obliged to have recourse to the *soukars* ... the usurers only derive advantage from this', *Tracts Historical and Statistical on India* (London, 1814), p. 86.

[23] *Replies to Bentinck's Queries Respecting Ryotwar System of Revenue Administration in the Presidency of Fort St. George*, India Office Records, Q. 29. Report of Collector Timmins dated 30 September 1840, *Parl. Papers*, H.C. 533, vol. X of Session 1852, Appendix 19.

[24] *Loc. cit.* In fact many collectors in the 1840s engaged in Settlement operations prescribed the collection of revenue after the harvested produce had been sold. See Court of Directors to Governor General 13 August 1851, See *Parl. Papers*, H.C. 533, vol. X of Session 1852, appendix.

[25] See Para. 296 of Government of India Resolution of 1 August 1822. This was essentially the work of Holt Mackenzie. *Selections from the Revenue Records of North Western Provinces* (Allahabad, 1872), vol. II, p. 68.

But neither the Madras nor the Bengal government was prepared to accept this advice. Mackenzie was roundly cautioned by the Governor-General not to cite Bentham as an authority in advocating the abolition of legal limitation of interest rates.[26] The Madras government felt that, since even England had not abolished the usury laws, it would be better to 'await the result of the further discussion of it in England ... than to introduce here upon general grounds so great an innovation'. Besides, the Board of Revenue was not sure whether the rates of interest and profits would be harmonised because they saw money being borrowed mostly for consumption purposes, and not for 'productive commerical purposes'.[27]

Such being the view of the policy makers, the All India Act XXIII of 1839 was passed consolidating the various presidency regulations imposing ceilings on the rates of interest. Within a decade and a half, however, Britain abolished the usury laws which had been on the statute book since the middle of the sixteenth century. In the same year (1853), the powerful Bengal Chamber of Commerce presented a petition to the Government of India for the repeal of the usury laws. Sir Barnes Peacock, the Law Member in the Council of the Governor-General, responded to this petition favourably and said: 'In my opinion it is just as impossible to regulate the rate of usury as that of any other article.'[28] Within six months a bill was presented by Sir Barnes Peacock and the Act XXVIII of 1855 was passed, repealing the earlier act. Neither Madras nor Bombay made a representation, and by convention, this meant assent. The North West Provinces also accepted the principle of abolition. Out of eleven judges who answered, nine favoured the repeal in very strong terms.[29] Even in the Legislative Council, opinion was so unanimous that the whole discussion did not occupy even five pages of the proceedings.[30] This was to the great liking of the banking circles, and as Charles Norris Cooke of the Bank of Bengal said with evident satisfaction, 'our legislators merely acted upon the spirit of the age, which was opposed to the absurdity'.[31] Even small businessmen welcomed the removal of the usury laws. When in 1858, the various collectors of the Madras Presidency were asked about the working of the Regulation, most of them reported that

[26]   Bentinck to Mackenzie, 24 October 1829, (*Bentinck Papers*, Nottingham University).
[27]   *General Report of the Board of Revenue to the Court of Directors, 1831* (India Office Records).
[28]   Minute on Usury Laws, July 1853, *Minutes of Sir Barnes Peacock*, India Office Records, pp. 24–5.
[29]   See *Papers of Act XXVIII of 1855* (National Archives of India).
[30]   *Legislative Council Proceedings*, 1 July 1854, vol. I, pp. 40, 184–5, 202–5, 680, 690, 746.
[31]   *The Rise, Progress and Present Condition of Banking in India*, p. 27. It must be noted here that not only in India, but also in many other countries, usury laws were repealed. See F. W. Ryan, *Usury and Usury Laws* (Boston, 1924), p. 57.

the mercantile community appreciated the enactment without reservation.[32]

The removal of the usury laws was the last act in a series of administrative measures and policies based on contract rather than custom. Before the advent of the British Indian society was controlled more by customary norms than by contractual principles. In this welter of customary dues and obligations based on status, the British injected contractual principles in which attorneys, judges and appeals, and courts assumed prominence.[33] The policies were no doubt leading India towards a commercialised and westernised system, but due to certain peculiar circumstances of the Indian economy, the developments were not always desirable. The abolition of usury laws, limitation acts, sale acts and other similar legislative actions gave coercive power to unscrupulous people who had economic relations with the actual tillers of the soil. The British–Indian Association, in a petition to the Governor General in Council in 1857, drew attention to the 'evil consequences of the abolition of usury laws', and pointed out that the rate of interest under the *mahajani* system did not represent the real value of money.[34] The notions that were behind these new legislations were alien to the ways of thinking of the large masses of Indian population.[35] No wonder the clever few who understood the principles were in an extremely favourable position to exploit the rest.

Not that exploiters and the exploited were absent in the past, but what happened was that the character of the relationships between them changed substantially as a result of British legislation. This could be clearly seen in the peasants' relationships with the land-holders and the money lenders. The process of change in the character of such economic relationships started with zemindars when, without a proper appreciation of the existing position, a new relationship was superimposed on the old. Before the establishment

---

[32] See Madras *Board of Revenue Proceedings*, 7, 15 and 28 January 1858, India Office Records, No. Range 313, vols. 78, 79 and 80, *passim*.

[33] Nineteenth-century observers were aware of this transition from customary norms to contractual relationships. See for example *The Black Conquest: Some facts in relation to the Administration of the Madras Presidency* published in 1886, pp. 12–13. See also Bernard Cohn, 'From Indian Status to British Contract' in *Journal of Economic History*, vol. XXI, No. 4, December 1961, and H. S. Trevaskis *The Land of Five Rivers* (London, 1928), pp. 288 *et seq*.

[34] See *Legislative Papers of Act XIX of 1857* (Joint Stock Companies) (National Archives of India).

[35] H. Lushington pointed out to the Select Committee of the House of Lords that the natives do not understand the British system of contract. *Parl. Papers*, H.L. 20 part III, vol. XXX of Session 1852–53, Q. 4595. See also W. G. Pedder of the Bombay civil service: 'Famine and Debt in India' in *The Nineteenth Century*, September 1877, p. 187. See also R. Carstairs, *The Little World of an Indian District Officer* (London, 1912), Chap. VII. Carstairs served in the Indian civil service from 1876 to 1903.

of courts, the zemindars as tax farmers could not extract the rent as a matter of course through the ordinary legal channels. But after the courts came into existence, obligations were easily enforced through judicial processes. In the same way, money lenders who were part of rural society secured increased power. The British brought with them their belief in the absolute right to property. Land became a valuable and saleable commodity, with the conferment of absolute ownership rights on farmers in the non-zemindari areas. Hence the farmer could do anything with his land, mortgage it, sell it, or buy it again. In the same way, with the conferment of absolute rights on the zemindars, they won the right to charge any amount of rent, and if the tenant refused to pay it, even to evict him.

LANDLORD–PEASANT RELATIONS

The imposition of British forms of revenue and judicial administration and the consequent changes in economic conditions and organisation posed sharply the landlord–peasant problem. Early discussions on the question took place between Sir Philip Francis, a Councillor of the Governor-General, Warren Hastings, and Sir John Shore, a functionary of the Government of Bengal. Francis was a product of his age, and advocated a strictly *laissez-faire* policy. His pious hope was that if the zemindars and ryots were 'left to themselves, they will soon come to an agreement, in which each party will find his advantage'.[36] He was not unaware that it was in the nature of the landlords to exploit peasants. But his views were of the pre-Malthusian period of optimism about the brotherhood of man. But Sir John Shore, who had also favoured a permanent settlement with the zemindars, nevertheless raised a doubt as to the ryot's security under the system proposed by Francis and Thomas Law. Shore perceived that such relationships as those between the zemindar and government and the ryot and zemindar were not as simple as Francis imagined. As Shore saw it, the duty of the government was to bring about a good relationship between tenants and landlords, which meant that when introducing new laws the government should not leave the question of landlord–tenant relationships to be decided by a free-for-all between the parties concerned.[37]

This objection was overcome by reference to British law as expounded by Justice Blackstone. Thomas Law cited Blackstone to the effect that, when

[36] *Original Minutes*, p. 131 (Minute dated 5 November 1776).

[37] See Shore's Minute dated 8 December 1789 in Firminger (Ed.), *The Fifth Report* (Calcutta, 1918), vol. II, p. 520. See also his Minute, 18 June 1789, *Ibid.*, pp. 113–14. See also Shore to Thomas Law, 23 January 1789, *Letters to the Board, Submitting by their Requisition, a Revenue Plan for Perpetuity* (Calcutta, 1789), p. 38.

once the lords of the manor had given permission for the villeins and their children to enjoy possession, then 'Common Law of which custom is the life' gave them 'title to prescribe against such Lords'.[38] Lionel Place of the Jaghire district in the Madras Presidency also found support in Blackstone for comparing the *pycarry* (known also as *khoodkasht ryot* in Bengal, a kind of sub-tenant or husbandman who cultivates the lands of others) with the copyholder of England.[39] It was such arguments that influenced Lord Cornwallis in enacting a settlement which reflected his firm belief that a process of natural selection would eliminate all bad landlords.[40] It would of course not be entirely correct to put the whole responsibility on Cornwallis. It has been pointed out by the historian of Indian administration that Cornwallis's proposal was discussed and assented to at the highest levels of policy making in Britain which at that time included the Prime Minister himself as well as Dundas and Charles Grant.[41] Apart from the very few experienced Indian civil servants, most of those who were involved in the decision concerning the vesting of the entire proprietary rights on the zemindars always tended to be influenced by what they were used to in England, which to them was the ideal system.[42]

But whatever might have been the origins of the policy, the hopes of Lord Cornwallis were not fulfilled concerning harmonious landlord—peasant relations. Zemindars freely indulged in oppression and exploitation of the tenants, through their agents as well as by the process of sub-infeudation. Between 1800 and 1810, rents nearly doubled in Burdwan, a district in Bengal.[43] Raja Rammohan Roy, himself a Bengali zemindar, admitted that the conditions of the cultivators had not improved although the income of the proprietors had increased.[44] Two related factors were responsible for the

[38] *Ibid.*

[39] Report on Jaghire, 6 June 1799, Firminger, *op. cit.*, vol. III p. 152. Likewise, John Hodgson of the Madras Board of Revenue said that it was not necessary to attach an importance to theoretical rights enjoyed by the tenants. The important thing was to give the rights he had always enjoyed. Applying Blackstone ('A subject in England has only the usufruct, and not the absolute property to the soil') he said, 'the ryot of India may rest contented with an usufructory right'. Firminger, *op. cit.*, (vol. III, p. 470.) The English copyholder also pays rent fixed by immemorial custom and that could not be increased. The record was the Court roll of the minor. The trouble and confusion rose in India because the English proprietor was a proprietor in the sense the zemindar in India was not, at any rate until 1793.

[40] See Minute dated 3 February 1790, *Ibid.*, vol. II, pp. 530 *et. seq.*

[41] J. W. Kaye, *The Administration of the East India Company* (London, 1853), p. 183.

[42] See Nathaniel Halhed's (himself an experienced Indian civil servant) perceptive comment in *A Memoir on the Land Tenure and Principles of Taxation* (Calcutta, 1832), pp. 91–2.

[43] See Minute of Harrington dated 3 July 1827, *Bengal Revenue Consultations* 11 October. 1827, India Office Records, Range 61, vol. 24, no. 10.

[44] See his *Expositions on the Judicial and Revenue System of India* (London, 1832), *p. 73*.

degradation of the Bengali peasantry. The population of Bengal continued to increase in the decades after the 1793 Settlement but without any appreciable rise in the opportunities for employment.[45] The growth in the agricultural labour force through a larger population as well as the displaced labour force from the declining cotton manufacturing centres resulted in an increasing demand for cultivable land.[46] Simultaneously the government conferred on the zemindars summary power to distrain the property and arrest the person of the cultivator, leaving him again no other means of redress against illegal or unjust distraint or arrest than the process of a law suit. The passing of new regulations like *haftam* and *panjam* (Reg. 7 of 1799 and Reg. 28 of 1802) gave ample powers to the zemindars to collect rents from the tenants. The peasants had little protection because the traditional government agencies were either abolished (e.g. *qanungo*) or subordinated to the zemindar (e.g. *patwari*). The power in the hands of the executive was limited and if the ryots had grievances, they had to go to a civil court to get redress. In any case the peasants could do little in the face of the new legal instruments of *haftam* and *panjam* possessed by the zemindars. The civil courts too could do little because the settlement was made with no previous survey, no record of rights and without even a defined method of assessment.

These being the conditions, there was very little scope for the operation of the common law so dear to Justice Blackstone and his Indian disciples. This state of affairs made many officials conclude that Cornwallis had been mistaken; and even the home government was concerned about the unexpected results of the permanent settlement. When the question of settling newly acquired lands came up, the Court of Directors thus cautioned the Government of India: 'the rights of individuals should not be compromised by premature decision'.[47] This policy of caution owed not a little to the entry into the India Office of James Mill who, in his *History of India*, had in unmistakable terms condemned the permanent zemindari settlement effected by Lord Cornwallis. In a letter to David Ricardo, James Mill had said, 'But I must now conclude, and go to talk about the Zemindars and ryots, and think of the means of protecting the latter against the former – no easy task.'[48] The East India Company received support from the Board of Control in this mat-

---

[45] The population in Bengal was 24 millions in 1787 according to W. Jones, 27 millions excluding Benaras in 1810 according to the *V Report*, 36 millions in 1835, and 67 millions in 1872. See C. D. Field, *The Regulations of the Bengal Code* (Calcutta, 1875), p. 62n.

[46] Sir Charles Trevelyan told the House of Commons Select Committe that the surplus population thrown out of the Dacca Cotton manufacture fell back upon agriculture. *Parl. Papers*, H.C. 527, vol. VIII of Session 1840, Q. 1950.

[47] Court of Directors to Governor General, 16 June 1815, *Revenue Letters to Bengal*, India Office Records, vol. IV, pp. 6, 129; vol. V, pp. 216–18.

[48] Mill to Ricardo, 14 August 1819, Sraffa (ed), *Works and Correspondence of David Ricardo*, vol. VIII, p. 53.

ter. In the second decade of the century, Cumming, the extremely influential secretary of the Board, pointed out that the permanent zemindari settlement had produced effects that were the very opposites of 'protection, moderation and encouragement to the great body of the people'. It had destroyed the hereditary rights of the landed gentry and ruined the old system of reciprocal rights and duties. Hence Cummin and the Board of Control were always' against the extension of the permanent settlement system to any other part of India.[49] The Court of Directors had realised that the rents payable by the tenants to zemindars were arbitrarily fixed by the latter and that the government machine was not strong enough to protect the former.[50]

Contrary to the Irish case where economic ideas were used to favour the landlord class, James Mill utilised the Ricardian rent theory to provide support for his policy of ignoring the landlords in the newly acquired areas where land tenures were being organised by the British. Mill and the Court of Directors saw to it that the zemindari system, in spite of the strength of the Cornwallis school in the Government of India, spread no further than the originally settled areas in Bengal. Regarding the already settled areas, as early as 1812, H. T. Colebrooks proposed to reopen the whole question and prepare afresh all pre-British records to fix the tenures and also settle the rent payable by the tenants to zemindars. This policy did not materialise owing to the colossal problem of locating the old records. After nearly forty years of service in India, J. H. Harington a Bengal civilian, proposed in 1827 a regulation to place the landlord–tenant relationship on a more satisfactory footing. This, too, came to nothing. On the one hand, civil servants like J. Pattle said that, where oppression existed, it was due to the agents of absentee landlords and so not all zemindars should be penalised for the fault of a few absentee landlords.[51] On the other hand, there were other civilians like Alexander Ross who thought such enactments would be objectionable 'on the ground that they would ⌈add⌉ to the injury of the Zemindars and other superior landholders'.[52] Ross conceived India as developing on the English agrarian model, and was hence satisfied that they were proceeding on the right lines. Harrington's proposed regulation would in fact have reduced the absolute power of the landholders, and consequently they would not be able to perform their functions. A few years previously, when a similar question came up, a Bengal civilian pointed out that in Britain the authorities had

[49] Note on Dowdeswell's Minute, 7 October 1819. *Home Misc.* India Office Records, no. 530, p. 21.

[50] Court of Directors to Governor General, 15 January 1819 (Revenue), *Bengal Despatches*, India Office Records, no. E/4/695, pp. 58–9.

[51] Minute dated 1 June 1827, *Bengal Revenue Consultations*, 11 October 1827, India Office Records, no. Range 61, vol. 24, no. 8.

[52] *Ibid*. Minute dated 6 March 1827, no. I.

not interfered in the landlord–tenant relations because they knew that 'what is for the benefit of one individual estate, must influence by its example, the general improvement of the country'. Although the policy makers were aware of the necessity of agriculture for the prosperity of the country, they did not think it essential to legislate 'for the express support of the husbandman. In all countries husbandry is a trade like every other profession, and as long as it is profitable or suits the habits, a man will follow it and no longer'. It is true that experience told the civilians that Indian landlords tended to oppress their tenants; but that could not be helped because Adam Smith himself had said, 'the principal attention of the Sovereign ought to be to encourage by every means in his power the attention both of the landlord and the tenant, by allowing both to pursue their own interest in their own way, and according to their own judgement.'[53]

In general one could say that the prevailing climate in the Bengal Presidency was against any interference. The zemindars' domination became an accepted fact of life to such an extent that the tenants, who in theory had substantial occupancy rights, became in fact tenants at will. The Cornwallis school which flourished in Bengal was satisfied with the state of affairs and was not willing to tamper with the existing agrarian relations. It was not until the 1840s and 1850s that serious doubts began to be expressed as to the wisdom of letting things alone.[54] This was in spite of the North Western Provinces being under a group of administrators who believed, to quote from R. M. Bird, a representative member of this group, 'I am entirely satisfied after every investigation and enquiry I can make, that there was under the former Government no agricultural class between Government and the cultivators . . . legalised landed proprietors were an invention of our own.'[55] There were also people who were convinced that 'the existing tribunals were insufficient for the attainment of rights or their protection' and that the revenue system needed change.[56] But as yet the officers who felt like this were few in Bengal and felt helpless against the law they themselves had created.

The explosive happenings of 1857 left their mark very clearly on the

---

[53] See Ravenscroft to Colebrooke & Deane, 1 January 1816, *Selections from Revenue Records of North Western Provinces: 1818–1820* (Calcutta, 1866) vol. I, pp. 266–70. The quotation is from the *Wealth of Nations*.

[54] Baboo Peary Chand Mitter drew attention as early as 1846 to the deteriorating landlord–ryot relations in Bengal. See *Calcutta Review*, vol. VI, no. XII, pp. 335 *et seq*. Judicial opinion was also becoming somewhat favourable to the ryots from 1845 onwards. See K. C. Acharya Chowdhoory, *Rent Question in Bengal* (Mymensingh, 1879), p. 12.

[55] Undated Memorandum, 'Further Thoughts Respecting Settlements' in (*Bentinck Papers*, Nottingham University).

[56] See Court of Directors to Governor General, 13 August 1851 (Revenue Department), *Parl. Papers*, H.C. 533, vol. X of Session 1852, Appendix 19.

actions of the British in India. In a search for allies, a pro-aristocratic bias began to colour British administrative policies. In Oudh, the policy of extending peasant proprietorships initiated by Dalhousie under the inspiration of John Stuart Mill was sharply reversed by Canning in favour of the landed aristocrats. Opinions were expressed by many an official in favour of implementing laws favourable to the growth and maintenance of a rich land-based aristocracy. Although the aim was frankly to secure political support, the whole policy was defended on grounds of *laissez-faire* liberalism to such an extent that a newspaper claimed that 'a large addition of the ablest revenue officers in the country was made to the liberal and scientific school represented among political economists by McCulloch and opposed by J. S. Mill'.[57] It would not be correct, however, to assume that a uniform shift towards *laissez-faire* and reactionary policies had taken place so far as India as a whole was concerned. As a matter of fact, in Bengal it was the other way round. The very first change in policy after the events of 1857 was to favour the peasants even at the risk of violating the dicta of orthodox concepts of free trade. It must be pointed out here that the orthodoxy of the inviolability of free trade between two parties had been under fire even in Britain at this time. It was John Stuart Mill who had come out against this rigid doctrine, indicating the limiting cases where the laws were not applicable. Mill was not against state intervention as such, and said that some rights should be given to the peasants so as to give them a stimulus.[58] Further support was derived from the writings of J. E. Cairnes who was also against applying an extreme form of free trade to land problems.[59]

The conditions of the Bengal peasantry were, however, so appalling that the originators of the Act x of 1859 had no necessity to turn to dissident economists for doctrinal support. Conditions were different in India, and orthodox political economy would not help. As Seton-Karr, a Bengal civil servant, said in an anonymous article in the *Calcutta Review*: 'the law of landlord and tenant ... in the east, must often be guided by principles at which even Adam Smith and Malthus might have been somewhat startled'.[60] The Lieutenant Governor of Bengal simply claimed that the Act was only an attempt to discharge the heavy obligations towards the peasantry of Bengal. Even before 1857, two officers of the Bengal civil service, Messrs Ricketts and

[57] *Opinions of the Press in India on the Tenant Right Controversy in the Punjab* (Lahore, 1869), p. 34.

[58] *Principles of Political Economy*, p. 332.

[59] See *Essays in Political Economy* (London, 1873), Chapter VI, the *Indian Economist* reprinted an article by Cairnes on Irish land tenures and claimed that his views on Ireland were applicable to India as well. 30 June 1874.

[60] Vol. XXIX, no. LVII, p. 153.

Stainforth, had made drafts of similar legislation although they were not carried out.[61] The intention of the Act x of 1859 was to restrict the absolute powers of the zemindars and give a measure of protection to the tenants. Accordingly the zemindars were declared not to have absolute rights over the land, and a tenant had occupancy rights if he had held the land for the previous twelve years. This was most revolutionary considering the concept a property prevalent in Britain at that time, but almost all the judges of the various local courts of Bengal, to whom the matter was referred, came out in favour of the Act.[62] Some of them even felt that the Act had not gone far enough if viewed from 'the sacred force of common law in this Country.'[63] While the predominant portion of official opinion, both on the executive and the judicial wings, was in favour of the Act, there were a few who felt that to violate free trade in land would have an adverse impact on the supply of capital and enterprise. In a Memorandum Charles Currie pointed out that

Rent is the surplus profits of land after deducting the wages of labour and the interest of capital expended on the land. The amount of rent therefore will vary according to the habits of industry and frugality of the cultivator, and the amount of capital expended in cultivation, any attempt arbitrarily to determine the rent of any land is an infringement on the rights of the landowner and liable to obstruct the development of the resources of the country.[64]

By proposing to give occupancy rights to the ryots and making him pay only 'fair and equitable rates' of rent (as its section v prescribed), the Act became such an infringement. Currie was convinced that agrarian relations in India were in 'a natural state, and there appears no necessity for deviation from the acknowledged principles of political economy'.

However, these criticisms did not have much effect, and the Act was strongly endorsed by the authorities of the day. In fact, in spite of all the criticism, the Act itself could not be construed as negating the faith in the market mechanism. Section VIII specifically left the rents of non-occupancy

---

[61] See Letter from the Board of Revenue to the Government of Bengal, no. 148, dated 27 April 1855. The Act as it was passed owed much to these drafts. *Papers of Act X (1859)*, Part I, (National Archives of India). For a critical contemporary assessment of Act x of 1859 from the peasants' point of view, see R. H. Hollingberry, *The Zemindari Settlement of Bengal* (Calcutta, 1879), Hollingberry was a civil servant and has used material from the *Papers of Act X (1859)* extensively in his work.

[62] Occupancy rights were granted to tenants of 12 years standing even in the 1830s by R. M. Bird and others of North Western Provinces.

[63] Minute of A. Sconce, a judge of the Sudder Dewany Adawlut, dated 19 May 1858, *Papers of Act X (1859)* (National Archives of India).

[64] 'Memorandum on the Bill for Amending the Law relating to Rent'; Minute dated 17 June 1858. The Board of Revenue of Bengal also expressed itself against this upholding of customary rates as against competition rates. See its letter to Bengal Government, no. 417, 1 December 1858, *Ibid*. See also the anonymous pamphlet, *Indigo and Its Enemies or Facts on Both Sides* (London, 1861), p. 78.

tenants to be settled by direct landlord—tenant negotiations. Besides, even for the occupancy tenants (for whom all the critics approved special favourable treatment), the Act permitted its policy to be set aside by private contract, unlike the Irish land legislation.

The Act was immediately acclaimed as the *Magna Carta* of ryots[65] because, in the words of the Viceroy, it was 'a real and earnest endeavour to improve the position of the ryots of Bengal and to open to them a prospect of freedom and independence which they have not hitherto enjoyed'.[66] But the Indian landlords, in which group the European indigo planters should also be included, were very vocal in their condemnation of state interference in the matter of the landlord—tenant relationship. Many pamphlets were published espousing their cause and meetings were held to put forward their views.[67] The gravamen of the charge was the excessive doctrinairism exhibited by the policy makers. One pamphleteer accused the government of being anti-landlord, and of making use of John Stuart Mill's ideas only to make its case respectable.[68] Another critic felt that in framing the Act x, its authors took into consideration only one — albeit very important — aspect of human behaviour, namely selfishness. Drawing extensively from Adam Smith's *Theory of Moral Sentiments*, he concluded that 'man's moral sentiments, or the unselfish rules which he prescribes for himself from his judgement of the conduct of others form part equally with the selfish rule of political economy in determining his actions'. In other words, Act x was based on the doctrinaire assumption that landlords were purely selfish, which in fact they were not, because their moral sentiments would prevent them from being conditioned solely by egotistic motives.[69] But if the Indian landlords did not like the

---

[65] A writer in the *Hindu Patriot* cited by H. C. Sutherland of the Bengal civil service, as a result of the passing of this Act, India has 'emerged from the dark depths of feudalism into the bright sunlight of constitutional freedom', See *Calcutta Review*, vol. xxxiv, no. LXVIII, January—June 1860, p. 247.

[66] Canning's Statement of Assent dated 29 April 1859. In the same assent he paid a generous tribute to Mr E. Currie for having 'established a lasting claim to the gratitude of the cultivators of soil in Bengal'. *Papers of Act X (1859)*, Part II (National Archives of India).

[67] See for instance *The Permanent Settlement Imperilled or Act X of 1859 in its True Colours* by a Lover of Justice (Calcutta, 1865); R. T. Larmour, *Notes on the Rent Difficulties in Lower Bengal* (Calcutta, 1862) The British Indian Association was a powerful pressure group operating on behalf of the zemindars and planters.

[68] I.P.H. *Propositions on the Land Tax in India* (Bombay, 1866), p. 55. According to the author, the Government of India have only done through the tenancy legislation, 'what the French Government was asked to do by the Communist sect in 1848 and thereabouts. The French Government was then asked to protect the labourer against the capitalist, as the Indian Government does in Bengal, or itself to become the capitalist (as the Indian Government does outside Bengal), and establish ateliers nationaux.' p. 44. He however concedes that although the Communist sect had the same theoretical aims as J. S. Mill, their practical means were quite different.

[69] *The Relations of Landlord and Tenant in India* (Serampore, 1863), pp. 28—9.

legislation and attributed it to doctrinaire thinking, the Act was admired in Britain, especially by those who had a sympathetic interest in the Irish land problems. One observer expressed his satisfaction that at last the Indian authorities had solved a difficult question by repudiating 'industrial feudalism and economic doctrinairism' in favour of 'customary Law and equitable principle'.[70]

In the 1860s, one oft-repeated criticism of tenancy legislation was that it misunderstood the basic purpose of rent in the economic system. It was claimed that increasing rent indicated increasing prosperity, for the necessity of having to pay the rent to the landlord provided a stimulus to the farmer and the peasant to produce more. By indulging in unproductive consumption, the landlord on his part augments the effective demand which has the effect of stimulating the economy via its multiplier effects. The arbitrary lowering of rents by tenancy legislation, however, operated in the opposite direction.[71] Another variant of this argument was that Act x of 1859 was 'sowing pauperism broadcast over the land'.[72] The reasoning was that the return which the tenants got out of cultivation, if arbitrarily fixed by custom, would be more than the return they would get if the rents were determined by competition. Because of this, the intensity of desire to take up the cultivation of new lands would diminish. In the absence, then, of the regulating effect of rent, the continuous process of economic development would be arrested. It was thus visualised that the economy would operate at a static level, with the standard of living continuously declining owing to the steady increase in population.

The tenancy Act passed in 1859 was in reality an innocuous law, and the Bengali landlords were not slow in evading the good intentions of its framers. Before the Act of 1859, there was no right of enhancement because by ancient custom the *pergunah* rate established limited rent. The Act gave security of tenure and occupancy rights, but the rent was liable to be increased. While the Act said that the rents should be 'fair and equitable', at the same time rents could be increased by due processes of law, provided the rent paid by the particular ryot was below the prevailing rate for similarly placed locations and also provided that the increased value of produce was not due to the ryot's own exertions but due to other external causes. Even the occupancy rights were confined only to those who had occupied the same patch of land continuously for twelve years. Besides the burden of proof of occupancy rested

[70] H. D. Dutton, *Ancient Tenures and Modern Land Legislation in British India* (London, 1870), p. 12.

[71] 'Capital and Land' in *Calcutta Review*, vol. XXXVIII, no. LXXVI, 1863, pp. 340 *et seq*. The author makes frequent references to Malthus' *Principles of Political Economy*.

[72] A. P. Webb, *Agricultural Bank and Supplemental Legislation for Agricultural Relief* (Meerut, 1883), p. 7.

with the tenants. The only possible proof was the issue of *pattas* (written settlement of the land revenue) which was inoperative for a variety of reasons. This meant that a predominant number of tenants were automatically excluded from benefiting by the Act. In any case the landlords, by frequently shifting the tenants from field to field, were able to make the twelve-year occupancy rule ineffective.

Another complicating factor which shows in bold relief the unhappy landlord–tenant relationship in Bengal at this time was the impact of indigo cultivation. Bengal had a virtual monopoly in the promotion of indigo, mostly in the hands of European planters. The planters acquired lands and rented them to peasants on condition that they grew indigo for them at fixed prices. In the 1850s and 1860s, the price of indigo was, if anything, stationary; whereas, owing to a number of factors, there was an increasing demand (and a consequent increase in prices) for other commodities like rice. The peasants were naturally eager to take advantage of the increase in prices (and also to compensate for the enormous increase in wages), but were unable to do so because of their contracts with the indigo planters. The European planters were very influential, and as the Commissioner of Sunderbans, J. H. Reilly, told the Indigo Commission in 1860: 'I consider the zemindari power in the mofussil to be omnipotent, and when once the planter is zemindar, nothing can oppose him.'[73] In spite of this, there were many disturbances, and the peasants' smouldering discontent was a cause of great worry to the administrators.[74] In general it is possible to say that many officials, apprehensive as they were of a repetition of 1857, were conscious of the problems faced by the ryots and made attempts to persuade the planters to be reasonable, which the planters of course resented.[75]

The planters seized the Act x of 1859 as a weapon to put indirect pressure on the ryots. While, on the one hand, they released the peasants from the contracts to cultivate indigo, on the other, the planters in their role *as zemindars*, demanded much higher rents. Their argument was that the

[73] Quoted in R. H. Hollingberry, *op. cit.* vol. II, p. 129.

[74] See Canning to Wood, Letter dated 30 October 1860, cited in Maclagan, *Clemency Canning* (London, 1962), p. 276. See for Grant's account of this encounter in his Minute dated 17 September 1860. *Papers Relating to the Cultivation of Indigo in the Presidency of Bengal* (Calcutta, 1860), p. 64. For accounts of the indigo disturbances see Blair Kling, *The Blue Mutiny* (Philadelphia, 1965), Chapter III and IV; and Campbell, *Memoirs*, vol. II, pp. 915–37.

[75] An author who was sympathetic to the cause of the ryots cited Mill's *On Representative Government* to show that the indigo planters were behaving exactly like all English colonists in oppressing the original inhabitants. John Murdoch, *Letter to the Rt. Hon. The Earl of Elgin on the Rent Question in Bengal* (Calcutta, 1863), pp. 21–2. The indigo planters on their side complained that they were being oppressed by members of the Indian civil service. See *Brahmins and Pariahs: an Appeal by the Indigo Planters of Bengal* (London, 1861).

peasants were provided lands at low rental because of the promise to grow indigo at specified prices, and hence if the ryots refused to honour their portion of the contract, there was no reason why the planters should be content with the low rentals. As the Act x of 1859 had specified that the 'fair and equitable' rates should be determined by the judiciary, both planters and zemindars and the ryots resorted to the courts for deciding upon the definition and calculation of fair and equitable rents.[76]

When the question as to what was the vague 'fair and equitable' rate of rent arose in the dispute between James Hills, a European indigo planter–zemindar, and Ishwar Ghose, a ryot,[77] the Chief Justice, Sir Barnes Peacock predictably gave a judgement which reflected, not only his convictions regarding *laissez-faire* and property rights, but also his displeasure of the tenancy legislation. According to him, rent meant only one thing and that was what the Classical economists – especially Malthus – had laid down:

A definition more useful for our purpose is that given by Mr Malthus in his *Principles of Political Economy*. He there defines rent to be 'that portion of the value of the whole produce which remains to the owner of the land after all the outgoing belonging to its cultivation, of whatever kind, have been paid, including the profits of the capital employed, estimated according to the usual and ordinary rate of agricultural capital at the time being'. The word 'outgoings' used in the above definition, must include a fair and equitable rate of wages for the labour employed ... whether that of hired labourers paid out of Capital, or the labour of the ryot himself or of his family, and also when the rent is paid in money, the labour and expenses of carrying the produce to market, or of converting it into money.

Rent, according to Peacock, was the consequence of the inadequate supply of land relative to the demand for it. Rent rises because of the increases in population and economic development; hence it was but proper that the owners of the land should get the benefit. His conclusion was inevitable because of his refusal to believe that zemindars were anything but absolute proprietors and the ryots no more than mere tenants at the will of the zemindars. He felt that it was an 'act of the greatest injustice' to raise the status of the peasant 'instead of leaving him as an agricultural labourer without capital or property'. It was natural also that he should turn a deaf ear to the lawyer on the other side who quoted John Stuart Mill to the effect that

---

[76] According to Sir Henry Maine, the landlords were not to be blamed for the legal controversy. 'It had a purely official origin and began in an idle verbal dispute as to what are the "rights of property".' Maine to Mill, 1 November 1868 (MSS at Johns Hopkins University Library: I am indebted to Mr Peter Jackson of the Hull University for drawing my attention to it.).

[77] See the judgement in James Hills *vs.* Ishwar Ghose, High Court of Calcutta presided by Chief Justice Sir Barnes Peacock and Justices Bayley and Kemp. Case No. 1607 of 1862, 30 August, 4 September, 1862.

custom influenced the determination of rents in countries such as India.

The judgement was a bombshell and it put the government itself in an awkward position. G. N. Taylor of the Viceroy's Council thought it was based on a 'doctrine which is full of danger and injustice to the whole body of occupancy ryots'.[78] And Sir Henry Sumner Maine, who was at that time the Law Member, felt that whereas the legislation was intended to soften the misery of the ryot, the judgement itself 'goes every length against the ryot'.[79]

In so far as it dealt with the economic aspect of the landlord–tenant relations, the judgement provoked three lines of criticism. The foremost of these rested on the case that in India economic or competition rents did not prevail. Arguing that in such instances only 'concrete historical inquiry' could bring out the truth, the *Calcutta Review* declared

Rent in this country is in reality, not rent at all in a Malthusian sense. The principles of political economy apply only to rents settled by free competition. In the Mofussil there is no such thing known ... The custom, then, or theory, of rent here, has always implied a limitation of the landlord's demand long before it reached the point assigned by Ricardo as the limit on his system.[80]

Another writer in the same journal pointed out the necessity of unrestricted mobility of resources and the availability of alternative investment opportunities in trade and manufactures for a successful functioning of a free trade economic policy in land. Neither of these preconditions was present in India, and there 'above all other countries, what Senior calls the Great Monopoly of Land exists beyond a doubt. And the ordinary rules of demand and supply are suspended, and inapplicable'.[81] Sir Henry Maine, applying the historical method, maintained that 'occupancy tenures are very old in the history of the world; open markets for land are comparatively new'. In India, 'the question at issue related to rents by *custom*, and not to rents by *competition*, and hence all quotations from politico-economical writers were entirely irrelevant'.[82] The whole confusion, according to Maine, was due to the wrong use of technical terms such as rent.

The second line of criticism flowed from the earlier one of the wrong use of nomenclature. The point was not 'rent' as understood by Malthus to be settled between the possessor of land and the user of it; it was really a

---

[78] Minute dated December 1864, Proceedings, August 1865, no. 24A. *India Legislative Consultations* July–August 1865, India Office Records, no. Range 208, vol. II; pp. 890 (1–13).

[79] Maine to Wood, 16 September 1863 (Halifax Papers, India Office Library).

[80] Vol. XLI, no. LXXXI, 1865, p. 161.

[81] *Ibid.*, vol. XXXIX, no. LXXVIII, 1864, p. 293.

[82] 'Oude Tenant Right' 10 July 1864, *Minutes of Sir Henry Maine*, p. 63 (India Office Library).

question of resources for public expenditure. The zemindars were only collecting the revenue on behalf of the government, and as such the government had every right to look into the question of the rate at which the resources of the ryots were transferred to the public fisc.

And, finally, it was argued that even if one did not question the application of the Classical theory to India, the calculation of rents on the basis suggested by Malthus would be impossible. If such calculations were based on inaccurate data, it would lead, in the words of H. Ricketts, to 'inconsistent and inequitable decisions, and all the subsequent confusion and distress'.[83]

The confusion enshrined in the Act with regard to fair and equitable rates was worse confounded by a series of conflicting judgements in the Calcutta High Court. In one case (Sri Narayan Ghose *versus* Kashi Prasad Mukherjea), the court declared that the adjustment must be 'according to the method of proportion, that is the increased rent must bear to the old rent the same proportion as the former value of the produce of the soil bears to its present value'. In another instance, the same judges who tried the previous case gave the verdict that the particular facts of each case should be given importance against any fixed unalterable principle.

In spite of all that was said against the judgement of Sir Barnes Peacock, it was at least consistent as a principle, although utterly devoid of any understanding of the sociological realities of the Bengal peasantry. Maine was no doubt correct when he said, 'Peacock's principle of rackrent has this great advantage, that it *is* a principle'.[84] However, in order to maintain this principle, he had to make unreal assumptions about the nature of zemindars and their rights over the soil.

As a result, the government was in a dilemma. They had originally introduced the legislation to improve the position of the ryots, but as the *Calcutta Review* said, the judgement of Peacock had 'made it a farce'. The government was asked to take words at their proper meaning; 'And if length of holding is to give rights to hold, fool not the unfortunate occupant by adding the words, "if nobody else wants your holding".'[85] The government, however, did not find the problem easy to solve, because Bengal was far too complex for any one principle to fit in adequately.[86]

Many suggestions were presently made in the face of the impasse created

---

[83] *A Few Last Words on the Rent Difficulties in Bengal* (London, 1864), pp. 6, 17–18.

[84] Maine to Wood, 11 September 1863, *op. cit.*

[85] Vol. XLI, no. LXXXI, 1865, p. 167.

[86] See Maine to Wood, 12 June 1864, *op. cit.* Samuel Laing who had been the finance member until two years previously said, 'This was a question which no one could precisely answer, and which had to adjust itself according to the disposition of the landowner, the power of resistance of the ryot, the example of other estates, and a variety of other circumstances.' *India and China, England's Mission in the East* (London, 1863), p. 36.

by the judgement. Sir Charles Trevelyan wanted to effect a permanent settlement between the peasant and the landlord 'somewhat in the way of our tithe
commutation in England'.[87] Ricketts proposed a complete settlement of the
rents based on a field survey and an exhaustive registry of all rights and.
interests in the land. What he wanted, in effect, was to settle Bengal under
the famous Regulation VII of 1822 applicable to the North Western Provinces.[88] 'Agricola', however, thought that this would be a Herculean task,
but suggested instead the appointment of a commission to compile a proper
register of various forms of tenure that might enable the district officers to
provide protection to those needy.[89]

Maine himself preferred some sort of a permanent sub-settlement which
would have violated the theory of property as well as theory of political
economy that Peacock had championed. Maine was conscious of the peculiarity of Indian social structure as well as the vagueness of the expression
'fair and equitable'; the words, he pointed out, 'when submitted to technical
tests, prove to mean anything or nothing'.[90] He agreed that 'all the ordinary
economic maxims are adverse to interference between landlord and tenant,'
but he declared 'in favour of regulating their relation by express law we have
only to urge the peculiar and exceptional constitution of Indian society'. The
argument he used to justify interference with the permanent settlement was
strictly legal and historical:

> If the permanent settlement was a compact, it was *pactum sine causa*, an engagement
> not made upon consideration, and entitled to be interpreted largely in favour of the
> party which gave everything and received nothing. If there were any consideration,
> it consisted in the general prosperity expected from the measure; and, if part of
> this has not been realised, but on the contrary a formidable political and social
> evil has resulted to any class of the population, we are surely not estopped by any
> principle of justice from abating the mischief.[91]

It may be mentioned here that whereas Maine stressed the peculiar aspects
of the Indian society to support a claim for state interference, officers with
experience of revenue settlement work felt no such need. H. C. Irwin, for
example, said, 'the stock assertion that tenant-right is opposed to the
principles of political economy is at present, perhaps, hardly in need of

[87] Wood to Maine, 2 August 1864, *op. cit.*
[88] See *The Rent Difficulties in Bengal, and How to Remedy Them?* (London, 1863) *The Real Difficulties in Bengal, and how to settle them* (London, 1861), p. 11. Trevelyan was also in favour of these recommendations of Ricketts. See Wood to Lawrence, 10 September 1864. Even Wood at a later stage toyed with the Ricketts proposal. See Wood to Lawrence, 10 December 1864 (*Lawrence Papers* India Office Library).
[89] See *The Rent Question in Bengal, or Should Act X be Altered?* (Calcutta, 1865).
[90] Minute dated 20 May 1864, *op. cit.*, p. 50.
[91] *Ibid.*

refutation'. Accepting the distinction made by J. S. Mill between the laws of production and the laws of distribution, Irwin pointed out that both these sets of laws (composing as they do the principles of Classical political economy) were based on certain behavioural assumptions regarding the desire for accumulation. Under these circumstances, a system under which the cultivator has no security needs to be corrected because of its harmful effects on incentives to capital accumulation.[92] Therefore it was concluded that any unsatisfactory tenant–landlord relationship deserved 'the most severe and summary condemnation upon all principles of political economy in any reasonable sense of the term'.

But whatever might have been the wishes of Maine and the moral support he received from many including the Secretary of State, no help was forthcoming to make Act x do what its framers had desired, and no support to have it amended.[93] The only way – and according to Maine, 'the best possible way' – to set things right at this stage was to act through the judiciary. This soon came about. A full bench of the Calcutta High Court was asked to give an opinion on this most involved question: Should the rent demanded by the landlord conform to the market rate or customary rate? If the customary rate was not being adjusted to fluctuations in the price movements, what other principle should be adopted?

The verdict of the full bench in the case (known as The Great Rent Case) between Thakoorannee Dossee *versus* Kashi Prasad Mukherjea reversed the earlier decision of Chief Justice Peacock and ruled that rents could be enhanced by the landlords only to the extent of the movement of the price level. John Stuart Mill was cited to show how the Indian rents were not Malthusian ones. Justice Norman said in the course of the judgement that Malthus' definition was only a 'statement of the mode in which, and extent to which, the Laws of supply and demand act upon rents, rather than a true definition of any rent that ever was, or in the nature of things will be, paid by a tenant to the owner of the land.'[94] Another Judge, Justice Trevor, accepted J. S. Mill's contention that, in India, customary rents were prevalent more often than economic rents, and hence the intentions of the framers of Act x of 1859 would be frustrated if the judgement of Sir Barnes

---

[92] See *The Garden of India or Chapters on Oudh History and Affairs* (London, 1880), p. 315.

[93] He had few supporters in either the Viceroy's Council or the Legislative Council. The Bengal Government as well as its Board of Revenue were opposed to fresh legislation. See his letters to Wood, 19 December 1863 and 5 February 1864, *op. cit.* Although Wood gave moral support, he was not in favour of particular legislation to solve only one aspect of a more general problem, a view the new Viceroy Lord Elgin did not share. Elgin to Maine, 25 February 1863 (Elgin Papers, India Office Library).

[94] See *India Legislative Proceedings*, July–December 1865, India Office Records, no. Range 208, vol. 11, pp. 890 (89). See also similar views expressed by Justice Jackson, *Ibid* Range 208, vol. 10, p. 41.

Peacock were accepted.[95] Norman recorded in his judgement that he saw the
Act x of 1859 as a

further Reform, to adopt Mr Mill's language, made by the present generation in the
interest of the ryot, and a partial return to the old state of things, entitling
ryots with right of occupancy acquired under the law by a twelve year occupancy to
obtain pottahs at a rent fair and equitable according to the custom of the country
and not according to the theory of English Political Economists, by whose analysis,
when applied to this country, all that is not comprehended in the wages of his labor,
and profit of the ryot's stock, must be the landholder's rent.[96]

This judgement settled the matter for a long time to come. One could easily
hazard the view that customary rates, which were very different from competitive rents, became the accepted policy. Between them, John Stuart Mill and
Ireland had effected a radical change in official economic opinion. Time and
again the Irish experience was cited to show how the Indian land tenures
should be treated with special care so as not to trench upon the rights of the
inferior landholders. For instance, the young settlement officer of Bareilly
criticised Act x of 1859 and advocated competition to govern the landlord–
tenant relationship: 'Why should the officers of Government step in to fix
the rent of land between landlord and tenant any more than the price of sugar
between buyer and seller? I am for free trade in land as well as in its produce,
and I am convinced that the cultivator would benefit in the long run.' But
A. Colvin, the experienced secretary of the Board of Revenue, chided the
settlement officer as follows:

It would be a curious reversal of our Irish experience if it did. 'In the long run'
peasants increase and multiply; and I don't see how greater competition for land
is to benefit competitors, whatever may be its effect on those who hold it in
proprietary position. To advocate free trade in land in Northern India seems to me
in a settlement officer to argue a strange forgetfulness of the mode in which the
respective interests in the land have grown and are growing under our rule.[97]

By the beginning of the eighth decade, many provinces had introduced
tenancy legislation using Act x of 1859 as the starting point. In some areas
such as Oudh, it met with stiff resistance from officers who believed in maintaining the upper hand of the landlords. To these officers, Classical liberalism

[95] For Justice Trevor's references to John Stuart Mill's *Principles of Political Economy*, see
his Minute of 5 November 1864 on the working of Act x of 1859, *ibid.*, Range 208,
vol. 10, p. 57.

[96] *Ibid*, Range 208, vol. 11, pp. 890 (39).

[97] Note by A. Colvin dated 31 December 1872, *Permanent and Temporary Settlements in North
Western Provinces* (Allahabad, 1873), Para. 31. The *Calcutta Review* remarked, "Anomolies
we must have under a paternal Government. As for example, – we fix the price of land –
though if a city were being starved by the Mahajuns, we would not fix the price of the
produce.' Vol. XLI, no. LXXXI, 1865, p. 163.

came in as a useful pretext to justify their policy.[98] In other areas such as Punjab, the tenancy legislation firmly corrected a pro-landlord policy effected a few years previously,[99] and in fact most provinces had to introduce some sort of tenancy reform, as the current was really too strong for the old orthodoxy.

As has just been seen, the Act x of 1859 reappeared unscathed after the severe jolt it had had in the Calcutta High Court. But the tenant's position was now only marginally better, for the economic circumstances were indeed all against the tenants, and oppression and agitation alternated with dismal monotony. The landlords wanted to squeeze as much out of the ryots as possible in spite of the protective legislation. Owing to the improvement of communications and of the jute trade, prices rose, and the question was raised who should benefit by the prosperity brought about by these external forces. The zemindars thought they should, and went about levying illegal cesses and arbitrary increases in rent.

Unlike the Irish peasants whose cause was espoused by articulate leaders like Parnell, the Indian peasants had no such support. The educated Bengali elite themselves came from the zemindari families and they used their resources in furthering their class interests. The growing frustration of the peasantry led to armed uprising on several occasions during 1873, 1874 and 1875. It was now becoming clear to the authorities that the Act x of 1859 was inadequate and that further legislation was necessary in the interests of stable agrarian relations. The Famine Commission in 1880 urged the government to make more effective the existing legislation protecting the tenants.[100] Ripon too, who was the Viceroy at the time of the release of this report, saw the need for such legislation to correct former mistakes. According to him, 'the misapplication of English ideas, the misuse of language borrowed from English law and the English rural system' were to a large extent responsible for obliterating in practice the tenants' rights that the Government of India had promised to uphold.[101] The Secretary of State also admitted the failure of the earlier legislation and agreed that fresh action was necessary.[102]

While an attempt was made by Sir Richard Temple in 1875 to put the

---

[98] See Jagdish Raj, *The Mutiny and British Land Policy in Northern India* (Bombay, 1966), Chapter VI.

[99] For an account of the passing of the Punjab tenancy Act, the reader is referred to G. R. H. Hambly, 'Richard Temple and the Punjab Tenancy Act of 1868' in *English Historical Review*, January 1964, vol. LXXIX, no. 310, pp. 47–66.

[100] *Report*, Part II, p. 118. *Parl. Papers*, Cmd. 2735, vol. LII of Session 1880.

[101] Governor-General in Council to Secretary of State, 21 March 1882, no. 6 (Legislative) *Legislative Department Proceedings*, April 1885 (National Archives of India). See also Ripon to Hartington, 24 March 1882 (*Ripon Papers* British Museum).

[102] Secretary of State to Government of India, 17 August 1882, no. 3 (Revenue). Philips, Pandey & Singh (Eds.), *The Evolution of India, and Pakistan 1858–1947: Select Documents* (London, 1962), pp. 631–2.

position of the occupancy ryot on a firm footing, it was however not until 1879 that the government took serious action by appointing the Rent Law Commission, whose report came out the next year. Between the publication of the report of the Rent Law Commission in 1880 and the final adoption of the Bengal Tenancy Act in 1885 there was continuous controversy. The two crucial aspects of tenancy legislation, viz. extension of tenancy rights and security of tenure by the curtailment of the freedom of the landlord to enhance rent, were again extensively debated. It must, however, be pointed out that the fundamental departure had already been taken in 1859, and all that the 1885 Act did was to extend the protection offered to the tenants. By not recognising the Bengal zemindar as the archetypal English landlord and by introducing the concept of 'fair and equitable' rates of rent, the absolute rights of the zemindar had already been clipped. This could be easily seen in the Bengal Tenancy Bill introduced in 1883. The aims of the Bill were:

1 Provision of occupancy rights to all settled ryots who had cultivated land in the same village or Estate for a period of 12 years irrespective of where they tilled.

2 Occupancy rights to become heritable and transferable.

3 Enhancement of rent subject to a maximum.

4 Compensation for ejectment.

5 Summary procedure for rent suits.

As Sir Courtenay Ilbert who introduced the Bill in the Legislative Council claimed, the Bill included the three 'Fs' (fair rent, fixity of tenure and free sale), but he denied that this Bill was inspired by the Irish Act of 1881.

Once again the champions of property rights and the law of contract were up in arms against the Bill. The Bill, claimed Chief Justice Garth of the Calcutta High Court, was based on a policy of confiscation.[103] The zemindars felt that the Bill was an affront to the sanctity of contract, and they reminded the Parliament in a memorial: 'Contract is the basis of transactions in civilized life, the first step in advance over patriarchical habits, and essential to the success of social and moral progress.'[104] According to them, the idea of violating property rights and the sanctity of contract was pregnant with danger. 'The importation of foreign ideas in the regulation of the ordinary relations of life in an oriental country,' they warned, 'for which the people are not ripe can only lead to harm.'[105] In another petition

---

[103] *Minutes on the New Rent Bill* (Calcutta, 1882), p. 16.

[104] Petition dated 1 July 1883, *Papers Relating to Bengal Tenancy Act*, vol. II, p. 346 (India Office Library).

[105] *Ibid.* The Committee of the Bhagalpur Landholders Association said that even if the ryots were ignorant, interference was not proper because 'where would it stop?' According to them, 'the remedy for this state of things is diffusion of education, and not legislative interference'. See their *Notes on the Revised Tenancy Bill 1884* printed in *Papers of Act VIII of 1885*, Part II, p. 688 (National Archives of India).

by the Central Committee of the zemindars, they claimed to have been made victims of political expediency 'based on the theories of the peasant proprietary school, that in all countries the land should be held by the people, and that landlords should be abolished.'[106] The transferability of occupancy rights came in for particular criticism, although that would have been well within the bounds of free trade; it was claimed that this would lead to whole-sale alienation of land to the money lenders.[107]

The framers of the Bengal Tenancy Act and its official supporters were not particularly anxious to hide the fact that they were interfering in landlord – tenant relations. While accepting the fact that property was sacred, they asserted (like the framers of Act x of 1859) that they were only fulfilling the obligations incurred in 1793,[108] and that state interference *per se* was not detrimental.[109]

The Act as it was finally passed was a compromise between the extreme attitudes of the zemindars who preferred little interference and the government of Bengal which was anxious to go far in the direction of tenant protection.[110] The Act was appreciated for its moderation and was used as a model for similar legislation in other provinces of India.[111]

The subsequent history of agrarian conditions in Bengal shows that even Ireland was an inappropriate model for India in the matter of land tenure reforms. At that time, it seemed to many members of the Indian administra-tion – influenced as they were by the agonising soul-searching that was going on in England concerning the Irish economic problem – that India was more

---

[106] Petition dated 17 November 1883, para 57. *Legislative Department Proceedings* (National Archives of India), April 1885.

[107] The Government countered this argument by reference to Statistics which showed that more transfers of land to other agriculturists than such transfers to money lenders took place. See A. P. Macdonnell's Memorandum dated 5 January 1884, *ibid*.

[108] See Government of India to the Secretary of State, 21 March 1882, no. 6 (Legislative), p. 47.

[109] C. A. Elliott, a settlement officer in North West Provinces, came to the conclusion after an empirical study that 'in all the points that denote the prosperous agriculturist, the protected tenant is 50 per cent better off than the tenant-at-will'. Hence it 'will hardly be possible in future for anyone to declare that the theories of political economy – so far as they bear on the advantages to the people of the *petite culture* – look very well on paper, but do not bear the test of actual experiment. Here, as with all true theories, the logic of facts agrees with the logic of the closet.' 'Influence of Caste on Rates of Rent', Report dated 16 January 1868, p. 417. *Selections* v. Vol. II, no. 15 (India Office Library). See also H. S. Cunningham's (member of the 1880 Famine Commission) views in his Minute dated 20 November 1884, *Papers Relating to the Bengal Tenancy Act*, vol. III, p. 1777 (India Office Library).

[110] See for further details of the passing of this Act, S. Gopal, *The Viceroyalty of Lord Ripon* (Oxford, 1953), pp. 190–4.

[111] See Dietmar Rothermund, 'The Bengal Tenancy Act of 1885 and its Influence on the Legislation in other Provinces' in *Bengal: Past and Present*, July–December 1967.

like Ireland than England. It was no doubt true up to a point, but there were fundamental differences strongly conditioned by social norms, not clearly perceived. Indian society was essentially hierarchical, and as an obscure pamphleteer remarked, the highest aspiration of the Bengali peasant was not 'like the French peasant, to have land, but to have a tenant who will bow down to him and call him Maharaj'.[112] In Ireland, the Catholic church minimised the rigour of any socio-religious inequalities, and therefore the problem there was basically one of providing fair treatment to the cultivating tenant. Many who were not dazzled by the new trail blazed by the Irish Land Improvement Act in solving the land tenure problems were afraid that both Act x of 1859 and the Act of 1885 were not going to make any great difference to Indian economic problems. In contrast to the dichotomy in Ireland of the absentee landlord and cultivating peasant, in Bengal the typical situation was one of the zemindar at the apex with a Theekadar, Occupancy ryot, Brahmin undertenant, Bania undertenant, and cultivating low caste peasant at various lower levels. All the legislation did was to provide the three Fs to the Occupancy ryot without doing anything to the tenure-structure at the lower levels. Thus in spite of the economics of John Stuart Mill, and in spite of all the sound and fury of the legislation, the Bengali agrarian situation remained the same for many decades to come.

RURAL INDEBTEDNESS

The removal of usury laws in 1854 was one of the final stages in the induction of the principles of non-intervention into Indian administration. But this policy had hardly been accepted when the crises over the landlord–tenant relationship reversed the trend. In the same manner, the problem of rural indebtedness enforced legislative action. This problem was especially acute in those regions where some form of peasant ownership in small holdings existed.

Money lenders (known variously as Mahajans, Sowcars, Shahs, Vanis, Marwaris and Banias) had always been part of the socioeconomic structure in rural India. Agriculture was a highly uncertain occupation because the Indian peasants were dependent on the monsoons. Famine conditions arising out of a failure of rains often left the village money lender as the only recourse for the poor villager. The money lender enabled the peasant to meet his immediate contingencies and, as Sir Richard Temple observed, 'with all his faults, the money-lender is a useful man, and often gives credit when it is most needed'.[113] Credit was required not only to meet emergencies but

[112] *The Relations of Landlord and Tenant in India* (Serampore, 1863), p. 21.
[113] Minute dated 30 August 1878, *Papers of Act XVII* of 1879 (National Archives of India).

also for the normal day-to-day business of agricultural operations and for conducting various social and religious functions. The money lender in most places became so involved with the financing of agricultural production that he was described by a judge of the Calcutta High Court as the 'capitalist of the concern, who practically bears all the expenditure, pays the rent, and takes all the profits'.[114] This was because the zemindar – especially in Bengal – was a mere rent charger, whereas the peasant cultivator was reduced to the status of a field labourer barely earning his livelihood.

Even if, to look at him in the most favourable light, the money lender were seen as the one thrifty person in an otherwise improvident population, able to provide needed help in extremity, yet his very situation inevitably led him to seize every opportunity for exploitation. The money lenders, however, were kept in reasonable check by two factors, custom and a legal or customary maximum rate of interest. During the pre-British days, the money lender was part and parcel of the integrated village.[115] Even if the villages were far from the idyllic autonomous village republics of the conception of Metcalfe or Marx, still the force of public opinion in the village prevented the money lender from striking harsh bargains as he was dependent upon the village elders for enforcing his claims on the debtors, as there was no organised judiciary to secure the recovery of loans.[116]

As the British suzerainty spread in India, British forms of law courts came to be established where 'contracts' were enforced rigorously. This system of an impersonal judiciary enforcing a written penal code freed the money lenders from their dependence on the village elders to back their claims. Still there were two more checks. Firstly, until the 1850s existing usury laws made it difficult for the money lenders to enforce claims in the civil courts beyond the legal rate of interest. Secondly, whereas until 1859 the limitation for money debt was twelve years, Act xiv of 1859 reduced the period of limitation to three years, which meant that the debtor had to renew the bond inclusive of outstanding interest.

The main charge was that the courts, contracts and the law of limitation introduced an impersonal element into what were essentially personal economic relationships in the villages. The effect of all this, in the words of

---

[114] J. B. Phear, *Indian Famines and Village Organisation* (London, 1877), p. 12.

[115] See Sir Malcolm Darling, *The Punjab Peasant in Prosperity and Debt* (Bombay, 1925), p. 202. See also A. P. Webb, *Agricultural Banks and Supplemental Legislation for Agricultural Relief*, p. 6. See also Sir Erskine Perry's Note on Deccan Riots. Dated 1 December 1877, India Office Records, Financial Department Collections, c/140, p. 182.

[116] It was claimed that similar results were to be found even when the peasants were ruled by feudal superiors. The *Indian Economist* eloquently expressed the idea that the peasant was 'no doubt the milch-cow of the zemindar or of the Sirkar, but the Marwaree was not allowed to finger the udder at all'. 22 January 1872, p. 148.

the Secretary of the Legislative Department of the Government of India, Mr D. Fitzpatrick, was 'to blunt the nice sense of honour which, under the Governments that preceded us, led debtors, as a general rule, to pay up their own debts . . . as in the case of many other laws we have passed . . . we have put people at arm's length from one another'.[117] The passing of the civil procedure code in 1859 gave the money lenders the power to select their form of process. It abolished the earlier regulation of 1827 which had exempted the peasants' necessary equipment from seizure for debt. Of course the legal system by itself would not have resulted in the money lender gaining the upper hand in the rural economy. Another circumstance was the money lenders' increasing willingness to extend the scale of their operations because of the increased supply of collateral which individual ownership created. The various forms of peasant proprietary created by the British land policies in both western India and the Punjab gave creditworthiness to the normally improvident peasants. Land ownership was made transferable, and owing to the settled conditions land values were showing an upward trend which meant the transformation of land into attractive property.

These were reinforced by other trends that heightened the possibilities of exploitation by the money lenders. There was, first of all, the enormous increase in population which,[118] with the natural reluctance to migrate on the part of the villagers, increased the pressure of numbers on the available cultivable land. The increasing cultivation of commercial crops like cotton made the peasants dependent upon the vagaries of the international price situation. Bombay's cotton, for example, after a spectacular increase earlier, experienced a sudden fall in the price level in the late 1860s owing to the unsettled conditions in the United States of America. It took time for the peasants to get rid of the expensive tastes acquired after the initial boom, while the regularity of rent collections by the government in cash made it necessary for the peasants to borrow money from the money lender.[119]

Thus the legal system, economic trends, a stable administration, the desire

---

[117] Note dated 2 September 1878. *Papers of Act XVII of 1879*, Part 1, p. 215 (National Archives of India). William Wedderburn an experienced Indian civil servant (and a very sympathetic observer of the Indian rural scene) pointed out how the money lender had drifted into a false position as a result of the British legislation. See his *A Permanent Settlement for the Dekkhan* (Bombay, 1880), p. 7.

[118] Estimates of population growth are all unreliable. The Deccan Riots Commission gave the increase as 45% between 1845 and 1875. Richard Temple in his Minute of 29 October 1878 calculated from the various Settlement Reports the growth in population to be 60% from 1820 to 1876.

[119] T. C. Robertson, who was for a long time in the Indian civil service, claimed that it was the punctuality and not the heaviness of land revenue that made the British rule unpopular! See *Remarks on Several Recent Publications Regarding the Civil Government* (London, 1829), p. 51.

to borrow and the willingness to lend were all responsible for the most important result, of 'the gradual transfer of ownership of the soil from its natural lords — the cultivators — to ... traders and bankers.'[120] Very often the 'natural lords' did not even get the normal market price because the frequency of famines in the 1860s and 1870s, by depressing the value of land temporarily, enabled the money lenders to buy at a cheap price large acreages of cultivated land. Thus C.H.T. Crosthwaite found the wholesale alienation of land to money lenders to be widespread in the whole of north India. In Kanpur district alone, out of 2311 villages, 60 per cent had been taken over from the improvident borrowers. 'From the Punjab, from Bombay, from Central India, everywhere the ancient owners of the soil are giving place to the trader and the usurer.'[121] Perhaps Crosthwaite was exaggerating about the percentage of land acquired by the money lenders. For instance Gerald Barrier's statistics for the Punjab shows that only between a third and one half of the total transfers were made to the money lenders between 1874 and 1896.[122] In general, it was not only the money lender who bought land, but also the other affluent ryots who lent money as a sideline. The ultimate effect was the increasing dichotomisation of the rural economy into 'landed' versus 'landless', with the number of the latter steadily growing.

This result was bound to happen when one of the parties was ignorant of the legal system and its implications. The British law-giver assumed that the people were thrifty, clever and capable of looking after themselves in all economic dealings. The aim was to impose as few restrictions as possible on the mobility of resources, and this was very necessary for economic development as well as to reduce the costs of administration. According to Adam Smith, the ideal economic system conducted its commercial operations free of obstacles, and many administrators in India — particularly at the top — sincerely believed that they were leading India to that ideal. Indeed a Law Member of the Viceroy's council felt sorry that, in India, the various Acts have not bothered to repeal Hindu laws 'which are notoriously in favour of the debtor'.[123] The Lieutenant Governor of Punjab too thought that the trend of land transfers was but natural, and remarked that the number of land sales

---

[120] S. S. Thorburn, *Musalmans and Money-lenders* (Edinburgh, 1886), p. 1. See also A. Harington's 'Economic Reform in Rural India' where he shows in detail the increased agricultural indebtedness in 1870s and 1880s. *Calcutta Review*, no. CLI, vol. LXXVI (1883), pp. 54 *et seq.*

[121] 'A Land Policy for Northern India' in *The Indian Economist*, 21 July 1873, p. 320. See also T. Morison, *The Industrial Organisation of an Indian Province* (London, 1906), pp. 103, *et seq.*

[122] *The Punjab Alienation of Land Bill of 1900* (Durham, 1966), p. 103.

[123] Minutes by Whitley Stokes, 13 April 1878. *Papers Relating to Act XVII of 1879*, Part I (National Archives of India).

did not exceed that 'which may safely accompany the natural and healthy development of wealth in a country in backward circumstances.'[124]

However, it was not easy for the administrators on the spot to be as detached as these theorists speculating about the inevitability of man's sufferings. It was perhaps natural for the Secretary of State to philosophise loftily: 'In all civilized societies there is a vast amount of suffering and destitution, very lamentable to contemplate, but which it is wholly out of the power of the State by any direct action to eradicate.'[125] The men on the spot especially the district officers, on the other hand, were guided by the twin considerations of maintaining the Raj as well as humanitarianism,[126] and were not prepared to remain silent spectators of the way the economic relations between the peasants and money lenders were drifting.[127] S. S. Thorburn of the Punjab civil service was explicit: 'I maintain, however, that we dare not in our own interests, as a handful of foreigners governing many millions, subject the dominant to the weaker classes amongst the people.'[128] And another civil servant declared in 1871 that the 'loyalty and contentment of peasant proprietors is of far greater importance than the maintenance of an economic principle'.[129] These problems needed to be tackled in a large way and 'not merely battered about with the small shot of political economists'.[130]

However, intent upon coaxing the Indian economic system onto the path trodden by European capitalism, the government had no alternative but to bow to the 'laws' of political economy. Political economists were indeed correct because the money lender was not receiving more than the market rate of interest, and if the rates were high that it was due more to the enormous risks involved in rural credit than to any inherent rapaciousness on the part of the money lender in lieu of unpaid debts seemed perfectly natural in the light of impersonal forces of economic 'laws'. But the widespread riots that took

---

[124] Proceedings of Home Department, Punjab, no. 4609, 23 December 1874, *ibid.*

[125] Secretary of State (Lord Cranbrook) to Government of Bombay, no. 4 (Legislative) 26 December 1878.

[126] Sir Richard Temple, Governor of Bombay, said while discussing this subject that there was no injustice in a legal sense but still it was 'unjust' in the sense that it was 'repugnant to the sense of natural justice as between man and man, that moral sense which is present in the minds of all men, whether educated or uneducated'. Minute dated 30 August 1878 (Temple Papers, India Office Library).

[127] See Justice Melville's Memorandum on Interest in Punjab, June 1872. *Papers Relating to Act XVII of 1879* (National Archives of India). An 'Indian Civil Servant' said as early as 1856 that protection of the Indian ryot from the money lenders was 'even more necessary when the matter is considered in a political point of view'. *Usurers and Ryots* (London, 1856), p. 13.

[128] *Musalmans and Moneylenders*, p. 88.

[129] From the Punjab Revenue Administration Report of 1871, cited by G. S. Chhabra, *Social and Economic History of the Punjab 1849–1901* (Jullandar, 1962), p. 329.

[130] Crosthwaite in the *Calcutta Review*, vol. LXIII, no. CXXV, 1877, p. 354.

place in 1875 in the Bombay Presidency – especially in the districts of Poona, Satara, Ahmadnagar and Sholapur – made even the sceptic authorities of the supreme government realise the seriousness of the situation. Like the 'moral economy' of the common people of Britain in the eighteenth and nineteenth centuries,[131] the Indian crowd also believed in certain moral–economic principles, and this was clearly seen in the opposition to the coming of the new men and new institutions that were altering the existing social order and upsetting the old pattern of allocation of resources based on established precedents. The crowds that rioted did possess a concept of economic order but this was neither coherent nor clear-cut, and at any rate seldom made explicit. This can be seen in the fact that the rioters' main object had been to destroy the bonds given to money lenders, not cause personal injury to them. The Bombay government was conscious of the fact that there was hardly any serious crime during the whole period of the rioting.[132]

A point to be noted here is that one could find anti-money lender elements in many other uprisings in India in the nineteenth century.[133] Even in 1857 the wrath of the *sepoys* was occasionally directed against the money lenders, although at that time the prime target was the British government in India. The Santhal rebellion in the mid-1850s was of course immediately aimed at the money-lending community. These were indications of the political dimensions that the existence of usurious money lenders could assume. Whereas the earlier riots only helped to form an opinion in the minds of some civil servants, actual legislation followed the Deccan riots of 1875. The Tank disturbances that occurred in the Punjab in 1879 were also aimed at money lenders.

That the problem of rural indebtedness caused by usurious money lenders should be sought to be solved by a reintroduction of usury laws was natural. During the 1840s and 1850s, such suggestions for using laws to protect people from indebtedness were usually met with criticism.[134] But from the 1860s onwards, usury legislation had many protagonists. In issue after issue, the *Indian Economist* espoused the cause. It claimed that the money lender of the time was 'the direct product of British Economical doctrines'.[135] It

---

[131] See E. P. Thompson, 'The Moral Economy of the English Crowd in the Eighteenth Century' in *Past and Present*, no. 50, February 1971, pp. 78–9.

[132] See Ravenscroft (Chief Secretary, Government of Bombay) to Hume (Secretary Agriculture, Revenue, Commerce of Government of India), 6 April 1877. *Papers Relating to Act XVII of 1879* (National Archives of India).

[133] See an interesting paper by Ian Catanach, 'Agrarian Disturbances in Nineteenth Century India' read to Australian and New Zealand Association for the Advancement of Science, August 1965.

[134] See for example *The Calcutta Review* which referred to Jeremy Bentham's work on usury regulation, vol. VI, no XII, 1846, p. 327.

[135] 21 March 1872, p. 103. See also the *Indian Observer*, 6 April 1872, pp. 216–17.

was the belief of these writers that the Classical theory of economic policy was applicable only to countries such as Britain where commercial civilisation was in its best state.[136] This had been stressed even in 1854, when one of the only two critics of the Usury Bill, Judge Colvin of Jaunpore, urged that the repeal of usury laws would be 'too much in advance of the Social state of the people'.[137] This point of view gathered much support in the 1870s.

The underlying idea was that in India economic relations were not between equals. Whereas the government assumed both the parties to be equally matched, the fact was that 'the village cultivator *cannot* be regarded as negotiating on equal terms with the astute and educated bania'.[138] In India, the main condition for abolishing usury laws (i.e. the existence of a 'commercial and highly educated people') did not exist. The peasant was no better than a school-child in so far as borrowing was concerned and, as Lord Salisbury said, 'unlimited discretion to borrow money seems to be as deadly to H.M.'s Hindoo subjects as to an Oxford freshman'.[139] The cultivator was indeed no match for the crafty and clever money lender;[140] 'unable to read, write or compute,' said the *Indian Economist*, 'The gross frauds upon him constantly being disclosed in our Courts takes the question of usury law out of the range of Benthamite reflections altogether.'[141] In other words, it was no use expecting such borrowers to be motivated by 'enlightened self-interest'.

The peasant was not a free agent, argued many, being indirectly forced to borrow money from the money lender owing to the punctual assessment of the land tax, although he was by no means directly compelled to borrow from the bania. Under such circumstances, the argument that there was nothing wrong with the economic policy itself but that only the people were wrong, was like 'putting up a saw-mill in an infant-school and then saying, "Poor little creatures, how sad that they should be so deplorably ignorant of machinery"'.[142] The fact that the peasant was ignorant of the ways of modern

[136] It is possible to find advocates for usury regulation for England even in the 1880s. See for example R. G. Siller who exhorted the government to supplant 'political economy' by 'God's Laws'! *Usury: A Paper Read Before the Somerville Club* (London, 1883), p. 14.

[137] See *Papers of Act XXVIII of 1855*, p. 74 (National Archives of India). Judge Gubbins of Banaras was the other critic.

[138] *Indian Economist*, 21 March 1873, pp. 198–9. Justice Melville of the Punjab High Court had also pointed out how the money lender in the Punjab 'takes an unconscionable advantage of the necessity, ignorance and carelessness of the borrowing agriculturist'. *loc. cit.*

[139] Salisbury to Wodehouse, 6 August 1875. See also Salisbury to Temple, 25 June 1875 (Salisbury Papers at Christ Church College, Oxford).

[140] Sir Raymond West who was a judge of the Bombay High Court compared the peasant and the money lender to a fly and a spider. *The Land and Law in India* (Bombay, 1873), para 22.

[141] 21 March 1873, p. 199.

[142] See W. G. Pedder, 'Famine and Debt in India' in *The Nineteenth Century*, September 1877, p. 196.

commercial life and was not altogether a free agent made him a poor judge of his own interests.

Such were the reasons given for the reintroduction of usury laws. But the usury regulations offended the policy of non-interference, a fact very well known to the advocates of such action. Although the repeal of the usury laws was an expression of the 'truest wisdom' in Britain, thought the *Indian Economist*, it was a 'cruel folly' in India. The paper explained that political economy was a useful tool in the hands of the legislators, but they should remember that, 'political economy *assumes* a certain condition of things, and then points out the principles which must govern the legislation therein'. But when the conditions changed, 'you must adopt new principles'.[143]

Probably the most influential argument in favour of state intervention for protecting the indebted villager from the money lender was provided by Judge Sir Raymond West of the Bombay High Court. He too agreed that interference in economic affairs was bad, but to stop all interference suddenly would be to make the condition worse, not better. 'Opium is a pernicious drug,' he said, 'yet its unreserved withdrawal may cause death.' Society was much more complex than economists allowed for. To think of the economic basis of society as a 'mere conflict of antagonistic interests' would be doing violence to the 'whole field in view'. This had actually been done by economists who had affirmed that maximum welfare would be attained by the uninterrupted action of each individual's self-interest. Hence Sir Raymond's warning: 'If through our blind faith in chance we abandon the existing organisation to influence that we see must be destructive, and let go our hold on the ordering of events, we may probably find by and bye that they have passed altogether beyond our control.'[144] Apart from these general considerations for the reintroduction of usury laws, it was held that the removal of the laws in 1855 had the effect of increasing abnormally the rate of interest, and this 'practically precluded all profitable investment – except to the money-lender – and struck at the root of all legitimate trade'.[145]

In spite of all the favourable comment on the usury laws, official opinion was still against it. The idea that the state had a duty to mitigate the sufferings of the people was no doubt accepted, not only in the area of rural indebtedness, but also in other areas such as famine and epidemics, but usury laws were not considered to be the proper remedies. In the Punjab, when the

---

[143] Issue dated 21 March 1872, p. 102. The remedy for rural indebtedness could be found only if the rulers 'remember that India is not England, and that Adam Smith's philosophy may be utterly inapplicable to a native community'. *Ibid.*, p. 103.

[144] 'The Land and the Law in India' included in *Selection from Papers on Indebtedness and Land Transfer* (Calcutta, 1895), pp. 18–19.

[145] Memorandum by 'Mephistopheles' to the Famine Commission, *Home Misc.* India Office Records, no. 796, p. 890.

district officers were asked about the desirability of the fixation of a maximum rate of interest, a majority accepted, but 'some of the most thoughtful reports, however, are against any alteration in the existing law'.[146] Writing in 1873, J. Monteath pointed out that persons with Indian experience were quick to attack political economy. If properly understood, experience in India was in fact the best means of correcting false theories. Indian experience had proved that any blanket ban on usury would only cripple the nation's trade and furthermore be very difficult to implement.[147] Even the Deccan Riots Commission felt that the usury law had the 'natural effect of placing the debtor in a worse position by the introduction of a practice which has sur-vived its cause, by which the debtor is compelled to co-operate in a fiction to evade the law.'[148]

The Deccan Agriculturists Relief Act, which was passed in 1879, was in the nature of a compromise. The need to protect the peasants was counterbalanced by the conviction of the unsuitability of usury laws. In their search for a method to stabilise the relationship between an improvident borrower and a conscience-less money lender, the authorities even toyed with the idea of introducing the French system of conciliation between debtors and creditors for small sums through the *juges de paix*, which dispensed with written pleadings and similar legal procedure.[149] This suggestion came to nothing.[150] The Act preferred the provision of proper legal instruments for checking oppression where it existed[151] to interference with the money market itself, the uninterrupted functions of which were considered a desideratum for the successful functioning of a commercialising economy.[152] It softened the rigorous application of the law of contract by authorising civil servants to examine the claims brought before them for fraud.[153] It also provided an

---

[146] Substance of Replies to Justice Melville's Memorandum of 11 June 1872, *Papers Relating to Act XVII of 1879* (National Archives of India).

[147] *Indian Economist*, 31 October 1873, p. 58.

[148] *Report of the Committee on the Riots in Poona and Ahmadnagar*, pp. 32–33, 69, 70, et. seq.

[149] Secretary of State to Government of Bombay (Legislative) no. 4, 26 December 1878. *Despatches to Bombay*, India Office Records, L/PJ/3/1498, pp. 268–9.

[150] Minute by T. C. Hope, 26 March 1879. *Papers of Act XVII of 1879* (National Archives of India).

[151] The Law member of the Viceroy's Council thought that the Act would actually complicate and mutilate the simple procedure but the Viceroy overruled him declaring that he approved the Bill 'not upon legal grounds ... but in reference to the social and political considerations'. Note by Whitley Stokes and Minute by Viceroy, 30 June 1879. *Papers Relating to Act XVII of 1879* (National Archives of India).

[152] In spite of this, the Act was criticised for example by *The Indian Spectator* which said, 'It has taken no cognizance of sound economic principles nor of the rules of human conduct which are everywhere the same, whether in semi-civilized Asia or advanced Europe.' Issue dated 8 October 1882.

[153] The Chief Justice of Punjab held in 1873 issued a circular to all Courts asking them to

insolvency clause that had been urged even as early as 1856.[154] The Act required mortgages to be properly registered. Instead of specifying a maximum rate of interest, it gave power to the judicial officers to determine the fair rate of interest depending upon the merits of each individual case. Still the problem of land transfer to the money lenders remained unsolved. If the peasant borrower could not repay the loan, he had to surrender his security which in most cases was land. This was not so in pre-British times, because the land did not represent transferable property and in any case, as pointed out by a civil servant, the feelings of the people 'in this matter is in accordance with the old Jewish law, which regarded the permanent alienation of land as impossible'.[155] The British innovations not only turned land into property, but also made it transferable.

The extensive land transfers had the effect of leaving the land cultivated by disgruntled and disheartened tenants who had formerly been owners. The new landlords preferred to rackrent the land rather than invest capital on it. The peasants, we are told, were reluctant even to use the water from the irrigation projects as the rewards would not reach them.[156]

This problem of land alienation was extensively debated in the late 1850s, and one of the suggestions – endorsed by the Secretary of State, Lord Stanley himself – that was seriously entertained was the introduction of a system of entails. This would have made the sale of land to pay off debts virtually impossible. Members of Indian administration were ranged on both sides, and those who opposed the proposal did so on both abstract theoretical grounds as well as on concrete practical considerations. There were some like H. B. Harrington who argued that because of the peculiar Indian habits, customs and institutions, the proposal to prevent land alienation through restrictive legislation would not succeed.[157] Others who argued against the proposal did so on more positive grounds. Many judicial and revenue officers felt that the situation was not yet serious enough to warrant such a heroic remedy. Indeed the direction in which the economic organisation was evolving seemed to them to be the appropriate one. If a system of entails were introduced, it would only retard the growth of Indian economy. For example J. P. Grant, Lieutenant Governor of Bengal, firmly argued against restrictions on what he called 'the natural, gradual and healthy movements of the social system

---

Footnote 153 continued

    see behind all claims to examine whether the decreed interest was exorbitant. *The Calcutta Gazette*, 25 April 1873.

[154] An Indian Civil Servant, *Usurers and Ryots: Being an Answer to the Question, Why does not India Produce more Cotton*, p. 13.

[155] Charles Raikes, *Notes on North West Provinces* (London, 1852), pp. 121–2.

[156] Ravenscroft to Hume, 6 April 1877, *op. cit.*

[157] Minute of 22 October 1858, *India Judicial Proceedings*, 16 September 1862, India Office Records, no. Range, vol. 66, pp. 1067–8.

whereby new men rise'. Any attempt to erect 'an impassable barrier between land and capital' seemed to him indefensible.[158] J. H. Batten, Commissioner of the Rohilcund division, looked to the future prospects of Indian economic development, and suggested that if a system of entails were introduced in India it would not only be 'theoretically objectionable' but would also exhibit a curious inconsistency in British policy. As he said:

they involve the anomaly of declaring that what is the highest wisdom in Ireland (a country in many respects resembling India in regard to attachment to soil, hereditary prejudice & c) is the highest folly in India. My respected lecturer, Professor Longfield, the judge of the encumbered estates court in Ireland, would, I fancy, hardly forgive me, if I were to lay down the proposition, that the greatest benefits have accrued in that country from getting rid of an impoverished and embarrassed squirearchy, and by substituting in their place capitalists in the shape of Dublin lawyers and Belfast merchants; but that in British India the great and healing measure is to proclaim the Hindoo Mitakshara; to create entails in the families of broken-down debtors, whose merits consist solely in their 'blue blood', and to expel from the soil all wealthy parvenus infected with the stain of trade.[159]

The predominant view was that it would be a retrograde legislative step to prevent the sale of land, because by preventing the infusion of capital in land it would result in India being permanently poverty-stricken. It was agreed that the improvident villagers all too readily alienated their land; but a blanket prevention of land sales was not the appropriate remedy as that derived from a wrong approach to the problem. John Strachey, the Collector of Moradabad, thought that

much of the difficulty which is found in dealing with such questions as this, arises from the notions with which English people are imbued on the subject of the interference of Government ... Hardly a thought has been given to the improvement of the condition of the agricultural community by other than legislative or administrative measures.[160]

If it was the desire to help the agriculturists, this should be done through positive measures. In India, the state being the landlord should make available the necessary physical inputs such as credit and irrigation to raise productivity. Prevention of land sales would not help the Indian peasants, and if anything it would only hurt their long term interests because economic development depended on the creation of saleable private property and the incentives available for capital formation.

---

[158] Minute of 6 June 1860, *Ibid.*, p. 1091. See also R. N. Cust, *Manual for the Guidance of Revenue Officers in the Punjab* (Lahore, 1866), p. 31. See also James Lean's (Judge of Mirzapore) Minute 28 April 1859, *Ibid.*, p. 1175. Lean's ideas were shared by many other judges of North Western Provinces like T. C. Plowden, A. Ross and I. B. Pearson.

[159] Letter from J. H. Batten to the Board of Revenue, 26 May 1859, *Ibid.*, p. 1148.

[160] Letter from John Strachey, 19 May 1859, *Ibid.*, p. 1162.

These arguments were accepted even by those who forcefully championed the need to curtail the wholesale alienation of land to the money lenders that were taking place. In their opinion, India was different and British political economy was inapplicable to Indian socioeconomic conditions. Sir William Muir, member of the North Western Provinces Board of Revenue, bluntly said: 'I believe a measure of this kind, however indefensible it may appear according to our European notions of Political Economy, would be in close accordance with the habits and customs of the country'.[161] Other members of the North Western Provinces administration like E. A. Reade, C. B. Thornhill, A. H. Cocks and Charles Raikes supported this view, and thought that only the restriction of the sale of land would prevent the landholder from borrowing beyond his capacity to repay.[162] There were a few civil servants like J. H. Batten who supported a system of entails for practical political reasons, in spite of being fully aware of its deleterious economic consequences. As Batten said, 'my political economy must bend before the force of local natural circumstances, and I must give a vote in favour of *some* remedy'.[163]

The controversy ended with no action being taken to restrict sale of land. While other considerations, such as the feeling that the old proprietors of land were not particularly helpful to the British rule in India during the events of 1857, played a significant part, the final decision owed not a little to the theoretical objections proffered by many officials against legislative prevention of land sales.

These theoretical objections were utilised once again in the 1870s, when the possibilities of the restriction of land alienation were being explored. Opponents of the measure once more contended that any attempt to prevent land transfers would be a violation of the principles of free trade, and would be fraught with serious consequences such as the depreciation in the value of land as security resulting in higher rates of interest, and destroying the habit of self reliance and industry.[164] Sir Evelyn Baring, the finance member in the Viceroy's Council thought that, not only were the problems faced by the peasants natural, but also that the government would be unable to mitigate the sufferings by its interference.[165]

This time there were numerous civil servants, however, who felt that state

[161] Minute of 20 April 1859, *Ibid.*, p. 1136.

[162] *Ibid.*, pp. 1126 *et seq.* See also Charles Raikes, *Notes on the Revolt in the North Western Provinces of India* (London, 1858), p. 173.

[163] *op. cit.*, p. 1148.

[164] Proceedings of the Home Department, Punjab, no. 4609, Minute dated 23 December 1874, *Papers Regarding Act XVII of 1879* (National Archives of India). See also letter to the Under-Secretary of the Punjab Government, 28 June 1872, *Ibid.*

[165] Minute dated 1 January 1881, *Legislative Department Proceedings*, Government of India, December 1881, K.W.(A) no. 49–90 (National Archives of India).

intervention was not only necessary but also that it would work. It was thanks to the persistence of district officers with such views as those of Thorburn, Denzil Ibbetson, Crosthwaite, and of judges like Sir Raymond West and Melville that a public opinion in favour of intervention by a paternal government was created. As has already been pointed out, the basic philosophy of the paternal government was that India was inhabited by a simple-minded population that could not take care of itself. For the maintenance of the Raj, it was necessary for the government to look after the interests of the people. All of these favoured measures to stop the land transfers. Thorburn suggested, for instance, that it be made illegal for money lenders 'to acquire any interest in arable or pasture land'[166] and that land revenue assessment for lands already taken over by money lenders and other zemindars from the peasants be doubled.[167] Judge West in his *Land and Law in India* justified such a course of action with his concept of 'protective ownership of the state in land'. His argument was that whereas unrestricted transferability of lands had worked well in Britain, it would not work in the same manner in India. The state should claim part ownership of the land for the sake of protecting the peasants from hurting themselves.

This view had its success only in the 1890s,[168] because of the resistance provided until then by the adherents of *laissez-faire* and *status quo* in the various decision-making organs. Even after the 1890s, when attempts were seriously made to introduce legislation to prevent land transfers, justification came from the apprehended political dangers, and not from the abandonment of Classical political economy.[169]

The improved legal procedure and the attempts to prevent land transfers were all negative measures. The problems of rural indebtedness, and the attendant question of land alienation arose out of a fundamental necessity of the village cultivator, viz. credit. That the money lenders were performing an essential service to agricultural operations was accepted by most. The relationship of the money lender and the peasant was likened by Sir William Wedderburn to that of capital and labour.[170] The Famine Commission also

---

[166] *Musalmans and Money-lenders*, p. 102.

[167] *Punjab-Revenue & Agriculture Proceedings*, 27–9 June 1899, India Office Records, Vol. 5608. I owe this reference to Dr N. G. Barrier.

[168] Many provinces initiated moves to prevent alienation of land. See *Selections from Papers on Indebtedness and Land Transfer*. The proposals made by the Central Provinces were entirely based on the work of Justice West. See the letter from the Government of Central Provinces to Government of India, 11 November 1889, p. 74.

[169] See N. G. Barrier, *The Punjab Alienation of Land Bill of 1900*, pp. 96 *et seq*. The Viceroy of India, Lord Lansdowne said in 1894 that interference was 'no doubt wrong from the purely economical point of view, but we have to deal with a serious political danger and I see no way out of it but this'. Quoted on p. 34.

[170] *A Permanent Settlement for the Dekkhan*, p. 6.

pointed out that the villager in India required the money lender, and any 'violent interference with the legitimate business of the rural banker would be disastrous, as it would result in the calling in of all agricultural loans and the transfer of this capital to some other field of investment.'[171] This was why, in spite of political considerations, no extreme measures were taken to wipe out the money lenders altogether.

One positive measure suggested to solve the problem of rural indebtedness was the formation of agricultural banks to bring down the rates of interest. If the government was concerned about the agriculturist with regard to credit, 'it should be thoroughly and in absolute supercession of the village usurer'.[172] It was claimed that it was well within the means of the government to provide credit facilities because of the enormous idle cash balances that could be put to good use. This would also not violate unduly the principle of non-inter-ference. First, the government was the landlord and no theory could be against a landlord giving advances to his tenants.[173] Secondly, in the words of another advocate of agricultural banks:

It is useless at this time of day to urge that private enterprise will be interfered with, for that argument was blown to the winds when Government found itself obliged to take up the management of transit companies, telegraphs, railways, steamboats, and post office and savings banks. As to the displacement of capital, what we have to consider is the greatest happiness of the greatest number, and not, as in this case, the ill-gotten gains of the grasping few.[174]

And thirdly, there were the examples of the successful French *Crédit Foncier* and other rural credit institutions of Continental Europe. John Strachey said as early as 1859 that 'the principles on which the *crédit foncier* is founded, however foreign they may be to English ideas, are quite applicable'[175] to Indian conditions. The experiments of Raiffeisen and Schulze-Delitzsch in launching successful agricultural credit institutions in Europe fired the imagination of Frederick Nicholson, Edward Maclagan, H. Dupernex and other Indian civil servants to seek suitable methods to provide credit, and stimulated them to prepare plans for organising similar institutions for India. Very little was done, however, and such progress as took place in this direction only occurred in the twentieth century.

Provision of credit was part of the larger problem of stimulating economic development. Many administrators realised that, even behind the necessity of

---

[171] *Report of the Famine Commission* (1880) Part II, Section IV, Chapter III, p. 130, *loc. cit.*

[172] A. P. Webb, *op. cit.*, p. 2.

[173] A. Harington in the *Calcutta Review*, vol. LXXVI, no. CLI, 1883, pp. 165 *et seq.*

[174] Patrick Carnegy, *Notes on the Indebtedness of the Agricultural Classes of India* (London, 1874), p. 13.

[175] See India Judicial Proceedings, 16 September 1862, India Office Records, no. Range: 206, vol. 66, p. 1163.

cheap credit, the fundamental cause of rural debt was poverty. If poverty could be eliminated, the resulting prosperity with its concomitant economic organisation would also eliminate the frictions in the economic relations between various classes of society.

CONCLUSION

The two issues discussed in this chapter, regulation of interest and tenant-protection, illustrate how powerful definite economic solutions could be in actual policy situations. In both these policy measures the problem was simple: should the government interfere between individuals who enter into voluntary economic relationships? Classical political economy gave a simple and unequivocal 'No' for an answer because any interference on the part of the government in the working of labour and money markets would result in misallocation of resources with undesirable consequences for future economic progress. This clear mandate which became a dogma in the minds of the members of the Indian administration especially in the first half of the nineteenth century, was responsible for this negative policy prescription being accepted with great tenacity. Indeed even when powerful pragmatic and humanitarian reasons were adduced for its removal, the policy-ideal was not discarded although minor changes were introduced in its implementation.

5

ECONOMIC IDEAS AND LAND TAXATION

The true defence of our system of taxation in India is, not that it is preferable to
any other, when judged according to the generally received principles of political
economy, nor even that it has been continued because we found it established,
but because we consider it to be utterly impracticable to raise the same sum in a
less exceptionable way.

The Court of Directors of the
Honourable East India Company

THE BEGINNINGS OF A LAND POLICY

For its sustenance, the British Raj depended to a large extent on the land, for
it was the resources that were secured from the agricultural sector that helped
the government to organise the administration, embark on conquests,
maintain law and order and make British India the brightest jewel of the
Empire.

Such diversion of resources was not easy. On the one hand, funds were
needed for the purpose of ruling a vast country like India; and, on the other,
it was by no means a light task to build a system of taxation that would be
satisfactory in all respects. To be operative the system should not conflict too
much with interests that were politically dangerous or potentially trouble-
some. Nor should it destroy the mainsprings of agricultural enterprise. At the
same time, sufficient resources had to be secured with little disturbance.
Throughout its history, the policy makers of the British government in India
found it convenient, therefore, to resort to the 'Principles of Political
Economy' for guidance to solve the problems that arose in devising systems of
land taxation. How they used these principles depended upon the times,
places and individuals concerned.

After an initial period of experiment and uncertainty, the taxation of land
was regulated by Lord Cornwallis on what is known as the permanent settlement. The landholders who were holding the land as hereditary tax officials
were given absolute property rights over these lands. The important clause of
this settlement was that the amount of tax such landholders had to pay was
fixed for ever. Cornwallis's justification for this was that a 'much more
advantageous tenure' would be needed to 'incite the inhabitants of this

country to make those exertions which can alone effect any substantial improvement'.[1] This had been the opinion of Sir Philip Francis who, as a councillor of the Governor General, advocated a permanent settlement of taxation in 1776.[2] People like Francis and Cornwallis could not conceive of a society where all land was owned by the sovereign. In that age of enlightenment, private property was considered a necessity for material progress.[3] Hence it seemed appropriate to Francis and Cornwallis to convert the existing hereditary tax-farmers who had certain proprietary rights into a full-fledged propertied class.

In the decade before the conclusion of the permanent settlement the Bengal tax system was a conglomeration of numerous taxes without any definite pattern because the zemindars not only collected land taxes but also levied many other petty taxes. Hence an important purpose of the permanent settlement with the zemindars was to set the tax system right. Thomas Law of the civil service, a pre-Cornwallis supporter of permanent settlement, cited Turgot's policy which aimed at removing the multiplicity of indirect taxes and substituting one direct tax. Law advocated the abolition of many petty duties that were being levied in Bengal at that time, and to support this policy, Law cited the French Physiocrat, Turgot.[1] The French Physiocratic school, of which Turgot was a distinguished member, considered agriculture as the sole source of wealth because that alone yields a *produit net*. As all taxes ultimately fall on this *produit net*, it was thought better to tax it directly. Hence, according to the Physiocrats, an efficient, economical and just tax system should consist of a single direct tax on agricultural rent. The tax was expected to diffuse itself ultimately throughout the community by means of appropriate increases in the price of raw materials.[5] About a third of the net product was suggested as the most desirable rate.

It is, however, interesting and somewhat surprising to see Francis citing authorities like Mirabeau and Montesquieu along with Sir James Steuart and Adam Smith, to justify an unalterable tax for the Bengal landholders.[6] What Mirabeau actually suggested was the fixing of the 'proportion' of the net product or rent to be taken by the state. The Physiocrats considered the

---

[1] Minute dated 18 September 1789, W. K. Firminger (ed.), *Fifth Report*, vol. II, p. 512.

[2] See his Minutes of 22 January 1776 and 5 November 1776. *Original Minutes of the Governor General and Council of Fort William on the Settlement and Collection of the Revenue of Bengal* (London, 1782), pp. 49, 126 *et seq.*

[3] See Montesquieu, *The Spirit of the Laws* (London, 1878, Nugent Translation), vol. I, pp. 65, 237. For a citation from this work see Francis to Lord North, *Original Minutes*, p. 8. See also *Wealth of Nations*, pp. 776, 853.

[4] See Law's Minute, 28 May 1790, Thomas Law, *A Sketch of Some Late Arrangements and a View of the Rising Resources in Bengal* (London, 1792) p. 187.

[5] See Luigi Einaudi, 'The Physiocratic Theory of Taxation', in *Economic Essays in Honour of Gustav Cassel* (London, 1933), p. 130.

[6] *Original Minutes*, pp. 123, 126, 127.

'proportion' to be very important and they did not raise serious objections to raising the total revenue derived from the agricultural sector. Although certain other sources of governmental income are also mentioned in the Physiocratic writings,[7] they preferred the bulk of the revenue to come from agriculture. Their ideal was to cause as little inconvenience as possible to the smooth flow of the economic system. If the *produit net* were properly taxed, it would cause no burden to the community. The Physiocrats believed 'certainty' as a necessary criterion for taxation; but it was 'certainty' of the proportion and not of the absolute amount. Even the other great influential writer, Montesquieu, who did not subscribe to many of their views. agreed with them on this point.[8]

This position of the Physiocrats was not accepted by Adam Smith. He maintained that a tax based on 'proportion' of the *produit net* would violate the tax canon of 'certainty', besides being also expensive to administer. Basically his objection to this sort of tax was that it would prove a great discouragement to land improvement. He favoured a fixed tax in absolute terms on agricultural estates, although he was not against a variable tax if sufficient precautions could be taken to make it work.[9]

It would be tempting to conclude that although Francis cited Physiocrats, the main doctrinal influence was that of Adam Smith, and thus reject the thesis that Francis derived theoretical support from the writings of the Physiocrats.[10] But there are problems in such an interpretation. For one thing, Francis' Minute is dated 5 November 1776, and the *Wealth of Nations* was published early in that year. Francis might have received the idea from Sir James Steuart's *An Inquiry into the Principles of Political Oeconomy* published about a decade earlier. Steuart, like Adam Smith, thought that a tax proportioned to rent was more equitable. But anticipating Smith, he did not consider it important. He advocated that the rent of lands should be valued once, and taxes fixed; and once fixed, Steuart wanted the tax rates to be perpetual.[11] He was not also against the levy of indirect taxes, as the Physiocrats were; like Adam Smith, he also believed in dispersing the tax

---

[7] The Physiocratic manual on public finances, Mirabeau's *Theorie de L'impot* (1761) mentions revenue from the *domaine* mint, post office, salt tax and tax on tobacco as desirable.

[8] *The Spirit of Laws*, vol. I, p. 227.

[9] *Wealth of Nations*, p. 784.

[10] B. Natarajan has argued that Smith's influence on Francis' proposals was complete. See 'Economic Ideas behind the Permanent Settlement' *Indian Journal of Economics*, January 1942. On the other hand, Firminger says, 'Francis views . . . were probably derived from French sources – Quesnay, Mirabeau, Turgot etc.' Introduction to *Fifth Report*, vol. I p. xviii. Ranajit Guha goes further and in an amply documented and highly stimulating study comes to the same conclusion more emphatically. *A Theory of Property* (Paris, 1963), pp. 96 *et seq.*

[11] *An Inquiry into the Principles of Political Oeconomy* (London, 1766), vol. II, p. 578.

burden and found indirect taxes useful as supplementary sources of income for the public exchequer. Although Francis had said, 'with respect to the revenue, which government should raise from the manufacture of salt and opium, I declare my opinion that it ought to be by way of duty only',[12] his general attitude towards taxation was, 'the fund of this Country is land. Nothing else ought to be taxed. There ought to be no custom-house.'[13]

Nevertheless it seems legitimate to conclude that Francis had in the main kept to the English tradition as exemplified in the writings of Steuart, Smith and Justice Blackstone, although he thought it fit to cite lengthy passages from the French economists as well. When we compare the general approach towards taxation and public expenditure of the Physiocrats and that of Adam Smith with those of Francis and Cornwallis, it seems that Francis and definitely Cornwallis were firmly within the English tradition. Physiocrats thought that state expenditure was not only not unproductive, but also was necessary.[14] In taxation also, while the Physiocrats emphasised taxing the *produit net*, they were not against taxation as such. Indeed many Physiocrats recognised the necessity of periodical reassessments of land tax. On the whole, they had what Warren Samuels calls a 'pervasive solicitude for what may be called the *constructive* facet of taxation and public expenditure'.[15]

On the other hand, Smithian economics underlined the essential un-productiveness of state expenditure and the need to restrict the size of the public sector. Francis leaves no one in doubt as to his attitude:

The whole demand upon the country, to commence from April 1777, should be founded on an estimate of the permanent services, which the Government must indispensably provide for; with an allowance of a reasonable reserve for con-tingencies ... I know not for what just or useful purpose any Government can demand more from its subjects; for unless expenses are collected for the express purpose of absorbing the surplus, it must lie dead in the treasury, or be embezzled.'[16]

After this estimate and the necessary taxation rates were once determined, they should never be altered. Cornwallis had similar ideas and even on the question of indirect taxation, unlike Francis, he followed his English forerunners.[17]

---

[12] *Original Minutes*, p. 68.

[13] *Ibid.*, p. 196.

[14] See for instance the view of Baudeau cited in Gide and Rist, *A History of Economic Doctrines* (London, 1946), p. 56n.

[15] W. Samuels, 'The Physiocratic Theory of Property and State', *Quarterly Journal of Economics*, February 1961, vol. LXXV, no. 1, p. 106. See also J. Johnson 'The Role of Spending in Physiocratic Theory', *Q.J.E.* Nov., 1966, vol. 80, no. 4, pp. 616–33.

[16] Minute dated 22 January 1776, *Original Minutes*, pp. 49, *et seq.*

[17] Ross (Ed.), *Correspondence of Charles I Marquis of Cornwallis* (London, 1859), vol. II, p. 472. Minute dated 10 February 1790.

Sir Philip Francis and, to a lesser extent Lord Cornwallis, were men of many parts, and they absorbed ideas and experiences throughout their life-time; hence it is not a rewarding exercise to attach any one particular influence on them absolutely. The protagonists of particular policies attached great importance to these authors. It does not, however, follow that they agreed with them in full. Francis and others used suggestive sentences and dropped the names of economists and thinkers like Montesquieu and Mirabeau to make their policies look respectable. Generally speaking, the Physiocrats as well as Classical economists were against arbitrariness in land taxation. This concern for a rational fiscal system was the main element in the economic policies of Francis and Cornwallis. They were not alone in this respect, as another early English administrator in India, Jonathan Duncan, when he became the resident and superintendent of Banaras in 1778, introduced policies based on a similar concern for a rational tax structure.[18] It is not surprising that the English administrators in India who had to bring order into disorganised agrarian systems, were utilising a mixture of Physiocratic and Classical conceptions of land taxation and free trade. Regularity of revenue (by means of a single consolidated land tax) and a smoothly running economy (by the avoidance of petty indirect taxes) were the desiderata of political supremacy.

While detailing the doctrinal influences on Francis, Law and Cornwallis, it would be proper to mention other practical considerations as well. Both the supporters and opponents of the permanent zemindari settlement agreed that 'the soil of right belongs to the natives'. And the government presided over by the East India Company by itself had no such right. The question really boiled down to who the 'natives' were who owned the soil. They were convinced that the hereditary tax collectors were indeed the landlords who could be compared to the English 'lord of the manor'. Even if it were not so, and the land belonged to the actual cultivators, the English government in India at that time did not have the means to ascertain those rights. It might even be dangerous to let loose among the population 'strangers' ignorant of the 'arts of cultivation in this soil and climate' to record the rights. On the other hand the cultivators were 'attached by custom, religion and prejudice to the authority of their ancient Masters'. So, instead of a few Europeans 'thinly scattered over the face of the country', the task should be left to the 'native masters'.[19] In this alliance of ideas and expediency in the formation of

---

[18] See V. A. Narain, *Jonathan Duncan of Varanasi* (Calcutta, 1959), p. 145.

[19] See Francis' Minute in the Revenue Department, 12 May 1775, (Francis Mss at India Office Library). The Settlement effected by Cornwallis with the zemindars used extremely rough and ready method to compute the tax payable. The principle used was that of 10/11ths of the then rent-roll.

policy, it would indeed be unjust to assign to either of the two the prime importance.[20]

NEW DIRECTIONS IN LAND REVENUE POLICY

After the governor-generalship of Lord Cornwallis, the settlement with zemindars on a permanent basis was espoused by his successor, Lord Wellesley, who declared that he was endeavouring to model 'this great empire' according to the example of Bengal.[21] In this he was encouraged by Henry Dundas, the President of the Board of Control until 1804. Lord Minto, who succeeded Lord Wellesley, and his Council – especially Henry Colebrooke – were great believers in large estates, property rights, fixed tenures and fixed taxation; and consequently they tried to introduce permanent settlement in the newly acquired regions of northern India.[22] This happened too in the Madras Presidency in the first two decades of the nineteenth century. A permanent settlement based on the Bengal principles was concluded in the Northern Circars (Coastal Andhra) in 1798. Members of the Madras Board of Revenue at that time such as Petrie, Garrow and Hodgson were all eager supporters of the Cornwallis system, and were anxious to push through reforms on those lines in Madras too.[23]

The Madras civilians, like their Bengal counterparts, took notice of contemporary economic and political thought and in their official writings cited passages from the works of the leading thinkers. For example, Adam Smith and William Paley were quoted to show that only self-interest and an exclusive right to one's own produce could motivate progress, and that

[20] H. R. C. Wright argues that the settlement with the zemindars had little to do with theory. Practical circumstances left Cornwallis no alternative. 'Some Aspects of the Permanent Settlement in Bengal' *Economic History Review*, II Series, vol. VII, December 1954, p. 213. A contemporary pamphleteer had suggested in 1792 that the ideal tax system was the one based on the ability to pay principle as enunciated by Adam Smith. However to assess the ability to pay would involve detailed investigation into the 'net receipts of the ryots'. As the existing administrative machinery was inadequate to properly enforce the ability to pay principle, the next best thing would be to conclude a permanent settlement with the zemindars. See John Stonhouse, *Thoughts on the Expediency of Settling & C.* (London, 1792), pp. 17–20.

[21] Wellesley to Dundas, 13 November 1800, Add. Mss 37,275, pp. 234–5 (Wellesley Mss at the British Museum). See also Wellesley to Dundas, 5 March 1800 in Martin (Ed.), *Despatches of Wellesley*, vol. II, p. 231.

[22] See Minutes of Colebrooke and Lumsden in *Selections of Papers from the Records at East India House* (London, 1820), vol. I, pp. 44–61. See also Imtiaj Husain, *Land Revenue Policy in North India* (Calcutta, 1967), pp. 69–73.

[23] The Madras Board of Revenue had impressed Dundas. See his letters to Wellesley Add. Mss 37,275, pp. 191–193, *loc. cit.* For the views of the Board, see *Report of Special Commissioners of Jaghire* dated 9 April 1802. *Madras Revenue Consultations: Proceedings of Special Commissioners 1802*, India Office Records, no. Range 283, vol. 67, pp. 1027 *et seq.*

only security of tenure could give a free hand to self-interest. John Hodgson thus pointed out that Smith's views on the duties of the sovereign indicated that the state should leave the landholders free, and he found support in Archdeacon William Paley's writings. Hodgson actually wanted to create new proprietors if they were not already in existence, because they would have a deeper interest in the soil than the government revenue collectors.[24] According to him, the raising up of a 'respectable body of land-owners, will introduce that just gradation of rank, which is so essential to the existence and prosperity of every well-ordered society'. This would also have the advantage of the people being 'relieved from the constant and vexatious interference of revenue officers ... and the government, of a great part of the expense of maintaining them'. Comparing the Indian zemindar to the 'tacksman' of northern Scotland, Hodgson quoted from Samuel Johnson's *Tour of the Hebrides* to speak favourably of the 'Tacksmen' and indirectly of the zemindars.[25] Montesquieu and Adam Smith were brought in to argue state ownership of land. Petrie, Cockburn, and Webbe, the Special Commissioners, in their report to the Governor of Madras, cited Montesquieu to show that 'of all despotic governments there is none that labours more under its own weight than that wherein the prince declares himself proprietor of all the lands. Hence the neglect arises.'[26] The existence of waste lands makes it necessary to provide incentives for cultivation. They also pointed out that Adam Smith's advocacy of the sale of crown lands was 'applicable to the sale of the circar or havelly lands of India and similar advantages may in progress of time be expected in proportion as the means of acquiring private wealth'.[27] Adam Smith was cited to show that taxation ought to be certain, and Blackstone came in handy to prove that the rights of undertenants would not be unduly sacrified.[28] It must however be remembered that the Madras Board of Revenue was also conscious of the ease with which land revenue could be collected. Whether the settlement was made with the zemindars or with the village chiefs, the number of taxpayers was reduced but the amount collected per taxpayer increased. This mode of taxation thus satisfied the two important criteria of taxation, economy and certainty. The interaction of the self-interest of the cultivators

[24] Hodgson wrongly ascribes the passage he cited from Paley in his Minute to David Hume. See for Hodgson's Minute, Firminger (Ed.), *Fifth Report*, vol. III, p. 485. It is interesting to see that Thomas Law also cited the same sentence from Paley to put forward a similar idea. See his *Remarks on the Ryotwarrey and Mocurrery Systems* (London n.d.), pp. 16–17.
[25] Firminger, vol. III, p. 482.
[26] Montesquieu, *The Spirit of Laws*, vol. I, p. 65. Francis also cited this passage in his Minutes.
[27] *Report on Special Commissioners on Jaghire, op. cit.*, p. 1064. See also pp. 1031–2, 1045–6, 1063.
[28] See Firminger, vol. III, p. 470.

and that of the zemindars would also result in a just division of the tax burden among them.

The Court of Directors were not impressed by the arguments of the advocates of permanent settlement and told the various governments in India that in order to formulate and implement any policy, 'a studious attention to the general principles of political economy' alone would not be sufficient. What was wanted, according to the Court, was 'an intimate knowledge of the character and manners the habits and prejudices of the Natives'.[29] But what worried the Court most was the severe financial stringency that the Company's Indian governments were experiencing in the first two decades in India.[30] Hence they were reluctant to limit the sources of revenue. Then there were the unfulfilled promises of the permanent settlement. In some areas, revenue was regularly collected but in most areas — including those in Bengal and Madras — the expectations did not materialise. It even resulted at first in the destruction of the old hereditary aristocracy. As the population was sparse in the 1790s, there was a great demand for tenants.[31] There was also no legal way by which the landlords could collect the rent from their tenants. Thus many zemindars found it difficult to pay their taxes regularly. When they failed to pay the taxes, the lands were taken from them and auctioned off. Most of the lands were acquired by the *nouveau riche* of Calcutta, who ruled their possessions through unscrupulous agents. Poverty was the invariable result of such rackrenting and mismanagement.[32]

[29] Court of Directors to Governor-General (Revenue) 15 January 1812, *Revenue Letters to Bengal*, India Office Records, vol. II, p. 53. Warren Hastings had made similar remarks when Francis cited economists to prove his point. Hastings said, 'The opinions of Montesquieu, Sir James Stewart and Doctor Smith, which are produced to show that an unequal assessment is attended with few or no inconveniences, may be just as to those countries, where the land-tax bears but a small proportion to the amount of the produce; and any attempt to alter the proportions of a land-tax, which have been established by ancient custom, might, as they suppose, give rise to those discontents which, amongst a high spirited people, every innovation is apt to excite; but the case is very different in Bengal.' *Original Minutes*, p. 143.

[30] See A. Tripathi, *Trade and Finance in Bengal Presidency*, Chapter III.

[31] See W. W. Hunter, *Bengal Mss Records* (London, 1894), vol. I, pp. 51, 62. According to J. C. Sinha about one half of the cultivable land was waste covered by jungles. *Economic Annals of Bengal* (London, 1927), p. 273.

[32] J. C. Sinha tells us that one third to one half of the old landed property changed hands as a result of public sales. *Ibid.*, p. 272. In an unpublished letter to the editor of the *Edinburgh Review*, Francis lamented the failure of the permanent settlement and declared 'I never meant that *my* plan should have been executed in this manner.' Eur.E 19, item 58, Francis Mss at India Office Library. The same tendency for the hereditary zemindars to sell out to new zemindars was witnessed in the permanently settled areas in Madras. See J. C. Morris (Acting Secretary of the Board of Revenue) to the Chief Secretary of the Government of India, 8 March 1832 (Bentinck Papers, Nottingham University Library).

The zemindari settlement and the several variants of it were not without their critics in India. Many civil servants had felt that additional investigation would be essential before coming to any permanent agreement. Cox and Tucker, two civilians who had been appointed to investigate the possibility of introducing a permanent settlement in the Ceded and Conquered Provinces of the Bengal Presidency, reported against the immediate introduction of permanent settlement because they found extensive waste lands that could be brought to cultivation.[33] Madras civilians like Munro, Thackeray, Chaplin, Ravenshaw and Bentinck were all against permanent settlement. Charles Grant, who had influenced Cornwallis in 1793 to decide on permanent settlement, had by 1806 become disillusioned with it.[34] Now that he had become a director of the East India Company, he began to use his influence to prevent the spread of the Bengal system.[35] Samuel Davis, who had served in Bengal during the time of the permanent settlement, became a director of the East India Company and was only anxious to 'unmask the effects of Lord Cornwallis's Code of 1793.'[36] Sir Thomas Munro, who was a critic of the system, became influential at the Board of Control when his friend John Cumming became its secretary in 1807.[37] John Sullivan, the assistant Commissioner of the Board of Control, had earlier served in Madras and had been a staunch supporter of the Munro–Read system of land revenue. With Lord Buckinghamshire becoming the President of the Board of Control in April 1812, the critics of permanent settlement gained complete control over the home government.

Whereas in 1811 the Court of Directors had said, 'from the principle of that (permanent revenue) settlement we have never thought of departing', by 1815 they came to the conclusion that permanent settlement was not conducive to the promotion of economic progress.[38] Before the Court committed itself to any alternative system, its main task was to wear down the

[33] See Minutes: R. W. Cox dated 23 July 1808 and H. St G. Tucker dated 23 July 1808, *Bengal Revenue Consultations,* 5 August 1808, India Office Records, R. 55, V. 13, No. 4, 5. See also I. Husain, *op. cit.,* pp. 63–8.

[34] See Ainslie Embree, *Charles Grant and the British Rule in India* (London, 1962), pp. 114–17. pp. 101–2.

[35] See Grant's letter to Minto, 17 January 1809, cited in I. Husain, *op. cit.* pp. 101–2.

[36] See K. A. Balhatchet, 'The Authors of the Fifth Report of 1812', *Notes and Queries,* New Series vol. 4, no. 11, November 1957, quoted in p. 478.

[37] For John Cumming's views, see his Minute on the 'Extension of the Permanent Settlement' *Home Misc.* India Office Records, no. 530. Munro's return to England in 1808 and his evidence to the House of Commons Select Committee also must have played a part in creating an opinion against the Bengal system, although nothing conclusive could be asserted.

[38] Court of Directors to Governor-General (Revenue) 1 February 1811, *Revenue Letters to Bengal,* India Office Records, vol. I, L/E/3/441, p. 533, 9 June 1815, *Ibid.,* vol. II, L/E/3/442, pp. 76–94.

old 'Cornwallis school' in India which was anxious to spread permanent zemindari settlement throughout the country.

The home government was neither happy with 'permanency' nor was it prepared to settle the amount with the zemindars or similar middlemen. The three disadvantages of the permanent settlement (with or without zemindars) were:

1 inelastic government revenues from taxation;
2 the absence of a cushion against a fall in the value of money; and
3 the necessity 'for a moderate participation at distant intervals, with the proprietors in the growing improvement of the country'.[39]

None of these criticisms could be levelled against that extreme antithesis of the Cornwallis Settlement, the ryotwar settlement, introduced by Alexander Read and Thomas Munro in various parts of the Madras Presidency from 1792 onwards. Read and Munro had succeeded in making settlements with the actual cultivators on a temporary basis. The cultivator had a direct tax-paying relationship with the government, and paid a rent only on the field he cultivated and not on the available waste land. The assessment was made in each village after a careful survey of the quality of land and, the economic position of the cultivators, as well as its past performances. It must, however, be mentioned that although the original settlements in various parts of Madras Presidency were concluded for short periods, Munro himself favoured a permanent settlement with the actual individual cultivators.[40] He thought that if tax rates were moderate during ordinary seasons, peasants would accumulate wealth. This increased taxable capacity could be put to good use during periods of war, when extra taxation could be resorted to without productivity being impaired.[41] Munro's intention was to create valuable property that was transferable, so that there would be some incentive to accumulate capital. He did not, however, aim at creating property where it was absent, but rather at discovering and recognising the proprietary rights of the cultivators, for this had not been done in the various settlements concluded with zemindars and other middlemen. However, the home government was so conscious of the existence of proprietary rights that it continued to demand detailed enquiries before introducing any new system.[42]

[39] Court of Directors to Governor General (Revenue) 15 January 1812, *Ibid.* vol. II, L/E/3/442, pp. 84–6 (para. 107).

[40] Munro to Archibald Obins, 20 June 1806, cited in K. N. V. Sastri, *The Munro System of British Statesmanship* (Mysore, 1939), pp. 22–5.

[41] See Munro's evidence before the House of Commons Select Committee on 5 April 1813, *Parl. Papers*, H.C. 122, vol. VII of Session 1812–13.

[42] Court of Directors to Governor-General (Revenue) 27 February 1810, 1 February 1811, 15 January 1812. *Revenue Letters to Bengal*, India Office Records, vol. I, pp. 411, 500–2; vol. II, pp. 86–7.

The Court of Directors neither supported a permanent tax settlement nor did they give support to annual tax revision. Their support was extended to a system where settlements were to be concluded with individual peasants for a reasonable length of time, 'ten, fifteen or twenty years'.[43] The policy was to fix an assessment on the lands on the basis of a survey and valuation for a period at the end of which the assessment would be renewed with or without alterations, depending upon the changed circumstances.

This compromise (that was neither 'permanent' nor 'annual') was the result of a quest for a system that would give the benefits of a permanent settlement without its finality. In spite of the Court's half-hearted enthusiasm for political economy as the sole guide to action, the Directors produced a large quotation from the *Wealth of Nations* to support their policy of a ryotwar system with long leases. It was pointed out that Adam Smith (in the words of the Court of Directors, 'one of the most enlightened writers on Political Economy'),[44] had said that the only important objection to a variable land tax was the discouragement to improvement. Smith had suggested, however, that a promise not to alter the rates of taxation for long periods of time would meet this objection.[45] Periodic upward adjustments in the tax assessment were found necessary for another pertinent reason. Unlike a highly 'improved state of society and for a people wealthy and prosperous' where the functions of the state were minimal, India, whose people were 'poor, indolent and ignorant', required a more active government. In order to produce a 'happy change in the character and fortunes of the Nation', the state must construct and maintain 'works of great public utility'. The Court argued that, if the amount of land revenue were to be fixed *in perpetuam*, the essential task of promoting national development could not be performed.[46]

As we have already seen, the Court of Directors was concerned about the fall in the value of money, which meant a fall in the real income of the government as well.[47] The Court held that its scheme of taxation would solve the problem, and cited from the *Wealth of Nations* to show that the real income of the government would not lag behind because, if the money income of the cultivators increased due to monetary causes, the government demand could be proportionately increased during the time of reassessment.

[43] *Ibid.* Letter of 15 January 1812, vol. II, p. 73. See also the letter of 16 June 1815 where it is said, 'it cannot be expected that under a lease for so short a period as two or three years much capital will be expended on improvement'. *Ibid.*, vol. IV, p. 129.

[44] *Ibid.*, vol. II, p. 72.

[45] *Wealth of Nations*, pp. 784–5.

[46] *Revenue Letters to Bengal*, India Office Records, vol. II, pp. 75–6.

[47] This aspect was repeated many times by the Court of Directors. See for example its Revenue despatch to Governor-General, 1 February 1811, *Revenue Letters* to Bengal, India Office Records, vol. I, p. 510.

The governments of Bengal and Madras challenged the Court of Directors regarding the validity of the land revenue policy, using arguments derived from a careful study of the *Wealth of Nations*. Bengal pointed out that there was indeed no error in referring to the principles of political economy in support of policies for India because of the peculiarity of the 'character, manners, habits and prejudices' of the Indian people, as was alleged by the Court of Directors. The principles of political economy were based on a fundamental assumption concerning human motivations, and this applied to all situations.[48] The government of Bengal correctly pointed out that Adam Smith supported the variable land tax only as a hypothetical case, and the conditions laid down by Adam Smith could not easily be attained. Smith had said that if ways and means could be devised so as 'to give not only no discouragement, but, on the contrary, some encouragement to the improvement of land', then the tax would be justified. But the government said, 'we maintain that no scheme can be devised by which a variable land tax shall not operate as a discouragement to agriculture, certainly not in opposition to Dr Adam Smith, but in perfect concurrence with the sentiments delivered by him'. Here the government cited the passage in which Smith had said:

The discouragement which a variable land-tax of this kind might give to the improvement of land, seems to be the most important objection which can be made to it. The landlord would certainly be less disposed to improve, when the sovereign, who contributed nothing to the expense, was to share in the profit of the improvement.[49]

The government was perhaps justified in making use of this emphatic statement and not referring to the qualifications couched in very uncertain terms through the usage of words like 'perhaps' and 'might'. The conditions of success of a variable tax as stressed by Smith were a proper survey, just arbitrators, perfect security, freedom of trade, mobility of resources, an extensive market, easy and safe communications, and 'unbounded' freedom to export. The Government of Bengal knew that these ideal conditions did not exist in India, whereas the Court of Directors had assumed that all these ideal conditions could be provided in the course of the routine administration of the country.

The Madras Board of Revenue argued that 'the Sovereign's share of the produce in India may with great propriety be regarded in the same light as the landlord's share of the produce in England'.[50] Once this is granted, the

[48] See Governor General to Court of Directors (Revenue) 17 July 1813, *Revenue Letters from Bengal*, India Office Records, L/E/3/18, p. 283 (para. 18).

[49] *Wealth of Nations*, Book V, Chapter II, Part II, art. I.

[50] Report of the Madras Board of Revenue, 28 January 1813, *Madras Board of Revenue Proceedings*, India Office Records, 28 January 1813, Range 290, vol. 60, pp. 826–32. Reprinted in the *Selections of Papers from the Records of East India House*, vol. I, pp. 558–72.

analogy of British tax system would fail in India because the Indian land tax would not be based on the actual rent of the landlord but the rent itself. The land tax in England was assessed according to a 'valuation of the rents derivable by the landlords or owners of estates', and the land tax was a certain portion of this rent according to such valuation. But the permanent settlement in India was rated according to a 'valuation of the produce: instead of being a *portion* of the landlord's rent, it is a portion of the produce equivalent to the *whole*'. If there were no middlemen, the government would be entitled to all this rent which was 'supposed to amount generally to the value of little less than one half, and in some situations to even more than one-half of the gross produce'. If this heavy burden of taxation were imposed on the landlords it would certainly be 'inconsistent with the accumulation of agricultural stock, and consequently inconsistent with any reasonable expectation of improvement'. This means that it would also 'be incompatible with the existence of any valuable property in the land'. The Madras Board of Revenue claimed that, without the possibility of accumulating property, 'the actual condition of the landholders generally is not that of *landlords* but of tenantry, deriving a subsistence from the occupation of agriculture'. On the other hand, if a permanent settlement (i.e. fixing the ultimate government demand) were concluded, it would stimulate their industry and would enable them, 'in progress of time, to pay with ease that which is now collected from them with considerable and increasing difficulty'.

The Board could not see any fundamental difference in a settlement either for a few years or for many years. In both cases, the 'knowledge of the assessment being liable to be raised ... must influence, in some degree, the value of the property ... more and more as the period of the term approaches'. Lease in terms of a fixed period was, according to the Board, 'altogether inapplicable, inexpedient, and calculated to perpetuate the present poverty of the landholders'. Besides, the Board was not unaware of Adam Smith's lack of enthusiasm in supporting a variable land tax because of the many qualifications he thought necessary.[51] The tax objective was simple. It was a trying time for the Government of Madras from the financial point of view, and hence the rates of taxation could not be reduced. But if the permanent settlement were concluded, in future at least the proportion of resources absorbed as taxation would go down. Although under an ideal tax system the state should absorb only one third of the gross produce, the 'public exigencies will not admit of so large an immediate sacrifice' (that is from one half to one third). In lieu of a reduction of the land tax, if permanency were at least conferred, the landholders could 'acquire, in progress

---

[51] *Ibid.*, especially paragraph 39.

of time, by their industry, that which the Government does not find itself in a situation to confer as a boon'.

On another major concern of the Court of Directors, the effect of the depreciation of money on the land revenue, the governments of Bengal and Madras gave reassuring answers. The Madras Board of Revenue doubted whether money in England had depreciated, because any such depreciation would not be confined to one country and must eventually spread throughout the world.[52] On the contrary, not only had there been no repercussions in India, but prices in India were actually falling. To arrive at this conclusion, the Madras Board of Revenue employed Adam Smith's method of using the price of corn as an index.[53] In order to emphasise its view, the Board pointed out that the wage movements, which normally closely follow price movements, had not shown any change during the previous twenty-five years.

Adam Smith had hypothesised that the price level could be affected by taxation, and while this was accepted by the Madras Board of Revenue, it discounted any particular concern arising from this:

there exists not at present any ground for apprehending loss from depreciation in the value of money, and with respect to providing against the disadvantage of a rise in the price of provisions or other commodities, occasioned by taxation, we submit that, even if practicable, it would be unnecessary, since that which causes the disadvantage brings with it its own remedy.[54]

The rise in the prices of tobacco and salt was thus explained away by pointing out the existence of the monopoly taxes, and not as being due to a secular decline in the value of money.

Taxation apart, the increased money supply was supposed to affect the price level. While prices in England could be increased due to the existence of paper currency, in India only an increased flow of precious metals could lead to that effect. But there were other factors to counteract increased supply of specie. First, as the Government of Bengal pointed out, 'there exist so many drains for the diffusion of it through every part of Asia . . . that its presumable; its [i.e. oversupply of money] . . . influence cannot, but at a very remote period indeed, be felt in this country.'[55] The Madras Board of Revenue pointed out the large export of precious metals to Asia and

---

[52] *Ibid.*, para. 52.

[53] *Ibid.*, para. 56.

[54] *Ibid.*, para. 58.

[55] Governor-General to the Court of Directors (Revenue) 17 July 1813, *Selections of Papers from the Records of the East India House*, vol. I, pp. 184 *et seq.* In Bengal, however, it would appear that prices were going up rather than down. Between 1793 and 1814, the price level had increased by 75%. This estimate was based on a survey conducted in Burdwan district by W. B. Bayley. See his 'Statistical View of the Population of Burdwan' *Asiatic Researches*, vol. XII, 1818.

Europe as having caused the decline in prices. Secondly, as the country was a developing economy with a growing population, any increased supply of precious metals would only be 'proportioned to the increase of the population, and the augmented stock of all the necessaries of life ... [thus] may still stand in the same ratio to the stock of consumable commodities'.[56] Finally, it was observed that the habit among Indians of hoarding would result in enormous sums being withdrawn from circulation, which surely must have a depressing effect on prices.

If, in spite of all the arguments, there occurred the unlikely event of currency depreciation, the Madras Board of Revenue suggested that a land tax could be levied in kind. But the Board did not pursue the matter, and made the suggestion as a possible last remedy. Probably the members of the Board were also aware of Adam Smith's objections to the collection of taxes in kind.

The Court of Directors were now convinced that, if it argued further in terms of abstract ideas, it would also get back counter-arguments in the same coin. Hence, while replying to the letters from Madras and Bengal, there was hardly any mention of Adam Smith or political economy, but the whole discussion reflects the current Classical economic thinking. The Directors laid down that the local governments should first ascertain how far the introduction of permanent settlement would affect the existing rights of inhabitants and the 'future interest of the State'.[57] To ask for the alienation of all future claims on the soil was, the Court wrote to Madras, an extreme 'proposition we are not prepared to accede'.[58] Permanent settlement involved a policy that would be 'irrevocable and unalterable'. In any case it was not necessary to have a body of middlemen to induce tenants to cultivate the waste lands because 'extension of agriculture' would automatically 'proceed as population advances'.[59] The Court charged the various Indian governments with concluding that temporary settlements would be incompatible with agricultural improvement. Permanent settlement only increased the income of the landlord and not that of the cultivator. After all, the Court was composed of traders and manufacturers, a class which was at that time bitterly opposed to the landlord class on the question of corn laws. The economic argument for the abolition of corn laws was that that would

---

[56] Governor-General to the Court of Directors (Revenue) 17 July 1813, *loc. cit.*

[57] See Court of Directors to Governor-General (Revenue) 6 January 1815, *Revenue Letters to Bengal*, India Office Records, vol. III, p. 406. See also the letter dated 17 March 1815, *Ibid.*, vol. IV, pp. 17 *et seq.*

[58] Court of Directors to Government of Madras (Revenue) 12 April 1815. *Selections of Papers from the Records of the East India House*, vol. I, p. 639.

[59] *Ibid.*, vol. I, p. 639 (para. 76).

increase 'profit' at the expense of 'rent', which was considered good for the country. The permanent settlement would have done the opposite: 'The effect of a permanent settlement ... is to augment the landlord's rent, not the profit of the cultivator; and it is from neglecting to make this distinction that an inference has been drawn, in our opinion, very unwarrantably, of the incompatibility of temporary settlements with agricultural development.'[60] The Court of Directors argued that there was no reason to suppose that the rent of the landlord would be automatically spent on capacity-creating investments. On the other hand, if the cultivator was well rewarded for his labour as well as his capital, he would have 'every necessary inducement to continue his industry, although there should be no surplus to be paid in the shape of rent to the landlord',[61]

The Court realised that, in the ultimate analysis, the efficiency of a tax system depended on nothing so much as its capacity to absorb resources with the least possible repercussions.[62] Thus these discussions silenced the supporters of permanent settlement in India. Whereas in south India, Sir Thomas Munro returned in 1814 and introduced a ryotwar system without much controversy, in northern India the making and execution of the new land revenue policy involved considerable discussion and compromise between various strongly held opinions.

LAND TAXATION IN NORTH INDIA

The discussion centred on how well a tax system such as the Madras ryotwar settlement could be adopted in the Ceded and Conquered Provinces, and there was a strong body of official opinion still not entirely in agreement with the policy favoured by the home government. The ryotwar system – because of the direct relationship between the peasantry and the government – involved a certain degree of state intervention in economic matters. This was anathema to many civil servants; as an anonymous civil servant declared, the 'most prominent feature in the ryotwar system and the most pernicious, is the excessive amount of interference on the part of the Government officers which it involves'.[63] Even the Governor-General, Lord

---

[60] Court of Directors to Governor-General (Revenue) 9 June 1815, *Revenue Letters to Bengal*, India Office Records, vol. IV, pp. 64–5. *Selections of Papers from the Records of the East India House*, vol. I, p. 303.

[61] *Ibid.*

[62] Court of Directors to Government of Madras (Revenue) 12 April 1815, *Selections of Papers from the Records of the East India House*, vol. I, p. 640.

[63] *Remarks on the Ryotwar System of Land Revenue as it Exists in the Presidency of Madras* (Madras, 1853), p. 19.

Hastings, who was rather sympathetic to some form of ryotwar tenure, thought middlemen inevitable in view of the administrative apparatus necessary for an adequate execution of the ryotwar system.[64]

But not all senior civil servants of the Bengal government were committed irrevocably, either to permanence or to the necessity of middlemen. It is from among this group that the seed of the reform of land taxation ultimately came. Holt Mackenzie, who was the Secretary of the Territorial Department in 1818, has been credited with laying the foundations of the new land revenue settlements of north India.[65] He was a brilliant student of Malthus at the East India College at Haileybury, and the teacher thought very highly of the student. Malthus said of Mackenzie's examination answers: 'Had that paper been drawn up by a mature man in three days, I should have thought it a considerable effort; and it was produced by Mackenzie, without books, in three hours.'[66] Mackenzie was accused by Sir John Malcolm of relying too much on political economy and deriving conclusions from broad assumptions. However he told the Governor-General that he will 'derive great and essential aid from him, but while you benefit from his information and talents you will be slow to be guided by his opinion and judgement'.[67] Bentinck, who had had ample opportunity of knowing Mackenzie's work closely, discounted such fears and said that, along with great talents, Mackenzie had also 'a perseverance and patience in the investigation of detail'.[68] When we look at Mackenzie's ideas as embodied in his Memorandum of 1 July 1819 and the Resolution of the Government of India dated 1 August 1822, Bentinck's judgement seems to stand. The Regulation VII of 1822, which sprang from the above two documents, laid down that settling land revenue should be preceded, among other things, by detailed enquiry and fixation of assessment in terms of the net produce of the land to be settled.

It has been suggested that the new land revenue policy enshrined in Regulation VII of 1822 was the outcome of the influence of James Mill's rigid espousal of the Classical theory of rent.[69] This thesis implies that the

---

[64] Minute of 21 September 1815, *Selections of Revenue Records 1818–1820* Part I, pp. 320, 321.

[65] See for an account of Mackenzie's life and work, T. G. P. Spear, 'Holt Mackenzie: Forgotten Man of Bengal' *Bengal: Past and Present*, Jubilee Number, 1967.

[66] Cited from a personal letter from Malthus to Robert Grant, by Grant at the East India House, 20 February 1817, *Asiatic Journal*, June 1817, p. 585.

[67] Malcolm's Memorandum to Bentinck, 24 January 1828, (*Bentinck Papers*, Nottingham University Library). See also Stokes, *op. cit.*, p. 94, F. J. Shore who had been a member of the civil service remarked in 1837 that MacKenzie 'was mainly guided by theory . . . was unfortunately deficient in that local knowledge and matter of fact experience, without which the fairest theories have failed'. *Notes on Indian Affairs*, vol. I, p. 183.

[68] Bentinck to Ellenborough, 30 September 1829, (*Bentinck Papers*, Nottingham University Library).

[69] Stokes, *op. cit.* Chapter II and S. C. Gupta, *Agrarian Relations and Early British Rule in India* (Bombay, 1964).

Classical economists conceived rent theory to be useful in formulating a policy of land revenue; and that the theory alone was responsible for Holt Mackenzie's formulation of the land revenue policy for north India.

When, however, we look into the formation of this policy, we find that the thesis is suspect. It is true that, while making policy, doctrines played a part, but it does not follow that the Ricardian rent theory was the doctrinal basis, or that theories alone determined the outcome. The Classical theory of rent – certainly the Ricardian version of it – was fashioned to study the long-run dynamics of the distribution of productive shares in a growing economy. Even when we look at the practical origins of the theory of rent, it was intended to buttress the respective views on the desirability of corn laws in England held by various economists. The theory of rent as such was applied to the Indian land revenue problem by James Mill through his very crucial assumption of state landlordism. Mill had the same ideas as many civil servants about the ill effects of a zemindari system which had not enquired into the existing proprietary rights on the soil. Just as the architects of the Bengal system assumed the zemindars to have possessed the same proprietary rights as English landlords, James Mill found it convenient to accept the view that in India the state owned all land.[70] Unlike Holt Mackenzie and other civil servants, he cared little for the proprietary rights of the actual cultivators. Partly due to his utilitarian beliefs against any aristocratic order and partly due to the past performance of the Bengal zemindars, Mill wished to avoid the mistake of creating any fresh propertied class. Hence he was not prepared to grant proprietary rights even to the actual cultivators, with whom it was proposed to settle the land revenue; he was satisfied that the peasants, if given property rights, would not exert themselves but would live like parasites on the rents.[71] Nor was he prepared to settle land taxation at low levels, as was the intention of Sir Thomas Munro and William Thackeray; rather, he wished to extract every iota of the rent element for the state. Since the state was the landlord, this would not represent a new tax jeopardising capital accumulation, but was merely the collection of rent. It is thus clear that James Mill had no sympathy for any type of capitalistic farming in India. The only other leading economist of the Classical school who said anything about the Indian land taxation was McCulloch, and he too did not favour capitalistic farming for India. Nor did he approve the ryotwar system. McCulloch recognised the failure of the efforts to introduce large scale capitalistic farming in India through the

[70] 'Such a thing as a feudal system or a liege lord, never had a moment's existence in India, nor was ever supposed to have, except by a few pedantic, and half-lettered Englishmen.' James Mill in *History of British India*, vol. IV, p. 102.

[71] Stokes, *op. cit.*, p. 110.

Cornwallis system.[72] While the landlord absorbed all the rent for unproductive consumption in the zemindari system, he thought the state extracted almost all of the rent element under the ryotwar system.[73] As McCulloch was a believer in the Classical orthodoxy, he took a poor view of the utility of public expenditure. According to him, the rent element should merge with the element of profit, so that both could go into the formation of capital. To achieve this end, he suggested some form of peasant proprietorship long before John Stuart Mill.[74]

As a general policy, the Classical economists would not favour frequent variations in land tax, the assumption of state landlordism, or small scale farming. They believed in private property in land and the consequent landlord–tenant relationship based on contract. It is clear, however, that they did not blindly advise for India a policy which they considered best under the conditions they were accustomed to in Britain.

As he was the assistant examiner at the India House James Mill could have exercised considerable direct influence in the matter of the formation of policy to calculate the rent based on a survey of rights and net produce. The acceptance of the idea that rent was to be computed scientifically on the basis of deducting cost of production from gross produce implies a knowledge of the current theories of rent on the part of the policy maker. And the fact that James Mill – with his zeal to spread the utilitarian message – was at the very centre of the policy-making apparatus indicates that he had ample opportunities of influencing the policy. But it has been pointed out that when the crucial decisions leading to the Regulation VII of 1822 were made, James Mill had not much opportunity to influence the outcome directly. Imtiaj Husain has shown that James Mill had written not a single policy-making despatch that went from the Court of Directors to India regarding the land revenue settlements. Even the despatch of 1833 which he wrote and contained important instructions had been anticipated by the Bengal government before its arrival in Calcutta.[75]

In many aspects, such as the net product criterion, there was hardly anything novel. Devendra Panigrahi refers to Section 27 of Regulation XXV of 1803 which had recognised net produce as the basic criterion for calculat-

[72] McCulloch's Notes to his edition of *Wealth of Nations*, vol. IV, p. 505. Note no. XX.

[73] See McCulloch's *Principles of Political Economy*, 4th Edn. 'Most parts of India are occupied by metayers, or tenants paying from two thirds to one third of the produce to government as rent; no wonder, therefore, that the occupiers are in the most abject state of poverty', p. 515n.

[74] McCulloch's Notes on *Wealth of Nations*, vol. IV, p. 515. See also McCulloch's anonymous paper in the *Foreign Quarterly Review*, vol. IV, August 1829, p. 484.

[75] See I. Husain, *op. cit.*, pp. 151, *et seq.* 240, 253.

ing land revenue.[76] Indeed it is possible to go further. In the 1790s, when settling the Baramahal districts in Madras, Alexander Read was influenced by James Anderson's theory of rent and even tried his hand at using net produce to calculate the tax assessment. Read pointed out that the gradations of soil from the best to the worst were infinite. At the lowest level, some lands had to be left uncultivated because of the soil's incapacity to reproduce even the required seed. Other soils yielded the cost of production. Better soils yielded a profit to the farmer in addition to the cost of production. Finally there were soils that produced a surplus over and above the cost of production and profit. The proprietor had a right to claim this surplus as his rent. Translating these ideas to his task of land assessment, he concluded that a soil assessment was necessary if a settlement was to be effected for a period of years and at the same time tax-induced distortion in allocation was to be avoided.[77]

Apart from the familiarity of such aspects, there were other aspects of Mackenzie's policy that were opposed to the spirit of James Mill's advocacy, but nearer to that of the teachings of Classical economics without the utilitarian emphasis. Proprietary rights were anathema to James Mill and yet Mackenzie was all along conscious of the necessity to recognise such rights wherever they existed and foster them.

Because of its enormous scope, Regulation VII of 1822 was found difficult to administer. Many critics thought the detailed surveys led to much injustice, and even Montesquieu was cited to support this criticism.[78] The cultivators would be harassed by the tax collector in the new scheme instead of by the landlord. In either case the attempt would be made to absorb all possible surplus produce. Critics like Sir William Sleeman, H. M. Spry, T. C. Robertson, H. D. Robertson, John Briggs, and many others, felt gradations of society were found as necessary in India as they were found acceptable in Britain. Even Holt Mackenzie had said that it would be desirable to 'secure what is so much wanted, a class of persons recognised as officers of Government, yet possessing a fixed and hereditary connection in land'.[79] He had very clear reasons for this requirement:

---

[76] *Charles Metcalfe in India* (Delhi, 1968), p. 83.

[77] See Alexander Read to David Haliburton (President of the Madras Board of Revenue) June 1793, *Baramahal Records*, Part VI, p. 2, and Part XXI, p. 119. It is also interesting to note that in some of the oldest Pergunah 'dustooroolmuls', Robert Mertins Bird was able to obtain, he found, 'of one and two centuries back, that from 1/8th to 1/7th was allowed as a deduction, for ploughing, and the remainder divided in equal' parts by the government and the cultivator. 'Further Thoughts Respecting Settlements' (*Bentinck Papers*, Nottingham University Library).

[78] *An Inquiry into the Causes of the Long Continued Stationary Conditions of India* (London, 1830), p. 82. See also H. D. Robertson, *Examination of the Principles and Policy* (London, 1829), p. 47, John Briggs, *The Present Land Tax in India* (London, 1830), pp. 445–6.

[79] *Selections from the Revenue Records of North Western Provinces*, vol. II, p. 156 (Memorandum of 19 October 1826).

The moral and political advantages derived from the existence of rent-holders is a separate question; they are indeed incalculable, where, as in our country, they give a body of men to manage almost the whole internal government of the country and to secure its political and civil freedom. We may hope that the landholders of this country may gradually be brought to contribute in their degree to the same ends here.[80]

Besides, Sir William Sleeman used typically Malthusian arguments for having unproductive consumers to keep the economy going.[81]

Holt Mackenzie was conscious of the nature of rent in economic theory, but he also comprehended the blurred relationship between rent, profit and wages in the Indian context. Realising fully that the individual peasant, even if freed from the permanently settled zemindar, would be unable to accumulate capital, he decided that the best course would not be to treat all on equal terms. As he put it, 'the whole rental of the village, if settled among such a host, would have little influence in raising them from beggary'.[82] Consequently he favoured the system where engagements could be concluded with *malguzars* (tax-paying representatives of a group of cultivators) rather than with all the peasants.[83] And to this class he would give 'that *portion* which we are *about* to *create* by a limitation of the Government demand'.[84]

In the meantime, there were administrators who were seeking fresh alternatives. The Bengal system, as we saw, had no future, and the Madras system too had defects in the eyes of the policy makers of North India. The new alternative was to be found in 'village communities'. Revenue settlement should be concluded with neither the big landlord nor the individual cultivator but with the village as a whole through its representative. Like Burke half a century earlier, Metcalfe and Briggs were[85] great admirers of Indian institutions and they were anxious to preserve them if they were found not detrimental to progress. The village communities were considered to be a medium course between the greedy and rapacious zemindar on the one hand, and, on the other, the ignorant European collector with his huge establishment. The supporters claimed that organisation

---

[80] Quoted in C. D. Field, *The Regulations of the Bengal Code* (London, 1875), p. 60n.

[81] *On Taxes or Public Revenue: The Ultimate Incidence of Their Payment* (London, 1829), pp. 84–5, 150 *et seq.* After having said that in India the administrators had not realised the importance of effective demand for the prosperity of the country, Sleeman wrote in a footnote: 'Since the Government has availed itself of the great talents, abilities, and application of Mr. Holt Mackenzie ... much clearer views have been had, and much more judicious measures pursued in this branch of our Indian administration,' p. 85n.

[82] Memorandum dated 19 October 1826, *op. cit.*, p. 148.

[83] He insisted on adequate safeguards for the cultivators as well. *Ibid.*, pp. 125–6.

[84] *Ibid.*, p. 148.

[85] Metcalfe's Minutes of 7 November 1830 and 3 February 1831 printed in the appendix to *Parliamentary Papers*, H.C. 735–III, vol. XI of Session 1831–2. See also Panigrahi, *op. cit.* Chapter 3. See for his views, Briggs, *op. cit.*, pp. 437–6.

of land tenure on the basis of village communities would prevent excessive subdivision of land and at the same time enable the village to exist without too much interference from the government officers. The government settled the assessment with a representative of the village community; it was later divided by the villagers among themselves.

When Bentinck became Governor-General, his immediate problem was to settle land revenue policy as the 1822 Regulation had become unworkable. Like the Governor of Madras earlier, he had wholeheartedly supported the ryotwar system of Read and Munro. But now he did not have the same enthusiasm for a system that required too much detailed investigation. He was no doubt reluctant to create new zemindars, but realising that landlords could perform a positive role in stimulating economic development, he decided to retain proprietary rights wherever they existed.[86] As most of the proprietary rights in the Ceded and Conquered Provinces of Bengal were vested in the hands of the village communities, Bentinck's decision was to conclude the settlements with such communities. But in quite a few estates, the rights of the landlords were left untouched subject only to the subordinate rights exercised by the cultivators. Whether the *malguzar* was conceived as a landlord or simply as a tax-paying representative, the aim of the land revenue policy at this time was to let the people themselves decide on the allocation of the total tax burden among themselves.[87]

Another important deviation from the Regulation VII of 1822 related to the policy of field assessment. According to this the revenue payable was calculated at the lowest level of the tax-paying community, i.e. the individual field, and the land tax was computed with reference to the cost of production and the value of produce. The new policy laid down that the total revenue payable of a village should be calculated first on the basis of fertility, location and population; then the revenue payable by individuals would be settled either by the proprietary joint communities among themselves or by the landlords. By making the 'fertility of the soil' a crucial element in the revenue assessment, Bentinck had remained within the fold of Classical rent theory. In other words, rent was the product of the original and indestructible powers of the soil and not of the cultivator who might use his ingenuity

---

[86] This was why he was reluctant to interfere in the landlord–tenant relations. According to him, it was unjust as well as difficult to fix the rent payable by the tenants to the landlords because rent would depend upon the seasons, crops, demand and similar matters of detail: 'There seems, indeed, no reason why the Government should interfere to regulate the wages of agricultural more than that of any other description of labour.' Bentinck's Minute, 26 September 1832, *Selections from the Revenue Records of North Western Provinces*, vol. II, p. 408.

[87] Holt Mackenzie's Undated Memorandum on Bird's Settlement (*Bentinck Papers*, Nottingham University Library).

to produce a more valuable crop. Metcalfe among others opposed this, and suggested that assessment should be made on the basis of the actual crops grown, because that alone gave an index to the cultivator's ability to pay.[88] But Bentinck was insistent because, as he told the Sudder Board of Revenue, soil assessment alone would provide the necessary incentive for the cultivator to grow more valuable (especially commercial) crops.[89]

The recognition of zemindari proprietary rights, assessment of only a part of the rent, and relaxation of the rigorous application of the net produce criterion, all meant a reduction of the Ricardian content in the formation of land revenue policy. The main reason for the change of policy from Regulation VII of 1822 to Regulation IX of 1833 was the administrative difficulties which had been encountered, as Eric Stokes has pointed out.[90] However, there was also the fact that the thinking of conservative economists of the day that found favour with a number of senior civil servants. Malthus was naturally the most influential of these conservatives, and for a variety of reasons he felt the necessity of landlords for the correct functioning of the economy. He saw in them unproductive consumers without whom the economy would collapse. Malthus specially mentioned this siphoning off the rent element as responsible for blocking the 'way of progressive cultivation' in parts of India.[91]

The fact that the leases were to be for thirty years shows the influence of Classical economics of the Adam Smith tradition, which advocated a rather prolonged leasing period.[92] The utilitarian version of political economy, if it had been strictly applied, would have meant an annual settlement, leaving no element of rent at all in the hands of the cultivator. Not only were thirty years to be allowed to pass before a resettlement but Bentinck allowed only two thirds of the rent element to be absorbed for the public exchequer, leaving the rest to the cultivators or landlords. In the revision of settle-

---

[88] See Panigrahi, *op. cit.*, pp. 114–15.

[89] Letter dated 7 April 1831, Appendix 82, *Parl. Papers*, H.C. 735–III, vol. XI of Session 1831–2, p. 313. The Court of Directors held similar views. See for example its letter to Bombay in *Selections of Papers from the Records of the East India House*, vol. III, p. 801. The Court of Directors was against assessment based on the value of the crops grown because that would act 'as a check on industry and discourage cultivation'. The Court made it clear that, in view of the possibilities of increased trade with Britain owing to the equalisation of UK sugar duties, no policy that might even remotely hinder agricultural growth should be tolerated. See Court of Directors to Government of India, 12 April 1837, reprinted in John Maskell (ed.), *The Circular Orders of the Board of Revenue from A.D. 1820 to 1850* (Madras, 1851), pp. 251–3.

[90] Stokes, *op. cit.*, p. 105.

[91] *Principles of Political Economy*, II Edn. pp. 154–5.

[92] James Mill had also advocated a 20 to 30 years duration between assessments and his reasons were identical with those of Adam Smith. See his evidence *Parl. Papers*, H.C. 320A, vol. V of Session 1831. Q. 3910, p. 367, and Q. 3972, p. 372.

ment that began in 1855, according to the Sahranpore rules, this was reduced to half.

If the 'policy' as it finally emerged had a meagre Ricardian–utilitarian content, there was even less of it when the policy was actually implemented at the district level where the collectors determined the amount of land revenue to be assessed. It is no doubt true that the officials were educated in political economy and were sufficiently imbued with certain value judgements based on the tenets of *laissez-faire* and utilitarianism. But when they actually settled the amount of land revenue, they were not entirely free agents to be guided solely by their theoretical knowledge.[93] In other words, Classical political economy in its widest connotation provided the 'ideal' for these civil servants, but they had to rely on their own discretion, and judge each case on individual merit.

LAND TAXATION IN BOMBAY

The conclusion to emerge from the foregoing is that Ricardian political economy with the utilitarian twist espoused by James Mill was only marginally influential on land taxation policy, and that other pressures, including the influence of conservative economists like Malthus also played a part. By the time the policy became fully operational, the doctrinal content had been reduced considerably to make way for pragmatic considerations. This could be seen when we look at the Bombay land revenue experiments in the 1820s. In the second decade, land revenue policy in Bombay was largely influenced by the ryotwar system, as civilians with Madras experience were in charge of revenue administration; by and large the gross produce criterion (that is, one third of the gross produce) was used for taxation, the objective being to encourage peasants with proprietary interest in land. There were odd civilians like Marriott, the district Collector of Northern Konkan who had suggested a similar rate to encourage the growth of property and middlemen.[94]

But in the mid-1820s, the idea of the net produce criterion as the best basis of taxation caught on, no doubt due to the experiments of Holt Mackenzie in the Ceded and Conquered Provinces of northern India. In his comment on Chaplin's Deccan Survey, the Governor of Bombay, Lord Elphinstone, had referred to the net produce criterion for land revenue

---

[93] See John Rosselli, 'Theory and Practice in North India: The Background to the Land Settlement of 1833' *Indian Economic and Social History Review*, vol. VIII, no. 2 June 1971, p. 145.

[94] The Court of Directors approved this scheme although it was 'liable to the strongest objections'. Revenue Letter to Bombay, 4 May 1825, *Selections of papers from the Records of the East India House*, vol. III, p. 779.

assessment and indicated that soil assessment alone would provide equal treatment of equals and would be completely neutral as between different varieties of soils.[95]

The most spectacular application of the theory of rent in land revenue assessment was made by J. D. Pringle in the Poona district in 1826. Pringle proposed to make cost of production an explicit item in the calculation of revenue assessment. He thought correctly (like Elphinstone) that the net produce must vary in relation to the gross produce in lands of different fertility. The gross produce criterion had the built-in bias in favour of the landlords possessing more fertile soils. This meant that the better soils would be cultivated first, and this would prevent a rapid expansion of cultivation. The concept of 'net produce' in Pringle's system was the same as 'rent' in Classical political economy, and it was to be arrived at after deducting the rewards for labour and capital from the gross produce. Although the state as the landlord would be within its rights to extract all the net produce, it would mean that there would be no 'property in the soil'. Pringle had been a prize-winning student at Haileybury under Malthus, and hence he could not think of an agrarian economy without its community of prosperous enterprising agriculturists and unproductive consumers. Therefore he proposed to levy only 55 per cent of the net produce so that it would enable the holders of fertile lands to accumulate capital and thus lead to a stable social order based on proper gradations. This was quite in keeping with the Malthusian economic thought.[96]

Unfortunately Pringle's survey aimed at great accuracy, and it was done with very unreliable instruments. When the assessments were completed, the burden was found heavy. The tax collectors used severe methods to collect the taxes with the result that large tracts of land were abandoned. It was rather ironical that, just at the time when the Pringle survey was proving a disaster, James Mill singled out Pringle for special praise in the House of Commons.[97] However the Governor-General of India, Lord Bentinck, was not equally impressed.[98] Indeed, the failure of the Pringle system had its impact on Bentinck's thinking when he had to struggle with the revision of the unworkable 1822 Regulation of the North Western Provinces.

In order to remedy the situation caused by the Pringle survey and settlement, H. E. Goldsmid and George Wingate were appointed to revise the

[95] Elphinstone's Minute, undated *Ibid.*, p. 854.
[96] For a succinct summary of Pringle's system, see A. Rogers, *The Land Revenue of Bombay* (London, 1892), vol. II, pp. 101 *et seq.* and *Gazeteer of the Bombay Presidency: Poona*, vol. XVIII, Part II, pp. 379 *et seq.*
[97] *Parl. Papers*, H.C. 320A, vol. V of Session 1831, Questions 3882, 3887, pp. 364-5.
[98] See his Minute 26 September 1832, *Selection of Revenue Records from North Western Provinces*, vol. II, Para. 49, p. 403.

earlier settlements. Wingate pointed out that the 55 per cent of the net product taken as tax represented inequality in taxation, and also showed that, while Pringle defined 'net produce' like the 'rent' of the economic theorists, in practice while making assessments, 'net produce' appeared different, because *no* 'no-rent' land was given as the bench-mark. Hence soil assessment had not been fixed on the 'rent of the land'.[99]

While making the revision, Goldsmid and Wingate concentrated on assiduous local enquiry into each individual holding and its past performances. What James Mill thought had been replaced by Pringle's 'scientific' system had once again come into operation. James Mill had told the House of Commons that the only criterion adopted for land revenue assessment by native administration was the cultivator's ability to pay, which was calculated by past performances.[100] The Wingate–Goldsmid survey was also determined on the same basis, and to justify this stand Wingate pointed out how the excessive assessments of the past, based as they were on the government monopoly of land, were responsible for what he called 'so striking an inversion of the usual course of society'. What he meant here was that economic development in India, unlike that in the West, was not proceeding towards the stationary state along with the increasing utilisation of all the nation's resources. He observed the paradox of a stationary state in India, with resources in a state of underdevelopment and population not growing as it does in a developing economy. In India the land was held by one monopolist, and consequently rent was not regulated by the competition between landholders and tenants,[101] but by tenants competing for land which was held by the government. Under these circumstances, even if the assessment were little above the correct competitive rate, it would have disastrous consequences because the excess 'goes on from year to year slowly but surely, exhausting the fountains of national wealth'. This is because 'every increase of rent must be accompanied by a corresponding reduction in the rate of profits, which forms the sole inducement to apply capital in productive industry ... this is a cause capable of prematurely checking, nay, barring altogether, any further progress of society at even the earliest stages of improvement.'[102] Here Wingate derived support from Malthus for his line

[99] Wingate to Mills 31 July 1839 in Appendix II, *Papers Relating to the Revision of the Assessment of the Indapoor Talooka* (Selections from the Records of the Bombay Government, New Series, vol. CVII), p. 139. See also p. 129.

[100] Q. 3901, *op. cit.*, p. 366.

[101] See for James Mill's views. Q. 3891, *Ibid.*, p. 365.

[102] Wingate to J. S. Low, 15 June 1839, *Papers Relating to the Revision of Rates of Assessment on the Expiration of the First Settlement in the Madha, Sholapur, Mohol, Barsi, Karmala Taluqs* (Selections from the Records of the Bombay Government, New Series, vol. CL), pp. 51–2.

of argument. Malthus had pointed out that 'bad governments and unnecessary monopolies ... modify this natural progress, and often occasion a
premature formation of rent'.[103] Wingate cited the following sentence from
Malthus in defence of his position: 'there is reason to believe that in parts of
India ... the progress of taxation on the land, founded upon the sovereign's
right to the soil, ... have forcibly and prematurely lowered the profits of
capital ... and have thrown great obstacles in the way of progressive cultivation'.[104] Wingate added that Malthus's view was 'strictly applicable to the
present condition of Deccan'. Over-taxation, then, was an evil that had to be
avoided by a careful enquiry into the cultivators' ability to pay, which in
turn could be ascertained only by past performance. Moderation in levying
taxes was essential, whatever method of assessment was used. In this context, controversy over the choice of the principle of assessment (whether
gross product or net product criterion) remained irrelevant. As we have
seen, even when a gross product criterion was used, cost of production was
taken into account in making an assessment. Chaplin's famous Deccan
survey, which preceded Pringle's attempts, had instructed the assessment
to be fixed 'after making the usual deductions on account of labour and
expense of cultivation, as well as the maintenance of the Ryot's family'.[105]

So in the settlements concluded by Wingate and Goldsmid, lip-service
was paid to the theory of rent, but in practice no rule was followed except
that of the tax payers' ability to pay.[106] Similarly, when the land revenue
settlement was made in Madras in the 1850s, no strict rule was followed,
although statements were made to express their adherence to the correct
'principles'. The Court of Directors had asked the Government of Madras
to use the net product criterion. But the entire policy making apparatus of the
Government of Madras (the Director of Survey and Settlement, the Board
of Revenue and the Revenue Department) utilised the gross product criterion.
The Board of Revenue, for example, while not denying that 'the views
expressed by the Court are correct in theory', nevertheless said they could
not be put in practice because of the insuperable difficulties of measuring
net produce.[107] The Secretary of State agreed with this and did not materially

---

[103] *Principles of Political Economy*, 2nd Edn, p. 153.
[104] *Ibid.*, p. 156. cited in Wingate to Low, *op. cit.*, p. 51.
[105] *Selections of Papers from the Records of the East India House*, vol. III, p. 848.
[106] Ira Klein has pointed out that throughout the nineteenth century the revenue system in
the whole of the Bombay Presidency did not make any revolutionary departure from the
traditional Indian methods of assessment or tenure as has been claimed. See 'Utilitarianism
and Agrarian Progress in Western India' *Economic History Review*, December 1965, vol.
XVIII, no. 3, pp. 576 *et seq.*
[107] Board of Revenue Proceedings 15 July 1857. Extracts in the *Collections to the Revenue
Despatches to Madras*, India Office Records, no. L/E/3/714. Collection no. 1.

alter the order of the Government of Madras that it did not 'wish that the Director of Settlement should consider himself hampered by the necessity of endeavouring to ascertain what may be the net produce of the land'.[108] Six years later, when Sir Charles Wood reviewed the land taxation policy of Madras, he once again instructed that the net product criterion be adopted. At the same time, realising that theory could provide no more than the 'ideal' component in the formation of economic policy, and that the application of this policy in its rigid form was impossible, he added that the assessment need 'not, indeed, to be worked out pedantically, or with any pretence to mathematical accuracy, but to be kept in view by every settlement officer in forming his assessments'.[109]

This instruction, not surprisingly, proved to be a dead letter because it was never seriously taken into account by the collectors making revenue settlements in the districts.[110] Thus in practice, the south Indian officials' attitude towards the 'theory' behind land revenue assessment was not very different from the attitude of their north Indian counterparts mentioned earlier.

THE QUEST FOR PERMANENCY AGAIN

James Mill had said that although theoretically 'permanency' of tax rates would give incentives to cultivators to undertake capital investment, in practice it would only convert them into rent-receivers as the economy progressed and cultivation extended.[111] For a variety of other reasons, apart from Mill's criticism, the Court of Directors did not consent to any form of permanent settlement whether with large landlords, village communities or peasant proprietors. However, in the decades after 1840 there appeared fresh proposals for permanent settlements, some favouring large landlords and others peasant proprietors. These proposals arose primarily because their proponents felt that the high assessments made during the earlier temporary settlements had substantially retarded capital formation in land.[112]

---

[108] Orders to the Revenue Department, dated 15 February 1858, *Ibid*. For the Secretary of State's letter, see Secretary to Government of Madras (Revenue) no. 5, 15 December 1858, *Revenue Despatches to Madras*, India Office Records, no. L/E/3/689, pp. 43–4.

[109] Secretary of State to Government of Madras (Revenue) no. 7 of 1864, 24 February 1864. India Office Records, L/E/3/697, paras, 10, 11.

[110] See Lord Hobart's (Governor of Madras), Minute dated 19 December 1873, India Office Records, no. L/E/3/762, Collection no. 21.

[111] *Parl. Papers*, H.C. 320A, vol. V of Session 1831, Q. 3976, p. 372.

[112] The belief that high taxation had retarded capital formation was held by numerous observers. As early as 1825, the official utilitarian organ claimed that after taxation and rent payments, 'absolutely nothing' remained for the cultivator. 'The ordinary sources of accumulating capital, and the inducements for increasing the productiveness of the soil (so little productive now) are destroyed.' *The Westminster Review* October 1825, p. 264. See also Harvey Tuckett, *The Indian Revenue System as it is* (London, 1840), pp. 148–9. Even

Permanency was espoused in India by many interests to encourage capital formation in Indian agriculture. British manufacturers, as we have already seen, in the 1840s had begun to look to India as the suppliers of agricultural raw materials – especially cotton – for their factories. The manufacturers were convinced that the Indian government absorbed a major portion of the produce through the land tax. Although the manufacturing interests talked about an all-India policy, their attention was mainly attracted to the condition, prospects and improvement of the principal cotton producing areas, particularly western India, which had a revenue system based on the periodic ryotwar settlement. The various manufacturing associations of Lancashire sent Alexander Mackay to report on the possibilities of stimulating the production of cotton and other staples through proper land tenure arrangements. Mackay held that the incentive to produce could only come from security of tenure and the prospect of enjoying one's own income. Whereas under the zemindari and the ryotwar system, the peasant was not sure of enjoying his surplus produce, a system based on peasant proprietary would give the needed incentive for the production of necessary raw materials.[113]

It is interesting to note that the doctrinal basis of peasant proprietary was provided by John Stuart Mill, and yet Mill himself had justified the traditional British–Indian land revenue policy of treating land as the property of the state.[114] Mill's support for peasant proprietary was enthusiastically accepted by many of its Indian protagonists.[115] This advocacy was possible in spite of Classical political economy because Mill had made an important distinction between land for investment of capital and land for subsistence farming, an argument frequently advanced.[116] The basic idea was simple enough: peasant proprietary provided the stimulus for the

Footnote 112 continued

those who denied the view that the land revenue system was responsible for low capital formation, nevertheless accepted the fact that capital was scarce in India. See *An Inquiry into the Causes of the long-continued Stationary condition of India* (London, 1830), p. 16.

[113] See Alexander Mackay, *Western India* (London, 1853), pp. 317–18. See also George Thompson, *Six Lectures on the Condition, Resources and Prospects of British India* (London, 1842), p. 29.

[114] *Memorandum of the Improvements* (London, 1858), pp. 3 *et seq.*

[115] See *Calcutta Review*, vol. XLVII, no. XCIV (1868), pp. 102 *et seq.* See also *Indian Economist*, 11 July 1870, 10 January 1870, 31 January 1874, and 31 October 1874. M. N. Nanavati said in 1872: 'The Bombay system aimed at, and has to some extent been successful in, creating a peasant proprietary; for the advantages of which I can here only refer to Mill's Political Economy, vol. I, Chap. vi, vii.' *The Revenue Survey and Settlement of the Bombay Presidency* (Bombay, 1872), p. 42.

[116] *The Calcutta Review*, vol. XXXIX, no. LXXVIII (1864), p. 298. The author said 'The effect of a land tenure like that which prevails in India is ... to bring the principle of population to act directly on the land, and not as in England, on capital.'

cultivators to accumulate capital without the surplus being drained away by either landlord or government. Unlike in Britain where rent played a part in providing an indication of the approaching stationary state, thereby encouraging emigration or the movement of capital from agriculture to manufacture, in India rent had no such role. Rent in India could not properly be identified as the reward for the possession of superior grades of soil alone.[117] India, being basically agricultural, with only two distinct classes, landlords and cultivators,[118] it was pointed out that the relationship between these two classes was more like the cottier tenancy of Ireland where rent was not dependent upon the different qualities of the soil.[119] The advocates of peasant proprietary visualised the abolition of landlords (government or zemindars or talookdars) and the conversion of the cultivators into enterprising farmers, with the help of funds that would otherwise have gone to the landlord.[120]

There was the other school of thought, according to which the peasants did not have the capacity to accumulate capital, and hence taxation should be concluded on a permanent basis, not with the peasant proprietors, but with the large landholders.[121] The remedy was in large-scale farming and the utilisation of the economies of scale. This would be possible only if the surplus generated by the landlords by their application of capital was free from taxation when the time came for resettlement. As against the permanent settlement with small peasant proprietors, this school advocated permanent settlement with large landholders. The warmest supporter of this cause was Colonel Baird-Smith, who found in northern India areas where revenue

---

[117] Emerson Dawson, *The Indian Land Question: A Timely Warning*, by Indopolite, p. 8. The author claims that this pamphlet was approved by John Stuart Mill. See the preface.

[118] Those who administered the revenue system of North Western Provinces, which had its inspiration from the Ricardian political economy, were also aware that the two classes that mattered were these two. The 'rent' meant only 'ryot or produce rent, paid by labourers, raising their wages from the soil'. See James Thomason, 'Remarks on the System of Land Revenue Administration prevalent in the North Western Provinces of Hindostan' dated 25 August 1849. Richard Jones' *Essay on Rent* was cited in defence of this definition. See *Directions for Revenue Officers in the North Western Provinces of the Bengal Presidency Regarding the Settlement and Collection of the Land Revenue* (Calcutta, 1858), p. 9.

[119] See *Calcutta Review*, vol. LI, no. CI (1870). Both Richard Janes and John Stuart Mill were cited in support, pp. 153–60.

[120] The *Calcutta Review* declared that the 'system of peasant property which has been everywhere except in England admitted to be eminently successful in raising the rustic population, and introducing habits of thrift and social economy'. vol. no. XXXIX, no. LXXVIII (1864), pp. 278–9. See also *The Famine in Orissa: The Permanent Settlement of the Land Revenue in India* (London, 1867), pp. 6–7.

[121] See for example the *Bombay Quarterly Review* Issue dated January–April 1858, XIII pp. 76–7. See the writings of Patrick Smollett of the Madras Revenue Service, *Cotton Supplies from India: The Government Monopoly of the soil* (Manchester, 1860), p. 26. See also his *India: A Lecture Delivered* (Glasgow, 1863), pp. 38 *et seq*.

settlements that had been concluded on a long term basis were able to with-stand the rigours of famine more easily than the areas with short term assessments.[122]

If the advocates of peasant proprietary received inspiration from John Stuart Mill, the advocates of permanent settlement with large landlords received it from the *laissez-faire* economists. One of the leading supporters in the mid-nineteenth century was Francis William Newman who was very appreciative of the Cornwallis settlement and critical of state ownership of land. According to him, the Indian tax system was most oppressive and needed changing.[123] On *laissez-faire* principles, the only way to improve the economy was for the government to avoid all interference by giving up its assumption of the ownership of land. Profits should be left to fructify in the hands of the enterprising farmer, and he should be allowed to enjoy the results of his labour unmolested. This would be possible only by limiting the government share in the total produce for ever.

The theoretical point at issue behind the new quest for permanence has to be seen in the hundred-year old controversy between the protagonists of land revenue as rent and land revenue as taxation. The fact, as everyone saw, was that the government was absorbing resources from the agricultural sector. What was not clear was how should this amount of resources be determined. Was it by the application of the theory of rent which would mean the absorption of the rent element only; or the theory of taxation which had no such limits? As has already been seen, the application of the rent theory to determine the taxable income was extremely vague. If the amount actually collected was below the full rental, the theory was not being followed, and if on the other hand, the amount collected exceeded the rental, it was encroaching upon profits. Consequently it was argued that land revenue was better treated as a tax, and a good tax was a moderate tax.

Further, it was suggested that the theory of rent was only a tool to explain the past and not a theory of policy useful for laying down rules. The theory of taxation on the other hand was intended to provide guidelines for the construction of a proper tax system. The advice given then was simple: treat the land revenue as a tax *de jure* as well as *de facto*; apply the canons of Adam Smith and levy a moderate tax; make it permanent to remove

---

[122] *Parl. Papers*, H.C. 29, vol. XL of Session 1862. Permanent settlement was frequently suggested as a sure remedy for the recurring famines. See for example, H. A. D. Phillips, *A Blacker Pamphlet or an attempt to Explain the Severity of the Late Famine* (Madras, 1878), J. Da Costa, *Facts and Fallacies Regarding Irrigation as a Prevention of Famine* (London, 1878).

[123] *Lectures on Political Economy* (London, 1851), p. 127. Newman was cited by an Indian pamphleteer to support permanent settlement. I.P.H., *Articles and Letters about the Indian Land Tax* (Bombay, 1866) p. 35.

arbitrariness in the levy of taxation as well as providing incentives for development.[124]

There was so much support for permanent settlement in India[125] that the Secretary of State was persuaded to issue a Revenue Despatch to India, dated 9 July 1862, in which he laid down that permanent settlement should be the ultimate policy for India.[126] It was felt that, in the light of increasing knowledge, the faults of the Cornwallis settlement would not be repeated should any settlements be concluded with landholders *for ever* in northern India. The policy was widely welcomed in Britain at the time.[127]

In spite of the considerable popularity of permanent settlement in the 1850s and 1860s, the policy had not much chance of finding a place in the statute book. It had to contend with the vehement criticism of John Stuart Mill who said that, if the policy of permanent settlement were introduced, it would have disastrous consequences.[128] Once again the theory of rent was resurrected to oppose permanent settlement even with the cultivators. The ideas of Richard Jones regarding the Irish cottier rent had been used to criticise the Indian land revenue system; indeed, his views had been a pillar of strength for the protagonists of a peasant proprietary system in India. This evoked many replies. Rent in India, it was held, was not solely due to the land—man ratio. Both custom and competition played a part in determining rent in India, as was inferred by Jones; but it was contended that the existence of rent in India was also due to the differences in soils. As H. S. Reid, Member of the Board of Revenue of the North Western Provinces, put it, 'In these Provinces extension of irrigation raises rent: in Ireland, increase

---

[124] W. S. Halsey (of the Civil Service) in a *Report on the Question of Temporary and Permanent Settlements as Applied to the District of Cawnpore* (London, 1871), said that 'There is a charm, as he (Sir William Muir) and Mr Mill rightly say, in the words "for ever"—such a charm in the ears of a native as few of us can appreciate, which, if combined with a reasonable reduction of the Government demand, would diffuse a spirit of contentment and satisfaction over the whole country, and for the sake of which we should be justified in giving up all prospective advantages, and which contentment and satisfaction will so contribute to the material wealth of the country, that when from the fall in the value of precious metals, or other causes, we are forced to turn our attention to other sources for revenue, we shall not find the slightest difficulty in raising it,' p. 18.

[125] The *Indian Economist* said in 1873, 'The *consensus* of opinion that existed in the North Western Provinces ten years ago in favour of permanent settlement.' Issue 21 March 1873, p. 203.

[126] Sir Charles Wood kept on warning the Viceroys that the permanent settlement should not be precipitated if there was any prospect of an increase in assessment. See Wood to Lawrence, 15 October 1864 (Lawrence Papers at India Office Library).

[127] See for example 'Sir Charles Wood's Despatch Recommending the Perpetual Settlement of the Land Revenue of India' *Economist*, vol. xx, 13 September 1862, pp. 1009–10.

[128] See *Dissertations and Discussions* (London, 1875), vol. iv, pp. 148–9. See also Mill to Maine, 1 January 1869, H. S. R. Elliot (ed.), *The Letters of John Stuart Mill* (London, 1910), vol. ii, p. 169. See also his *Principles of Political Economy*, pp. 326–7.

of population', and added that the 'Indian ryots, especially in canal-irrigated districts, do not breed and multiply like Irish Cottiers'.[129] Auckland Colvin, Secretary of the Board of Revenue, pointed out that those who used Richard Jones to support the thesis that variations in the qualities of soil did not have an impact on the rent really misunderstood him. He said correctly that, 'Jones does not say that improvements do not affect the outturn of different lands, and consequently their rental value to the proprietor, but that with peasant cultivators the *existence* of a rental value is in no way dependent on qualities of the soil.'[130] This meant that Classical political economy did not entirely lose its relevance in India. Rent did not enter into cost of production, and hence a tax on rent was not a tax on industry. The difference between England and India was that the operation of the law moved sluggishly in India because of the lack of availability of non-agricultural employment opportunities for labour and capital. Otherwise, in essentials, there was no difference because 'still the price of produce, must, at least, be such, as to enable the cultivator to subsist, and to replace the little capital necessary for his operations'.[131]

Thus the theoretical arguments behind the proposal of permanent settlement had to contend with the objections of John Stuart Mill as well as many Indian civil servants. In any case, a desire for state intervention had entered official thinking because of the realisation that economic development, necessary to reduce the rigours of famine, could be stimulated only by the visible hand of the state. This made it difficult to give a wholehearted support to a crude *laissez-faire* economic policy which, if applied to the land revenue policy, would have meant an inelastic tax structure. As it was, public revenues were inelastic and the scope for any spectacular increases in indirect taxation was limited.[132] The silver crisis, depreciation of the value of the rupee, and increased expenditure on public works and famines made the rulers cautious of any policy which attempted to reduce public revenues.

Lord Salisbury, the Secretary of State for India in the 1870s, was concerned about the controversy and explored the possibility of a formal enquiry. He wished to know

1 whether Indian landlords on the British pattern were possible or not;

[129] Reid's Minute on 'Permanent versus Temporary Settlements' dated 15 April 1873. *Permanent and Temporary Settlements, North West Provinces*, para. 7.

[130] Note by A. Colvin, dated 31 December 1872 *Ibid.*, para. 18. See also W. C. Pedder of the Bombay Civil Service in the *Indian Economist* 15 July 1871, p. 323.

[131] *Calcutta Review*, vol. XII, no. XXIV (1849), p. 465.

[132] See evidence given before the Select Committee of the East India Finance by various civil servants. J. H. Morris, a settlement officer from Punjab called permanent settlement to be a 'most suicidal act'. Q. 589. The Select Committee, itself recommended that the policy of the 1862 despatch be postponed. *Parl. Papers*, H.C. 363, vol. VIII of Session 1871.

2 whether a fixed settlement does or does not stimulate the occupier to improve the land; and

3 does the system make people prosperous enough to consume other articles sufficient to recoup the revenue through indirect taxes?

Salisbury's intention was not really to rake up an old controversy, and yet that was what happened when in 1874 the Governor of Madras and his Council violently disagreed on important issues of policy concerning the land revenue settlement. The Council wanted to continue the old survey and re-settlement of land revenue policy, whereas the Governor, Lord Hobart, argued the case for a permanent settlement. In the Secretary of State's council, there were people like Sir Louis Mallet, who rejected the old survey and settlement system because it was an 'experiment of Government on a large scale, founded on communistic principles', based on an assumption of state ownership of land. For Mallet the choice was clear. 'There are two irreconcileable principles at last brought face to face. On the one hand, the principle of private property and free exchange; on the other, that of State property and monopoly.'[133] Sir Henry Maine, while denying that the Indian land revenue system was based on communistic principles, nevertheless accepted the idea that Indian land revenue in practice was a tax and it should be treated as such.[134] But those members of the Council who had served in the Indian civil service, like Sir Erskine Perry, thought that the subtle distinctions between rent and revenue were meaningless and 'belong to the class of what the French call *speculations oisives*'; hence it was not advisable to 'start any speculative theories to inflame the young civilians fresh from Adam Smith and Ricardo into crusades' against the existing system.[135]

Lord Salisbury's view was essentially pragmatic.[136] He was not concerned whether he called it rent or revenue so long as 'we get the money';[137] but he pointed out the necessity of correct definitions because the vocabulary of the Indian civilians

is derived with more or less fidelity from the writings of political economists. They have been required to study the science closely before they could undertake our service, and their minds were fresh from a close application to it when, for the first time, they came into contact with Indian life, and were trusted with a share of Indian Government. To the modern Indian statesman the refined distinctions of the economical school are a solid living reality, from which he can as little separate his thoughts as from his mother tongue.

---

[133] Mallet's Minutes 3 February 1875 and 12 April 1875. 'Survey Settlement, Madras' *Financial Department Collections*, India Office Records, no. C/138.

[134] Maine's Minute, 13 March 1875, *Ibid.*

[135] Perry's Minutes 8 March 1875 and 15 May 1875, *Ibid.*

[136] Salisbury to Northbrook, 2 April 1874 (*Northbrook Papers*, India Office Library).

[137] Salisbury's Minute 26 April 1875, *Financial Department Collections*, India Office Records, no. C/138.

Salisbury was afraid that if the rent theory were upheld, the Indian civilians would go about extracting the entire rent element. This would be undesirable because in the rural districts capital was scarce and consequently heavy taxation retarded capital formation. This injury 'is exaggerated in the case of India, where so much of the revenue is exported without a direct equivalent'. He added, 'As India must be bled, the lancet should be directed to the parts where the blood is congested . . . not to those which are already feeble from the want of it.' Thus on strictly pragmatic grounds, Salisbury decided to treat land revenue as a tax. But again on very similar pragmatic grounds he rejected permanent settlement. The finances of the government were such that permanent settlement could not be implemented. The old policy had to continue he thought, but the resettlements should be moderate and should not take advantage of 'inflated prices'. The important thing according to Salisbury was to 'disavow language belonging to the rent theory'.

In India the viceroys as a rule were pragmatic. Lord Mayo, the viceroy in the early 1870s was formerly an Irish landlord, and this fact made John Stuart Mill anticipate a pro-landlord bias in him.[138] Mayo was, however, conscious of the many consequences of permanent settlement with the landlords and hence was willing to continue the system of periodical settlements.[139]

Indeed, during Mayo's viceroyalty, an assault was made on the Bengal permanent settlement itself *via* the proposed education and road cesses on land revenue. It was claimed by the protagonists of these earmarked taxes that they would not only increase the elasticity of the land tax proceeds, but also lead to the provision of much needed local infrastructure. However, the Government of Bengal – no doubt influenced by the agitation conducted by the Bengal zemindars – opposed these proposals on the ground that they violated the basic canons of taxation. H. L. Dampier, Secretary to the Bengal government, asked the Government of India to refer to John Stuart Mill's *Principles of Political Economy* (Book v, Chapter 2) where it is indicated that taxation should be equal. In communicating the views of the Governor of Bengal, Sir W. Grey, Dampier said that in Bengal the permanent settlement was an unalternable tax and hence 'any cess which may be levied in Bengal cannot be imposed on the same principle, but must be treated as taxation proper, and fixed in accordance with the equitable principle of equality of taxation'.[140] He conceded that had the land revenue been merely 'rent' instead of a 'tax', the proposed local taxes would have been valid.

---

[138] Mill wrote to Sir Charles Dilke on 9 February 1869 that 'what will happen under the Irish landlord who is now Viceroy, I dread to think.' Elliot, *op. cit.*, vol. II, p. 188.

[139] Lord Mayo's Minute on 'Permanent Settlement of North Western Provinces' dated 7 February 1871, Add. 7490, Part 14 (Mayo Papers at the Cambridge University Library).

[140] H. L. Dampier to the Secretary of the Home Department, Government of India, 30 April 1869 (Mayo Papers at the Cambridge University Library).

The Government of India denied the arguments of Dampier and Grey. A. P. Howell of the Viceroy's Council categorically declared that the Government of India

has never held, I believe, any other theory about the land revenue than that propounded by Mr Mill. The land revenue has been repeatedly declared to be, not taxation, but rent ... Indeed the main drift of Mill's argument is that the land *should* bear some of the burdens of the increasing requirments of the progress of society, because the landlords 'grow richer as it were in their sleep without working, risking, or economising', and this is exactly the view of the Government of India.[141]

Although the Viceroy, Lord Mayo, prefaced his remarks by discounting the applicability of Mill's arguments to the Indian case, he nevertheless supported the cess on grounds of necessity, as well as on the basis of British practice, and declared that the permanent settlement should not be used by the zemindar to 'evade his just share of the taxation of the country'.[142] Mayo was greatly influenced by the secretary of the newly created department of agriculture, Alan Octavian Hume, who argued that local taxes were based on the benefit principle but at the same time that 'absolute equality and uniformity' of taxation as demanded by the Bengal zemindars was not possible in practice. In addition to equality as a canon of taxation, Hume pointed out other considerations such as justice and convenience that had to be taken into account in framing tax policy. In Bengal, the people were like orphans in need of protection, and hence the principle of taxation to be followed must enable the government to achieve its objective of protecting the people.[143] Further, Hume argued that it was necessary to provide infrastructure for Bengal and the local cesses were as good and equitable as any other method. In any case, he continued, there was no precedent elsewhere for the zemindars' reluctance to pay local taxes. Local rates rested on entirely different principles from those of other taxes. Drawing on an English comparison, he said: 'No sane man, who has compounded for his land tax in England, expects to be therefore exempt from tithes, or, even if he was compounded for both, to be therefore exempt from any drainage or poor rate that the local Boards may see fit to impose.'[144]

The Government of India received ample support even from the Secretary of State, Lord Argyll, in its attempt to widen the tax base. His argument was that India required education, roads, irrigation and other services for

---

[141] Minute dated 28 May 1869 (Mayo Papers). This passage was later incorporated in the Government of India's despatch to the Secretary of State, 31 December 1869, no. 19 (Education) of 1869.
[142] Governor General in Council to Secretary of State, 31 December 1869, no. 19 (Education) of 1869.
[143] Memorandum on 'Local rates – Bengal' dated 19 January 1871 (Mayo Papers at Cambridge University Library).
[144] *Ibid.*

future economic development. The state had to extract all available surplus from the people to provide the required infrastructure without of course placing undue burdens on certain sections of the community. It did not matter how the extraction of the surpluses was designated. It is true that Argyll believed in creating private property in land for promoting economic development in India; but at the same time he made it clear to the Viceroy that this wealth should be accessible 'to such demands as arise from time to time out of the duty and the necessity of our applying to its conditions the knowledge which belongs to a more advanced civilization than its own'.[145] He concluded that as the Bengal zemindars had large unutilised taxable capacity (evidenced by the large proceeds of indirect taxation on luxuries) they were fit objects of additional taxation through local rates based on land.

Lord Northbrook, who succeeded Mayo, drew his inspiration from John Stuart Mill and Sir Henry Maine, and firmly believed that landlords in India could not be created on the English model. According to him, 'Land tenures in India differ so widely from those in England,' that 'our ideas and arguments hardly apply at all.'[146] He thought that the creation of landed property by introducing permanent settlement would not solve any problem. Moderate assessment, he thought, would go a long way to increase the productive capacities rather than permanency.

After Northbrook's viceroyalty, economic conditions fluctuated so wildly that the Government of India was in no position to consider fixed taxation. It only remained for the Secretary of State's dispatch of 1883 to abandon formally any idea of permanently limiting the land revenue. The idea lost its popularity so quickly that B. H. Baden-Powell was able to write in 1892 that 'There are now very few persons in Indian experience who are likely to entertain any such proposition with favour and for official purposes the question is dead and buried.'[147]

CONCLUSION

To sum up the experiments by the British Raj over a century, we can confidently state that economic ideas played a major part in the discussions though the policies as they finally emerged did not reflect the extent of the theoretical discussion.

[145] Secretary of State to Governor General in Council, 12 May 1870, no. 5 (Education) of 1970.
[146] Mallet, *Thomas George, Lord Northbrook*, p. 73.
[147] *Land Systems of British India* (Oxford, 1892), vol. I, p. 341. See also the Resolution by the Government of India dated 16 January 1902, *Land Revenue Policy of the Indian Government*, pp. 1–49.

Two branches of political economy aided the administrators in policy making, the theory of rent and the theory of taxation. The use of either depended on the conception of land rights the particular policy maker entertained. If it was felt that the state was the proprietor of all land, the theory of rent was utilised. If, on the other hand, the conception of the state was 'individualistic' (i.e. the state viewed as the sum of all its parts), with no special proprietary rights over the land, theories of taxation were resorted to.

In the Classical view, the public sector had only to perform the functions associated with the allocation branch and not with the distribution or stabilisation branches. To put it differently, the state must confine itself to the production of pure public goods and only in exceptional cases provide even merit wants.[148] If public expenditure were confined to these 'unproductive' items (that is, in terms of the categories of Classical economics), any resources that were diverted from the productive endeavours of the private sector would represent so much less resources for capital accumulation. Under these conditions, the golden rule was to keep public expenditure, and therefore taxation, as low as possible.

Once, however, taxation was found necessary, it was to conform to the canons of taxation enunciated by Adam Smith and thus not upset in any way the existing allocation of resources. Direct taxation would be ideal if the tax came out of the surplus, thereby falling on the residue. In the Classical division of factor-rewards, wages and profits go to reward labour and capital, whereas rent remains as the residual surplus available for the possession of the land. If, however, the state was the supreme landlord and the cultivators only leased the cultivated or cultivable portions of land, then the state was entitled to the rent after making allowances for the expenses incurred by the cultivator on wages and capital. In this case, the state must obey the rules like any good and prosperous landlord. This is the reason for the part played by private property in economic development in the discussions surrounding land taxation.

Whichever view was adopted in framing the guidelines, by the time they were translated into operational policies they were substantially modified by resistances such as ease of administration, the necessity to preserve public revenue and above all gathered experience. These practical exigencies explain why the role of theory in shaping positive policies declined as we move towards the second half of the century.

---

[148] For definitions of fiscal terms such as 'public goods' and 'merit goods' see R. Musgrave, *Theory of Public Finance* (New York, 1959).

6

ECONOMIC IDEAS AND TAXATION POLICIES

There is hardly a source of Indian Revenue that political economy would quite approve if there were a choice

Lord Lytton

In questions of taxation in India, it seems to me that political considerations are fully as important as a perfect agreement with the principles of political economy

Lord Northbrook

INTRODUCTION

Until the imposition of an income-tax in India in 1860, virtually all taxation except land revenue was indirect. In a way, this predominance of indirect taxation was not counter to prevailing economic opinion in Britain. Both Adam Smith and Malthus had described indirect taxes as not very welcome although necessary.[1] Ricardo thought that indirect taxes on luxuries were to be preferred to income and other direct taxes.[2] McCulloch felt that practicability was more important even than equity and hence indirect taxation was to be preferred to direct taxation, as the former stimulated ingenuity and invention.[3] As a rule the Classical economists preferred *no* taxation to any particular form of taxation. If indirect taxes affected the allocation of resources, direct taxes had the disadvantage of reducing the capital resources available for investment. Hence it would be very difficult to deduce a set of policy prescriptions regarding taxation that would find favour with all Classical economists. The only set of criteria which every economist accepted were the four canons of taxation prescribed by Adam Smith: certainty, economy, convenience and equality. These canons, however, did not specify the types of taxation that would be appropriate under all conditions; so the policy to be adopted would really depend upon circumstances.

As the resources gathered through land taxation were found inadequate,

[1] See Shehab, *Progressive Taxation* (Oxford, 1953), p. 32. Sraffa (ed), *op. cit*, vol. VI, p. 118.
[2] See Carl Shoup, *Ricardo on Taxation* (New York, 1960), pp. 214, 219, 222–3.
[3] *A Treatise on the Principles and Practical Influence of Taxation and Funding System* (London, 1845), p. 151.

the Court of Directors during the Company Raj took recourse to many forms of indirect taxation since it was hostile towards any form of direct taxation. The administrative machine, in any event was not adequate to levy successfully a direct tax. When they once did allow a direct tax on houses in Bengal, Bihar and Banaras, there was a great agitation that soon 'assumed an alarming aspect'.[4] This particular house tax was not very different from a progressive tax on houses that Adam Smith had blessed. Nor was the tax novel to the Indian sub-continent because a very similar tax (which was according to the Court of Directors, 'of the nature of an Income tax') had existed in the Deccan and Carnatic. The house tax was given up and the Court developed such a distaste for direct taxes that they were not happy even with taxes on necessities, for they 'differ but little from direct taxation; that they are liable to nearly the same objections with direct taxes'.[5] Indirect taxes, then, were preferred, but the choice of the particular indirect taxes was influenced by many factors, such as the ease of collection, the necessity to stimulate economic development, the aim of channeling the maximum possible benefit to Britain, and finally the dicta of orthodox economic theory familiar to the Court of Directors. It was fully realised that 'imposts upon the indispensable necessaries of life have, by raising their price, a natural tendency to raise the wages of labor, in so doing to increase the price of manufactures and ultimately to injure the trade of a country'.[6] Secondly, indirect taxes have the effect of 'intercepting a large portion of the produce of its land and labour, before it has circulated through the community in the way of exchange, and performed in some respects the functions of a re-productive capital'.[7] In spite of these two powerful objections, financial necessity made it imperative to resort to indirect taxes because of the facility of collection. Indirect taxes, as the Court of Directors told the Government of Madras,

possess the recommendation of being productive, of being easy of collection, of being in one sense equal, and if they are not heavy of not being very oppressive. Accordingly [that] they have been resorted to by all Governments and the state of society in India certainly furnishes a better apology for a deviation from the strict rules of political economy in matters of taxation than is to be found in the manners of any European Nation.[8]

[4] Court of Directors to Governor-General (Secret Revenue), 16 September 1817, para. 7, p. 636, para. 12, pp. 658–9. *Bengal Despatches*, vol. 59, India Office Records, E/4/674.

[5] Court of Directors to Governor-General (Revenue), 16 June 1815, *Revenue Letters to Bengal*, India Office Records, vol. IV, pp. 259, para. 168.

[6] Court of Directors to Madras (Revenue), 24 April 1811, *Despatches to Madras*, vol. 47, India Office Records, E/4/907, pp. 252–3, para. 95.

[7] Court of Directors to Madras (Revenue), 12 April 1815, *Selections of Papers from the Records of the East India House*, vol. I, p. 640.

[8] Letter of 24 April 1811, para. 97, pp. 257–8, *op. cit.*

The same considerations made the Court of Directors advise the Government of Bengal to resort to the 'Renewal of old than in the establishment of new Taxes', because people would have been used to them.[9]

Accordingly, a variety of indirect taxes was levied during the nineteenth century in India. First, there were the many inland duties – a legacy of the pre-British period when India had split into many small political entities – which, by preventing a free flow of goods and services, helped to stunt the growth of internal trade and commerce; abolition of them would certainly have benefited the Indian economy, and it would also have helped the British traders in India and the British manufacturers in England, providing them with cheaper raw materials. Secondly, there were levied from time to time import duties on cotton textiles; although the removal of these would be contrary to the interests of the new Indian industries, the policy of removing them would not have violated the free trade doctrines of the economists. And, thirdly, there were certain taxes like export duties and differential tariffs for goods imported to India, which were not only inimical to the interests of Indian economic development and trade but also did not conform to any economic theory.

INTERNAL TRANSIT DUTIES

A miscellany of town duties, internal transit duties, and *octroi* duties were commonly levied during the Mughal period. When the British rule became firmly established in India, it was decided to reorganise the tax structure so that the selling operations of the East India Company would not be hampered by imposts levied every now and then during the transport of commodities from the ports of disembarkation to the markets. In 1802, the collector of customs at Banaras suggested that it would promote the use of British goods if they were to pass everywhere free of duties after getting clearance at the Calcutta customs. The Court of Directors approved this suggestion and from then on customs duties on imported goods were paid only at Calcutta.[10] But the problem of transit duties remained as far as internal trade was concerned. These were levied on most articles at various places and at variable rates.[11] The duties were refunded if the commodities were exported,

[9] Court of Directors to Governor-General (Revenue), 16 September 1812, para. 14, *op. cit.*

[10] Court of Directors to Governor-General (Revenue), 27 June 1804, *Revenue Letters to Bengal*, India Office Records, L/E/3/441, vol. I, pp. 5–7, para. 14.

[11] The dispatch of the Court to the Governments of Bengal, Bombay and Madras dated 29 July 1814 provided the basis for the remodelling of the Indian tariff system. This despatch specifically asked for the inland transit duties to be retained as T. P. Courtenay, the President of the Board of Control said he was not against their abolition because they were not harmful to British exports to India. Courtenay's Report, 25 January 1814, *Home Misc.*, India Office Records, no. 523, pp. 97 ff.

but export duties had to be paid in that case. The town duties were usually local sales taxes based on consumption. While the Regulation IX of 1810 consolidated the general duties leviable, the basic principle as well as the difficulties that it gave rise to remained operative until 1836.

This system was attacked from time to time by certain civil servants. Holt Mackenzie, the secretary of the Territorial finance department, used the doctrines of free trade to attack the inland and transit duties. According to him, the duties 'seriously hinder the commercial intercourse of the country'. The taxes not only increased the cost of production but were also responsible for much corruption. By aggravating the natural price of goods brought to the market, this system tended towards monopoly by making it difficult for individuals with small capital to embark on business.[12] Lord Ellenborough, who was the President of the Board of Control in 1829, wrote to the Governor-General that he wished to see the transit duties abolished. His argument was that taxes in general prevented the growth of private property. Abolition of inland and other duties would help the formation of private property in addition to giving encouragement to the production of cotton and other raw materials so essential for British industries.[13] Bentinck also had similar views,[14] and suggested in 1830 a policy involving the removal of internal transit duties. The Court of Directors, while accepting the justice of the views of the Indian authorities – especially those of Mackenzie – nevertheless warned the government against 'the impolicy of risking anything by an experiment, in the present state of your finances'.[15]

Bentinck was not very much against town duties where the resources so obtained could be earmarked for the development of the town in which they were collected.[16] The Court of Directors, however, disapproved such allotment of particular funds to particular purposes, and laid down the rule that expenditure should always be governed by the necessity of the particular item and the convenience and ability of the state to meet it.

---

[12] Minute dated 23 June 1825, *Bengal Separate Consultations*, India Office Records, Range 164, vol. 16, no. 23.

[13] Ellenborough to Bentinck, 19 May 1829 and 2 January 1820 (*Bentinck Papers*, Nottingham University Library).

[14] Even when he was at Madras, he had sympathetically treated requests for abolishing transit duties there. See an interesting Memorandum written at the turn of the eighteenth century, *Observations by a Very Intelligent Merchant Recommended to the Attention of Lord Bentinck* (*Bentinck Papers*, Nottingham University Library).

[15] Court of Directors to Government of Bengal (Separate: Salt, Opium and Customs), 10 June 1829, *Bengal Despatches*, vol. 110, India Office Records, E/4/725, pp. 812–15. Court of Directors to Governor-General (Separate: Customs), 30 May 1832, no. 2. *Bengal Despatches*, vol. 119, India Office Records, E/4/734, pp. 1392–3.

[16] Bentinck's Minute on the Military Board, 1831 (*Bentinck Papers*, Nottingham University Library). (Bentinck was favourably reviewing a similar proposal by Mr Adam in his Minute 22/2/1823.)

Not deterred by these rebuffs, Bentinck appointed C. E. Trevelyan, then a young civil servant, to investigate the whole question of inland transit and town duties. The report he submitted contained a devastating attack on the inland customs and town duties on the basis of the arguments of Adam Smith. Unlike Ellenborough, Trevelyan was not worried about the total tax burden, but he was rather concerned with the burden of the tax on industry. Reflecting the new economic thinking of Parnell[17] and the Manchester school, he argued that division of labour and capital accumulation were necessary but at the same time these were limited by the extent of the market. The available market in India was being split into tiny parcels by the imposition of inland and town duties, like the petty German principalities.[18] Trevelyan argued against internal customs between regions, advancing the same reasoning as that used by the Classical economists. Trevelyan also held that as government expenditure was essentially unproductive the abolition of inland duties would result in greater *productive* capital formation in the hands of the capitalists. Besides, the tax collectors who were 'not only unproductive, but *destructive* labourers', would enter the productive labour force.[19] In essence, his conclusion was that the inland and other duties prevented the natural flow of resources along the most profitable channels.

Although their attention was drawn to Trevelyan's report by the Governor-General, the Court of Directors refused to abolish the inland and other duties.[20] In the meanwhile, the Lieutenant Governor of the North Western Provinces, Alexander Ross, acting on the advice of his Board of Revenue, abolished the customs houses in his territories without waiting for orders from either the supreme government or the home government. The censure of Alexander Ross that followed was not due to the principles at issue but the Court's desire to reprimand him for what they felt to be a constitutional impropriety. Ross' policy, however, was followed in Bengal, and within a short time all the customs houses in Bengal were scrapped. When Lord Ellenborough came to India in 1842 as the Governor-General, he cleared India of practically all these inland duties.[21] The ending of inland duties was inevitable, as the whole of India was already being united and forged into a single economic unit.

[17] Sir Henry Parnell, *On Financial Reform*, published in 1830, advocated direct taxation and demonstrated the gains from avoiding taxes on inputs. His arguments were derived from the writings of Classical economists and had great impact on the economic policy of Sir Robert Peel in the 1840s.

[18] *A Report Upon the Inland Customs, and Town Duties of the Bengal Presidency*, p. 4.

[19] *Ibid.*, p. 170.

[20] Ellenborough to Chairs, 18 March 1835 and reply by Chairs, 2 April 1835. *Parl. Papers*, H.C. 533, vol. x of Session 1852.

[21] Abolition of Transit duties. Bengal Act 14 (1836) Bombay Act 1 (1838) and Madras Act VI (1844).

THE DIFFERENTIAL TARIFF SYSTEM

Until 1810, British manufacturers received no special preference in the Indian market over the products originating from Europe or America. Before 1787 some taxes were levied on imports from countries other than Britain, but they were abolished under instructions from the Court of Directors, who wanted to increase commerce as well as to prove 'to other nations the sincerity of our desire to afford to them the enjoyment of trade in our Indian possessions upon the most extensive and liberal footing'.[22] However, this policy was not consistently followed in spite of the growing strength of free trade opinion in Britain. Already in 1807, while searching for sources of revenue, the Court of Directors considered charging extra duties on foreign (i.e. non-British) goods and ships, following the benefit principle.[23]

The Government of Bengal introduced a system of discriminatory taxation for the first time in 1811 when Regulation III was introduced providing that goods brought into India in non-British ships were to pay twice the amount of duties. Cotton goods imported in British ships paid $7\frac{1}{2}$ per cent *ad valorem*, where goods imported in other ships paid 15 per cent *ad valorem*. The British manufacturers who were at that time clamouring for the ending of the East India Company's monopoly were pleased with this arrangement although some of them would have liked even more protection in the Indian market against foreign competitors.[24]

Already the President of the Board of Control had sent a detailed report to the Court of Directors asking them to remodel the tariff system of India so as to encourage imports from Britain. He told the Court that they should not consider only 'their mercantile interest', and their tax system should no longer be based on their rights and privileges alone, but 'regulated by the general principles of political economy'.[25] But Courtenay's (the President of the Board of control) political economy was different from that of the Classical economists. He started from the position that the 'free and un-burthened export of its manufacturers is unquestionably according to all received principles of political economy, an advantage to the exporting country'. He proposed to give these advantages solely to Britain and India,

---

[22] Secret Letters to Bengal, 3 November 1787. Courtenay said that this letter was originally written by Henry Dundas instructed by Pitt himself after the Convention with France on 31 August 1787. See his Report, *Home Misc.* India Office Records, no. 523, pp. 12–13.

[23] See Draft of Court of Directors to Bengal (Separate: Customs) 6 November 1807. Although the above remarks were removed by the Board of Control in the final despatch, it shows their views. *Bengal Despatches*, vol. 47, India Office Records, E/4/662, pp. 832–3.

[24] See a letter from De Dunstanville, a Cornish tin mine owner and signed by five other copper and tin mine owners to the President of the Board of Control. Dated 18 July 1814. *Home Misc.* India Office Records, no. 61, pp. 237, 241–4.

[25] *Loc. cit.*, pp. 5–6.

hence his suggestion for removing all export duties and the reduction of import duties. When an official at the India Office suggested that no reduction was necessary on imports because imports were going up, Courtenay's answer was: 'a trade which consists in the transport of manufactures from one part of the empire to another is to a country like England a national interest and carried on by navigation it is a concern of state policy. To encourage such a trade is to encourage British industry, British shipping and British finance.' So he proposed a double duty on commodities that were imported into India on non-British ships. Courtenay's suggestions were accepted in full by the Court of Directors, and the local governments were instructed to alter the tariff policy according to his principles.[26]

It is not very difficult to understand the significance of such a policy once the prevailing circumstances are known. France was still the enemy of the British, and the Battle of Waterloo had not yet been fought. Hence this was not a period in which Britain could be expected to encourage international trade. Pitt's free trade policy, begun in 1786, was short-lived, and the reaction in favour of protection, which started in 1793 with the Peninsular War, did not subside until after 1820. Having instituted a policy it was difficult to change it, although the circumstances were no longer the same. The Court of Directors were unwilling to reduce the differential duties of foreign nations because they were found to be 'desirable with a view to the interests of our revenue as well as to guard against a competition unfavourable to British commerce and shipping'.[27] Even when the Court felt that foreign trade ought to be increased, they specified that it must not 'imply a *sacrifice of some greater interest*', and also that it 'should be in favour of those states which grant peculiar advantages to British traders'.[28]

Having established a tariff system in India favourable to Britain, the British government pursued a crude mercantilist policy even in respect of Indian imports into Britain. Simultaneously with the imposition of import duties to suit British imports into India, the British tariff was made stiffer

[26] Court of Directors in Bengal (Separate: Customs) 29 July 1814, *Bengal Despatches*, vol. 65, India Office Records, E/4/680, pp. 297 *et seq*. Courtenay in his Report did not hide the fact that his consideration was not necessarily the well-being of India. 'The experiment to be tried is a measure of encouragement to the importation of those articles into India, is not simply an experiment upon the capacity, or with a view to the advantage of India, but is an experiment also, the success of which would be beneficial to the commerce and industry of Britain. It is therefore peculiarly a question for decision in this country.' *Loc. cit.*, p. 130.

[27] Court of Directors to Bengal (Separate: Customs) 18 June 1817, *Revenue Letters to Bengal*, India Office Records, vol. V, p. 318.

[28] Court of Directors to Bombay (Separate: Customs), 10 September 1828, *Bombay Despatches*, vol. 55, India Office Records, E/4/1050, pp. 45–6. *Italics mine*.

for Indian commodities entering Britain.[29] In fact, protection was demanded and given to the prosperous and powerful British shipbuilders against the relatively youthful Indian ship-building industry. By 1814, the nascent Indian ship-building industry was beginning to damage the well established British shipbuilders because its cost structure was found economical by the British users of merchantmen. Hence the British shipbuilders clamoured for a duty on India-built shipping to achieve the 'desired reciprocity' which would make the buyer indifferent as to where he purchased his ship. It was pointed out by the British ship-building interest that, although the principle of reciprocity 'involves the considerations of advantages and disadvantages as between merchants and manufacturers only, national considerations' were also 'a distinct part of the subject, and must be contemplated by those who rule with more enlarged views of general policy'.[30]

Even when there was no competition between Indian and British goods, Indian goods were treated in Britain as if they came from an independent country. Indian exports of sugar to Britain were particularly affected. The West Indies was India's main competitor in the British market, but Indian sugar had to pay a much higher rate of duty to enter the British market, 37 shillings per hundredweight as against only 27 shillings.[31] West Indian sugar was also given a subsidy of 3 shillings per hundredweight for every ton re-exported from Britain. The Indian manufacturers, however, were confident that if the duties were equalised India would be able to export more to Britain. In addition to the dutiable goods, there were items like silk the import of which was totally prohibited in Britain.

While the differential tariff was not much criticised, other aspects of the British tariff – especially the preferential treatment given to the West Indian sugar – were vigorously opposed. Many civil servants in India complained of unfair treatment by the British government.[32] One civil servant wrote anonymously that the unfair tariff was violating 'common justice' and was not consistent with the 'fair principle of reciprocity', and owing to the special relationship between India and Britain, whether protection was beneficial to Britain or not, it should never have been against India.[33] Others

---

[29] See for the table of rates, *Parl. Papers*, H.C. 735–II vol. X of Session 1831–2, pp. 591–607.

[30] See 'Reasons for Imposing a Duty on India-built shipping' (1814). Add MSS. 38,410, p. 331 (Liverpool Papers at the British Museum).

[31] When it was proposed to increase the tariff preference granted to West Indies sugar in 1813, an important argument was that Indian sugar would adversely hit British shipping interest as against India built shipping. See House of Commons debates *Hansard*, 1 Series, vol. XXVII, p. 201–5, 26 November 1813.

[32] See for the views of Sir Thomas Munro, Minute, Arbuthnot (ed.), *op. cit.*, vol. I, p. cxxix.

[33] *Free Commerce with India: A Letter to the President of the Board of Trade* (London, 1825), by a Madras Civil Servant, pp. 10–11. Metcalfe also demonstrated against the unjust

said that had India been independent, she would have pursued a protectionist policy and even now should be permitted to do so.[34] Montgomery Martin suggested a system of reciprocity between Britain and India and a uniform commercial system, in order to consolidate the empire as in the German states.[35]

Whereas only a handful of Indian civil servants criticised the British tariff against Indian goods, a variety of interests fought for the equalisation of duties on East and West Indian sugar, and political economy was a convenient tool. First, the East India Company had the problem of remittances from India;[36] second, the free traders who thought that exports could not be increased without taking anything back;[37] third, the general public which anticipated cheap sugar, if the duties were equalised or removed;[38] and fourth, perhaps the leading lights of the anti-Slavery movement who were connected with the agitation to equalise the duties on West and East Indian sugar. Sir John Shore, Charles Grant, and others who belonged to the Clapham sect had all been connected with India. Their attacks on slavery were more against the West India interest than any other, and they too used the language of political economy.[39] This was also one of those practical

---

Footnote 33 continued

distinction which he thought was preventing the introduction of European enterprise into India. See his note on Ellenborough to Bentinck, 11 October 1829 (*Bentinck Papers*, Nottingham University Library). See also *Letter to the Author of a View of the Present State and Future Prospects of the Free Trade and Colonisation of India* (London, 1830), pp. 24–5. Edward Thornton, *India, its State and Prospects* (London, 1835), p. 84.

[34] Gavin Young, *An Essay on the Mercantile Theory of Wealth* (Calcutta, 1832), pp. 2, 59, 76–7, 84. Young advocated an independent economic policy based on Mercantilist principles for India. He used both the infant industry argument as well as the example of America's succeessful experience with tariffs. See also *Historical Sketch of Taxes on the English Commerce in Bengal*, pp. 146–7, 154. Mss Eur D. 283 (India Office Library).

[35] *Parl. Papers*, H.C. 527, vol. VIII of Session 1840, Q. 4114. See also John Bell, *A Comparative View of the External Commerce of Bengal During the Years 1831–2 to 1832–3* (Calcutta, 1833), p. 3.

[36] See views of the Collector of Masulipatam to Madras Board of Revenue, 6 April 1836. This was in reply to a query regarding methods to improve trade between India and Britain. The same answer was given by the Collector of Rajahmundry, 14 November 1834, who said 'reduce the duties and to give no advantage to other colonies'. *Home Misc.* India Office Records, No. 791, pp. 252, 589.

[37] See John Prinsep, *Suggestions of Freedom of Commerce and Navigation more Especially in reference to the East India Trade* (London, 1823), p. 24.

[38] Captain Maberly in the House of Commons said for example that Britain should get rid of the West Indian Colonies ('From the time of Adam Smith, down to the present day, every intelligent writer on political economy had condemned our colonial connections') so that on the one hand Britain would be relieved of the enormous defence expenditure and on the other 'sugar could be procured at a comparatively moderate price from the East Indies.' *Hansard*, II Series, vol. XII, p. 1085, 18 March 1825.

[39] See for example the views of a Bengal Civil servant sympathetic to the tenets of the Clapham Sect, S. S. Brown, *Home Letters* (London, 1878), p. 219.

problems in which economists like Ricardo, McCulloch and John Stuart Mill voiced their opinions most vehemently.[40]

This question came up in the House of Commons in the summer of 1827, and John Stuart Mill in an anonymous article in the *Parliamentary History and Review* attacked in unequivocal terms the preference shown to the West Indian sugar. He claimed there was no legitimate justification for the extra duties levied on Indian sugar. 'If the duties were equalised,' Mill argued,

the taxed commodities either could, or could not, be obtained at less cost from the East Indies than from the West. If they could, the discriminating duties are a tax on the people of England, to enable the West Indians to carry on . . . losing business. If not, the duties are meant for no purpose except to ward off a danger which does not exist; they ought, therefore to be repealed.[41]

Much as the Indian government and the East India Company were concerned about the discrimination in favour of West Indies, there was little they could do to alter the situation.[42] West Indian interests were too strong in Parliament for equalisation to become a reality.[43] There were many petitions favouring equalisation sent to William Huskisson at the Board of Trade in the 1820s, but in spite of his free trade views, Huskisson was too much the politician to do anything against a powerful force in Parliament, and he was reluctant to bring about the equalisation, thinking that it 'would bring ruin on the West Indies'. His remedy was to induce the West Indian planters to reduce their sugar output voluntarily rather than through removing the preference enjoyed by them in Britain.[44]

Eventually the preference enjoyed by West Indian sugar was taken away in 1836 during the administration of Sir Robert Peel, who, more than anybody else was responsible for the adoption of a *laissez-faire* economic policy in Britain. West Indian planters did indeed argue on mercantilistic lines for the perpetuation of the discriminatory tariff,[45] but when the whole

[40] Sraffa (ed.), *op. cit*, vol. v, pp. 479–83, McCulloch's Edition of *Wealth of Nations*, vol. IV, p. 529, and McCulloch's *Literature of Political Economy* (London, 1845), p. 93.

[41] Volume dated 1826–7. Quotation is from a photostat copy of Mill's Article at the LSE Library, p. 59. Mill did not regard West Indies as a separate country (i.e. economically speaking) and thought that trade with it should 'be amenable to the principles of the home trade'. See *Principles of Political Economy*, pp. 685–6. Book III, Chap. 25.

[42] See the debate held at the East India Company on 19 June 1822, *Asiatic Journal*, September 1822, p. 256.

[43] West Indian interests in British Parliament had considerable political influence until the great reform Act of 1832. See L. J. Ragatz, *The Fall of the Planter Class in the Caribbean 1763–1833* (New York, 1928).

[44] See Huskisson's Memorandum on Sugar duties, Add. Mss 38,744, pp. 206–8 (Peel Papers at the British Museum).

[45] See for instance their Memorandum to Sir Robert Peel, dated 16 March 1835, Add. Mss. 40, 417, pp. 109 *et seq.* (Peel Papers at British Museum).

British tariff structure was undergoing a thorough transformation on free trade lines, their argument had little effect on policy makers.

Even after the equalisation of West and East Indian sugar duties, the impact of the total system was favourable to British industry, and it did not stimulate industrial activity in India to any appreciable extent. Imports from Britain were allowed to pass through the provinces without any obligation to pay transit duties, while Indian goods were not so exempt until the transit duties were abolished. There were heavy export duties on raw cotton exports to any country other than Britain. We have already seen how British industry had a strong tariff wall to protect it against overseas competition. Some goods like silk and taffeta were prohibited imports until 1824, and even afterwards they were charged 20 to 30 per cent *ad valorem* duties.

From time to time, Indian officials advocated the abolition of the differential duties in favour of British manufacturers, although the British free traders were silent on this issue. Holt Mackenzie came out against this type of discrimination in India's tariff structure. As early as 1825, he wrote that 'it appears to me to be doubtful whether it is founded on any just principle', and he held that English industry was strong enough to withstand foreign competition without 'special favour'.[46] Trevelyan said that it was possible to justify discriminatory taxation on the basis of Adam Smith's dictum that defence was more important than opulence, but he was not sure whether the existing situation warranted such serious violation of the principles of free trade economic policy.[47] The Government of India also advocated the abolition of all distinctions regarding the place of produce.[48] But the Court of Directors was not willing to remove the discriminatory tariff.

By 1850 the English fiscal system was fully based on the principle of free trade. The Indian government too, under the Earl of Canning, desired the introduction of similar legislation, and proposed, among other things, an equalisation of the duties paid by British and foreign manufacturers.[49] Following the Crown takeover of Indian administration, it was the Secretary of State, and not the Court of Directors, who was now responsible for the formation of Indian policy. Lord Stanley, the Secretary of State, concurred with the opinions of the Government of India and said that as the 'enlightened legislation' of recent years in Britain has removed the discriminating duties,

---

[46] Minute dated 23 June 1825, *Bengal Separate Consultations*, no. 23, India Office Records, Range 164, vol. 16.

[47] *A Report upon the Inland Customs*, p. 152.

[48] Governor General to Court of Directors (Separate Customs) 1 October 1830, no. 4 of 1830, *Bengal Letters Received*, vol. 112, India Office Records, E/4/133.

[49] Already by the Act VI of 1848, the special protection given to British ships had been removed. All goods exported or imported on foreign ships were required to pay only the duty that was charged on such goods if they were exported or imported on British ships. In defending this policy, the Court of Directors said: 'Ships are not the cause, but the instruments and consequences of extended commerce; and to protect the shipping at the

it was 'equally desirable that the same principle should be applied to the commerce of the Queen's dominions in India'.[50] The new tariff system based on these ideas came into operation in 1860.

CUSTOMS DUTIES ON IMPORTS

Along with the removal of the differential tariff, import duties were introduced into' the new tariff scheme. The Secretary of State had no objection at all to those duties on goods 'which are used as luxuries by the richer classes of the community without the imposition of any injurious check on consumption'.[51] Thus the British manufacturers not only lost their preferential treatment over other nations but were also put in an unfavourable position compared with the Indian producers of cotton textiles. Only two years previously, it had been remarked that, while a strict free trader would 'object to these differential duties between British and foreign goods', the burden on British imports into India by itself was not much and any increase would not therefore be unreasonable.[52] But the situation had altered by 1861, as the import duties particularly affected the Lancashire cotton textile manufacturers; from then onwards, until the taxes were repealed in 1882, the Lancashire manufacturers carried on an agitation for the removal of these duties. In this agitation, they derived much support from the free trade policies advocated by Cobden and Bright. The gradual reduction and the eventual removal of import duties used to be ascribed to the belief of the policy makers in free trade. In other words, the policy makers were supposed to have thought that trade between India and Britain, if left customs-free, would bring equal benefit to both countries.[53] However, in the light of the available evidence and the recent researches of R. J. Moore, Peter Harnetty and Amales Tripathi, we may legitimately feel somewhat sceptical about this view. It is possible to say that a belief in these principles encouraged the policy makers to conform to the wishes of vested interests more readily than

Footnote 49 continued

   expense of the commercial interests, must of necessity involve the absurdity of sacrificing the end to the means.' Court of Directors to the Governor General in Council, no. 3 of 1846 (Separate Revenue), *Parl. Papers*, H.C. no. 511, vol. IX of Session 1847–48, p. 444. Governor-General in Council to Court of Directors (Separate Revenue) no. 5 of 1857, 23 February 1857. *India and Bengal Letters Received* E/4/268, India Office Records.

[50] Secretary of State to Viceroy (Separate Revenue, Customs), no. 4 of 1859, 7 April 1859, Separate Revenue Dispatch to India, India Office Records, No. L/E/3/622, pp. 124–5. While the discussions were going on *in camera*, the *Economist* came out in favour of the abolition of the discriminatory tariff in India, vol. XVII, no. 816, 16 April 1859, p. 418.

[51] Secretary of State to Viceroy (Separate: Customs, Revenue) 7 April 1859, *op. cit.*, pp. 143–4. *loc. cit.*

[52] W. E. Forster, *How We Tax India?* (Leeds, 1858), p. 28. A liberal politician and sometimes member of Gladstone's Cabinet.

[53] P. E. Roberts, *History of British India* (Oxford, 1938), p. 455. See also J. Ramsay Macdonald *The Government of India* (New York, 1920) p. 129.

they would have done otherwise. But what is clear is that, without the motive force of interested parties, such principles by themselves would have had little chance of being implemented.

After the cataclysmic events of 1857, the financial problem was the main consideration to such an extent that one of the great protagonists of free trade, James Wilson, had to resort to indirect taxation on imported goods and justify it on the plea that 'necessity has no law'.[54] The Secretary of State informed Wilson that Manchester manufacturers were unhappy with the Indian tariff, for it was hitting them 'while treating Bombay leniently'.[55] And this was in spite of the fact that 10 per cent on manufactured goods and 5 per cent on yarn was all that the Indian government levied on imported goods. Even these low tariffs were not to the liking of the Manchester Chamber of Commerce, which passed a resolution that to retain customs duties in India was not in keeping with a nation wedded to a *laissez-faire* economic policy.[56] The Chamber might have maintained its pressure, but as Sir Charles Wood said, Wilson's 'known free trade opinions kept sober people quiet and steady'.[57]

In the 1860s the Lancashire manufacturers had the added problem of raw material shortages due to the American Civil War. Manufacturers thought that if with protection the Indian cotton textile industry grew, they would not only have to compete with the nascent Indian industry for markets but also for raw materials.[58] Petitions were presented and pressure was exerted. Apart from the stock arguments of free trade, the Lancashire publicists argued that the tariff was only protecting inefficient hand manufactures. The effect was the prevention of any large increase in foreign trade, whereas 'to acquire an increased interchange of products with other countries is the aim of every aspiring nation'. Inefficient hand manufacturers were being protected, and labour and capital were prevented from moving to the production of export commodities. If the protection given to inefficient manufactures were removed, it would not mean unemployment because 'if we should throw the native weaver out of that employment, we in doing so only lead him to a more profitable one, and advance his own conditions'.[59]

Although the Secretary of State realised that the Indian import duties

---

[54] Wilson's Financial Statement, 18 February 1860. *Annual Financial Statements*, p. 19.

[55] Wood to Wilson, 3 April 1860 (Halifax Papers India Office Library).

[56] With remarkable prescience, H. T. Prinsep had said in 1853: 'A tax of 10 per cent on the manufactures of England imported into India, such as is levied on those of India brought to England, would create an outcry at Manchester that no government could stand against.' *The India Question in 1853*, p. 24.

[57] Wood to Canning, 16 September 1860 (Halifax Papers, India Office Library).

[58] From *Manchester Examiner & Times* 29 October 1861, cited in Silver, *Manchester Men and India Cotton* (Manchester, 1964), p. 165.

[59] See James Mann, *The Cotton Trade of India* (London, 1860), pp. 26, 28.

were not hurting the Lancashire cotton textile industry, he nevertheless asked the Viceroy to explore possibilities of reducing the duties.[60] Both the Viceroy and the finance member were receptive to the idea. Samuel Laing, the finance member, like the British cotton manufacturers at this stage, was more worried by future prospects rather than by the immediate loss of a market.[61] Accordingly he reduced the duty on yarn from 5 per cent to $3\frac{1}{2}$ per cent, but retained the duty on manufactured goods at 10 per cent.[62]

The problem rose again in the 1870s with the cotton slump. Manchester merchants turned their attention once more to India, which was quite natural under the circumstances. When foreign investments dropped in the 1870s this could have resulted in a considerable drop in British exports as well. But it was the crucial demand for British goods (especially cotton textiles) overseas and particularly in the primary producing colonies such as Australia and India that prevented a severe contraction in production. The manufacturers advocated a lower salt tax to increase the effective demand for cotton goods. A sound income tax was also recommended because it was felt that the Indian merchants were not taxed as heavily as their counterparts in Britain.[63] The Chamber of Commerce also viewed the growth of the Indian cotton textile industry with considerable alarm. From a mere four mills in 1858 with about 2000 workers, the Indian cotton textile industry had grown into seventeen mills with 10 000 workers in 1869, and to fifty-eight mills with 40 000 workers in 1880.[64] This phenomenal growth was ascribed to the five per cent *ad valorem* duty on cotton imports. In its Memorial to the Prime Minister, Gladstone, the Manchester Chamber of Commerce said that as a consequence of the import duty a protected trade in cotton manufacture was being developed in India.[65] The Manchester manufacturers carried on a sustained agitation against these duties, claiming that this removal became increasingly important with the fall in the value of silver which was having a favourable effect on the Indian exports and on unfavourable impact on English exports to India. The Prime Minister was told: 'the levying of such duties ... is inconsistent with the commercial policy of this Country and subversive of the soundest principles of political economy and free trade'.[66]

[60] Wood to Elgin, 25 February 1862, 3 March 1862, *op. cit.*

[61] See the statement dated 16 April 1862, *Annual Financial Statements*, p. 86.

[62] For an elaborate treatment of the customs duty controversy, see Peter Harnetty, 'The Imperialism of Free Trade: Lancashire and the Indian Cotton Duties, 1859–1862' *Economic History Review*, vol. XVII, no. 2, August 1965.

[63] Resolution of the Manchester Chamber of Commerce 19 October 1870, Redford, *Manchester Merchants and Foreign Trade* (Manchester, 1956), vol. II, p. 26.

[64] S. D. Mehta, *The Cotton Mills of India: 1854–1954* (Bombay, 1955), p. 233.

[65] Redford, *op. cit.*, vol. II, p. 28. See also the *Economist*, 7 November 1874 vol. XXXII, p. 1339. See also the *Indian Economist*, 10 January 1870.

[66] Redford, *op. cit.*, vol. II, pp. 28, 29.

Lancashire publicists also conducted a regular pamphlet war to influence public opinion.[67]

The abolition of customs duties was, however, opposed by many people in India. S. S. Bengallee of Bombay argued that the customs duty was not protective in character, and in addition to that it also satisfied other requirements (e.g. equity) of a good tax.[68] There were many others who contested the view that protection was harmful to the long run interests of the country. A columnist in the *Times of India* referred to the past development of cotton textile and woollen manufacturers in Britain in terms of the protection they had from India for cotton textiles and from Ireland for woollen manufactures. It was true that protective tariffs had, under certain circumstances, misallocated resources, but on balance they were beneficial.[69] Kashinath Trimbak Telang pointed out that the custom duties, by providing protection, had enabled large quantities of previously idle capital to be invested in India profitably, and remarked that 'Bombay with her protectionist system had not gone to rack and ruin, but has been exhibiting, on the contrary, a striking development'.[70] Most of the arguments opposing abolition used the 'infant industry' argument made respectable by John Stuart Mill in his *Principles of Political Economy*. Another critic of abolition said that the objections raised in England against customs duties were from the standpoint of English political economy, which was by no means universally accepted. He specially referred to the writings of Friedrich List, Karl Knies and other members of the German historical school who had consistently opposed the free trade ideas of English Classical political economy from the standpoint of protection for infant industries.[71] To the frequently made charge that protection had the effect of increasing the price level, Telang cited David Syme's article in the *Fortnightly Review* (April 1873) to show that as a result of protection prices had ultimately fallen in the USA and France.[72]

A large number of Indian civil servants were against abolition, especially those in the upper echelons of service, worried by the financial stringency caused by famines, the fall in silver and the necessity of public works. They

---

[67] W. E. Taylor, *Letters on the Indian Import Duties* (Manchester, 1876), pp. 5–15. See also R. Raynsford Jackson, *India and Lancashire: An Answer to Recent Arguments* (London, 1876), pp. 7–8.

[68] *A Letter to the Right Honourable Lord Lytton against the Contemplated Repeal of the Duties on the Import of Foreign Cotton Goods into India* (Bombay, 1877), p. 7.

[69] *Articles on Indian Finance* (Bombay, 1883), p. 18.

[70] *Free-trade and Protection from an Indian Point of View* (Bombay, 1877), p. 24.

[71] *Articles on Indian Finance*, p. 18. See also *The Indian Problem Solved* (London, 1874), p. 392.

[72] Telang, *op. cit.*, p. 9. David Syme with his rich Australian experience was in a much better position to appreciate the protectionist viewpoint. In his *Outlines of an Industrial Science* published in 1877, he made a long critical comment on the abolition of Indian import duties.

were naturally unwilling to give up any source of revenue. They knew that the alternative to customs duties was income tax, and this was anathema because of its direct, inquisitorial nature. Indian opinion as gauged by the British administrators was against the repeal of customs duties as well as against any introduction of income tax. Samuel Laing, who had been a finance member, said in 1872 that if India had been independent, without any doubt she would have increased import duties in preference to an income tax.[73] Lytton, the Governor-General wrote to Lord Salisbury, the Secretary of State, at one stage that he and his finance member Sir John Strachey were the only members of the government who were for the repeal of the customs duties on cotton imports.[74] Even the Viceroy's council felt that these 'duties are levied at a very small cost and at a minimum of inconvenience to the people,' and they cause no discontent'.[75] These considerations were more important for practical administrators than mere theories, as another senior civil servant pointed out: 'The advocates of abolition quote political economy, and gain the easy victory which always falls to those who take their stand on first principles and irrefutable theories.[76] The civil servants' difficulty was that they had to be on the defensive, having no theoretical basis for their views. Bred in an atmosphere of free trade, most of them were reluctant to embrace the protectionist viewpoint without strong reservations. Hence the Indian civil servants found themselves opposing the removal of the duties while agreeing that imports duties were harmful to the country.[77]

An important aspect of policy making in this issue was the political importance of the Lancashire lobby in the Commons. The lobby was in a position to threaten the Conservatives with electoral defeats in the Lancashire constituencies. The Secretary of State, Lord Salisbury, wrote to the Viceroy that the whole issue had become political, and that Parliament, when 'its attention is drawn to the matter, will not allow the only remnant of protection within the direct jurisdiction of the English Government to be a protective duty, which, as far as it operates at all, is hostile to English manufacturers'. Difficult as it was, he still managed to secure the withdrawal of a motion on Indian tariff policy in the House of Commons in 1876.[78]

---

[73] *Parl. Papers*, H.C. 327, vol. VIII of Session 1872, Q. 7475.

[74] Lytton to Salisbury, 25 April 1877 (Lytton Papers India Office Library).

[75] Proceedings of the Separate Revenue Department, January 1875, *Parl. Papers*, H.C. 56, vol. LVI of Session 1876.

[76] Note of dissent on the Report of Committee for valuation of tariffs by Alonzo Money, a Member of the Board of Revenue, *Ibid.*

[77] See Speeches of T. C. Hope, Sir William Muir, Ashley Eden and Lord Northbrook. Proceedings of the Viceroy's Council, 5 August 1875, *Ibid.*

[78] Salisbury to Lytton, 24 March 1876 (Lytton Papers, *op. cit.*). Members of Salisbury's council like Drummond, Ellis and Cassels were against any reduction or elimination of the import duties in India.

The strong Lancashire lobby in Parliament was not easily silenced. Being the leader of the Conservative Party, Lord Salisbury was particularly anxious about the fate of the impending by-elections. 'We have a certain grumbling agitation going on in the manufacturing districts about the cotton duty,' he wrote in 1877 'and it may possibly affect the Salford election at this unlucky moment.'[79] In fact, Salisbury's idea in sending Lord Lytton to India as Viceroy was to carry out some of his policies, of which the abolition of import duties was one, Lytton's predecessor, Lord Northbrook, having been unwilling to relinquish import duties and having emphasised that the 'Manchester demand is unreasonable, not supported by the facts of the case, and should be resisted'.[80]

Lord Lytton, however, had an intractable finance member of the Council who was unwilling to give up the import duties on cotton. The obvious solution was to get rid of the finance member, and to this end Lytton wrote to Salisbury for help: 'I believe, with the assistance of an able Finance Minister, who cordially adopts our point of view, I should be able to deal a death blow to the cotton duties.'[81] Lytton's choice was Sir John Strachey, who had also been recommended to him by his friend Sir James Fitzjames Stephen for a different purpose.[82] The finance member, Sir William Muir, was therefore conveniently promoted to the India Council, and Strachey was appointed to succeed him.[83]

In spite of Strachey's presence and his own 'wild ambition to get rid of customs duties altogether',[84] Lytton was unable at that time to go beyond a few concessions. But the decisive moment came two years later in 1879. Increasing unemployment in Lancashire made the position of the Conservatives none too easy. With a general election approaching, the Conservative constituency parties of Lancashire made many efforts to influence the Secretary of State to remove the Indian import duties which they thought were responsible for the slump in the cotton industry. To cite an example, the President of the Blackburn Conservative Association did not hide his Party's position *vis-à-vis* Indian tariff policy:

It is felt that we have been very unfairly treated by the Government with reference to the abolition of the Indian import duties, and I feel certain that the prospects of

---

[79] Salisbury to Lytton 13 April 1877 (Lytton Papers, *op. cit.*).

[80] Northbrook to Mallet, 6 September 1875 (*Northbrook Papers*, India Office Library) cited in Edward Moulton, *Lord Northbrook's Indian Administration 1872–76* (London, 1969), pp. 194–5.

[81] Lytton to Salisbury, 11 April 1876 (Lytton Papers, *op. cit.*).

[82] See my forthcoming monograph tentatively titled, *Monetary Thought and Management in India: Studies in their Interaction in the Nineteenth Century.*

[83] See Lalit Gujral, 'Background to the Appointment of Sir John Strachey as Finance Member in 1876' *Journal of Indian History*, no 119, August 1962, pp. 359 *et seq.*

[84] Lytton to Salisbury 16 February 1877 (Lytton Papers, *op. cit.*).

of the Conservative party are such as to give no hope for the return of any Conservative candidate in this division of the Country, without something done immediately in the way of reducing or rectifying the duty.[85]

Lord Cranbrook, who had succeeded Lord Salisbury as Secretary of State, forwarded this communication to Lytton, adding that unless something was done the Conservatives stood to lose fourteen seats in Lancashire.[86] Lytton accordingly repealed the whole of the import duties on cotton except for a few minor items. All his councillors with the exception of Strachey opposed the repeal. However, the Viceroy used his extraordinary power of veto to circumvent the majority decision in the Council. Even at the London end, the Secretary of State faced stiff opposition for his free trade policy.[87]

The remaining few items in the customs tariff were repealed during Ripon's viceroyalty in 1882. Knowing full well that the pressure from English manufacturers was responsible for such a course of action, in order to assuage the feelings of the Indians, the Secretary of State advised the Viceroy to stress 'as much as possible on the Indian arguments in its (abolition of the import duties) favour'.[88] This is of course what the viceroys were always doing.[89]

Sir Louis Mallet, who had been sent to India to investigate the problems connected with customs duties during the viceroyalty of Lord Northbrook, had remarked that the duties were condemned by every English economist.[90] Lytton too claimed that the 'Manchester people have on their side all the best economists'.[91] In spite of such assertions, the economists were not all of them such unqualified free traders. John Stuart Mill's arguments for protecting infant industries is too well known to need elaboration here. Henry Fawcett, the most influential economist on Indian affairs, was also against the repeal of the cotton duties. He denied that the duties were falling on

---

[85] Hornby to Starkie, 7 February 1879, Enclosure to Cranbrook to Lytton, 15 February 1879. (Lytton Papers, *op. cit.*).

[86] Cranbrook to Lytton, 23 February, 1879 (Lytton Papers, *op. cit.*).

[87] See S. N. Singh, *The Secretary of State of India and His Council* (Delhi, 1962), pp. 123–5.

[88] Hartington to Ripon, 23 December 1881 (*Ripon Papers*, British Museum).

[89] See for example the defence of the abolition of custom duties in the *Budget Statement*, 1876–7.

[90] See enclosures to Lytton to Salisbury, 12 March 1876 (Lytton Papers, *op. cit.*).

[91] Lytton to William Muir, 12 June 1876 (Lytton Papers). It cannot be said that the British members of the Parliament who had championed free trade for India believed sincerely in it. To give an instance, Henry Chaplin while advocating government action said, 'I confess I am totally unable to comprehend the doctrines of modern Free Trade. They seem to me to have degenerated into nothing but a cry for "cheapness at any cost" no matter how it is produced.' *Hansard*, III series, vol. CCCXXXVI, p. 1888 4 June 1889. Another famous MP for Lancashire John Cheetham went so far as to say that 'if India was to be left to private enterprise he had no confidence in it' and he hoped for something better than 'the usual stale answer, namely that it was contrary to the rules of political economy'. Cited by Grampp, *The Manchester School* (Stanford, 1960), p. 125.

goods which were also being produced at Bombay. As the incidence of the duties was on the fine fabrics used by the upper income groups, he concluded that their repeal 'would reduce the amount of taxation paid by the wealthy, and would consequently still further increase the inequality in the taxation borne by the poor'. He further argued that, as the Government of India was running continuous deficit budgets, it would be unwise to give up any source of revenue unless it had found 'some other less objectionable form'. As the duties curbed imports, they were found doubly useful. On the one hand, they brought in revenue, and on the other, they reduced the pressure on external payments in gold. Fawcett thus concluded that the repeal of the duties would be harmful and pointed out the danger of applying free trade policy too rigidly. 'In considering questions of taxation,' Fawcett said, 'nothing can be more unwise than to conclude that that particular tax must be the best which is most in accord with the Principles of economic science'.[92]

Supporting Fawcett was the most respected practical financial administrator of the day, W. E. Gladstone, who opposed the repeal on financial as well as on moral grounds.[93] Even Sir James Fitzjames Stephen whose opinions Lytton valued did not seem anxious to remove customs duties regardless of the financial problems, as he wrote to Lytton: 'If I were you, I would do nothing at all about the cotton duties till I had well meditated on the spot and with full advice from the financial department.'[94]

It cannot be overemphasised that the issue was not decided by free trade doctrine but was the outcome of successful political pressure.[95] As Sir Evelyn Baring, Ripon's finance member, himself admitted, 'I have always held that a very considerable portion of public opinion in England is free trade more by accident than by conviction.'[96] There was some justification for Baring's complaint, because he was upset by the reluctance of the British government

---

[92] *Indian Finance: Three Essays* (London, 1880), pp. 76 *et seq.* Cliffe-Leslie also argued along the same lines. See *Fortnightly Review*, November 1870 for his article.

[93] Gladstone's Speech in the House of Commons, *Hansard*, 12 June 1879, 3rd Series, vol. CCXLVI, p. 1746. One must note here that at this time Gladstone was in opposition When he came to power, Lord Hartington, his Secretary of State for India, had caused all the remnants of customs duties removed irrespective of the financial considerations!

[94] Stephen to Lytton, 16 March 1876 (Stephen Mss at Cambridge University Library).

[95] Sir Richard Temple who was an Indian civil servant turned British politician advised Manchester merchants: 'it cannot be expected that, as British electors, you will submit to such duties being imposed in a country like India, which is under the absolute control of the Government in England, and which does not enjoy the blessings of a responsible – I would rather say an irresponsible – Government of its own. My advice to you is that you do not submit to it – (Hear Hear), and that you do not cease to agitate till those injurious duties are withdrawn (Hear Hear) . . .' (Address dated 15 March 1881). Manchester merchants were of course more successful than other interests such as the coal exporters who grumbled that their trade would be affected by the weakening of the infant cotton industry in India!!

[96] Baring to Ripon, 14 January 1883, Add. Mss. 43 598, p. 122 (*Ripon Papers*, British Museum).

to establish free trade between India and Britain for silverware. The import of silver plate was virtually prohibited in Britain by the law of compulsory hall-marking.[97] This particularly affected Indian exports to Britain. The Chairman of the Goldsmith and Silversmith's Free trade Association petitioned to the Viceroy, Lord Ripon,[98] who referred it to Gladstone, but he was not willing to introduce free trade for the ostensible reason that it would throw the silverplate workers in England out of employment.

Customs duties were originally levied because of the acute financial stringency experienced by the government. But for the attention bestowed upon them by the Lancashire manufacturers, the customs duties would have remained part of the Indian tax structure although they violated some aspects of the theory of Classical economic policy. The British parliamentary system was such that decisions were made by and large as a result of successful political horse-trading. It so happened that Classical political economy pointed towards the repeal of the customs duties. Even if it had been otherwise, the process of decision making being what it was, the outcome would not have been different.[99] It is difficult to concur fully with a recent interpretation that the influence of British mercantile interests on the formation of Indian economic policy was 'mild', and that far from being economic imperialism, it was a case of a genuine gift of sound economic policy to India.[100] It is true, as we have already observed, that there were Indian civil servants who resisted pressure from British business interests, but it should not be forgotten that if a particular policy happened to be vital, the final decision almost always went against Indian interests. In the last third of the century, according to a Lancashire Member of Parliament: 'we leaned upon the consuming power of our Indian fellow-subjects for a vast portion of our trade ... [I am] one of several members who represented manufacturing constituencies whose very existence rested on their trade with that great

---

[97] See Edward J. Watherston, 'Indian and other Foreign Productions in Silver, and Why they are virtually prohibited from importation into the U.K.' *Journal of the East Indian Association*, Vol. XIV, 1882, pp. 27–37.

[98] Petition dated 2 November 1883, Add. Mss. 43,634, pp. 30–31 (*Ripon Papers*, British Museum). See also C. W. Dilke, *Problems of Greater Britain*, Vol. II, p. 103.

[99] This could be seen from the fact that, although the hold of the Classical theory of economic policy over the prevailing economic opinion had slackened, the policy decision regarding the 1894–5 customs controversy followed the Classical prescription. This was when the British mercantile interests were able to apply pressure to introduce an excise duty on Indian manufacturers to offset the effects of a fresh customs duty which had become necessary owing to severe financial embarrassment. See for an account of this controversy, Peter Harnetty, 'The Indian Cotton Duties Controversy: 1894–96', *English Historical Review*, vol. LXXVII October 1962. See also C. J. Fuchs, *The Trade Policy of Great Britain and Her Colonies since 1860* (London, 1905), pp. 272 *et seq*.

[100] See Ira Klein, 'English Free Traders and Indian Tariffs, 1874–1896' *Modern Asian Studies*, vol. V, Part 3, July 1971, pp. 251–70.

country, and which, if that trade were withdrawn, would be at once deprived of all employment.'[101] British politicians were not blind to this aspect of the Indo-British economic relationship. Even those who were not professional politicians, and even those whom one would have expected to display magisterial impartiality, supported policies which favoured British interests. Economic theory was merely a convenient adjunct. For example Sir Henry Maine, while a member of the India Council, combined theoretical and political arguments in favour of repealing the cotton duties. He asserted at first that if India ceased to produce cotton textiles, she would 'be restored to her natural productive vocation. I have heard no answer to the economical argument'. But when confronted by the critics among Indian civil servants such as Sir William Muir who complained that during the formation of Indian economic policy undue attention was being paid to the Lancashire lobby, Maine snapped, 'There could be no worse result of Indian financial policy than that the opinion of the North of England should become indifferent to topics of Indian Government.[102]

Adherence to free trade was certainly not a major factor in the formation of Indian tariff policies over the years, especially when British interests involved. After all, when import duties on salt are taken into account, we see that this was neither a case of free trade nor a sacrifice of British interests. British salt manufacturers frequently tried to have the customs duties levied on imported salt removed, and used theoretical arguments to support their case.[103] However, the duties on imported salt were never abolished in India because there had always been a countervailing excise duty on locally manufactured salt. In fact, by suspending the government-managed production of salt in Bengal in 1863 and retaining the high level of excise taxation, British policy enabled the English salt manufacturers to penetrate the Indian market more easily, and thus cause the downfall of the Bengal salt industry.[104] Hence it would not be an exaggeration to say that British interests were never sacrificed when Indian tariff policies were framed whether they conformed to received economic doctrine or not.

[101] Slagg of Burnley in the House of Commons, 20 February 1888.
[102] Minute dated 13 July 1879. India Council Minute Book, India Office Records, no. C/128, pp. 367–70.
[103] See G. Wilbrahm, *Thoughts on the Salt Monopoly in India* (London, 1847) pp. 51–4, and D. C. Aylwin, *A Pamphlet on Salt Trade* (London, 1846), pp. 24–6.
[104] The suspension of government production of salt was the result partly of the pressure exercised by the English salt manufacturers, and partly the *laissez-faire* beliefs of G. Plowden the Salt Commissioner who recommended in 1856 the abolition of all forms of Government involvement in the production of salt. See for a detailed discussion, T. Banerjee, *Internal Market of India 1834–1909* (Calcutta, 1966), pp. 247–8; and R. C. Dutt, *The Economic History of India in the Victorian Age* (London, 1900), Chap. IX.

DUTIES ON EXPORTS FROM INDIA

While import tariffs were the subject of fierce controversy, export duties continued to be levied without much agitation. It is not difficult to perceive the reasons why, as a general policy, export duties did not receive approval from the Classical economists. Primarily they prevented a free flow of international trade. The Court of Directors were also conscious of the disadvantages of export duties,[105] and yet exports duties were part of the Indian fiscal system, with taxes on the export of salt-petre, foodgrains, indigo and other commercial crops for quite a long time. Until the discriminatory tariff was abolished, Indian products paid double export duty when exported to countries other than Britain. Holt Mackenzie, a youthful Trevelyan and Swinton of the Revenue Board were all vehemently opposed to such export duties even in the 1830s. Mackenzie had in his mind a simple form of the Classical theory of international trade when he found fault with the export tariff. He pointed out that normally the balance of payments between nations should adjust itself, but in the case of Indo-British trade, one country was a tributary to the other. Hence it is 'equally important for both countries that the tribute should be paid through the medium of a profitable export commerce, and no efforts should be spared to avert the alternative of exporting bullion or trading at a loss'.[106] Trevelyan compared these taxes to the Spanish *Alcavala* taxes eloquently condemned by Adam Smith, and said that the duties served no other purpose than checking the expansion of Indian exports.[107]

English manufacturers – especially the cotton magnates of Lancashire – had begun in the 1840s to examine the possibility of securing agricultural raw materials. Free trade also had almost achieved its final goal in 1846 with the reforms of Sir Robert Peel, notably the repeal of the Com Laws. Both these factors combined to initiate a fresh policy aimed at freeing India of its export duties. In an important despatch, which incidentally had received the blessings of John Stuart Mill, the Court of Directors stated:

---

[105] Court of Directors to Madras (Revenue) 24 April 1811, *Despatches to Madras*, Vol. 47, India Office Records, E/4/907, pp. 230–1.

[106] Minute dated 23 June 1825, *Bengal Separate Consultations* No. 23, India Office Records, Range 164, vol. 16.

[107] *A Report upon the Inland Customs*, p. 150. It must be noted that Trevelyan did not always remember these objections to export duties! He proposed as part of customs duty reorganisation 'to levy an export duty of five percent on the trade with England with the exception of cotton which ought to be free on account of the competition of America. This would be an entirely new duty on indigo and tobacco, and an increase on everything else'. Trevelyan to Bentinck, 21 December 1835 (*Bentinck Papers*, Nottingham University Library). Again when Trevelyan became the finance member in the 1860s, he proposed to introduce export duties on a variety of goods such as tea, jute, wool, coffee, hides, sugar and silk.

Such export duties cannot fail to some extent to restrict the demand for these articles, and to render them less able to compete with the similar products of other countries ... must of necessity operate as checks to their exportation. All these duties may, therefore, be pronounced to be objectionable in principle, and ought to be abolished, with, perhaps, the single exception of indigo; considering that India produces about $\frac{5}{6}$th of total supply, this article may bear a considerable export duty without affecting the demand, and the revenue may consequently be benefited without injury to the produce.[108]

This despatch was received warmly by the Government of India, and the acting president of the Governor-General's Council, T. H. Maddock, said that export duties were 'radically wrong' and were 'invariably more injurious to the public than beneficial to the Government'. Maddock was not prepared to treat indigo separately because it was 'not entirely without rivals', and even if India had a monopoly, export taxes only on indigo might result in an outflow of capital from indigo interests to other enterprises; and such tax-induced reallocation of resources would be harmful.[109]

After pointing out the financial difficulties that might necessitate a postponement of the repeal, Maddock said that export duty on cotton should be repealed without delay because it would enable the British manufacturers to secure cheaper raw materials.[110] This advice fell on the receptive ears of of the Court of Directors who accordingly sanctioned the removal of export duties on cotton while retaining those on other raw material exports.[111]

In the 1850s, while the discriminatory tariff system was abandoned, export duties on Indian goods were not removed although such a measure was part of the reform of customs proposed by the Governor-General, Canning, in 1857.[112] The Secretary of State was reluctant to give up export duties mainly because of the pressing financial situation of the government. 'Without defending in theory', he wanted the continuance of export duties on one condition; if the goods met with competition, he advised the government to repeal the duties. If any good possessed 'the actual or virtual monopoly, Her Majesty's Government would suggest . . . the expediency of attempting to obtain an increase'.[113]

Export duties, too, grated on certain trading interests, and pressures

[108] Court of Directors to Governor-General in Council, No. 3 of 1846 (Separate Revenue), *Parl. Papers*, H.C. 511, vol. IX of Session 1847–8, pp. 443–4.

[109] Minute, 23 June 1846, *Ibid.*

[110] Minute, 17 June 1847, *ibid.*, p. 472.

[111] Court of Directors to Government of India (Separate Revenue), No. 5 of 1847, 31 December 1847, *Ibid.*, p. 475.

[112] Governor-General in Council to Court of Directors, No. 5, 23 February 1857 (Separate Revenue), *India and Bengal Letters Received*, India Office Records, E/4/268, para 2.

[113] Secretary of State to Viceroy (Separate Revenue, Customs), 7 April 1859, No. 4, p. 138, *loc. cit.*

were exercised to remove them. In Britain the Manchester Chamber of Commerce was concerned about the impact of export duties on the cost structure of raw materials and it gave its support to individuals connected with India who were agitating for their removal.[114] In India, the exporters – most of whom were British – were able to prevent the imposition of any new export duties.[115] But, on the whole, the removal of export duties was not pursued with any sense of urgency.

In 1870, when the question of export duties was brought to the attention of the government by Sir Richard Temple, the Viceroy, Lord Mayo, in spite of being 'fully alive to the many objections that attach to all export duties, and especially to export duties on staples which compete in foreign markets with the produce of other countries',[116] had to postpone their removal because of deficit budgets and precarious finances. He overruled the Secretary of State's warning that it was 'more important for the general interests of the Country to preserve the trade than to maintain the revenue, even if the two objects were not incompatible'.[117] Sir Richard Strachey's warning to the government that export duties on agricultural raw materials was tantamount to reducing the fertility of the soil, and that they had serious allocational effects,[118] did not have any impact on Mayo's decision to retain them.

Every time the question of the retention, introduction or abolition of export duties came up, it was claimed that 'theory' was against export duties but 'necessity' required them. The problem of economic policy to be solved in the context of Classical economic thinking centred around two sets of

---

[114] Manchester Chamber of Commerce discussed on 24 July 1865 the 'impolicy of export duties in India especially on salt petre'. John Dickinson, Walter Cassels, Sir Arthur Cotton and Robert Knight were invited to participate.

[115] Trevelyan defended the export duties on coffee and tea that he had proposed in 1865 on the benefit principle: 'as the cultivation is carried on in wild frontier and mountaneous districts, the public expenditure is more than usually heavy, both for making roads for the conveyance ... and for providing the machinery for civilised administration'. *Parl. Papers*, H.C. 179, vol. XII of Session 1873, Q. 979. This proposal had been defeated. Lord Lawrence who was Viceroy ascribed it to the non-official English business community. 'English community ... objected also ... to the small export duties on tea, coffee, jute & C and succeeded in getting them disallowed.' Lawrence to Sir Stafford Northcote, 28 March 1867. Add. MSS. 500 23, p. 37 (Northcote Papers, the British Museum). However, Lawrence was criticised in England even for considering the imposition of export duties. *The Westminster Review* said that, the very fact of the proposal 'have received the sanction of the Viceroy at all, implies a want of apprehension on the part of his Excellency at once of the fundamental principles of political economy and of the established commercial policy of England'. July–October 1865, New Series, vol. XXVIII, p. 205.

[116] Governor General in Council to Secretary of State, 11 January 1870, (Separate Revenue, Customs) No. 3 of 1870, India Office Records, No. L/E/3/638.

[117] Secretary of State to Viceroy, 10 March 1870 (Separate: Revenue), No. 6 of 1870, India Office Records, Separate Revenue Despatches to India, No. L/E/3/625, para. 5.

[118] Speech in the Legislative Council, 31 March 1871, *Proceedings of the Legislative Council of India*, vol. X, p. 446.

questions: (1) does India possess a monopoly of the taxed commodities? and (2) is the overseas demand for the produce sufficiently inelastic so that the incidence would be on the overseas consumer rather than on the local producer? If the answers were both positive, then Classical economic theory had nothing against export duties.[119]

During the drafting of the despatch of Argyll to Mayo, a minor controversy took place about the desirability of levying export taxes. The original draft prepared by the permanent under-secretary, F. M. Prideaux, more or less rejected export duties as violating 'theory'. But Herman Merivale, at that time an under-secretary, saw nothing wrong in export duties; he referred to the ideas of John Stuart Mill to show that export duties were relatively harmless to the economy because 'the incidence falls chiefly – or even in some cases wholly – on the foreigner'. Merivale's interpretation depended on Mill's attitude towards the Indian exports of opium to China. Owing to the Indian opium monopoly and the price fixed by the government, the tax element in the price was borne by the overseas consumer. Merivale's conclusion was that 'although I am not sure that his reasonings apply to export duties on *necessaries* (which is the case here) yet I should think it rash to assume economical conclusions different from his'.[120] Prideaux took objection to this argument, and had himself as early as 1846 sent a despatch from the Court of Directors recommending the abolition of the 'export duties on all articles except indigo of which India was supposed to have almost a monopoly'. Prideaux mentions how he showed the draft to John Stuart Mill and secured his 'full approval'. Opium trade was a special case, and according to Prideaux, it should not be cited in situations where the commodities exported did not have a monopoly. He also made it clear where Mill's sympathies stood: 'I think I may fairly claim Mr Mill's authority as opposed to export duties *en gros*, although he may admit exceptions *en detail*.' The fact was that the Indian rice and paddy exports had to contend with the exports from Vietnam and Thailand. In general Prideaux held the view that export duties on rice, paddy, indigo, saltpetre and similar raw produce were changing the export trade, and ended with the warning: 'It is easier to destroy a branch of commerce than to revive it.'[121] Although a majority of the Council

---

[119] See for example J. R. McCulloch, *Principles of Political Economy* 5th Edn, p. 114. McCulloch in a letter to Trevelyan (27 January 1859) said, 'in truth there is no general objection to them; for in their case everything depends upon circumstances.' *Parl. Papers*, H.C. 179, vol. XII of Session 1873, Q. 927. J. S. Mill had similar views although he was not in favour of using export duties with a view to making the foreigners bear the tax burden. See *Principles of Political Economy*, p. 853.

[120] Marginal comments on the draft of Secretary of State to Viceroy in Council, 10 March 1870, *loc. cit.*

[121] Prideaux's comments on the above. *Ibid.* See also W. F. Marriott, 'Indian Political Economy and Finance' *Journal of the East Indian Association*, vol. XVIII, 1874, p. 14.

favoured Prideaux's opinion, the matter was finally left in the hands of the Government of India.

The Government of India never really got over the idea that the foreign consumer could be made to bear the burden provided the exporting country had monopolistic control over the commodity. As Sir William Muir, the finance member for Lord Northbrook, said after retaining the export duties on lac, opium and indigo while abolishing the export duties on all other commodities: 'We have practically almost a monopoly, and so the duty, serving to raise the price, falls on the foreign consumer.'[122]

INCOME TAX

The economic policy of the mid-century proponents of *laissez-faire* in relation to taxation was to abolish all indirect taxes that curbed investment and distorted the price structure. In general, direct taxes on income and property were preferred to indirect taxes as it was believed that they led to fewer distortions in the market structure. McCulloch had already drawn attention to the allocational neutrality of direct taxes on profits, although he did not give his unqualified approval to it because of its adverse impact on capital formation.[123] Indian supporters of income tax in the 1860s and 1870s used this argument frequently, and indeed Major W. G. Marriott said, 'The principal thing touching taxation which modern political economy has taught us, is the advantage of so imposing it that it shall be distributed, and fall on no particular industry.'[124] This policy was also held by James Wilson, founder-editor of the *Economist*;[125] and true to his convictions, he introduced an income tax for India very soon after becoming its first finance member.

Such a development was probably inevitable in India. Already there were many practical objections to the levying of further indirect taxes, even if Wilson could overlook the theoretical objections; in fact, as we have seen earlier, he had introduced indirect taxes that violated Classical fiscal policy. Taxation of the land was an inelastic source of revenue, and at that time the existing assessments themselves were being lowered. Hence, to meet increasing government expenditures, fresh sources of public revenue were necessary.

---

[122] Proceedings of the Council of the Government of India, 5 August 1875, *Parl. Papers*, H.C. 56, vol. LVI of Session 1876.

[123] *Taxation and Funding System*, p. 73.

[124] 'Indian Political Economy and Finance' *op. cit.* p. 14. Lord Lawrence, while recommending an income-tax stressed that 'It interferes with no trade; it hampers no industry.' See Governor-General in Council to Secretary of State, 10 November 1868 (Financial Department, Separate Revenue), No. 28 of 1868, para. 17, India Office Records.

[125] The *Economist* on the Finance of India, 19 February 1859, vol. XVII, No. 808, p. 194. See also Scott Gordon, 'The London *Economist* and the High Tide of Laissez-faire' *Journal of Political Economy*, vol. 63, December 1955, p. 479.

The introduction of a direct tax on income would, it was thought, give the advantages of free trade and at the same time secure an elastic source of funds for the public fisc.

Not only elasticity, but even equity, demanded a change in the structure of the fiscal system in favour of direct taxes. Wilson in his Financial Statement defended his income tax as having been 'based upon perfect equality and justice to every class of the community'.[126] Sir Richard Temple, finance member during the viceroyalty of Sir John Lawrence, was a staunch advocate of income tax for India and defended it staunchly on the grounds of equality of incidence.[127] The equity aim of Lawrence, Temple, Wilson, and other proponents of income tax for India in the third quarter of the century was designed to bring in those sections of society that were not contributing anything to public revenue. Their objective appears to have been to reduce the regressive character of the tax structure by introducing proportional taxation of income. Redistribution of income or property through progressive taxation was certainly not part of their policy. Wilson had earlier said that it was no part of the functions of fiscal arrangements to equalise the conditions of men'.[128]

Some caution is necessary while underscoring the equity motive in the formation of a tax policy crystallising in favour of an income tax. Throughout the 1860s, 1870s and 1880s, British manufacturers had been attacking Indian attempts to levy import duties. The British–Indian finance members had to take note of these views and some, like Temple, were in favour of direct taxation because it would have justified getting rid of indirect taxes – particularly customs duties.[129]

As against the policy of introducing direct taxes in place of indirect taxes, some members of the administration, for example Trevelyan, argued on the authority of Adam Smith that indirect taxation was more suitable to India for many reasons. First, 'indirect taxation brings the whole of the population

[126] *Annual Financial Statements*, p. 15.
[127] Minute dated 12 March 1872 (Temple Papers, India Office Library).
[128] Speech in the Legislative Council, 14 April 1860, *Proceedings of the Legislative Council of India*, Vol. VI, p. 376. Progressive taxation was still a hotly debated subject and any mention of its connection with India was frowned upon. Wood wrote to Wilson, 'Overstone was horrified by the report of a graduated income tax; but the reality will, I hope, give him some comfort, for it is no more than we do here, easing it off at the lower extremity.' Wood to Wilson, 26 March 1860. (Halifax Papers, India Office Library.) It is interesting to see that earlier economists were not critical of progression in taxation. Adam Smith had advocated a progressive tax on houses. See *Wealth of Nations*, p. 794. See also James Mill, *History of British India*, vol. I, pp. 250–1. But the mid-century economists had come round to support proportional taxation. See for example John Stuart Mill in his *Principles of Political Economy*, p. 808.
[129] Temple's address to the Manchester Chamber of Commerce, 15 March 1881. *Conditions and Prospects of British India*.

under contribution at the time, and in the manner most convenient to them, with a minimum of interference with their personal comforts and habits'.[130] Secondly, Trevelyan was afraid that many public servants would be needed to run the income tax department, and the consequence would be 'the gross violation of another of Adam Smith's rules, namely to take out, and keep out, of the pockets of the people as little as possible that does not come into the Treasury'.[131] Finally, Trevelyan even had an answer for those who advocated an income tax on equity grounds. India's prime objective at that time was a large accumulation of capital, and as the prevailing rates of interest were exorbitant, large profits alone would provide the needed incentive for businessmen to accumulate capital. He thus implied that by impinging upon profits direct income taxes reduced the incentive to save and invest.[132] Samuel Laing argued against income tax on the score of the tax administrator's problems such as the difficulty of defining and computing the net income, fighting tax evasion and so on.[133]

There were of course the usual political objections to income tax. While not opposed to the tax in principle, a very powerful section of Indian official opinion nevertheless pointed out that it might be difficult to collect and, further, might prove politically dangerous because the attitude of Indians towards public revenue and expenditure was not suited to this new impost. For example, the Officiating Commissioner of the Narbada Division, Mr W. B. Jones made this special plea:

Of the four cardinal maxims of taxation, two, viz., the maxims that a tax ought to take from the pockets of the people as little as possible over and above what it brings into the coffers of the State, and that every person ought to contribute according to his ability, depend in great degree on the acceptance by the people of the fact that a certain sum has inevitably to be raised. Now this is just what the people of India will not believe. They look upon the resources of Government as illimitable, and hail the exemption of one of their members as an act of generosity on the part of the State; it scarcely occurs to them to regard it as an injustice to themselves. To them a Government which appropriates all that it collects displays its own greed and not its regard for their interests ... Direct taxation on Western principles is therefore peculiarly odious to our subjects, and we should look in vain if we expect that our

---

[130] Trevelyan's evidence to the East India Finance Committee. *Parl. Papers* H.C. 179, vol. XII of Session 1873, Questions 890, 896, 897.

[131] *Ibid.* Ripon also found income tax sinning 'grievously against Adam Smith's fourth canon of Taxation'. See his note on Colvin's Memo of 10 June 1884 (*Ripon Papers* British Museum).

[132] Laing had earlier argued that income tax would reduce the flow of foreign capital. But George Warde Norman, the economist whom Wood consulted, assured the Secretary of State that it was not so. See Norman to Wood, 13 September 1861 (Halifax Papers, India Office Library).

[133] Laing's Minute 19 July 1861, India Office Records, *India: Financial Consultations*, July–August, 1861, No. 127, pp. 834–43.

taxes will meet with popular appreciation or the reverse, according to the approach to or recede from theoretical perfection.[134]

Whatever might have been the arguments for and against an income tax for India, none of the finance members who desired it found it easy to introduce. Just as the customs duty was anathema to the Lancashire manufacturers, income tax was heartily disliked, not so much by the illiterate masses of India, as mentioned by W. B. Jones, but by the more literate sections of society, the zemindars and other aristocrats, members of the civil service, and the non-official British community in India.[135] It was a predictable reaction on the part of the Indian moneyed classes to be reluctant to pay any new taxes. Many members in the upper echelons of the Indian administration, such as Trevel-yan, Mortimer Durand and William Mansfield, who had looked upon the zemindars and other members of the Indian aristocracy as strong allies of British rule in India, were apprehensive of the possible effects of their reluc-tance to bear any additional burden through income taxation. There was also the opposition from the British civil servants who were unhappy about the reduction in their income which income tax would cause, particularly after 1873, when the price of silver began to fall. Even a supporter of income tax like Sir Charles Wood thought it expedient to warn Wilson about the 'danger in touching the lower ranks of the army'.[136] Even more vociferous against the income tax were the non-official British in India, like the traders, planters, attorneys, journalists and others, and their opposition was a real source of worry for those viceroys like Sir John Lawrence, who desired to in-corporate an income tax in the Indian fiscal structure.[137] All these elements — Indian moneyed classes, the non-official Britishers overtly, and the members of the Indo-British civil service covertly — made common cause to oppose the income tax, and their main argument was that it violated the cardinal taxa-tion principle of equal treatment of equals because it fell 'exclusively upon the middle and upper classes of this country, who comprise less than one-thousandth part of the whole population, is unjust'.[138] The impact of the sus-tained criticism from these pressure groups was considerable. Lawrence,

[134] Letter to the Secretary of the Chief Commissioner of Central Provinces, 3 October 1872, *Reports on Taxation in British India 1872*, p. 401.

[135] The power of the pressure groups was such that Wilson was worried about his income tax bill till the last minute of his life. We are told by his daughter that the last coherent words he spoke were, 'Take care of my Income tax'. Barrington, *The Servant of All* (London, 1927), p. 311.

[136] Wood to Wilson, 9 April 1860 (Halifax Papers, India Office Library).

[137] See letter of Lawrence to Sir Stafford Northcote, dated 28 March 1867 Add. Mss. 50 023, p. 37 (*loc. cit.*, British Museum). See also J. M. Maclean, *The Indian Deficit and the Income Tax*, pp. 4–6.

[138] From a Resolution passed at a public meeting of Indians and Europeans in Calcutta Town Hall on 18 April 1870, cited in G. R. G. Hambly, 'Income Tax Controversy in India, 1869–1873', *Contributions to Indian Economic History.*, No. II, p. 11.

Mayo and others who had supported the imposition of income tax publicly, nevertheless voiced their misgivings in private in view of the determined campaign conducted by those opposed to the tax. It was surprising to see even such a sympathetic observer of the Indian administration as Henry Fawcett being influenced, however indirectly, by pressure groups. Fawcett, whom Lord Ripon admired greatly, was against income tax because he was concerned about the unpopularity it might acquire if it was associated with the repeal of cotton duties. Fawcett's opinion probably was a decisive factor in Ripon's decision not to have the income tax proposed by his finance member, Sir Evelyn Baring.[139]

In 1867–8, a variant of an income tax called a licence tax on trades and professions, but the incidence of which was mainly on the petty Indian traders living in the cities, was imposed at 2 per cent on incomes of Rs 200 per year and above. The tax was deliberately designed to appease the powerful pressure groups of the official and non-official British community in India. As Lawrence confessed to Northcote: 'It was mainly in deference to their views that the License tax was adopted this year in preference to an Income tax.'[140] There was very little justification for the tax except that it would bring some money to the public purse, and even the government publicly acknowledged that 'A License Tax must of necessity be unequal in its incidence.'[141]

As early as 1859 Wilson had made it clear that the government should take its stand upon some 'intelligent principle in taxation and stick firmly to it'. Otherwise 'vacillation and hesitation' would ruin everything in the country.[142] But the history of the Indian income tax at least up to 1886 had been exactly one of vacillation and hesitation.

In spite of strong theoretical support and urgent financial necessity, pressures emanating from many sources, operational difficulties, and even some straightforward administrative inequities and blunders[143] were responsible for the intermittent usage of the income tax in India between 1860 and 1886.

139 Fawcett to Hartington, 23 December 1881. Add. MSS. 43 567, pp. 168–71. It seems Gladstone was also against income taxation for India. Gladstone to Ripon, 24 November 1881 (*Ripon Papers*, British Museum).

140 Lawrence to Northcote, 28 March 1867, Add. MSS. 50 923, p. 37 *op. cit.*

141 A reply to the various Memorials. See Viceroy to Secretary of State 20 April 1867, No. 12 of 1867 (Financial: Separate Revenue) India Office Records, Separate Revenue Letters, L/E/3/165. Even in 1859 there was this controversy whether income or license taxes should be levied and the Viceroy's Council was equally divided. Wood told Wilson while giving freedom to act: 'Putting Licenses in wide classes would not be so just but would be more practicable. Income tax is according to English ideas. License according to Native ideas. I do not feel that I can give an opinion worth much on this.' Wood to Wilson, 10 November 1859 (Halifax Papers, India Office Library).

142 Barrington, *Life of Walter Bagehot*, quoted in p. 309.

143 Inequity of not subjecting the salaries paid in UK out of Indian funds to income tax. Income tax was also not deducted from interest payments on overseas, especially British debt.

After 1886, however, conditions changed and the earlier opinion that the tax was difficult to administer was no longer held with conviction. It seemed as though the nature of direct taxation and the need for it had been understood by the people. The problem therefore was no longer, 'shall we impose direct taxation?' but 'in what form shall direct taxation be imposed?'[144]

The financial needs of the government, created no doubt by the repeal of cotton duties, falling exchanges and famines, was so great that any new source of taxation was welcome. The events of 1857 were fast receding into the limbo of history, no further trouble of that kind was anticipated, and the Indian nationalist movement was also favourable to direct taxation on income. Although at the first session of the Indian National Congress, held in 1885, a proposal for income tax had been voted down, at the same time a broad-based license tax which would apply to the incomes of previously untaxed groups, such as members of the civil service and other professions, was approved.[145] After 1886, income tax gained 'greater and wider popularity among the nationalist circles, particularly as it became evident that its abandonment would lead to the imposition of other taxes'.[146] Once the income tax was introduced in 1886, it was given unqualified support by the Indian educated elite, and the only regret expressed was that it was not sufficiently progressive. In 1887, during the third Session of the Indial National Congress, a delegate who moved a resolution calling for the abolition of income tax was shouted down.[147]

The main reason why the tax entered permanently into the Indian tax structure was the acceptance of the tax in Britain. Although Galdstone promised to abolish it in 1874, he suffered a decisive defeat in the general election of that year. But when he returned to power in 1880 he neither abolished the income tax nor was he pressed to do so.[148] Besides, as Shehab points out, there was a notable increase in social legislation in Britain, and Joseph Chamberlain in his 'Radical Programme' envisaged a greater volume of state expenditure and higher levels of taxation as tools of social reform.[149] But already this

---

Footnote 143 *continued*

Blunders of abruptly changing tax rates in the mid-year as well as frequent tampering with the rates.

[144] See Colvin's Memorandum on 'Direct Taxation and the License Tax' 14 May 1884. Add MSS. 43 586, p. 4 (*Ripon Papers*, British Museum).

[145] See Briton Martin, Jr., *New India 1885* (Berkeley, 1969), pp. 303–4.

[146] Bipan Chandra, *The Rise of Economic Nationalism in India* (New Delhi, 1966), p. 524.

[147] *Ibid*, pp. 524–8. See also S. C. Srinivasa Charier (Ed.), *Political Opinions of Raja Sir T. Madava Row* (Madras, 1890), p. 19, and D. A. Taleyarkhan, *Selections from my Recent Notes on the Indian Empire* (Bombay, 1886), p. 280.

[148] See Seligman, *The Income Tax* (New York, 1911), pp. 172–3.

[149] *Progressive Taxation*, p. 190.

principle was tacitly accepted in India. As Ripon's finance member pointed out, 'If the country is to advance, the civil expenditure *must* grow. It would often be false economy to check it.'[150]

Thus direct taxation received acceptance not because it was a *neutral* tax but because of changing attitudes regarding the role of government expenditure as well as the inelasticity of the Indian tax structure.

CONCLUSION

This survey of the non-land taxation resorted to in the nineteenth century in India reveals that while politicians and civil servants were very much concerned with appropriate criteria for individual taxes, they seldom devoted any attention to the larger problem of correct fiscal policies. As the tax structure was evolving and as new taxes were being slowly introduced into the system, one could note rumblings of criticism which charged the authorities with failure to utilise the 'principles' of political economy in devising the tax structure. However, the problem was that one could hardly speak of a set of 'principles' that could provide precise guidance to the policy makers. Replying to Rickards' reference that India was not following a 'sound principled system of taxation', R. D. Mangles of the East India Company's Court of Directors correctly remarked: 'until he can bring the Political Economists of *Blackwood's Magazine* to repose in sweet concord with Mr McCulloch ... until there be somewhat more of community of sentiment with regard to *Principles* than at present exists, I scarcely think that the Governors of British India would be justified in abandoning the present system.'[151] This 'existing system' was largely a result of a steady trial and error method adopted by successive generations of civil servants subject as they were to a multitude of influences. Enough evidence has been provided to show that of these, effective political control of the British Parliament over Indian economic policies and financial stringency were crucial. In so far as an evaluation of individual taxes was made, more stress was laid on whether they conformed to the celebrated Adam Smith's tax canons of equality, certainty, convenience of payment and economy in collection or not, rather than whether the proposed taxes had serious allocational effects.

---

[150] Baring to Ripon, 26 September 1881, Add. MSS. 43 596, p. 203 (*Ripon Papers*, British Museum).

[151] *A Brief Vindication of the Honourable East India Company's Government of Bengal From the Attacks of Messers Rickards and Crawfurd* (London, 1830), p. 174. Mangles had served for a few years in the Bengal civil service. A similar opinion was expressed by Sir George Campbell in 1859: 'I believe taxation in so vast an empire to be a matter of experiment and gradual elaboration. I do not think that, it is possible successfully to introduce at once a complete and detailed system elaborated by any theorist.' *Our Finances* (Lucknow, 1859), p. 5.

7

POLITICAL ECONOMY AND A POLICY OF ECONOMIC DEVELOPMENT

to make the people of that Country consumers of the manufacturers of England
we must first make them *rich* ... the real interests of both Countries are the same

Lord Ellenborough to Lord Bentinck
19 May 1829

OBJECTIVES OF ECONOMIC ACTIVITY

The problem of elucidating the process of economic development runs as a major thread through the history of Classical political economy. Even when individual economists from Adam Smith to John Stuart Mill structured specific policies such as taxation to given objectives, their main concern had been the nature and causes of the wealth of nations. Seen in this light, the various specific economic policies adopted by the Indian government which emanated from the Classical economists could be said to have aimed at the larger objective of Indian economic development. However, from time to time Indian administrators thought of economic progress itself as an objective and sought guidance from received doctrine for framing appropriate policies. In this chapter we shall examine the nature of those policies and the part played by economic thinking in their formation.

Even before the publication of Adam Smith's *Wealth of Nations*, prevailing economic opinion had swung against the notion that a mere accumulation of precious metals was tantamount to increasing national prosperity. The aim of all activity, according to both the Physiocrats and the English Classical economists, was the net increase of consumable goods. As consumption of goods is not possible without the production of goods, production assumed great importance in the thinking of the economists. Increased production of goods was the means to an improvement not only in the material conditions but also in the moral condition of the people.

Once the confusion and piracy characteristic of the era of Robert Clive had ended, and the British government began to exercise some supervision over the government of the East India Company, a semblance of a national policy towards India could be discerned. The servants of the East India Company who were in charge of administering the territories had also imbibed the teaching of the Classical economists and were of the opinion that the objectives of a

proper government should be to stimulate the production of goods and services and not merely to stock the exchequer with gold and silver.[1] This meant
that as the ruler of vast territories the Company should not view public
revenues as part of the trading assets of a merely commercial organisation.
Following Regulation II (1793) of Bengal, Regulation II (1803) of Madras gave
expression to this view: 'Collectors shall administer the public revenues to the
advantages of the State, the happiness of the people, and the prosperity of
the country; and shall suggest such propositions to the Board of Revenue as,
in their judgement, may be calculated to augment and improve those
revenues.' Throughout the period of British rule in India this opinion was
expressed by both the official and non-official sections of British opinion.[2]

As we have seen in chapter 2, the possession of India was considered advantageous for Britain. But to secure the benefits of India, it was necessary for
India to achieve economic development; at the same time such development
should be complementary to the way the English economy was moving.
Within a decade of the opening of the Indian markets for the British manufacturers, it became clear that the old Indian handicraft industries were
redundant. The official mind was proceeding towards a policy of converting
India into a strong and stable supplier of raw material goods. In the words of
the House of Lords Select Committee, 'The chief manufactures of India
having been supplanted to a great extent by the manufactures of England,
not only in the market of this country, but in that of India itself, it has become
an object of the deepest interest to improve the productions of the soil.'
The Committee questioned its witnesses intensively on the possibility of
improving the production of raw silk, raw cotton, sugar, tobacco, indigo and
similar technical crops.[3] The policy makers themselves found it convenient

---

[1] See for example the views of an early administrator, Malet to the Governor-General,
8 August 1788, in *Charters and Treaties*, India office Records, vol. X and in a Memorandum
written for Governor William Bentinck of Madras, the author said, 'The wealth of a nation
does not consist anywhere in the quantity of gold and silver it contains, but in the ex-
changeable value of the annual produce of its lands and labour.' 'Cursory Remarks on the
Principles Applicable to the levying of Customs House Duties' (1804). (*Bentinck Papers*,
Nottingham University Library).

[2] *Remarks on the affairs of India* by a 'Friend of India', p. 4. See also J. T. Mackenzie, *The
Trade and Commerce of India* (London, 1859), p. 5; P. B. Smollett, *India: A Lecture
Delivered*, p. 45; and John Bell, *A Comparative View of the External Commerce of Bengal
during the Years 1831–2 to 1832–3*, pp. 3–4.

[3] Minutes of Evidence and Report from the Select Committee of the House of Lords on the
Affairs of *the East India Company*, vol. I, p. iii. *Parl. Papers*, vol. V of Session 1830. See also
George Larpent's evidence. Q. 2771, 2773. See also Trevelyan's evidence, Q. 1951. Contemporary pamphlet literature affords ample proof of the wide prevalence of this view of
international division of labour. See for example G. F. Hughes (of the Bombay
Civil Service): 'The resources of both countries England and India are so dissimilar that
they could act to their mutual advantage. India may remain as the field of nature – and
England that of art.' *Letter to Charles Grant* (London, 1834), p. 9. Such examples could
easily be multiplied.

to believe that they were only assisting a natural and inevitable process of the international division of labour.

This is not surprising, if we consider the theoretic support of the economists and also the actual need for raw materials of the British producers. Among the leading economists, Ricardo was particularly interested in this aspect of the problem. In a speech he delivered at a meeting of the proprietors of East India Stock, he agreed that 'great injury was inflicted on the manufacturing class' of India due to cheap, machine-made textiles from England. But Ricardo would not let this worry him: instead he asked, 'In what commodities those exports were paid for?' His answer was, 'Those who exported must have got a return in something else they had not before had. If we send cotton goods to India they must be paid for.' He then proceeded to explain how these cotton goods could be purchased only with other goods, which means the establishment of 'new branches of trade'. Thus he concluded that, ultimately, both countries were benefited.[4]

It is however futile to complain that the British rulers in India did not promote a balanced economic growth of both sectors of the economy, agricultural and industrial. It was a universally held opinion that India was thinly peopled, as the administrators found large tracts lying uncultivated; W. W. Hunter has pointed out that until the 1870s overpopulation was unknown in India.[5] In such an economic situation, profits on stock employed in agriculture were bound to be high. Hence there was no reason for the introduction of industry, or for that matter for inefficient industry to be propped up artificially. The criterion was the rate of profits and not self-sufficiency. Current economic thought was also favourable to economic development through agriculture. According to the Classical economists, investment in agriculture had far more beneficial effects on the economy than anything else. Adam Smith had remarked that 'no equal capital puts into motion a greater quantity of productive labour than that of the farmer'.[6] Industrial development could take place only with a strong agricultural base, and that too only when the law of diminishing returns set in in agriculture. Ricardo had said that it was investment in agriculture that 'first gives the notion and the means of establishing Manufactures'.[7] Malthus too imputed much importance to agricultural development as part of the general economic progress of any country.[8] John Wheatley, a neglected but capable economist of the period who was a resident of Calcutta in the 1820s, applied this idea

[4] As reported in the *Asiatic Journal*, April 1823, pp. 371–2. Sraffa (Ed.), *Works and correspondence of David Ricardo*, vol. V, p. 482.
[5] See Skrine's *Life of Hunter*, p. 393.
[6] *Wealth of Nations*, p. 344.
[7] Ricardo to Brown, 13 October 1819, Sraffa (Ed.), *op. cit.*, vol. VIII, p. 103.
[8] See my *Malthus and Classical Economics*, p. 159.

cogently to the problem of the economic future of India. He contended that England had enormous possibilities to increase its own national wealth through the productive powers of its colonies, especially that of India. But according to him the crux of the problem of utilising the productive power lay in the ability of a country to produce an agricultural surplus; there was absolutely no possibility of 'establishing a prosperous state of things, either in England, India, or any other country, without providing a large agricultural surplus'.[9]

Even before Britain emerged as a great industrial nation, the British rulers in India decided to strengthen Indian agriculture. Lord Cornwallis, for instance, wrote to the Court of Directors as early as 1793:

Although agriculture and commerce promote each other, yet in this country, more than in any other, agriculture must flourish before its commerce can become extensive. The materials for all the most valuable manufactures are the produce of its own lands. It follows therefore that the extent of its commerce must depend upon the encouragement given to agriculture, and that whatever tends to impede the latter destroys the two great sources of its wealth.[10]

Both Adam Smith and the earlier phase of Indian economic policy were influenced by the Physiocrats. The fact that the Physiocrats had some influence on the minds of early Indian policy makers need not be surprising. Any ruler of a predominantly agricultural community with possibilities of considerable development would naturally have notions similar to those of the Physiocrats. According to them, the strategic variable was the net product, and this could be augmented only by a systematic development of agriculture.[11]

The policy that agrarian development would ultimately lead to commercial and industrial development was never to be dethroned in the nineteenth century, although it is true that there were occasions when the state encouraged the promotion of some specific industrial undertakings. It must be mentioned that before 1813 there was an attempt made by the East India Company to encourage systematically the production of cotton textiles in India. This was because the Company was still actively engaged in the export business from India, and the government had also the problem of enormous remittances to home. These remittances were mainly incomes from interest on loans, savings from salaries, profits on shipping, indigo, and so

[9] See John Wheatley, *A Letter to the Right Honourable Charles Watkin William Wynn, President of the Board of Control on the Latent Resources of India* (Calcutta, 1823), pp. 9–11. See for similar arguments Edward Thornton, *India: Its State and Prospects*, pp. 68–9, 86.

[10] Letter dated 6 March 1793, Ross (Ed.), *Cornwallis*, vol. II, p. 556.

[11] See W. J. Samuels, 'The Physiocratic Theory of Economic Policy' *Quarterly Journal of Economics*, vol. 76, February 1962, pp. 150–1. See also R. L. Meek, *The Economics of Physiocracy* (London, 1962), p. 22.

forth. Remittance payments were a recurring annual unilateral payment, and the Indian government did not relish the idea of exporting bullion every time. Hence permission was sought for the encouragement of such exportable goods to effect 'an exchange of the demand, which England holds upon India with those countries which incur annually a commercial debt to Bengal'.[12] Henry St George Tucker who had had a hand in drafting this despatch always had a dread of a depletion of the 'circulating medium'. If a unilateral transfer of capital in the form of exporting specie were kept continuously, Tucker was afraid it would result in 'grave consequences'. Hence his and the Bengal government's concern was to promote the production of all types of goods – manufactures as well as raw materials.[13]

Having lost its trading monopoly in 1813, the East India Company did not maintain the same interest in encouraging manufactures in India. The isolated instances when the government actively promoted the founding of industrial establishments could be explained by referral to specific circumstances, and these cases certainly do not represent the execution of a particular policy. To give the example of the Porto Novo iron works founded by Mr J. M. Heath, an Englishman, the East India Company provided active help. But before Heath got permission, he had to assure the Government of Madras that 'there is no possibility that the iron made by me in this Country should ever displace a pound of English iron from the home market, and in this Country'.[14] In fact he pointed out that the reason for the establishment of the factory was to 'render England independent of foreign countries for the supply of iron which is required to be converted into steel ... we are now entirely dependent upon Sweden and Russia for every bar of iron that is to be converted into steel, the most important of all objects in the arts.'[15]

Although agriculture was to be the means of promoting economic progress, there could not be said to be a policy aimed at improving all aspects of agriculture. The need to make Britain self-sufficient was a factor that played no mean part in the selection of goods that were to be given active encouragement. Apart from those special cases, agricultural development was to be left to a 'free and unfettered market'. As for the agricultural raw materials

[12] Governor-General in Council to Court of Directors, 23 August 1809, *Bengal Letters and Enclosures (Financial) Received*, India Office Records, no. L/F/3/2, pp. 282 *et seq.*

[13] *Memorials of Indian Government* (London, 1853), pp. 385–6, 491–2. See also C. E. Trevelyan, *A Report Upon the Inland Customs*, pp. 174–5.

[14] J. M. Heath to the Governor of Madras, 27 October 1824, *Madras Public Proceedings*, 19 November 1824, India Office Records, Range 245, volume 58, pp. 3820–40.

[15] Heath's evidence before the Select Committee on East India Produce, *Parl. Papers*, H.C. 527, vol. VIII of Session 1840, Q.4589.

required for Britain, the Company was given advice and it acted upon it.[16]

Throughout the period of the East India Company's rule in India and even a decade after the takeover by the Crown, various British interests had been putting pressure on Indian governments to promote the cultivation of cotton in India, and the Indian government had done as much as they could.[17] The private correspondence of the successive secretaries of state and viceroys shows the extent of the pressure applied by British mercantile interests on Indian authorities to stimulate the production of commercial crops in India. To give an example, Edmund Ashworth of the Manchester Chamber of Commerce in a series of letters addressed to Lord Mayo said that it was imperative for India to produce cotton more efficiently, and frankly pointed out that 'the continued scarcity of cotton and the unpromising prospect of any early increase of supplies are seriously affecting the industrial and commercial interests of Lancashire,' and that the Government of India should 'lend a helping hand in the matter'.[18] Such a demand was always couched in language that stressed the mutual benefits to be reaped by both of the countries: 'We have machinery and steam power for weaving, India has the cultivators and land for growing cotton, without limits', said an East India Merchant, adding: 'Why should our looms ever stand idle, or the Indian expose his bare back to the sun?'[19]

However, the hypothesis that Britain deliberately converted India into a raw-material-producing country could be easily overemphasised. In fact, it might have been expected that Britain would have shown a more active interest in making India a strong source of raw materials and food stuffs. What is surprising is that the government took the few measures it did to encourage the production of cotton and similar products because of the almost unanimous opinion in favour of non-intervention except in the area of the provision of public works.

The famines of the 1860s and 1870s demonstrated that the agricultural sector was hopelessly overcrowded. It was during this period that many doubts were raised as to the wisdom of a strategy of development based on

[16] See advice given by the naturalist Sir Joseph Banks to Henry Dundas. Letter of 15 June 1787, cited in V. T. Harlow, *The Founding of the Second British Empire* (London, 1952), vol. II, pp. 287–8.

[17] See Mackay, *Western India*, p. 59. For a history of the attempts to encourage cultivation of cotton by the introduction of better seeds, better methods of curing and so on, see *Parl. Papers*, H.C. 369, vol. 27 of Session 1852–3, pp. 49 *et seq*. See also H. H. Spry, *Suggestions Received by the Agricultural and Horticultural Society of India* (Calcutta, 1841).

[18] Ashworth to Mayo, 5 February 1869 (Mayo Papers at the University of Cambridge Library). Ashworth was a persistent advocate for the creation of a separate department of Agriculture and Statistics.

[19] *Letter on the Sacrifice of the Immense Resources of India under the Present and the Necessity of Immediate Reform* (Liverpool, 1853), pp. 7–8.

agriculture alone. After the famines of 1860, industries and their development were suggested as part of economic progress; as a pamphleteer put it,
the poverty of India 'lies chiefly in the fact that she has to depend on
agriculture alone ... How to create an industrial population in India is the
problem of problems ... it is her "Life problem"!'[20] Other people connected
with the Indian administration expressed similar ideas.[21] A few articulate
Indians also began to challenge the concept of the territorial division of
labour still held in reverence by the majority of official opinion.[22] In the
same way some organisations in Britain supporting the Indian case argued for
both industrial development and state intervention.[23]

Such a policy of diversification of occupation was given prominence by the
Famine Commission in 1880 presided over by Sir Richard Strachey. However, official opinion did not take much notice of the expressions urging
government encouragement of industries. If anything, the famines
strengthened the policy makers' resolve to promote agricultural development.[24] This is seen especially in the 1860s and 1870. The Governor-
General in Council wrote to the Secretary of State that 'we can hardly hope
that India will become a great manufacturing country, until, at any rate
her people have made the fullest use of her bountiful soil, and her climate,
ordinarily so propitious to agriculture'.[25] The same point was made by a
contemporary observer who said that farming communities in Australia,
New Zealand and America enjoy 'substantial comfort on the profits of their
field produce', and hence there was 'no prima facie reason why the ryot
in India ... should not do the same'.[26] The road to Indian prosperity, then,

[20] An Indian Student, *India Before and After the Mutiny* (Edinburgh, 1886), pp. 124–6.
[21] See F. C. Danvers, *A Century of Famines* (London, 1878), p. 20. See also Hunter to Argyll,
12 April 1889, quoted in Skrine, *op. cit.* p. 395. Emerson Dawson, a Madras journalist,
pointed out that whereas land is subject to diminishing returns, there was scope for
increasing returns in manufacture. See *The Indian Land Question: A Timely Warning*
(London, 1865), pp. 28–9; H. J. S. Cotton, *New India* (London, 1886), p. 103; R. H. Elliot
in the London *Times*, 10 September 1874.
[22] See for the views of Diwan Rangacharlu, the lone Indian member of the 1880 Famine
Commission, V. L. D'Souza, *Economic Development of the Mysore State* (Bangalore, 1937)
p. 16. See also (Ardeshir Dinshaw) *British Policy Respecting Famines in India* (Bombay,
1874), p. 7.
[23] East India Association, *The Indian Problem Solved*, p. 359.
[24] This was not entirely out of tune with the informed opinion of even those who favoured the
exploitation of India's industrial potential. They all were conscious of the linkage effects of
a good agricultural base. As A. G. F. Eliot James in a book that was concerned mostly with
the possibility of industrial development nevertheless remarked at the end, 'But the fact that
India's real wealth is in her land must not be lost sight of.' *Indian Industries* (London, 1880),
p. 370.
[25] Governor General in Council to Secretary of State, 8 June 1880, No. 38 (Home Revenue and
Agriculture Department), *Parl. Papers*, Cmd. 2732, vol. 53 of Session 1880, p. 160.
[26] *The Influence of English Trade and American Protection by the Development of India* (Calcutta,
1883), p. 8.

lay in its ability to increase the productivity of its rural sector, and its capacity to widen the markets for its agricultural products.

LAISSEZ-FAIRE AND A DEVELOPMENT STRATEGY

Whether it was due to a changing concept of national objective or to the necessity of possessing an economic colony, the need for an economically strong India was much appreciated. But the issue was how to make India economically strong. Classical economists visualised an automatic mechanism – provided the state did not intervene – which generated economic growth towards the Classical limits of the stationary state. If only the correct institutional structure were provided, economic development should not be difficult to achieve. The basic ingredients were free trade, which provided scope for increased productivity of labour via greater division of labour, and capital accumulation which enabled the country to maintain a greater quantity of productive labour.[27] The entire system depended upon the cardinal socioeconomic feature of all societies undergoing transformation into full-fledged capitalist economies, namely the existence of property rights including landed property. When McCulloch declared in 1845 that 'it is idle, therefore, to think that a right of property in land can ever be advantageously dispensed with. Its establishment is, in fact, the grand source of civilization'[28] not a single nineteenth-century British economist would have dissented. The Classical economists had also given importance to non-economic factors such as primitive habits of thought, customs and native institutions which had a repressive influence on the process of economic development. In such circumstances, the benefits of free trade could not be achieved unless society were purged of all these growth-inhibiting characteristics, and such purging could only be done by state legislation.

Looked at from this broad perspective, Indian official opinion endorsed the Classical view of economic policy for development. The general aims of policies pursued during the famines, the tax policies and the various policies concerning the adjustment of economic relations were all intended to remove obstacles to the functioning of the market and bring about an ideal allocation of resources. As far as the land revenue policy was concerned, in its ideal form it was to identify agricultural classes, create private property, define precisely the existence of property rights in land, and construct a judicial system to uphold the agrarian organisation so that capital accumulation could take place.

Private property could be created only by the combined operation of

---

[27] See H. Myint, *Theories of Welfare Economics* (London, 1948), p. 12.
[28] *A Treatise on the Principles and Practical Influence of Taxation and the Funding System*, p. 50.

productive power and individual effort; and, as C. E. Trevelyan said, what was required was the 'freest possible scope to interested and benevolent enterprise'.[29] In order to bring about the combination of these two circumstances, the British rulers correctly understood the need for certain social and political preconditions, for example, the type of state intervention contemplated by utilitarian economists such as James Mill who visualised legislation to reform the structure of Indian society and character. With his vast theoretical knowledge of India, Mill was certain that the field for 'Agenda' was far greater in India than in advanced countries. His ambition and aim was to sweep out all the old institutions and build a new society where the application of Bentham's calculus would enable the achievement of the greatest good. Intervention in this category consisted mainly of measures to make society capable of utilising the benefits of free trade.

The other type of state intervention, that of the formulation of a programme of economic development, was a comparatively minor affair. The prevailing attitude put its faith in the 'invisible hand', rather than the 'visible' hand of the state; and active intervention in economic spheres was popular neither with the Haileybury-educated civil servants nor with the Court of Directors. Although the East India Company was a vestige of the by-gone age of Mercantilism, it believed and followed in India the spirit of the age. As early as 1787 the Court advised the Government of Bengal to refrain from interfering with the free market processes.[30] Thus from the beginning of the nineteenth century, the idea of non-intervention was entertained and adhered to. All that the government should do was to provide a system whereby people could exercise their rights freely. Indeed, commerce 'languishes under the interference of authority,' warned John Prinsep in 1823, 'even when most sincerely exerted for good'.[31] Even when the British government specifically requested the East India Company to encourage the production of strategic commodities like hemp (so much needed by the Royal Navy) in India to break the Russian monopoly,[32] it failed to stimulate the local governments into action. For example, in the mid 1850s, when the Crimean War stopped Russian supplies of hemp and flax, British authorities requested the Government of Madras to explore the possibilities of providing state encouragement for the production of those commodities. The Madras Board of Revenue however declared that apart from moderate taxa-

[29] *Parl. Papers*, H.C. 527, vol. VIII of Session 1840, Q. 1829.
[30] See Court of Directors to Bengal, 2 November 1787, India Office Records, *Secret Letters to India*, vol. I, no. 27, para. 17.
[31] *Suggestions on a Freedom of Commerce and Navigation more Especially in reference to the East India Trade*, p. 1.
[32] See Court of Directors to the Duke of Portland, 8 September 1807, India Office Records, *Home Misc.* no. 816, p. 130.

tion (to permit capital accumulation) and the improvement of the means of communication (to widen the market), the government could do very little to promote economic development. In their view, 'Any attempt to stimulate production by bounties reduced assessment, or direct purchases of the crop' would be objectionable, as 'such a course would interfere materially with the operations of the regular trader ... it might hereafter be found that the product so raised was profitable only from the special advantages shown to it, and was in reality less profitable than others which it had thus displaced.'[33]

Writing at a time when, in Britain, Lancashire interests were pressing the secretary of state actively to promote the cultivation of cotton in India, another writer said emphatically that the duty of the government was simply the protection of life and property and the provision of facilities for enforcing the fulfilment of contracts and public works; but 'anything like competition with private enterprise could only end in disaster'.[34] It was hard for those connected with Indian administration to imagine that government-managed enterprises would be profitably run. For example, ever since the railway age began in India in the 1850s there were engineers belonging to the various departments of public works who periodically speculated on the possibilities of developing an iron and steel industry in India to meet the demand created by railway construction.[35] When in 1860 the government asked Thomas Oldham to report on the possible manufacture of iron and steel by the Government of India, he unequivocally stated: 'The successful establishment of such works demands an unceasing care and attention, such thorough identification of the interests of those conducting, with the success of the scheme, and such entire devotion of energies and time as it is not in human nature to expect from any one not personally (and pecuniarily) involved in the work.'[36] At the most, the government could only provide encouragement and perhaps moral support to schemes already worked out by individual entrepreneurs. Even Lord Mayo, who had done a good deal for promoting Indian economic development, had this to say: 'On principle I am averse to Government's bolstering up particular private speculation by advances of capital. Let us put all available information ... let us endeavour to stimulate in all legitimate ways the invention of all mechanical applian-ces ... but let all private enterprises ... [must] depend for success on their

---

[33] See *Selections from the Records of the Madras Government*, no. XXIII, pp. 2, 137 *et seq.*
[34] J. T. Mackenzie, *op. cit*, pp. 10 *et seq.* See also Thomas Briggs, *The Development of the Dormant Wealth of the British Colonies* (London 1868), p. 13. See also A. Mackay's influential report, *Western India*, p. 59.
[35] See for example F. Tyrrell's Remarks dated 18 May 1864, India Office Records, L/PWD/3/208, p. 27.
[36] *Report on the Present State and Prospects of the Government Iron Works* (Calcutta, 1860), pp. 26–7.

own capital, industry, and intelligence.'[37] Hence one could infer that throughout the nineteenth century government as well as a sizeable section of economic opinion thought of economic development in terms of individual effort and accumulation of riches.[38] People could not be made to gather riches but could be encouraged to do so by the provision of all facilities. The state itself could not invest capital argued the Classical economists, for that would be detrimental to proper economic growth. If government activity increased unproductive expenditure that would involve a reduction in the supply of capital available for the labour product. Even if the state invested only on productive items it meant no gain to the community as it involved only transfer of funds from private to the public sector.[39] On political grounds they all objected to state intervention. Whereas Conservatives thought state intervention to be an intrusion into their privileges, Whigs hated all state activity and the Radicals felt it would only augment aristocratic prerogatives.

The argument that state intervention was absent in India was questioned some years ago by Gallagher and Robinson who posed the question, '*In the age of Laissez-faire* why was the Indian economy developed by the State?'[40] That British policy in India was intended to create a prosperous India has already been noted. It is true that there was a desire to turn India into an economy complementary to British economy. The surprising thing is that India was not, as alleged by Gallagher and Robinson, 'subjected to intense development as an economic colony'. It would be nearer the truth to say that India was prevented from being an independent economic nation. State intervention there certainly was, and it was of two types in nineteenth-century India, direct and indirect. Direct participation by the state was limited to the construction of public works which, as will be seen, was a special case; and the construction of public works did not mean the denial of the *laissez-faire* economic policy. Indirect state participation to stimulate economic development would have involved measures such as protection to infant industries, subsidies and the provision of technical advice. While some experiments were conducted from time to time with imported seeds, and some spasmodic action taken in the direction of improving the quality of raw produce

[37] Note by Lord Mayo, 29 July 1869 (Mayo Papers at the Cambridge University Library).

[38] It must be remembered that one of the cardinal virtues cherished by the Victorian English society was the concept of self-help so ably propounded by the best-selling author Samuel Smiles. The popularity in India of the value of individual effort could be gauged by the fact that Smiles' most famous *Self-Help* was translated into numerous Indian Languages. See Asa Briggs' introduction to the Centenary edition of Smiles' *Self-Help with Illustrations of Conduct and Perseverance* (London, 1958), p. 7.

[39] See B. A. Corry, *Money, Saving and Investment in English Economics* (London, 1962), pp. 62 *et seq.*

[40] 'The Imperialism of Free-trade' *Economic History Review*, 2nd series, vol. VI 1953, p. 5.

manufactured, it cannot be said that there was any actual and sustained policy of the systematic fostering of Indian agriculture or industries through these methods.

Agricultural development policy throughout the first three quarters of the nineteenth century basically meant (1) widening the market, (2) enabling capital accumulation by a properly structured fiscal system; and (3) removing apathy and the force of custom by encouraging British settlers to demonstrate the benefits of cultivation for the market. This policy took for granted that technical progress would automatically transform Indian agriculture. But the evolving agrarian conditions in India impressed observers and others concerned in policy formation that a more active policy was required to achieve agricultural development. It was during the viceroyalty of Lord Mayo that a new policy emerged which stressed the positive contributions that the state could make in stimulating agricultural development. Policy makers became increasingly aware of the importance of labour-saving devices and other physical inputs for increasing productivity in the Indian agricultural sector. A contemporary writer said in 1871 that 'If we are to progress at all in India, we must leap at once from the native "hal" to the steam-plough, and the sooner we recognise this fact the better.'[41] Though not in these flamboyant terms, the idea that greater mechanisation was necessary to resurrect Indian agriculture gained vogue among those connected with Indian administration. Reporting on the very question of agricultural implements to the Under-Secretary of State for India in 1868, Major-General Fred Cotton said that the government must take upon its head to do research on the appropriateness of particular tools, and provide immediate advice and help to the needy agriculturists. Admitting that Indian peasants lacked the means to own large machinery, he said that they could take advantage of government-hired machinery 'which as in the case of the travelling thrashing machine, is all that the small farmers trust to do in England. In this way, expensive machinery might be brought into general use throughout India.'[42] In a series of trenchantly written monographs Major A. F. Corbett argued the vital necessity of spreading good farming techniques such as the use of manure, deep ploughing and crop rotation among the villagers, and castigated the one-shot solution (through irrigation) to all problems of agricultural productivity.[43] This stress on the supply of physical inputs could be clearly

[41] C. S. Thomason, *The Public Works Department of India Why so Costly?* (London, 1871), p. 19.
[42] 'Report Upon the Agricultural Implements', 7 August 1868 (Mayo Papers at Cambridge University Library).
[43] See *Notes on Agriculture and Sanitation* (1868), *Is Irrigation Necessary in Upper India* (1870) and *The Climate and Resources of Upper India* (1874) Mayo had read with admiration the first two books, but it appears that Col. J. C. Anderson (Inspector General of Irrigation) to whom Mayo sent copies, was not so impressed. (See Anderson's Memo in the Mayo Papers.)

seen in Mayo's policy which resulted in the setting-up of an agricultural department to coordinate and encourage measures to improve the agricultural resources of the country.

By the last decade of the century it was accepted by most local governments that 'active intervention to lead and assist agricultural progress' was 'absolutely necessary'. Indeed the Agricultural Committee appointed by the government of Madras said that the government should have a 'definite policy, and should be thoroughly organised and properly equipped with supplies, with effective agents, and also with the means of testing its first results under varying conditions, and of disseminating and demonstrating successful results in the eyes of the people'.[44] This was possible because there was a growing awareness among many administrators in the last three decades of the century that any extreme application of *laissez-faire* ideas in the matter of promoting economic prosperity was mistaken, even as they had come to similar conclusions with regard to policies relating to famines and economic relations. It is not asserted here that allegiance had suddenly shifted from *laissez-faire* to state interventionism, but that doubts were expressed on the extreme position of *laissez-faire*. It was claimed by many that what was acceptable economic policy in Britain need not be so for India because the socioeconomic features were different in the two countries. For example, making a pointed reference to Herbert Spencer's *Social Statics*, in which *laissez-faire* is propounded in its extreme form, H. C. Irwin of the civil service said that the extent to which *laissez-faire* was practicable depended on (1) 'the strength of the spontaneously progressive element among the people'; and (2) 'the degree of homogeneity which prevails between the people'. As both were absent in India, Spencer's arguments were invalid for application in India.[45] Similar ideas were expressed by numerous civil servants and others so often that a believer was forced to remark: 'it must be confessed that India, in spite of its close connection with the most enlightened of Commercial nations, is a stronghold of all the economic heresies from which we have escaped'.[46] But it would appear that in late nineteenth century Britain, opinion was not unanimous on this issue. For example when in 1876, the Political Economy Club met to celebrate the centenary of the publication of the *Wealth of Nations*, a liberal politician –

[44] *Report of the Agricultural Committee* (1888), p. 6.
[45] *Calcutta Review*, no. 120, vol. LX, 1875, pp. 213–30. See also *The Indian Observer*, 13 May 1871, pp. 227–8; J. Forbes Watson, *Remarks on the Development of the Resources of India* (London, 1858), p. 12; *A Lecture on the Material and Social Effects of English Rule in India* (Salisbury, 1878), by an Anglo-Indian of Fifty Years Service, p. 7; W. M. Thorburn, *The Great Game* (London, 1875), p. 3; and Minute by Sir C. A. Elliott, 11 December 1879, *Parl. Papers*, Cmd. 3086–1, vol. LXXI of Session 1881, p. 188.
[46] *British Rule in India Financially and Economically Considered* (London, 1885), p. 34.

economist, W. E. Forster, remarked that they could not 'undertake the *laissez-faire* principle in the present condition of our politics or of parties in Parliament, or in the general condition of the country'.[47] He was by no means the only economist to doubt the validity of a *laissez-faire* economic policy, as there was a strong body of influential economists such as Leonard Courtenay, Arnold Toynbee[48] and Viscount Goschen who saw and applauded the positive aspects of state intervention.

However, when it was a question of encouraging sectors of the Indian economy that would have damaged certain sectors of the British economy, the government observed strict neutrality. The glaring example here was the question of protection to the infant cotton textile industry. We have seen already how the tariff on imported textiles levied for revenue reasons was abolished on the ground that it had a protective effect. In the nineteenth century, protection for infant Indian industries was never favoured in spite of the support it received among Indian economists and a small section of British public opinion.

Another glaring instance was the question of supporting the proposals for making iron and steel in India. After the railway age began in India it became clear that India had to explore the possibility of making some of the required stores. The government accordingly made attempts – but on a very modest scale – to investigate the possibility of exploiting indigenous mineral resources. Experimental works were constructed in De Chauri in the Kumaon district in 1856 and at Burwai and Barakar in the early 1860s. Even these very minor experiments were opposed by Trevelyan who was the Finance Minister in the early 1860s. According to him the amounts would have been better spent on cotton roads and irrigation projects. He thought that by setting up iron works 'we are competing at public expense, against the English iron trade'.[49] But Elgin, the Viceroy, and Henry Maine, the Law Member, both were of the opinion that these experiments would be a sort of prelude to the entering of private enterprise. Whenever funds were required for expansion the utmost caution was exercised by the government. At the time of transferring the iron works to the private sector very little

---

[47] Political Economy Club, *Revised Report of the Proceedings at the Dinner of 31 May 1876 held in Celebration of the 100th Year of the Publication of the Wealth of Nations* (London, 1876), p. 50.

[48] We are told by a former student of Toynbee that he was responsible for effecting a change in the attitude of Oxford economists regarding state intervention from one of hostility to healthy support. Until his death in 1883, Toynbee served as a tutor at the Balliol College, Oxford to the candidates for the Indian Civil Service. See Lord Milner's Introduction to Toynbee's *Lectures on the Industrial Revolution* (London, 1890), pp. xxv–xxvi.

[49] Quoted in S. K. Sen, *Studies in Economic Policy and Development in India 1848–1926* (Calcutta, 1966), p. 41.

encouragement was forthcoming. When W. P. Andrew, the indefatigable promoter of railway companies, asked for a guarantee (similar to the railway guarantees) to exploit the resources of iron-ore in the hope that 'India will shortly become independent of England for supply of iron',[50] he was refused. Even the licence-deed came after such a long time that it was no use to raise the needed capital. No other form of encouragement was given to other intending operators of the iron works. When Lord Ripon, a staunch believer in *laissez-faire*, himself proposed to give a few innocuous concessions to operate the Barakar Iron Works efficiently, the proposals were negatived by the Secretary of State, thanks to the immense influence wielded by the powerful English iron and steel manufacturers.[51]

Thus the early history of Indian cotton textile and iron and steel industries shows that, when the interests of Britain and India clashed, government policy remained neutral at its best. But the neutrality was itself sufficient to foster British interests. Hence on close examination the argument that India was turned into an economic colony by systematic state intervention has not much basis in fact.

CONCLUSION

We have argued that for the Indian administration development meant agricultural development, and notwithstanding a shift in the climate of opinion towards the last decades of the century, development was to be achieved through individual initiative without *direct* government assistance. However the story is different when we come to *indirect* government intervention in economic affairs to encourage economic development. Both the theory of the classical economists and the policy of the British Raj were not averse to this type of state assistance for promoting economic progress. We shall take up this matter in the next chapter.

---

[50] W. P. Andrew, *Tramroads in North India, in Connection with the Iron Mines of Kumaon and Garhwal* (London, 1857), p. 52. According to Andrew, 'The manufacture of native iron for rails is second only in importance to the construction of railways themselves in India.' p. 36.

[51] Ripon ruefully remarked: 'It is, we presume, certain that the establishment of the iron and steel industry would be viewed with disfavour by the persons interested in the manufacture of these articles in England.' Quoted in S. K. Sen, *op. cit.*, p. 43.

8

THE STATE AND THE POLICY FOR
ECONOMIC DEVELOPMENT

The solider who shields the peasant while he is cultivating his field from the
annoyance of the foe performs his part towards the improvement of the land;
and the Magistrate, whose duty it is to give security to property after it is
acquired, contributes more even than the capitalist himself towards the public
prosperity. Let it not be imagined, therefore, that the revenues of a state lose
all powers of reproduction from the moment that they pass into the chest of the
collector.

> Court of Directors to the Government of Bombay
> 10 January 1810

INTRODUCTION

The Classical theory of economic policy was never wholly averse to state
intervention in economic affairs: indeed the state had to play a significant
part in bringing about socioeconomic changes, so that rapid economic
development was made possible. Whereas James Mill thought that such
changes could be rapidly introduced by legislation, the Court of Directors
before his arrival at the India Office thought that the process of preparing
Indians to make them enjoy the pleasures of free trade was a slow and gradual
affair. The Directors also came to the view that the public sector had a
definite function to perform from a different point of view. In order to
defend public expenditure on the provision of what are called public goods by
modern economists, the Court even criticised Adam Smith and Quesnay for
making the unrealistic distinction between productive and unproductive
labour.[1] According to the Court of Directors, the expansion of the public
sector was not in itself wrong, but all depended upon how the public
revenues were spent. The Court of Directors were fully aware of the external
economies created by public expenditure, and the Directors were prepared to
intervene to provide these services. Successive governor-generals and
secretaries of state throughout the century had much the same attitude
towards public expenditure. Even Lord Argyll, who is so often dismissed
as the typical Whig-zealot for *laissez-faire*, stated that although 'the true

---

[1] See Court of Directors to Bombay, 10 January 1810, *Parl. Papers* H. C. 306, vol. X of
Session 1812–3, para, 168.

wealth of a wise and just Government lies in the growing wealth of its people' and that the best fiscal system was the one which 'encourages the accumulation and enjoyment of capital in private hands', nevertheless this wealth should always be accessible 'to such demands as arise from time to time out of the duty and the necessity of our applying to its (Indian economic) condition the knowledge which belongs to a more advanced civilization than its own'.[2]

There was thus hardly any question about the desirability of the state performing certain indirect functions to generate external economies for promoting the path of capitalist development. In so far as we can generalise they fall into a pattern as follows:

1 Security of property (physical and legal)
2 A Financial infrastructure (monetary system)
3 Promotion of entrepreneurship
4 Education
5 Public works and public utilities

Both the formulation and execution of policies and priorities concerning specific areas of public expenditure for economic development were dependent on considerations of immediate urgency and the availability of financial resources. Although it was understood that all the items listed above generated considerable external economies, it was equally realised that the costs and benefits were difficult to define and calculate. As the first four items were considered to be pure public goods, it was unanimously accepted that the state should provide them out of its own finances. However the provision of public works and utilities was difficult as there was the possibility of at least partly internalising costs and benefits. In other words, while the states's interest in the construction of public works and utilities was accepted, the question of the actual execution of a public works policy was subject to a fierce controversy, involving as it did areas of *laissez-faire* and Classical theory of economic policy.

SECURITY OF PROPERTY

British rulers in India from Cornwallis to Curzon and English Classical economists held one firm belief in common: the necessity of a strong state. As has been pointed out by William Grampp, Classical economists concentrated their attention on economic freedom and not political freedom.[3] In order to safeguard the former, they were prepared to surrender something

---

[2] Secretary of State to Governor-General in Council, 12 May 1870 (Educational).
[3] 'On the Politics of the Classical Economists', *Quarterly Journal of Economics*, vol. LXII, no. 5, November 1948, pp. 728–9, 736.

of the latter. They believed in the rule of law, no doubt, but rule of law could not be maintained without the strong hand of authority.

Unless people could enjoy their property, there would be little desire to accumulate riches. Hence if 'ignorance and violence' render 'persons and property insecure', there would be no economic progress either. Consequently the state's task according to the Classical economists was to provide security of property. McCulloch and James Mill were two of the economists who specifically mentioned security of property as a primary requisite for the economic development of India.[4] The official organ of Benthamite Utilitarians said with emphasis that security of property was tantamount to developing the sources of wealth and hence the most important incentive to capital formation in India. The state could develop India, said the writer, by 'giving to the people every possible security against misrule . . . by placing every check upon the natural rapacity of the few, and affording every protection'.[5]

From the beginning, governors-general in India were committed to providing security of property for the sake of promoting economic development. As early as 1793, we find Lord Cornwallis stressing that 'If we wish to render the country opulent, and the people happy, our great aim must be to establish security of person and property.'[6] The anxiety of the East India Company to maintain law and order was a political as well as a commercial necessity. Being a commercial organisation in origin, it knew that profitable trade and capital accumulation could not be carried on when political uncertainty prevailed.[7] Even the available capital vanished very often from circulation, to be hoarded and not invested profitably because of the lack of security.[8] Paucity of capital was not of itself a serious problem. The problem as perceived by Sleeman and others was one of utilising the available capital in India that lay scattered and not properly utilised because of the inhibiting institutional structure.[9] It was individuality and security of property that

---

[4] McCulloch's *Principles* (1 Edn.) pp. 78, 74 and note XX of his edition of *Wealth of Nations*. Robert Rickards cited from McCulloch to show how insecurity destroyed the Turkish economy and said that similarly insecurity generated by Moslem invaders prevented India from registering economic progress. See his *India* (London, 1829), vol. II, pp. 369–70, 374–5. See also Stokes, *English Utilitarians and India*, p. 140.

[5] *The Westminster Review*, October 1825, pp. 265–6. See also Munro's evidence on 14 April 1813 to the House of Commons Select Committee, *Parl. Papers*, H.C. 122, vol. VII of Session 1812–3.

[6] Minute dated 11 February 1793, *Correspondence of the Honourable Court of Directors of the East India Company and the Governor General in Council Respecting the Permanent Settlement of Land Revenue* (London, 1825), p. 25.

[7] See Court of Directors to Madras, 24 April 1811 (Revenue), Madras *Despatches*, vol. 47, India Office Records, E/4/907, pp. 335–6, para. 138.

[8] John Chapman, *Cotton and Commerce* (London, 1851), p. 111.

[9] *Rambles and Recollections*, vol. II, pp. 61–2.

provided stimulus to exertion, thanks to which 'wealth accumulates; invention is excited, theoretical and practical knowledge widely diffused'.[10] Thus a stable administration providing security of property was considered a prime necessity for economic development.

MONETARY SYSTEM

It became obvious very early to the British rulers of India that security of property by itself was not adequate, and that it had to be supplemented with the proper financial infrastructure that would enable a viable commercial economy to develop. Throughout India at the beginning of the nineteenth century coins differed in denomination and intrinsic value even within the same district. Yet in every region, thanks to the fluctuating rates and the operation of 'Gresham's Law', the weaker currency gained the upper hand in circulation. There was an almost complete absence of any standard of value because of the different kinds of coins circulating. Under such circumstances exchange economy was in effect no more than a barter economy. Money could not perform the function of a store of value which in its turn hindered investment. This chaotic monetary system was an immediate concern of many Indian civil servants especially when a framework of administration had been partially established. For instance, Sir Thomas Munro as early as July 1800 wrote to the Marquis of Wellesley about the necessity of introducing the same coinage and currency system all over India to prevent money changers from profiting at the expense of both the government and the people: 'There is perhaps no code of regulations that could be framed for the extension of agriculture and commerce and for the advancement of the general prosperity that would so surely and so speedily attain these ends as the single measure of establishing a uniform currency to serve both as the current money and as the money of account upon the three Establishments.'[11] And Lord William Bentinck claimed that impediments to 'commercial intercourse' such as lack of a uniform currency imposed 'a considerable burthen on the trade with all the disadvantages of a direct tax but without any countervailing benefit to the public finances'.[12]

The disorganised state of the currency structure was a source of worry for

---

[10] See Gavin Young, *A Further Inquiry into the ... Colonial Policy* (London, 1828), p. 91. Rickards said, 'The political economists instruct us that property is a primary necessity for progress, and that the security of property, are the basis of all improvement in human society.' *India* vol. II, p. 368. See also Lt Col James Caulfield, *Observations on Our Indian Administration Civil and Military* (London, 1832), p. 88.

[11] Add. MSS. 13,679, f. 37. (Wellesley Papers at the British Museum)

[12] Despatch to the Court of Directors (Finance Dept.) 10 November 1829, *Financial Letters and Enclosures Received from Bengal*, India Office Records No. L/F/3/25.

the Court of Directors too, and they accordingly decided to act. After investigating the mint-masters' accounts and consulting various government papers and authorities on the subject, the Court of Directors framed a despatch on 25 April 1806 which was sent to all three local governments in India. This despatch was the basis on which Indian monetary policy was formulated for the next three decades.[13]

The basic idea behind the proposals of reform was the indispensability of a monometallic currency system for India. In coming to this conclusion, the Court of Directors derived great comfort from Lord Liverpool's recently published *Treatise on the Coins of the Realm in a Letter to the King*. They wrote, 'we think his Lordship has established the principle that the money or coin which is to be the principal measure of property ought to be of one metal only'. Following Lord Liverpool, they emphatically stated that to adjust the relative values of these two metals 'according to the fluctuations in the values of the metals would create continual difficulties, and the establishment of such a principle would of itself tend to perpetuate the inconvenience and loss'.

It is significant that the Court of Directors cited Liverpool's treatise for theoretical support for their policy conclusions. Up to the end of the eighteenth century two main aspects of monetary management were discussed in the writings on currency. One concerned currency and currency institutions, in other words, the question how the currency system ought to be organised and administered. The second dealt with the analysis of the functions of money, that is the place of money in the national economy. Eighteenth-century writers came to certain theoretical conclusions, and on the basis of these recommended some practical measures. According to them, money's most important task was to 'circulate' commodities. As for the mechanical aspect of circulation, they believed in the impracticality of a dual standard. At the same time the economists had a good deal to say about the quantity theory of money, effects of money values on various classes of people, the rate of interest and so on.[14] But, by and large, it was the first aspect of the

---

[13] This despatch is printed as a House of Commons Sessional Paper in 1898, H.C. 127, vol. LXI of Session 1898. It is not possible to say who exactly was the author of this document. The 'Chairs' (Chairman and Deputy Chairman of the Court of Directors) of 1806, William Fullarton Elphinstone and Edward Parry, and the Chief Examiner, Samuel Johnson were all definitely responsible. It is also possible that the previous 'Chairs' Charles Grant and George Smith might have had a hand in its preparation because the Court of Directors had informed India even in 1805 that they were thinking about sending instructions to reform the coinage system in India: 'the general subject of the Indian coinage will soon come under our consideration, with a view to the establishment if possible of one general currency for the whole of the greater part of the Company's territories'. Letter dated 13 March 1805. *Revenue Letters to Bengal*, vol. I, pp. 93–4, para. 23, India Office Records, L/E/3/441.

[14] See for a summary of eighteenth century monetary theory, D. Vickers, *Studies in the Theory of Money 1690–1776* (London, 1960), Chapter XIII.

corpus of monetary theory that the policy makers of India found useful during the first three decades of the nineteenth century when they were groping for a means of establishing a stable currency system, where only near-chaos existed. Liverpool's views, as Feavearyear rightly pointed out, were 'no more than a summary of the best opinion upon the subject at the time'.[15] Although we find in his treatise a digest of previous thought and copious references to his predecessors like Locke, Harris, Petty, Adam Smith, Steuart and others, his was the first complete scheme for managing a mono-metallic currency with subsidiary token coins.

Having decided on a strictly monometallic currency system for India, the Court of Directors simply stated that 'in applying this argument to a coin for the general use in India, there cannot be a doubt in our opinion that such coin must be of silver'. Since their authority, Lord Liverpool, had recommended a monometallic gold currency, the proposal of a silver currency by the Court of Directors was somewhat unusual. It is not, however, al-together surprising as Steuart had given support to this proposal earlier. Locke, Harris and Massie, also writing before Liverpool, had favoured silver monometallism. Generally speaking, economic opinion at the turn of the century was largely in favour of gold monometallism. Liverpool himself agreed that the choice of the right metal 'is a very controverted point, and more difficult than any of which I have to treat'.[16] His criterion for the choice of the basic metal was simple: it depended upon the commerical transactions of the country. At an earlier period, 'silver coins were the more common currency of the country, because they were better adapted to the extent of our commerical transactions at that time. But great payments were even then frequently made in Gold coins'.[17] Thus Liverpool decided on gold coins for England because it was rich and a country 'where great and exten-sive commerce' was being carried on.[18]

The Court of Directors were not unaware of the poor state of the Indian economy. Although Bengal may have had a number of wealthy individuals, very few transactions involved great sums. The Court of

---

[15] *The Pound Sterling: A History of English Money* (London, 1963) p. 175. Liverpool's Treatise was not published until 1805 but the ideas contained in it 'had been presented in its substance to the Privy Council Committee in 1798, and probably had been urged on his associates even earlier'. F. W. Fetter, *Development of British Monetary Orthodoxy 1797–1875* (Cambridge, Mass 1965), pp. 57–8. Liverpool's ideas were accepted by all leading economists for the next few decades. Ricardo, for example, gave his full approval. See his *High Price of Bullion* (1811), Sraffa edition vol. III, p. 65 *et seq.*

[16] *Coins of the Realm* (London, 1880 edn.), p. 140.

[17] *Ibid.*, p. 151.

[18] Ricardo saw the question in a different light. Gold became the standard because it was over-valued. Even before gold became acceptable to people, it was the 'intention of the legislature to establish gold as the standard of currency in this country'. *op. cit.* pp. 68–9.

Directors' assessment of the Indian situation was based on Sir John Shore's elaborate Minute on the currency situation in Bengal.[19] Shore was an advocate for silver monometallism because he rightly perceived that even the smallest possible gold coin was 'unfit for the purpose of general circulation'. Gold coinage, he felt, would only lead to hardship to the people, and the gainers would be the professional money changers. Shore however stressed the necessity of an auxiliary gold coinage because if a gold coin were issued then it would obviate the necessity of importing large quantities of silver during crises. He suggested the issue of a gold coin which 'should be received by convention only' so that it would then 'circulate as far as the state of society will admit'. Bearing this advice in mind, the Court of Directors suggested in their despatch that gold coins of the same denomination, weight and fineness as that of the standard silver coins might be issued without tying them to a fixed ratio.

The reason given by the Court of Directors in suggesting the change from the Mughal Sicca Rupee weight of $179\frac{2}{3}$ troy grains to 180 grains was to 'fix the gross weight in whole numbers'. But probably they were also aware that 180 troy grains is equal to one *tola*, a standard Indian weight followed all over India. The issue of half rupees, quarter rupees and one rupee pieces was authorised for 'general convenience'.

Just as Liverpool suggested a gold currency with silver and copper as subsidiary token currency, the Court of Directors suggested for India silver as the standard and copper as the token currency. The Court of Directors' instruction is very similar to what Liverpool said on this subject.[20] They recommended a copper coinage of low denomination. The weight of this coin was to be so adjusted, giving due consideration to the cost of the copper and of the minting of the coins, as 'to leave a profit on its issue'. This would have 'the good effect of preventing the melting of the coins, as its value in currency would be something more than the value of the metal'.

We thus find, that the Court of Directors suggested for India a system of currency based on the currently accepted ideas on the subject. This was noted by a number of writers and appreciated. Roger Ruding for example, said of the scheme, 'This design is well worthy of the Company, and proves that it entertains enlightened notions of the true principles of coinage.'[21]

---

[19] Minute of Governor-General Sir John Shore, 29 September 1796, Bengal Public Consultations, 3 October 1796. India Office Records, Range 4, vol. 44, pp. 385–440. See also Regulation XXXV of 1793 of Bengal, and Court of Directors to Bengal, Letter in the Public Department, 25 May 1798, *Fort-William India House Correspondence*, vol. XIII (Ed. P. C. Gupta) (Delhi, 1959), pp. 77–8.

[20] *Coins of the Realm*, p. 173.

[21] *Annals of the Coinage of Great Britain and its Dependencies* (London, 1817), vol. II, p. 112n.

It is, however, one thing to formulate a scheme on paper six thousand miles away from the place for which it is intended, and an entirely different thing to put it into practice. It took nearly thirty years for this neat plan to be accepted and adopted by all the governments in India.[22]

The establishment of a uniform currency for India in 1835 was only the beginning, and the question of Indian monetary policy in the next six decades became highly controversial one in which British monetary ideas played a significant part in forming the opinions of the contending parties. Lines were as clearly drawn among the Indian administrators as they were among

TABLE 2

Period	Problem	Alternative solutions and their authors*	
		View 1	View 2
1850s 1860s	Inadequacy of circulating medium	Introduction of gold currency	Retention of existing system
		Sir Charles Trevelyan *Sir Richard Temple* Viscount Goschen J. R. McCulloch J. E. Cairnes	*James Wilson* G. W. Norman G. Arbuthnot
1860s	Introduction of paper currency	A fixed proportion of coins to notes issued	Full coin backing for notes issued
		James Wilson 'Banking School'	*Sir Charles Wood* 'Currency School'
1870s 1880s	Silver depreciation	Managed currency through bimetallism	Automatic silver currency
		Sir David Barbour J. Shield Nicholson H. S. Foxwell	*Lord Ripon* W. S. Jevons R. Giffen H. Fawcett W. Bagehot
		Managed currency through an artificial gold currency	
		Col. Baird Smith *Sir Richard Strachey* 'Ricardo's Ingot Plan'	

* Individuals whose names are italicised were important members of Indian administration involved in the monetary policy discussions.

[22] See my paper 'Economic ideas and the Foundations of the Indian currency system' in *Indian Economic and Social History Review*, December 1974.

the British economists. Consequently alternative policies were pursued with great fervour, as the accompanying summary table will indicate.[23]

Although contradictory ideas were held by the different participants of these controversies, each of them unanimously believed in the need for a proper monetary framework for the working of a commercial economy which in its turn was essential for economic development. In other words, a strong and stable currency system was part of the British approach to Indian economic progress. As this approach was also strongly free trade oriented, automaticity in the structure of the Indian currency system was accepted as the policy 'ideal' to be striven for. In spite of the counteracting influences of sectional interests and alternative viewpoints, the strength of this bias towards an automatic currency system could be seen in the fact that it was not until 1893 (and even then under very heavy pressure) that the system established in 1835 was altered.

ENTREPRENEURIAL CLASS

Security of property and stable financial institutions lead us to the problem of the formation of an entrepreneurial class to channel the available capital into correct investment. Classical economists understood the necessity of entrepreneurs but assumed their existence. As no clear distinction was made by the economists between interest and profit, 'entrepreneur' does not perform any important function in their analytical apparatus. Just as it was assumed that a man with capital would automatically invest it, the Indian policy makers thought that, if a class with wealth were created, it would automatically increase the total investment.

The problem faced by the Indian government from Cornwallis to Curzon was twofold. One was the problem of atomisation of land holdings, the other was the problem of unduly large estates. The first was economically disastrous while the second was politically explosive. Hence the general policy throughout the century was to fight both these tendencies in land-holdings in order to create sufficient 'concentration of capital' but without its sheer size developing into a serious political problem. Capital was a great desideratum for economic development; as Rickards pointed out, 'no fact is perhaps better established in political economy than that industry cannot in any of its branches be promoted without capital'.[24] Capital accumulation could only take place when a portion of the annual profits is saved from being con-

---

[23] This subject of the interaction of British monetary ideas and Indian economic policies has been treated exhaustively elsewhere. See my forthcoming monograph tentatively titled *Monetary Thought and Management in India: studies in their Interaction in the Nineteenth Century* and my 'Economics and Economists in the Formation of a Monetary Policy for India (1873–1893)'. *History of Political Economy.* vol. XI no. 1, 1977.

[24] *India*, Vol. II, p. 200.

sumed, as in the case of subsistence farming. Hence, for the sake of long-term interests, it was necessary to foster a middle class. In the various contending schools of thought concerning land tenures, one could find a broadly similar aim, notably creation of an agriculturist who would have the incentive to apply capital to land and raise productivity and production. This was also the ideal society according to the Utilitarians and Natural Right theorists as well as to the political economists. Economists from Adam Smith to John Stuart Mill thought that the most desirable form of society was one where moderate inequality coupled with a large number of middle sized fortunes prevailed.[25] The founders of permanent settlement, especially Cornwallis, are usually accused of deliberately creating a class of landlords through the permanent settlement with the zemindars.[26] But their intention seems to have been the creation of an agricultural middle-class rather than a landed aristocracy.[27] This favourable opinion towards the middle class is very clear if we look into Cornwallis' attitudes towards one of the pillars of aristocracy, the institution of primogeniture. Primogeniture was one of the time-honoured devices to maintain an aristocratic system. But this institution came under heavy fire in the eighteenth and nineteenth centuries under the influence of liberal individualism and rationalistic egalitar-ianism.[28] Adam Smith himself condemned primogeniture as unfavourable to agrarian development. As it saved large estates from being broken up and as large landholders could not improve their whole property, primogeniture was thought by him to be detrimental to society. Primogeniture artificially maintained the size of the farms more than was justified by individual ability to accumulate property.[29]

Lord Cornwallis' ideas on primogeniture are somewhat similar to those of Adam Smith. Although he was responsible for the creation of a propertied class he was against large estates. To break up such big estates, Lord Cornwallis passed Regulation XI of 1793, and later extended to Banaras by Regulation XLIV of 1795, which abolished primogeniture in the few cases where it still prevailed.[30] Justification for this according to Cornwallis

---

[25] See R. Schlatter, *Private Property* (London, 1951), pp. 249 *et seq.*

[26] James Mill, *History of British India*, vol. V, p. 438.

[27] In the words of John Hodgson: 'It is not by tehsildars, that we are to expect improvements will be made in the appearance of the country ... whenever we observe such improvements, they will generally be found to have been made by the middling class of people, standing in society between the manufacturer and cultivator, that is, by merchants, landholders, and men of property.' See Firminger (Ed.), *Fifth Report*, vol. III, pp. 485 *et seq.* See also vol. II, p. 511. See also F. D. Ascoli, *Early Revenue History of Bengal* (Oxford, 1917), p. 67.

[28] Article on 'Primogeniture' in *Encyclopaedia of Social Sciences*.

[29] *Wealth of Nations*, pp. 361–2.

[30] See Evelyn Cecil, *Primogeniture: A Short History of its Development in Various Countries* (London, 1895), pp. 173–4.

rested on 'the good policy of dismembering these very large zemindarries, the evils attending which become every day more strongly impressed upon our minds'.[31] While it is easy to infer that Cornwallis was interested in creating a set of large proprietors who would have the incentive to invest capital on the lands at the same time the landlords would not be too affluent or influential to cause political uneasiness.[32] Even Francis, who originally proposed a zemindari settlement, did not have in mind the creation of an Indian aristocracy. He wanted the larger estates to be subdivided, leaving the relatively smaller ones intact. To this end, he advocated a 'new law of inheritance' that would bring into being a standardised size of zemindaries, each paying about Rs two lakhs of revenue annually. In justification of this measure, Francis cited a passage from David Hume which said: 'Such moderate estates, as require economy, and confine the proprietors to live at home, are better calculated for duration.'[33]

In pursuing this policy of creating an agricultural middle class, Cornwallis and his spiritual predecessor Francis conformed to the ideas being developed in Europe at that time. Apart from political objections, Adam Smith had written that unlimited division of labour was not possible in agriculture.[34] At the same time, the Physiocrats had said that the chief obstacles to agrarian growth were small, subsistence-scale, capital-starved farms.[35] This could be altered only by pumping enough capital into agriculture. As small farmers could not do that, the Physiocrats recommended that 'the lands employed in the cultivation of grains be combined, as much as possible into large farms exploited by rich farmers'.[36] In addition to these ideas, British agrarian experience pointed out to these policy makers the need for large farms and wealthy proprietors willing to inject capital. H. J. Habbakuk has shown how, in the second half of the seventeenth and the first half of the eighteenth century, small freeholders sold their lands

---

[31] Governor-General in Council to the Court of Directors, 6 March 1793, Ross (ed.), *Cornwallis*, vol. II, p. 554.

[32] Cornwallis had said, 'It is immaterial to Government what individual possesses the land, provided he cultivates it, protects the ryots, and pays the public revenue' (Minute dated 18 September 1789, Firminger, *op. cit.* vol. II, p. 512). Compare this statement with that of a contemporary philosopher admired by Cornwallis, Archdeacon William Paley, who said, 'What we call property in land, as hath been observed above, is power over it. Now it is indifferent to the public in whose hands this power resides, if it be rightly used; it matters not to whom the land belongs, if it be well cultivated.' *The Principles of Moral and Political Philosophy* (1824 reprint), p. 453.

[33] *Original Minutes*, p. 59.

[34] *The Wealth of Nations*, p. 7.

[35] See R. L. Meek, *The Economics of Physiocracy*, p. 24.

[36] Quesnay cited by Warren J. Samuels, *op. cit. Quarterly Journal of Economics*, February 1962, p. 156. See also Henry Higgs, *Physiocrats* (London, 1897), pp. 30–1. Higgs points out how by a rich farmer Quesnay means not one who simply cultivates his land 'but an entrepreneur'.

and joined the big farmers on lease.[37] Arthur Young, the influential spokesman of the British agricultural interest in the eighteenth century. specifically mentioned large farmers being responsible for agrarian prosperity.[38]

The 'middle class' that grew out of the Cornwallis system actually came to be a parasitical class.[39] Instead of improving their estates through the injection of technical improvements, the new landlords ruled their lands through unscrupulous agents who rackrented, levied extra cesses and tormented the tenants in the manner of the agents of England-based Irish landlords. The estates in many cases were carved up into smaller pieces and sublet. Inferior holders of tenures followed the same practice, and a new and large class of mere annuitants was created. It could not be expected that this class would have injected more capital into land to make it productive. Apart from the possibility of rackrenting, there was the far more profitable way of investing the available capital in the form of usurious lending. Ordinary profits in agriculture could not compete with the gains to be made in the money market.[40]

The Court of Directors was disappointed that the 'acquisition of hereditary property has not stimulated Industry in the degree that was expected'.[41] When it was perceived that the Cornwallis system had miscarried, doubts began to be expressed as to the possibilities of creating a dynamic class of agrarian entrepreneurs. These initial doubts later crystallised into firm policy.[42]

Already Alexander Read, Thomas Munro and others were engaged in developing a peasantry with a direct connection with the government. Their idea was to convert the rackrented tenants into an independent entrepreneurial (but small-scale) farming community. They were irked by what William Thackeray called 'the justification of policies by a quotation from Montesquieu or Aristotle'.[43] The problem for these reformers was that they had to contend with an important argument derived from the economists

[37] 'English Landownership, 1680–1740' *Economic History Review*, vol. x, no. 1, February 1940, pp. 14–5.

[38] *The Farmers Tour* (1771) cited in Bland, Brown and Tawney, *English Economic Documents* (London, 1933) p. 531.

[39] See Chap. 5 above.

[40] See Benoy Chowdhury, 'Some Aspects of Peasant Economy of Bengal after the Permanent Settlement' *Bengal: Past and Present*, Jubilee Number 1967, p. 148.

[41] Court of Directors to Governor General (Revenue) 21 March 1806, *Revenue Letters to Bengal*, vol. I, India Office Records, L/E/3/441, p. 174.

[42] George Canning, President of the Board of Control to the 'Chairs', 16 August 1817, *Letters from the Boards*, vol. IV, India Office Records, p. 449.

[43] Thackeray's Minute 4 August 1807, Appendix 31, *Fifth Report*, Parl. Papers H.C. no. 377, vol. VII of Session 1812, pp. 984 *et seq.* Munro in his Report on Canara dated 9 November 1800 had similar views. *Ibid.*, pp. 908 *et seq.*

about the possibilities of 'economies of scale' in large farms as well as the capacity of large landed proprietors to accumulate. This argument on economies of scale was skillfully demolished by Thackeray in his defence of the ryotwar settlement, and in the process he denied the validity of using economic ideas of the West under the entirely different conditions in India.[44] Thackeray pointed out, first, that all great civilisations were based on small farms as the viable economic units. The exception was England, and there it was due to the existence of primogeniture. Here Thackeray noted that 'Arthur Young's precise investigations and deep reasonings apply to the agriculture in England ... but not to mootahdarry and ryotwarry', and added that in England increased productivity did not result from mere size. Such increases in productivity arose 'from turning out the people, who could produce but little; and putting in one good farmer, whose skill, industry and stock, enabled him to raise more produce than all the ten could do before'. The English landlords were not only efficient farmers, but also 'philosophic improvers, who have brought down all the secrets of chemistry to assist mother earth, in performing her task'. But the Indian landlords were more like the French landlords who were profligates and spendthrifts.[45] According to Thackeray, Indian landlords wasted the rents received in all types of unproductive goods.[46] In this process the country was 'impoverished, by being obliged to support this swarm of drones; it is impoverished by having so many hands withdrawn from useful labours'. Another point he made was that

The earth generally produces, in proportion to the labour and expenses bestowed upon it. The division of labour, so important an advantage in manufactures, has little effect on agriculture. If this is the case in Europe (and the best authors, especially Adam Smith, seem to think so) great capitals can do little in Indian husbandry, by promoting division of labour.

In any case, large estates have a tendency to disappear owing to great increases in population and consequent sub-division; and hence there was no point in maintaining them artificially. There was also the moral problem involved in creating afresh inequalities for the sake of satisfying the assumption that inequality was an essential condition for any well-ordered society.

[44] Alexander Read, one of the founders of the Ryotwar System and himself a serious student of contemporary economic writings was not however as vehemently opposed to the application of economic theory to India as Thackeray was. See *Baramahal Records*, vol. XXI, p. 119, para. 40.

[45] Although Smith is not quoted, Thackeray must have in mind the section in the *Wealth of Nations* (Bk. III, Chap. II) in which he points out how great landed proprietors seldom improve their land, and how small proprietors improve their lands.

[46] See also the extract of a letter from Thackeray (dated 1 May 1805) in *Madras Secret Letters*, 12 February 1806, India Office Records.

If in the process of economic change inequalities occur that could not be helped, but 'we must let them all start fair'. The problem in India was not the small size of farms but the lack of sufficient capital accumulation owing to the heavy land tax. Thackeray's advice was to keep the land tax low and settle the tax payments direct with the small cultivator, for this would make them efficient and thrifty; 'circumstances form habits, and small estates would form frugal swains'. These arguments provided great support to the home government in their determination to avoid permanent settlement with the zemindars anywhere in India.

However, the increasing population was having the effect of atomisation of landholdings leading to a state of subsistence farming. As we have already seen, the despair of creating a dynamic middle class was also responsible for the advocacy of colonisation into India during the late 1820s and 1830s by people such as Metcalfe, Bentinck, Young and others.[47] It was expected that the colonisation from Europe would perform the functions of an entrepreneurial middle class and thus lift India from the prevailing poverty level.

While many civil servants advocated colonisation, there were some who persistently advocated the creation of a middle class. Sleeman pointed out that India lacked a middle class 'which is the basis of all that is great and good in European societies'.[48] The reason why India was not progressing economically was stated to be the atomisation of holdings that prevented the rise of a stable middle class. Many of these civil servants were afraid that the introduction of the ryotwar system might lead to further fragmentation of cultivated land. They preferred medium sized holdings wherein the landlords would be able to employ labourers in economical cultivation.[49] As there was not a great demand for labour, the Indian peasants were unable to get extra work to supplement their income from farming. Comparing the economic condition of English and Indian peasants, G. Ravenscroft, a Bengal civil servant, said that the miserable economic position of the Indian peasant was due to 'the want of demand for day labour and the system of small cottage farms'. The Indian peasant was compelled to maintain himself and his family 'solely upon the profits of his land after deducting the rent, which from the

---

[47] *Alexander's East India Magazine* said 'Our expectations of any beneficial exertion on the part of the Native landholders have died away. During the period of forty-five years in which they have enjoyed ... they have scarcely made a single effort to improve their estates of agricultural skill ... It is, therefore, to the settlement of Europeans in India, with their characteristic energy and skill that we must look for that progress in agriculture.' vol. XIV, no. 84 November 1837, p. 404.

[48] *Rambles and Recollections*, p. 73: *A Journey Through the Kingdom of Oude in 1849–1850* (London, 1858), vol. II, p. 251. *On Taxes and Public Revenue*, p. 336. See also F. J. Shore, *Notes on Indian Affairs*, vol. I, pp. 46–50.

[49] See the Minute on Taxation and Revenue by Robert Rickards, *Parl. Papers* H.C. 306, vol. X of Session 1812–13, para. 129. See also his *India*, vol. II, p. 344.

small breadth generally in the occupation of a tenant, and the low price of grain even if he held it rent-free, would not give him the comforts of life enjoyed by the cottage farmer in England'.[50] Demand for labour could only increase with an accumulation of capital. But how could capital accumulation take place if the operating units were small? It was thought that large-scale farming with the attendant effects of rapid capital accumulation and increased demand for productive labour would result in prosperity.[51] Thus the grand conclusion arrived at by these disciples of Classical economics was simple: the economic condition of a majority of the Indian rural population could only be solved by the creation of employers for them.[52]

Although civil servants like Sleeman were emphatically opposed to an aristocratic class they nevertheless wanted the law of primogeniture to be applied to India to prevent such splitting of estates.[53] It is interesting to see the similarity between the views of McCulloch, Malthus and Sleeman. Among the Classical economists, Malthus supported primogeniture for the very reason that James and John Stuart Mill opposed it. Malthus advocated primogeniture not because it was an aristocratic institution but because it forced the second and subsequent sons to take up commerical and trading pursuits thus swelling the ranks of the middle class.[54] But the Mills thought that, as primogeniture concentrated property in an artistocracy, the only way to create a middle class was by splitting them into many smaller estates. Surprisingly McCulloch agreed entirely with Malthus in this respect.[55]

While these ideas for the creation of a class capable of enterprise and capital accumulation were widely endorsed, it is not possible to say that a

50 Ravenscroft to Colebrooke & Deane, 1 January 1816. *Selections from Revenue Records of North West Provinces: 1818–1820*, vol. I, pp. 268–70, para. 18.

51 See *Edinburgh Review*, March 1824, p. 5. See also (Major H. D. Robertson) *Examination of the Principles and Policy of the Government of British India* (London, 1829), pp. 47 *et seq.*, pp. 102 *et seq.*

52 See Alexander Ross's Minute dated 6 March 1827, *Bengal Revenue Consultations* 11 October 1827, India Office Records, Range 61, vol. 24, para. 14.

53 *Rambles and Recollections*, vol. II, pp. 246–7; F. J. Shore said that 'The system of equal distribution of landed and other real property among sons and co-heirs, is the curse of any country in which it obtains.' *Notes on Indian Affairs*, vol. II, p. 363. See also the anonymous *An Enquiry into the Causes of the Stationary Conditions* (London, 1830), p. 89; John Wheatley, *A Letter to the Right Honourable Charles Watkin William Wynn, President of the Board of Control*, pp. 11–12; Henry H. S. Spry, *Modern India: with illustrations of the Resources and Capabilities of Hindosthan* (London, 1837), vol. II, pp. 11–6; and A. P. Webb, *Agricultural banks and Supplemental Legislation for Agricultural Relief*, p. 8. Webb proposed that there should be no sub-division of estates below 15 acres, and wanted the introduction of primogeniture and consolidation of already dismembered estates.

54 *Principles of Political Economy* (II Edn.), pp. 373, 376, 380.

55 *Treatise on the Succession to Property Vacant by Death* (London, 1848), p. 28. See also the *Edinburgh Review* (July 1824), which criticised Adam Smith's views on primogeniture, p. 360.

systematic policy towards that end was pursued. The various land tenure and taxation policies had this objective in view but owing to structural reasons, the consequences were very often not anticipated. The land revenue policies of the period between the 1830s to 1850s nearly all tended to clip the powers of the rural elite without necessarily creating an agrarian middle class capable of generating capitalist agriculture.

The prevalence of liberal ideas and the events of 1857 led to the formation of an opinion in favour of making a renewed attempt to create a middle class through the introduction of a permanent settlement of the Bengal pattern.[56] However, the support that the agricultural middle class received in the 1850s and 1860s was misplaced, especially since at that time the man—land ratio was going against man. For it was a fact that the growing middle class that came out of the zemindari areas was composed mainly of annuitants living on land, government servants and westernised bourgeois of the cities who were incapable of acting as vehicles to promote economic development either through agriculture or manufactures. In the first half of the nineteenth century, there was growing a small class of people in Bengal whose origins could be traced to zemindaries but who were involving themselves in trading and commercial activities. But the financial crash that overtook them in the 1840s seems to have wiped out all entrepreneurial spirit from the growing middle class in Bengal.[57]

To conclude, by and large when a 'middle class' was advocated, it was an agricultural middle class somewhat similar to the yeoman-farmer of England; in other words, people with capital would employ labour in agricultural pursuits to grow foodgrains or technical crops to sell in the market. While it was recognised that entrepreneurship could be fostered through the creation of objective conditions for its development, in practice due to strongly held divergent opinions as to the nature of the class capable of entrepreneurship no stable policy was pursued throughout the period. There were, of course, observers who realised that what the Indian economy needed most were industrial entrepreneurs.[58] Indeed such a type of industrial bourgeoisie

---

[56] *The Calcutta Review*, vol. XXXVIII, no. LXXV (1863), pp. 119–20, p. 145. The reversal of the Oudh land revenue policy in favour of the landed gentry was welcomed generally by the English press as a measure conducive to the growth of a middle class. The *North British Review* for example was happy that the Oudh talookdar was in the way toward becoming a 'respectable Country Gentleman', 'India Convalescent', vol. XXXIV, no. LXVII, February 1861, p. 17. See also *Westminster Review* New Series vol. XXVIII, July–October, 1865, pp. 189–91. See above Chapter 5.

[57] N. K. Sinha, 'Indian Business Enterprise: Its Failure in Calcutta (1800–1848)' *Bengal: Past and Present*, Jubilee Number, 1967, p. 121.

[58] See for example Professor H. Green of the Bombay Educational Service, *Three Lectures on Political Economy* (Delivered before the Students' Literary and Scientific Society of Bombay)(Bombay, 1853), pp. 19–20. See also *The Calcutta Review*, vol. XXXIX, no. LXXVII (1864), p. 114.

showed its appearance (even without active assistance from the state) especially in the development of cotton textiles in Bombay in the second half of the
nineteenth century. In spite of the economists' opinion in favour of the rising
industrial capitalism, in practice no support was given to it; actually the
various policies based on *laissez-faire* (e.g. tariff policy) as well as state
intervention (e.g. labour legislation) had an adverse impact on the rise of a
stable and strong urban–industrial middle class.

EDUCATION

Education, even according to Adam Smith, was necessary for accelerating
economic progress, as it tended to increase efficiency, reduce population, and
encourage entrepreneurial ability.[59] Although not always motivated by these
considerations, the policy makers in England as well as India realised the
importance of education for Indian economic progress. Education was seen as
the golden means of bringing about social changes that were essential for promoting economic development in India. The caste system for example was
found quite early in the century to be the 'most effectual method that could be
devised by the ingenuity of man to check their improvement and repress their
industry'.[60] Antiquated social institutions were the result of ignorance which in
its turn could be cured only by government supported education programmes.

As early as 1813, the Charter Renewal Act specified that at least Rs
100 000 be spent on 'the revival and improvement of literature and encouragement of the learned natives of India and for the introduction and
promotion of a knowledge of the sciences'. However it was during the
governor-generalship of William Bentinck that a semblance of an education
policy emerged as a result of the protracted controversy on various aspects
of Indian education. Most of the participants in this controversy believed
that there was a strong link between the educational attainment of the people
and their material well-being. The broad aim of the policy was the introduction of Western ideas into India through the English language so as to
stimulate its moral and material progress. From the time of Bentinck, it was
accepted that the state had to play an important part in education, and the
fundamental reason why Western ideas were chosen for dissemination among
Indians was that in the minds of the leading architects of that policy, Indian
literature and sciences were viewed as basically 'irrational' whereas Western
ideas were based on scientific principles.[61]

[59] *Wealth of Nations*, p. 769.
[60] Court of Directors to the Government of Bombay, 10 June 1810, *op. cit.* See also
William Birkmyre, *The Wealth of India and the Hindrances to its Increase*, p. 14, for making
the identical point eighty years later.
[61] See for example the views of Lord Macaulay: *Speeches by Lord Macaulay with his Minute
on Indian Education.* Edited by G. M. Young, p. 351.

Sir Henry Maine pointed out that as Indian thought lacked concern for 'precision in magnitude, number and time',[62] Indians needed proper education in Western science if material progress were to be achieved in India. This policy was quite in line with the Utilitarian-inspired movement in Britain in the 1820s for the diffusion of useful knowledge among the common people, although, as Professor Stokes has shown, James Mill himself did not believe that India would immediately benefit from Western education before it became prosperous through good and efficient government.[63]

The policy enunciated by Sir Charles Wood in his famous 1854 despatch differed from the earlier policy only regarding the agencies for imparting education, but not with its broad aims of providing Western education through the English language so that both India and Britain could benefit.[64] Later commentators, whether official or non-official, warmly upheld the idea that expenditure on education had an immediate and practical return in the shape of increased tempo and efficiency of all economic activity,[65] and hence exhorted the state to provide appropriate educational facilities.

Thus it was not only economists but also the Indian policy 'ideal' which accepted the necessity for certain types of public sector activity. The next problem was the extent of such intervention, and although budgetary constraints imposed their own impeccable controlling mechanism, administrators were still anxious to acquire a guideline from theoretic considerations. Sir Alexander Grant, who was for some time Director of Public Instruction of the Bombay Presidency, lamented the fact that whereas in Bombay only $1\frac{1}{25}$ per cent of the total revenues was spent on education, in Britain the figure was 3 per cent and even that 'mere supplements to the ancient educational foundations'. According to him, the important question that should be 'entertained as a part of a science of state-economy: What proportion of a State's revenues ought fairly to be expanded on the education of the people?'[66] At least a tentative answer was necessary, he concluded. Needless to say, no answer was forthcoming.

[62] Quoted in Sir John Strachey, *India Its Administration and Progress* (London, 1911), p. 297.

[63] *English Utilitarians and India*, pp. 57–8.

[64] See for an elaboration of Wood's views Syed Nurullah and J. P. Naik, *A History of Education in India during the British Period* (Bombay, 1943), p. 204.

[65] See for example: Major Davidson, *Proposed Scheme for the Future Education of the Agricultural Classes in Western India* (Edinburgh, 1873), *passim*; *The Political Economy of Indian Famines* (Bombay, 1877), by 'Mentor', p. 31; and Sir Richard Temple, *Oriental Experiences: A Selection of Essays and Addresses Delivered on Various Occasions* (London, 1883), Chapter IX. See *The Calcutta Review* (vol. XXXIX no. LXXVII, 1864, p. 114), in which the author claimed that Western education will encourage 'thrift and abstinence – and we use the word as Senior uses it'.

[66] *Some observations on Educational Administration in India* (Edinburgh, 1868), p. 6.

PUBLIC WORKS

As we have seen, Classical economists visualised economic development as being a process initiated and put in motion by the dynamism of the individual entrepreneurs. But it was equally part of the Classical theory of economic policy that public works were a necessary framework 'within which private economic activity could be successfully carried on'.[67] A considerable programme of public works would enable the private entrepreneurs to function in a manner calculated to maximise total output.

Public works meant, in the context of Indian administrative practice, (1) state works including official buildings, military barracks and similar unprofitable items; (2) railways, canals, roads, lighthouses, posts, telegraphs and similar projects that provided transport and communications; and (3) irrigation projects.[68] Items (2) and (3) comprised projects that were necessary for 'the advancement of the material prosperity of the people'. It was stated clearly in various official reports that public works were essential, and should be constructed by the state with the sole criterion of whether a particular project was capable of generating a profit or not. As a government report pointed out

The obligation on the Government in respect of the construction of these Works is hence essentially based on the idea of their being *profitable* in a pecuniary point of view; not of necessity to the Government as capitalists, but to the entire body politic of the State. If it cannot reasonably be predicted that such a work will be *profitable* in this sense, it should not be undertaken.[69]

It was thus clear in the minds of Indian policy makers as well as their advisers (especially in the second half of the nineteenth century) that these works stimulated economic development. The editor of the London *Economist*, James Wilson, who later became the finance member of the Viceroy's Council in India, wrote a Memorandum for Sir Charles Wood in which he said: 'as the great works of irrigation are completed and the railways and means of

[67] R. D. C. Black, *Economic Thought and the Irish Question* (Cambridge, 1959) p. 162.
[68] There was also a classification made on the basis of productive and preventive public works. Productive works were defined as those which yielded an annual income which covered at least the interest on capital outlay including 'interest for a period subsequent to the commencement of each work during which no income is obtained'. Preventive works were those which did not reproduce even the interest on the capital expenditure. This distinction between productive and preventive works arose out of the technically different functions of the public works. One was to protect the people from the rigours of famine, whereas the other was intended to promote the general prosperity of the country. See Lord Salisbury's despatch to Viceroy, 23 July 1874, no. 9 (Finance). *Letters to India on Finances*, India Office Records, no. L/F/3/3/699, p. 562.
[69] *Report of a Committee on the Classification of Public Works Expenditure and the Various Returns Exhibiting the Operations Which are Required by the Government of India*, p. 3.

internal communication are concluded, the impulse that will be given to the internal trade and foreign commerce of India, will be of a very remarkable character'.[70] Lord Elphinstone was reflecting current opinion when he said that the country would 'have improved much more under a more liberal expenditure on works of irrigation or roads'.[71] A number of officials of the government stressed the necessity and desirability of enhanced expenditure on public works, especially in view of the government owning the land.[72] Even those civilians like Thomas Briggs who disputed the claim of the government being the landlord advocated the construction of public works.[73]

The advocates of public works visualised the benefits accruing as a result of their construction in terms both of stimulating demand (in Smith's terms 'widening the market') as well as increasing supply through physical inputs to augment productivity. It was the opinion of most economists in the Indian administration that the extent of the market was limited in India because the rural population had a limited range of demands, due presumably to ignorance and poverty; the village self-sufficiency system as it stood, it was argued, was responsible for this attitude, as it supplied to the villager all his few wants.[74] Since Indians did not see the possibility of enjoyment through the possession of greater income, a situation developed in India of a highly inelastic schedule of the supply of effort in terms of income.[75] Not until the Indian was educated to appreciate the consumption of more and more goods and services would he produce more. Colonisers could help this process of education by demonstrating the pleasures of an increased standard of living. This could also be done by increased international trade. As one M.P. put it, increased demand from Britain for the Indian agricultural produce would

[70] Memorandum dated 11 June 1853 (Halifax Papers, India Office Library).

[71] Select Committee of the House of Lord, *Parl. Papers*, H.C. 533, vol. X of Session 1852, Q.2135.

[72] See Strachey's Minute dated 19 May 1859, *Home Judicial Proceedings*, 16 September 1862, cited by Thomas Metcalfe in *Journal of Modern History*, December 1962, p. 396. Identical views had been expressed in 1836 by Sir Arthur Cotton. See his Minute 6 May 1836, India Office Records, L/PWD/3/206, pp. 159–60. Sir William Muir said much the same thing in 1877. See his Minute 12 June 1877, India Office Records, *Financial Department Collections*, C/140, pp. 110. See also the *Calcutta Review*, vol. XLII, no. LXXXIII, 1866, pp. 100 et seq. and the *Westminster Review*, vol. LXXII, no. CXLI, July–October 1859, pp. 160–1.

[73] *The Development of Dormant Wealth of the British Colonies and Foreign Possessions*, p. 13.

[74] See the evidence given by Warren Hastings and Thomas Munro. *Parl. Papers* H.C. 122, vol. VII of Session 1812–13. See also Court of Directors to Madras (Revenue) 24 April 1811, India Office Records, E/4/907, p. 393.

[75] See for instance an example given by J. A. Rivett-Carnac, in his *Many Memories of Life in India, at Home and Abroad* (Edinburgh, 1803), p. 130. For other instances see William Tennant, *Indian Recreations: consisting chiefly of Strictures on the Domestic and Rural Economy of the Mahommedans and Hindoos* (Edinburgh, 1805), vol. II, p. 148; and G. Banbury's Report on the economic condition of Chinglepat district, 13 April 1874, *Madras Revenue Department Proceedings*, 24 February 1875 (Tamilnadu Archives).

confer a value to the estates, and then 'cultivation could be carried on as an object of gain, rather than to procure a wretched subsistence'.[76]

Whether it was for facilitating the colonisers or for stimulating international trade, better communications were necessary. While the water carriage between the chief cities of India and Britain had widened the market for both the countries, as foretold by Adam Smith, it had not had much appreciable effect on internal demand. For stimulating internal demand, improved internal communications were necessary.[77] India now had 'freedom of commercial intercourse', and she needed only a better system of communication to make her prosperous.

Quite early in its administration, the East India Company saw the necessity of opening up inland markets and adopted this as a basic policy.[78] But little constructional activity like the laying of roads or the digging of canals was carried on during the regime of the Company, and as Bentinck wrote to Ellenborough, 'I really believe that there is not one middle-sized county in England, in which there is not more laid out on general improvement per year, than all the three Presidencies put together.'[79] The few such works undertaken were very effective, and on the basis of these results the authorities were urged time and again to construct roads and similar public works.[80] The administrators perceived a positive connection between roads and economic development. Henry St George Tucker, for instance, said 'It is true that in a rude state of society, roads must in general follow the track of cultivation, but in its more advanced stages, roads produce cultivation, and in every stage they promote agriculture and commerce in a greater or less degree.'[81] According to the Indian administrative thinking, accumulation was possible only when the class of capitalists (or entrepreneurs) functions. The opening up of new communications increased the value of property, giving incentive to the further accumulation of wealth. This argument was re-

---

[76] Robert Rickards in the House of Commons, *Hansard*, 1 series, vol. XXV, p. 517, 2 June 1813. John Chapman who promoted the Great Indian Peninsular Railway said 'A constant market, and that alone, I apprehend, would make them willing learners of any improvements.' *Cotton and Commerce of India*, p. 10.

[77] See J. S. Mill, *Principles of Political Economy*, p. 130.

[78] Approving the scheme of opening a canal by the agent at Hedgelle, the Court of Directors said, 'upon a general principle we are much disposed to give our approbation to works of this kind'. See Court of Directors to Governor General in Council (Revenue), 29 January 1813, *Revenue Letters to Bengal*, vol. II, para. 37, p. 269, India Office Records, L/E/3/442.

[79] Letter dated 5 November 1829. *Bentinck Papers* (Nottingham University Archives).

[80] Report on the Revenue administration Bareilly district, dated 14 July 1843, *Selections from Public Correspondence of Government of North West Provinces*, vol. I, p. 19. See also a Report by the Collector of Canara, 26 February 1836, India Office Records, *Home Misc.* no. 791, p. 527.

[81] Minute, 1 August 1832 (*Bentinck Papers*, Nottingham University Library).

peatedly used in connection with all forms of transport in general and rail-ways in particular. In a despatch drafted by John Stuart Mill the Court of Directors put the point with reference to a railway extension scheme in these words: 'The great probability of a rise in the value of land at Howrah when a greater portion of the railway is opened, is a reason for effecting this improvement at an early period.'[82] More than roads, railways attracted great attention as the possible remedy for Indian poverty. Advocating railways for India, the London *Times* in 1847 said that railways would end famines, check sickness, provide 'new impulses and opportunities for civilization', and the 'commercial results of the enterprise would be equally extensive'.[83] W. P. Andrew, quoting with approval Sir Henry Parnell on roads, said that the extensive agricultural and mineral resources were not being exploited only because of the distances involved. Hence in order to apply 'capital and enter-prise, directed by science', railway systems were necessary.[84] Hyde Clarke, a contemporary railway economist, painted a rosy picture of the consequences of railways in India and held that they would stimulate economic develop-ment more than any other factor.[85]

In India too, on economic grounds railways had powerful champions in the top administrative hierarchy.[86] Viscount Hardinge, who was the governor-general of India when the possibility of introducing railways in India was seriously discussed, wrote to Sir Roberl Peel: 'If we can proceed with our railway through the heart of the country, we shall make rapid strides in wealth and stability, for steam here would be the greatest instrument of civilization for the people.'[87]

[82] Court of Directors to Governor General in Council (Public Works Department), no. 22, 1 July 1857, *India and Bengal Despatches*, India Office Records, E/4/845, p. 87.

[83] Issue dated 27 August 1847.

[84] *Indian Railways* (London, 1848), pp. 28–9.

[85] *Practical and Theoretical Considerations on the Management of Railways in India* (London, 1846), p. 5. A number of other publications said the same. See for instance *Railways in India: Their Present State and Future Prospects* (London, 1855), p. 24. Even Karl Marx for once approved a policy of the British rulers of India. See his paper in *New York Daily Tribune* entitled 'The Future Results of the British Rule in India' in issue dated 8 August 1853. See Marx & Engels, *The First Indian War of Independence 1857–59*, p. 36. Similar ideas were expressed by an Indian student of the writings of Fawcett, J. S. Mill and Thorold Rogers. See Framjee R. Vicajee, *Political and Social Effects of Railways in India* (London, 1875), pp. 25–7.

[86] Most of the arguments for railways concentrated on the external economies to be generated. There is at least one instance when a detailed study of the costs and benefits of introducing railways was undertaken. In 1836, a study was made to calculate the alterna-tive costs of providing materials to a dam site. Comparison was made between bullock carts in ordinary roads and railways. See *Madras Journal of Literature and Science*, October 1836. Similarly in the same year, Sir Arthur Cotton made detailed comparisons between the costs per ton-mile by road, by canal transport, and by railways. Report dated 6 May 1836, India Office Records, L/PWD/3/206, pp. 157–8.

[87] Letter dated 9 January 1848, Add. Mss 40,475, p. 284. (Peel Papers at British

If public works related to transport increased the demand for Indian products, then irrigation projects enabled the Indian economy to increase its productivity. Irrigation, it was rightly claimed by many, provided an insurance against monsoon failures. India's population was concentrated along the river valleys and so it was thought that if irrigation canals were properly cut through sparsely populated areas, people would be attracted, thus dispersing population from the congested areas.[88] India being a large country, it was inconceivable that rains would fail at the same time over the entire area.

Between demand oriented policy towards the construction of transport – mainly railways – and supply oriented policy towards the construction of irrigation projects, a choice had to be made in view of the inadequate resources at the command of the Indian government. Although Lord Lytton pontificated in 1877 that 'they are no less out of place than arguments as to the relative value of food and air', in practice for several reasons policy swung towards railways. In the first place, there were some administrators like Major A. F. Corbett who were critical of the view that irrigation was the sole remedy for low agricultural productivity; and others like the collectors of Coimbatore and South Arcot who pointed out that for the types of crops that were required for exports (e.g. cotton, sugar cane) irrigation was not necessary.[89] Secondly, for at least three decades in the nineteenth century, a controversy raged between two contending schools. One maintained that the limited resources available should be concentrated on the construction of irrigation projects. India possessed considerable water resources as well as labour. The problem was the periodic failure of rains which caused famines. Under these circumstances, if the available water was stored properly, the problem of the lack of water could be solved, and even deserts could perhaps be brought under cultivation. In addition to the provision of water for cultivation, canals could be used for water transport. By the application of steam engines, fast transport too was possible. The foremost champion of this school was Sir Arthur Cotton who in his time had built the famous Cauveri, Godavari and Krishna irrigation projects. He calculated that the result of these projects had increased enormously public revenues through water rates and/or increased rent of the irrigated land. The projects had given high rates of return on the investment made amounting to $23\frac{1}{2}$ per cent (Cauveri), 45 per cent (Godavri), 16 per cent (Krishna) and 30 per cent (Western Jumna Canal). Besides these

Footnote 87 continued
  Museum). See also Court of Directors to Governor General in Council (Legislative) 7 May 1845, no. 11 of 1845, *India and Bengal Despatches*, India Office Records, E/4/783, pp. 797 et seq.
[88] A. P. Webb, *Agricultural Banks and Supplemental Legislation*, p. 9.
[89] Madras Board of Revenue *Proceedings* R./313/V./78, India Office Records.

direct returns, Cotton and his followers believed that considerable indirect returns also flowed by their effects on the promotion of economic development. According to this school of thought, similar results could be expected all over India. Hence Cotton proposed that the government should suspend the construction of railways and devote Rs10 000 000 per annum for ten to twenty years and build 10 000 miles of canals. He estimated that the cost of the 10 000 miles of major canals would cost about Rs30 000 000 in all, and the rest he proposed to spend on feeder roads and canals.[90]

On the other hand, there was a strong body of opinion that was critical of the claims made by the protagonists of irrigation-cum-canal projects. Some critics, like Patrick Smollett, dismissed the figures given by Cotton as having been cooked up.[91] Even the mildest criticism of Cotton said that he was 'too apt to exaggerate the success achieved'.[92] The uniform opinion was that what was applicable to the Madras Presidency was not applicable to all India. Irrigation was separate from canal transport and any attempt to combine the two would end in an utter waste of valuable water resources. Not all rivers were as perennial as the rivers that had been dammed up for irrigation purposes. Besides, much water would evaporate when used extensively for canal transport. Neither would the costs of constructing the irrigation projects be as low as Cotton expected nor would its return be as high.[93] The main desideratum in India was cheap transport because increased production was not important. Even during the famines, India exported considerable quantities of foodgrains. Hence it was considered that cheap railways were the correct solution.

Thirdly, whether it was the construction of irrigation projects or a railway network, the sustained agitation of the British industrial interests in favour of them was vitally important. From the 1840s onwards, the Lancashire cotton merchants maintained pressure for increased expenditure on communications and railways rather than for irrigation projects. Long before the

---

[90] Sir Arthur Cotton wrote a series of pamphlets on the subject. See his evidence to the House of Commons Committee on Public works in India. *Parl. Papers*, H.C. 312, vol. IX of Session 1878–9, Q 2722, 2751. See also his criticism of railways as a barrier to famines in *The Famine in India* (London, 1866), pp. 12–13. Among Cotton's supporters were Lt. Col. C. W. Grant of Bombay Engineers (*Indian Irrigation Being a Short Description of the System of Artificial Irrigation and Canal Navigation in India*, London, 1854, p. 25) and Lt. Col. F. H. Rundall of the Madras Engineers (*Notes on the Report of the Ganges Canal Committee Convened by Government of India*).

[91] Smollett, *Cotton Supplies from India*, p. 9.

[92] Thornton, *Indian Public Works* (London, 1875), p. 102.

[93] While it was true that some projects gave very high return to capital invested, the overall return was 7.3% (1875–6), 5.13% (1876–7) and 5.15% (1877–8) for all the constructed irrigation projects in India. See R. B. Buckley, *The Irrigation Works of India and their Financial Results* (London, 1880), p. 189.

actual stoppage of raw cotton imports from the Southern States of America, many manufacturers realised the danger of depending exclusively upon American sources of raw cotton.

In the beginning railways were suggested mainly for enabling Lancashire to procure raw cotton easily from India, but in the 1870s and 1880s, railways were also advocated to stimulate Indian demand for British products.[94] Hence the generally held opinion that the subject of railways 'was of the first importance to Lancashire'.[95]

Authorities at the highest level of the Indian administration were conscious of the influence wielded by the Lancashire manufacturers. Even an important personage like Lord Halifax preferred not to go too much against the wishes of the Lancashire manufacturers. It is also true that the interests of English industry were the same as those of the English economy. Halifax wrote to Dalhousie that the Manchester people cared for only the growth and transport of cotton from India, and 'if I can satisfy them that these points will not be neglected, I hope to keep them all in good humour. They are however a powerful body in the House of Commons, and besides this I think they are right in their object.'[96] Even when a decision had to be made for simple matters such as the choice of railway lines, the outcome always favoured the Lancashire interests, as for example: 'I am sorry to postpone the Jubbalpore line; but it is more important to complete the line up the Ganges, and from Bombay to Nagpore and the Nerbudda. In the present anxiety about cotton, I would not delay anything which opens a cotton field.'[97] British mercantile interests were not alone in successfully applying pressure; for British planters in India, too, managed to have certain projects carried out to suit their particular interests.[98]

[94] Evidence of G. Lord before Royal Commission on Depression of Trade and Industry, *Parl. Papers*, Cmd. 4797, vol. XXIII of Session 1886, Q. 5293, 5298. British iron and steel industry also looked to the expansion of Indian railways for an increase in the demand for its products. See W. Birkmyre, *The Revival of Trade by Development of India* (Glasgow, 1886), p. 10.

[95] Bright in the House of Commons, *Hansard*, 3rd Series, vol. XCV, p. 927.

[96] Wood to Dalhousie, 24 March 1853 (Halifax Papers at India Office Library). Cranborne (later Lord Salisbury) referred to the pressure from the Manchester Chamber of Commerce and wrote to Lawrence that if what they wanted was not done they may 'get a resolution of the House of Commons which will force upon the Indian government much more active steps in the matter'. Cranborne to Lawrence, 16 October 1866 (Lawrence Papers at India Office Library).

[97] Wood to Laing, 26 March 1861, *ibid.* Again while discussing the scheme for navigating Godavari river, he wrote 'The indirect effect which they cannot fail to have in contributing most materially to the supply of the English cotton market would render it incumbent on government to undertake them at the earliest possible period.' India Office Records, L/PWD/3/523. Collection no. 41.

[98] Wood to Madras Government, 23 August 1864, India Office Records, L/PWD/3/504, pp. 172–3. Argyll to Madras Government, 27 September 1869, *ibid.*, p. 288.

In spite of considerable support for the construction of public works, in the first half of the nineteenth century, owing to a tenacious belief in balanced budgets,[99] the amount spent on such works was seldom more than two per cent of total expenditure.[100] Even as late as 1875, an official of the India Office remarked, 'Public works have always formed rather a weak side of Anglo-Indian administration.'[101]

This low-level activity in the area of public works construction was certainly not due to any theoretical beliefs. Dogmatic objection to state participation in the erection and maintenance of public works was neither accepted at the India Office nor at the various local governments. It must be remembered here that Classical political economy as expounded by John Stuart Mill was not against state intervention. Mill's statement, 'In the particular circumstances of a given age or nation, there is scarcely anything really important to the general interest' which cannot be done by government, was quoted with approval by John and Richard Strachey in defending state participation in the construction of public works. Similar was the opinion of W. T. Thornton who was an official of the India Office as well as a close associate of John Stuart Mill.[102] Such economists approved Mill's principle of the superiority of nationalisation over private management of natural monopolies such as roads, railways and canals.[103]

Indeed the point at issue was not the desirability or otherwise of public works, but how best the available finances and expertise ought to be used to achieve the maximum results.

FINANCE FOR PUBLIC WORKS

With the increasing requirements of public works in the decades following the Crown takeover of Indian administration, budgetary surpluses proved inadequate. Current administrative thinking was against committing public finances to heavy future interest payments without any adequate return,

---

[99] The Court of Directors wrote to India: 'It is absolutely indispensable to the character of our administration and the permanent welfare of the important interests committed to us that our Disbursements should in time of peace be brought to an amount below that of our Revenue.' Letter 8 December 1827 (Territorial Finance Department). Similar views were again explicitly expressed in their letter of 9 October 1850 to the Governor General of India and their letter to the Government of Madras on 6 December 1850. See John Maskell (ed.), *The Circular Orders of the Board of Revenue* (Madras, 1851), p. 3.

[100] See Ambedkar, *Provincial Finance* (London, 1925), p. 19; and Seccombe's evidence before the Select Committee of the House of Commons, *Parl. Papers*, H.C. 312, vol. IX of Session 1879, Q. 758. Even the amount that was actually spent was mostly for unproductive civil and military buildings. See J. & R. Strachey, *Finances and Public Works of India*, (London, 1882) p. 87.

[101] W. T. Thornton, *Indian Public Works* (London, 1875), p. 1.

[102] *Loc. cit*, p. 9.

[103] See J. & R. Strachey, *Finances and Public Works of India*, pp. 407–8.

sufficient at least to recoup interest payments. It was quite against the spirit of Classical public finance that resort should be made to borrowing for public undertakings; as Sir Charles Trevelyan wrote to Lord Elgin in 1863: 'The Financial principle that the expenditure of the year should be provided for by ways and means raised within the year is the basis of our English system and it is not less necessary for the consolidation of the one we are constructing in India.'[104] But with an increasing acceptance of the desirability of public works and the state's accepting responsibility for their construction, public debt was the only available means of finance. Hence the principle of financing public works only through current budgetary surpluses came under attack. Here the controversy was between those who thought of public works as business enterprises and expressed caution against borrowing money without making sure of an adequate return, thus placing burdens on the future generations; and others who thought of public works in terms of infrastructure and urged loan financing because expenditure on public works was social overhead capital formation that generated immeasurable but ample external economies.[105] To build public works entirely out of budgetary surpluses, as John Dickinson said, would throw 'the whole cost on the present generation who can only receive a comparatively small proportion of their profits.'[106]

In 1864 a policy was adopted by which the state was permitted to construct irrigation works out of borrowed capital. Some members of the administration like Sir Charles Trevelyan were afraid that too much expenditure too suddenly on public works would have unfavourable effects on the economy.[107] Keeping in view these ideas, the secretary of state, Sir Charles Wood, insisted that irrigation expenditure should proceed gradually and that the projects should be remunerative 'to the extent at least of defraying the interest of the capital expended in constructing them'.[108]

The famines of 1866 made it necessary to have projects that would normally be classed as unproductive but would nevertheless be required on

---

[104] Trevelyan to Elgin, 14 February 1863 (Elgin Papers, India Office Library).

[105] See John Strachey, 'Observations on Some Questions of Indian Finance'. Finance Department Collection, India Office Records, C/137, p. 31, Richard Strachey's evidence, *Parl. Papers*, H.C. 327, vol. VIII of Session 1872, Q.6990, 6992, and 6999. See also 'The Government of India: Its Liabilities and Resources' *The Westminister Review*, vol. LXXII, no. CXLI, July–October, 1859, pp. 160–1.

[106] *A Letter from John Dickinson* (Tract 576 of India Office Library). Manchester merchants also were of this opinion, see Silver, *op. cit.*, pp. 94–5.

[107] Cited by Governor-General to Secretary of State, no. 53 (Financial) 9 April 1864, *Parl. Papers*, H.C. 105, vol. 50 of session 1867, p. 51. Mansfield was one member of the Council who thought that this was a 'grave economical error' and said that the progress of all public works would adapt itself to the available resources. 'The process is self-adjusting, and does not anywhere lead to convulsions.' Minute dated 5 February 1866, *ibid.*, p. 63.

[108] Secretary of State to Governor-General, no. 266, 30 November 1865, *ibid.*, p. 50.

the larger grounds of famine prevention. Lawrence, Mayo and Northbrook were all anxious to increase government expenditure on irrigation and railway projects.[109] Such enthusiasm was not to the liking of Lord Salisbury[110] who had succeeded Lord Argyll as secretary of state in 1874, and other India Office bureaucrats like Sir Thomas Seccombe, Sir Erskine Perry and Sir Louis Mallet. They all thought that the expansion of the public works department was essentially the child of the engineers in the Indian administration. It was the opinion of these economist–administrators that borrowing should be resorted to only for emergencies and not for ordinary developmental purposes. Perry got his opinions confirmed by the financier Baron Rothschild, the economist Newmarch and a capitalist Kayser.[111] It was also their contention that money borrowed in the United Kingdom added to the remittance problem created by the currency crisis. Above everything else, these economists – especially Mallet – were not believers in the merits of state interference and held the very opposite views to John Stuart Mill.[112] Mallet put this point trenchantly against Mill's idea that natural monopolies like railways, canals and irrigation projects should be nationalised. According to Mallet, railways are only partial natural monopolies and by nationalising them, the state makes them into full monopolies.[113] In view of the above attitude of the India Office, it is not surprising that Salisbury told the Government of India to exercise the greatest care in undertaking to construct any project out of borrowed funds. Unless a project earned (or promised to earn) more than the costs involved in borrowing the capital it should not be undertaken. Salisbury wanted a rigid enforcement of this rule.[114]

[109] See Seccombe's evidence to the House of Commons Select Committee on Public Works, *Parl. Papers*, H.C. 312, vol. IX of Session 1878–9, Q. 400.

[110] Earlier when he was the Secretary of State for India (1866–7), he had encouraged Lord Lawrence to go ahead with the latter's active policy of constructing public works. See his letters to Lawrence, especially 16 October 1866 (Salisbury Papers at Christ Church College, Oxford).

[111] Perry to Northbrook, 26 May 1879 and 6 August 1879 (*Northbrook Papers*, India Office Library).

[112] An Indian pamphleteer (favouring Mill's arguments) pointed out that railways were practical and natural monopolies, and hence should be in the State sector. *Indian Railways: An Argument for a Government Monopoly in Preference to Private Enterprise* (Calcutta, 1884), p. 4.

[113] Note on 'Public Works Policy: 1882' Add Mss 43,587, p. 5. para. 34 (*Ripon Papers*, British Museum). Salisbury had great respect for Mallet's view, and had once told Northbrook that Mallet's services were irreplaceable in the India Office.

[114] Secretary of State to the Viceroy, 23 July 1874, no. 9, Letters to India on Finance, India Office Records, L/F/3/3/699. This policy was largely upheld by the House of Commons Select Committee, *Parl. Papers*, H.C. 312, Vol. IX of Session 1878–9. Seccombe in his evidence said how it was the tendency of the Indian Government to increase public works expenditure and it was the tendency of the India Office to curb such expenditure. Q. 470–472.

Such an emphasis on the direct returns of public works projects evoked much criticism because many of the projects that were required for famine protection could not be undertaken, partly because of the paucity of budgetary surpluses and partly because of this ban on loan-financing. Hence the Government of India time and again referred to the enormous indirect benefits (necessary but not measurable) generated by projects even when they were not profitable.[115]

But this criticism did not have much impact and the practical effect was a reduction in the amounts expended on public works. It was not until the recommendations of the Famine Commission became known that the need to construct preventive public works was once again emphasised. But we have to wait until 1901–3 when the Irrigation Commission (Chairman Sir Colin Scott Moncrieff) introduced a system by which government conceded forward planning of irrigation requirements.

PRIVATE ENTERPRISE AND PUBLIC WORKS

Given that public works were needed and in the absence of adequate financial resources, it was suggested that the state should persuade private capitalists to undertake the construction of those public works in which at least some of the costs and benefits could be internalised.

Major irrigation projects had always been in the public sector in the first half of the century. But owing to the development of the joint-stock companies as a distinct form of business organisation, the Court of Directors as early as 1857 formulated a set of principles to be followed with regard to the construction of irrigation projects by private joint-stock companies. The principles were similar to the conditions attached to the guarantee given to the railway companies.[116] The view of the Court of Directors was shared by many, including those who were in opposite camps of the 'advantages of irrigation' controversy. Sir Arthur Cotton, who was a champion of irrigation, wrote that the government should invite 'the boundless resources of private enterprise and capital to aid the State by undertaking works of irrigation'.[117]

---

[115] Government of India to Secretary of State, 7 April 1876, no. 135. 'Financial Department Proceedings, 1876, India Office Records, vol. 962. This was urged in private letters also. For example Sir Richard Temple told Salisbury that much as he disliked public debt in theory, 'still for the purpose of canals and railways I would incur debt – A country with a larger debt and with railways and canals is richer far and safer and stronger than a country with a smaller debt and *without* those works.' Letter 29 January 1875 (Temple Papers, India Office Library). See also, Buckley, *op. cit.*, p. 172.

[116] See Canning's Minute on 'Private Companies for Canals and Irrigation' Dated 29 November 1858. *Home Department Revenue Branch, Proceedings* dated 11 February 1859, no. 1/4 (National Archives of India).

[117] *Results of Irrigation Works in Godavari District* (London, 1866), p. 10.

On the other hand, Patrick Smollett who saw nothing good in the big irrigation projects felt that works of improvement should be left to the landlords
themselves, and emphatically declared that 'these public works should not be
left to be designed by the paid servants of the State with the resources of the
Government treasury at their command'.[118] Alexander Binnie, who had lived
in India for twenty years, pointed out the wasteful employment of engineers
and the inefficient utilisation of its resources by the public works department
in India. He regretted that insufficient importance was given to the 'advantages of public competition, joint-stock co-operation, or private enterprise'.[119]
There was some support for this view among the members of the Indian
administration. Lord Canning gave three reasons for letting the private
companies undertake the irrigation projects, but none of the reasons was on
account of any dogmatic belief in *laissez-faire*.[120] The first advantage was
the introduction of English capital, and he said it was not merely English
capital as such, but 'free and mature English enterprise which we desire to
see introduced and developed in India'. The second reason was for conserving
the limited managerial services at the command of the government. And
finally he thought that public expenditure on public works normally fluc-
tuates owing to political factors, whereas private companies would not be
subject to the political exigencies. There were also others like E. T. Trevor,
secretary of the Bengal Board of Revenue, and many local officers who
believed that as a general rule public works construction should be left to
private enterprise.[121] The advocates of private sector irrigation projects
anticipated a massive influx of British capital into India. Sir Arthur Cotton,
for example, was certain that India would get a large share of the £100
million unemployed capital at 4 per cent interest.[122]

However, within the government, the predominant view was in favour of
government participation, construction and maintenance rather than one of
mere control. This view was held even by those who, like the collector
of Masulipatam felt: 'it is no libel on human nature to say that the man who
invests capital certain of 5 per cent interest hoping for more will not be as
prudent in his calculations and cautious in his investment as the man who
risks his all. The law by which the welfare of the community is secured by the

[118] *Op. cit.*, p. 15. Smollett said 'the public works department is ... the most overgrown,
expensive, unmanageable, and corrupt in the empire'. p. 16.

[119] *Public Works in India: A Letter Addressed to the Rt. Hon. W. E. Gladstone* (London, 1881),
p. 5.

[120] *Op. cit.*

[121] Home Department, Revenue Branch, Proceedings dated 4 November 1859, 1/4 National
Archives of India. Similar views were expressed by some collectors of the Madras
Presidency in 1858. See *Madras Board of Revenue Proceedings*, India Office Records,
Range 313, Vol. 79, pp. 1189–91; and vol. 81, p. 2221.

[122] Cotton to Mayo, 23 October 1868 (Mayo Papers at the Cambridge University Library).

self interest of individuals is in political economy what gravitation is in astronomy and any measure that weakens it is impolitic.'[123] A large number of local officers of the Madras Presidency favoured government control of irrigation projects because according to them the private sector lacked sufficient experience.[124] The Government of Bombay pointed out that, considering the success achieved by the government in irrigation undertakings of the past, it was possible that the 'government might largely increase their own revenue, while they would add to the general wealth and prosperity of the Country, by a judicious outlay in such works'.[125] It was pointed out by many officers that British private capital flowed into the irrigation companies only because of the guaranteed interest and so the government itself should enter the capital market. Further, the companies almost always utilised the officers of the various engineering services of Indian government. Captain W. S. Sherwill (Superintendent of Embankments) pointed out that when private enterprise took on the construction of irrigation projects the government had to act as projector, guarantor, supporter, superintendent and arbitrator. At the same time, however, the company as the capitalist draws the profit.[126]

Another criticism centred on the fact that private enterprise need not necessarily imply efficiency nor public construction mean waste. It was felt that, while the doctrine of non-interference was good for England, it might not be so for India.[127] Even Lord Canning, in spite of detailing the advantages of private companies, was in favour of government participation. He felt that any system of irrigation would most intimately affect the interests of the Indian peasants. Hence

interference of Government in the management of these works must be close and constant, call it if you will, so vexatious and intolerable ... I deduce therefore that in such cases the management must not merely be controlled by Government, but must be taken entirely into its hands ... There are many solid objections to the Government coming practically and directly into the position of a carrying company; therefore Railways even if executed by Government must, as soon as they are complete, be handed over to private parties to be worked. But with irrigation works, the case is exactly the reverse. Such works even if executed by private Associations must, as soon as they are complete, be transferred to the direct administration of Government.[128]

---

[123] *Letter to the Board of Revenue*, 20 January 1858, India Office Records, Range 313, vol. 79, pp. 1180–1.

[124] See *Madras Board of Revenue Proceedings*, India Office Records, Range 313, Vol. 78, pp. 137–8; Vol. 79, p. 1238.

[125] B. H. Ellis (Acting Secretary of the Government of Bombay) to Cecil Beadon (Secretary of Government of India) 18 December 1858, *Home Department Revenue Branch, Proceedings* dated 11 February 1859 (National Archives of India).

[126] *Proceedings*, 4 November 1859, India Office Records, no. 11/12, *op. cit.*

[127] See Ellis to Beadon, *op. cit.*

[128] Canning's Minute dated 29 November 1858, *op. cit.*

After Canning's viceroyalty, executive opinion had been almost unanimously in favour of government construction and maintenance of irrigation canals.

When the problem of public works was extensively debated in the mid-1860s, feeling was heavily in favour of government construction. Criticism by the lone dissenter, Sir Charles Trevelyan, did not carry conviction, partly because he did not want to replace private with public responsibility entirely and partly because as governor of Madras a few years previously he had not been favourable to the idea of giving the management of the canal system to private companies. He felt that as the canal system would be very profitable, there was 'no speculation, but a simple investment of undoubted productiveness, which belongs to the public, and ought not to be alienated in favour of private individuals'.[129] Critics of joint-stock companies were of the view that none of the benefits usually associated with joint-stock companies would accrue when irrigation projects were involved. If in addition, a guaranteed interest were given to the irrigation companies, the shareholder would lose all interest in checking the management. In any case, as Lord Cranborne wrote to Lawrence, 'nothing is so bad as "private enterprise" which starts with a concession and then gets capital by driblets afterwards on the strength of it'.[130] The consensus was that irrigation projects should be constructed and maintained by the state, a view not surprisingly shared – considering the circumstances – by Thomas Bazley of the Manchester Chamber of Commerce who said: 'I am strongly in favour of all the public works of India being established as government property.'[131] This was the policy of the Government of India in 1865, and it continued until the end of the British rule in India.[132]

While there was a consensus of opinion on the irrigation works that they should only be constructed by the government, the policy towards railways alternated between direct state participation and indirect encouragement through guaranteed interest on the invested capital. Among the earliest advocates of a coordinated railway policy was Sir Arthur Cotton who reported

[129] G.O. no. 2848, 7 December 1859, Public Works Department Proceedings (Tamilnadu Archives). See also Lawrence to Napier, 21 September 1866. (Lawrence Papers at India Office Library).

[130] Cranborne to Lawrence, 16 October 1866 (Salisbury Papers at Christ Church College, Oxford). Lord Lawrence was very much against private sector irrigation projects. See for his views: *Parl. Papers*, H.C. 179, vol. XII of Session 1873, Q. 4759, 4760 and 4763. He had the support of the governors of the three Presidencies, see for example, Denison to Lawrence, 8 December 1864. See also Wood to Lawrence, 2 December 1865 (Lawrence Papers at India Office Library): See also Maine's Minute 'Irrigation Works and State Railways' 8 November 1866, *Minutes of Sir H. S. Maine*, pp. 108–9.

[131] Bazley to Mayo, 9 August 1869 (Mayo Papers at Cambridge University Library).

[132] See Governor General to Secretary of State, 7 April 1864 (no. 23) and Secretary of State to Governor General, 8 August 1864 (no. 39), *Parl. Papers*, H.C. no. 105, vol. 50 of Session 1867.

in 1836 to the Madras Board of Revenue that authorities in India should prevent a haphazard development of railways. His visit to Britain in 1830 enabled him to observe how because railways were originally allowed to be built by private enterprise, it was found later difficult for the state to organise a proper framework of transport 'without an extensive interference with established private rights'. He pointed out that as India was starting from scratch, the state itself should plan, build and manage a railway system from the beginning.[133] F. W. Simms, however, who was sent to India in 1845 by the East India Company to investigate the possibilities of introducing railways, came back with optimistic hopes and suggested that the construction of railways should be left in the hands of private investors subject to carefully made regulations and conditions.[134] Lord Hardinge, who was governor-general at that time, was a firm believer in the virtues of private enterprise and wanted active help to be given to it.[135] Hardinge was succeeded by a man who, while he was the president of the Board of Trade, had had the unhappy experience of observing the chaotic growth of British railways.[136] Dalhousie naturally wanted to have Indian railways built according to a plan. But beyond exercising a control Dalhousie did not want to bother the government with small details, arguing that 'the conduct of an enterprise which is undertaken mainly for commercial purposes, and which private parties are willing to engage for, does not fall within the proper functions of any Government'.[137]

But the English 'private parties' were not willing to come forward to build railways, although they were vehemently against state construction.[138] In the 1840s, the money-market had been depressed as a result of the reaction to the extensive speculation in railway stock. Hence it was felt that investment would be forthcoming only if underwritten for a certain rate of interest by the state. In other words, investors were prepared to invest at public risk. Both the influential newspapers of the day, the *Times* and the *Economist*, supported the move to provide a guarantee.

There was, however, a good deal of opposition, and while the Court of Directors were thinking about the guarantee system in 1845, the then

[133] Report 6 May 1836, India Office Records, L/PWD/3/206, pp. 110 *et seq.*
[134] See Report. *Parl. Papers*, H.C. no. 68, vol. 41 of Session 1847, pp. 4–6.
[135] Minute dated 28 July 1846, *ibid.*, p. 23.
[136] Major J. P. Kennedy who was appointed by Dalhousie in 1850 as the first Government railway engineer, said in 1849 that railways in India should not commit the errors of the British system which consider railways as mere private enterprise. 'They ought assuredly to be classed amongst our most important national works, whether the cost of their construction may have been provided from private or public sources.' *A Railway Caution or Exposition of Changes Required* (Calcutta, 1849), p. 2.
[137] *Parl. Papers*, vol. 76 of Session 1852–3, p. 134.
[138] See Daniel Thorner, *Investment in Empire* (Philadelphia, 1950), Chapter VI.

president of the Board of Control, Lord Ripon, voiced his misgivings.[139] Ellenborough, of course, roundly condemned the system as a profligate waste of public money.[140] T. H. Maddock of the Governor-General's Council thought that the guarantee would 'encourage persons to embark in speculations based on no reasonable calculations of ultimate profit'.[141] However there was hardly a whisper of criticism from the point of view of Classical theory of non-interventionist economic policy.[142]

The opposition to the provision of guarantee was not effective against the combined pressure of two interest groups. One group consisted of some directors of the East India Company and their relatives (as Lord Ellenborough put it, 'friends and connections'[143]) who were interested in the railway speculation. The other group was the Lancashire merchants who, having realised the inability of the Indian government to undertake to build the huge transport network, wanted encouragement at least to be given to private enterprise to construct a railway system in India. As we have seen elsewhere, Lancashire hoped to get raw cotton from India, and thus free themselves from dependence on the United States of America for raw material.

Reluctance of British capital to flow into India, absence of sufficient local Indian capital,[144] budgetary deficits, reluctance to increase public debt for development purposes, and the realisation of the necessity of railways in India for a variety of reasons, made the Government of India agree to provide a guarantee to the British investors, even though they were aware that it could not 'be defended on any abstract principles of political economy'.[145] Guarantee was also necessary to attract the ample funds from institutional investors who were prevented by their terms of association from investing on anything other than securities.[146]

From time to time attempts were made by some of the Indian adminis-

---

[139] Ripon to Hardinge, 7 March 1845, Add. Mss 40,871, pp. 303–4 (*Ripon Papers*, British Museum). The Court of Directors were by no means unqualified supporters of the guarantee system. They had written to the Governor General that the system was 'liable to many objections and likely to prove very unsatisfactory'. Letter of 7 May 1845 (Legislative) para. 8, India Office Records.

[140] Ellenborough to John Cam Hobhouse, 25 December 1846, *Home Misc.* no. 844, India Office Records, pp. 284–6.

[141] Minute dated 1 May 1846, *Parl. Papers*, H.C. 68, vol. 41 of Session 1847, p. 18.

[142] Chapman came nearest to this approach when he said that the guarantee system involved an entire departure from the principles on which all legislation regarding trade of the Government of India were based. See his *Cotton and Commerce*, p. 327.

[143] Ellenborough to Hobhouse, 25 December 1846, *op. cit*, p. 285.

[144] See *Indian Railways and Indian Finance* (Bombay, 1869), p. 44.

[145] Evidence of Juland Danvers, *Parl. Papers*, H.C. 327, vol. VIII of Session 1872, Q. 2049. See W. J. Macpherson, 'Investment in India Railways: 1845–1875' *Economic History Review*, vol. VIII, no. 2, December 1955, p. 180.

[146] See W. Balston, *Scinde and Punjab Canal Company* (London, 1859), p. 5.

trators to suggest state construction of railways after seeing the enormous wastage during the construction of railways by inexperienced British operators.[147] But the secretary of state, Sir Charles Wood, was firmly on the side of private enterprise and wrote to Samuel Laing that it would be a 'new thing if government work is done cheaper than work managed by private persons'; and as to the complaints concerning waste, he said: 'I have a strong notion that no Railroad in England was ever constructed without a good deal of what after enquiry might fairly have been called waste and jobbing.'[148] It was also the opinion of many in the late 1850s that the system of guarantees had outlived its utility and its abolition was therefore urged.[149] Sir Charles Wood saw to it that no change was effected.

This policy of guaranteed interest was reversed in 1869 when Sir John Lawrence protested against it. Sir John had tried to take the responsibility of constructing railway lines even in 1866 because he found the guarantee had resulted in over-capitalisation in the railway companies. It was his conviction that the government could borrow more easily and construct the lines at a much less cost.[150] Although he had the support of the finance member, W. H. Massey, there was opposition from other members, Sir William Mansfield, G. N. Taylor, H. M. Durand and Sir Henry Maine.[151] All of them opposed the idea that the private companies tended to be extravagant and emphasised the uncertainty of leaving the construction of railways to government agencies. In the words of Mansfield, 'governments in India, and Secretaries of State, are somewhat ephemeral. Policy is apt to vary according to immediate exigencies, or the personal views of the ruling statesman of the day.' Maine advocated that government should concentrate on irrigation projects and leave the construction of railways to private enterprise. He was certain that 'No amount of determination in the Government, as constituted at any given time; no degree of positiveness in publicly stating an intention, can afford such security for the prosecution and completion of a line of Railway, as is given by its concession to a Company.' It was also felt by Lawrence's critics that the railway companies under the system of guarantee had done much to develop the railways, and hence the criticism of the system was 'unjust and impolitic'. There was little that Lawrence could do in the face

[147] See N. Sanyal, *Development of Indian Railways* (Calcutta, 1930), p. 64.
[148] Wood to Laing, 9 April 1861 (Halifax Papers at the India Office Library).
[149] Vernon-Smith in the annual Financial Statement presented to the House of Commons on 18 February 1859; and Peacock's Minute dated 25 April 1857, *Minutes of Sir Barnes Peacock*, pp. 100–1.
[150] Minute dated 8 October 1866. *Railway Letters from the Government of India* (1866), India Office Records, L/PWD/3/65, vol. 26.
[151] Minutes, H. M. Durand (13 October 1866), W. N. Massey (20 October 1866); Mansfield (2 November 1866); Maine (8 November 1866) and Taylor (13 December 1866). *Ibid.*

of such criticism from his colleagues in the Council. But he tried again in 1869 and pointed out once more that the system of guaranteed interest placed burdens on the government because the losses were borne by the government without profits ever being made to make good the losses.[152] Although those in favour of the continuance of the guaranteed interest system did not criticise the idea of state intervention, criticism was at least implied in their objection to the removal of the guaranteed system. To this, Lawrence replied:

the Government of India has for several years been striving to induce capitalists to undertake the construction of Railways in India at their own risk, and on their own responsibility, with a minimum of Government interference. But the attempt has entirely failed, and it has become obvious that no capital can be obtained for such undertakings otherwise than under a guarantee of interest, fully equal to that which the Government would have to pay if it borrowed directly on its own account. It is an abuse of language, to describe as an interference with private enterprise, what is only a refusal to support private speculators and to guarantee them from all possible loss by the credit of the State; or to allege that the investment of capital by private persons is hindered by the Government executing works, when private persons refuse to do so at their own risk.[153]

The secretary of state at this time was the Duke of Argyll, who allowed himself to be convinced by the viceroy.[154]

Although the government gave up the guarantee system, government construction of railways languished after 1869 because it was bound up with the general question of financing public works through public borrowings.

The Famine Commission thought that both types of public works (productive as well as protective) were needed to make India strong to resist the famine difficulties. The Government of India came to the conclusion that it had to fall back once more on private enterprise as the means to construct railways.[155] In order to encourage the private enterprise, the Government of

---

[152] Minute dated 9 January 1869, para. 9. *Railway Letters from the Government of India*, India Office Records, L/PWD/3/69, vol. 30.

[153] *Ibid.*, para. 11. This despatch was drafted by Richard Strachey and accepted by Lawrence without any reservation. See J. & R. Strachey, *Finances and Public Works of India*, pp. 90–1.

[154] See his Financial Statement presented to the House of Commons on 23 July 1869. See his Despatch to Government of India dated 15 July 1869 (no. 42 of 1869) in which he accepted the policy of state construction. In Britain such active state interference for promoting public works was widely welcomed. Indeed Sir Thomas Bazley, a leading light of the Manchester Chamber of Commerce, urged the Government to acquire all existing railway lines which, as Arthur Silver points out, was 'a rather advanced suggestion for laissez-faire England'. *op. cit.*, p. 267.

[155] See Sir Evelyn Baring's Minute dated 31 May 1881, Add. Mss 43,575, p. 500 (*Ripon Papers*, British Museum). He was against the guarantee system although he proposed it. See his evidence before the Gold and Silver Commission, Q. 7087. *Parl. Papers*, Cmd. 5512, Vol. 45 of Session 1888. Lord Ripon's Minute dated 14 June 1881, Add. Mss 43,575, p. 513. (*Ripon Papers*, British Museum).

India proposed a guarantee for railway construction. The secretary of state, however, failed to perceive the urgency of the situation and wrote back saying that productive public works should be left to the unaided private enterprise, or in his words, 'capital should be raised on the *exclusive security of the success of the undertaking*'.[156] As for protective works, 'I can look to no other agency than that of the Government.' The secretary of state did mention that, should private enterprise fail, 'a system of modified guarantee might be adopted'. But the view at that time in the India Office was against any form of guarantee.[157] The new system of modified guarantee was ushered in in 1884 after the House of Commons Select Committee had reported in its favour. This system continued until 1924.

CONCLUSION

What we have seen in this chapter should be adequate to dispel the notion that somehow the deeply held belief in a rigid *laissez-faire* approach to economic growth was responsible for the British administration doing hardly anything to promote economic development. Neither was the Classical theory of economic policy rigid concerning the role of the state in economic development nor was Indian administration blind to the benefits conferred by the active participation in economic affairs. It is no doubt true that the average member of the Indian administration had only an appreciation and belief in what one might call the popular conception of *laissez-faire* economic policy. But once doubts crept in as to the efficiency of that economic policy, and reference was made to the writings of economists for clarification, the problems multiplied for the policy maker. This is because of the lack of precision in the Classical theory of economic policy. It would be substantially correct to say that this theory of economic policy was largely inspired by Adam Smith's writings. Indeed, barring minor modifications here and there, it is entirely Smithian in its outlook. It is true that, broadly conceived, the ideal for the nineteenth-century economists was *laissez-faire*. But this has meant many things to many people, and is susceptible of many interpretations. The Scottish philosophical tradition stressed comprehensiveness even if it meant sacrificing logical precision.[158] For example, after referring to Smith's *Wealth of Nations*, it is possible to come to any conclusion regarding economic policy – absolute non-interference, relative non-interference and even some sort of

---

[156] Secretary of State to the Governor General, 8 December, 1881, no. 365 (Financial), *Letters to India on Finances*, India Office Records, 1/3/772, para 14.
[157] See J. Danvers, 'The Progress of Railways and Trade', *Journal of the Society of Arts*, vol. XXXVII, no. 1898, 5 April 1889, p. 457.
[158] See A. L. Macfie, *The Individual in Society: Papers on Adam Smith*, p. 22.

collectivism. Smith's nineteenth-century disciples were equally indefinite about the ideal economic policy. J. L. Mallet, a regular participant in the famous Political Economy Club discussions, recorded in his diary on 25 June 1830: 'most subjects belonging to that science are so involved in doubt and difficulty, that the moment you quit the great road and general principles, you find yourself in crooked lanes, a cul de sac. At our club, we early found it necessary to cease coming to any conclusions.'[159]

It was generally agreed that the state should play hardly any part in the economic life of the country. It was also agreed that there were exceptions and qualifications, but unfortunately, as Jacob Viner has expressed it clearly, these exceptions and special cases 'were rarely, if ever, integrated with the *laissez-faire* part of their doctrine in such a way as to disclose the principles by which the proper time and form and degree of departure from *laissez-faire* could be judiciously determined'.[160] The average Indian civil servant with vague notions of *laissez-faire* thus received no help from the texts, and to add to his perplexity and indecision, he found even leading practitioners of that discipline such as Fawcett, Mill and Wilson talking and acting with respect to economic policy of India as though they had never heard of the concept of *laissez-faire*. The consequence of this indefiniteness and lack of unanimity in what mattered most to policy makers was that they usually chose what suited their particular ideological stance. A confirmed Cobdenite like Sir Louis Mallet naturally found most congenial the ideas of Frederick Bastiat, the French exponent of the Classical economic liberalism, optimist, and friend of Cobden. On the other hand, Sir Richard Strachey, with his paternalistic attitude towards India, found John Stuart Mill to his liking because of the latter's liberal approach towards the functions of government. In addition to ideological stance, political and financial realities also influenced the final policy outcome.

This meant that Classical political economy gave almost a *carte blanche* to the Raj to do what it pleased, offering appropriate defence for almost any position taken. The remarkable thing is that this freedom was not utilised to any great extent in the nineteenth century so as to make a mockery of the eclecticism in political economy. In fact what the Indian government *did* was entirely within the scope outlined by Adam Smith as 'Duties of the Sovereign' and later modified by John Stuart Mill in his discussion on limits of the 'Province' of government.

---

[159] Political Economy Club, *Minutes of Proceedings 1819–1820*, p. 218.
[160] 'The Intellectual History of Laissez-faire', *Journal of Law and Economics*, October 1960, vol. III, p. 62.

9

CONCLUSION

The high and loyal principles which actuate all our ... officers would, I am fully persuaded, prevent any wilful deviation from the instructions laid down by competent authority. But where theories are strongly held, they often insensibly influence the course of action, and lead unconsciously to interpretations and inferences in accordance with these theories.

Sir William Muir
Lieutenant-Governor of North Western Provinces
in 1868

I was thus in a good position for finding out by practice the mode of putting a thought which gives it easiest admittance into minds not prepared for it by habit; while I became practically conversant with the difficulties of moving bodies of men, the necessities of compromise, the art of sacrificing the non-essential to preserve the essential. I learnt how to obtain the best I could, when I could not obtain everything ... to be pleased and encouraged when I could have the smallest part of it.

John Stuart Mill
(on what he learnt as an adviser
to the East India Company)

The theme of this monograph is the baffling area of the relationship between economic ideas and economic policy. The variables are so many, the problems so confused, and the time span so great that it is impossible to give any precise answer to the question: 'What influence, if any, did economic theory exert on economic policy?' The theory/policy link is not constant over time, nor is its nature the same in different areas. One can think of this nexus only in terms of a continuum, that is, it can be discerned only relatively, and not in any absolute terms. Many conditions must be met before it becomes possible to make definite statements concerning the influence of a particular theory on a particular policy and its implementation. This is so because in the area of economic policy there are few problems which have unique solutions that would satisfy everyone. Alternative solutions affect different groups differently with the result that no solution will have universal approval. It must be borne in mind that each case of the exercise of economic policy is unique, and that each one of them would have to be judged separately to ascertain the element of doctrinal influences upon it. We need also to emphasise that even when all the conditions are highly conducive to the influence of a particular theory on a particular policy, we cannot be absolutely certain that theory was decisive because the policy was formed within the context of a certain unique and complex historical situation which no amount of research can reproduce completely within our mind. At best our findings could be a correct approximation, but never the absolute truth.

Within the limits of evidence, our conclusions in broad terms are clear. Although the economic policies formulated and executed in India were the work of many individuals scattered over a vast area and spanning considerable lengths of time, it is possible to discern a slender connecting thread. All the elements ultimately form a pattern, in spite of their being diffused by the workings of a system of government peculiarly susceptible to all kinds of pressures. This thread linking up the various aspects of British economic policy in India was no other than Classical liberalism very broadly conceived. It is difficult to find a one-to-one correspondence between the theoretical structures and the ultimate policy measures. However, the economic opinion that prevailed in Britain in the nineteenth century would not have seriously disapproved the conception of economic policies conducted in every sphere in India. Even with the worst possible interpretation of the motives of the British Raj, it cannot be denied (with certain glaring exceptions) that the policies leaned more towards a free trade orientation than towards any crude conceptions of the beggar-my-neighbour policies of the so-called Mercantilist writers of the seventeenth and eighteenth centuries. In other words, the national objectives of Britain were sought through the application of the Classical theory of economic policy.

The Classical theory of economic policy that flowed from the writings of Adam Smith and his successors provided the 'ideal' in all aspects of Indian economic policy. While, in the first half of the century, ideals were sought to be applied to concrete situations, as the century progressed conditions became more and more unfavourable for theory to make any direct impact on the ideal and on the practical components of economic policy. Whether it was a question of inexorable concrete circumstances, of blind historical forces, or of opportunistic and selfish motives, the fact remains that the 'ideal' in almost all policies in the nineteenth century was provided by the outlook of Classical economic liberalism, as the accompanying table shows.

The question arises immediately as to why the 'ideal' economic policies were sought to be modified for purposes of implementation? If the answers

TABLE 3 *Economic policy ideals*

Policy	Ideals
Colonial policy	The ideal was to achieve the free flow of resources without any impediments, and for India to form part of a system of international division of labour.
Famine policy	The ideal was to let the market allocate the scarce food resources.
Economic relations	The maintenance of free trade. Individuals should be able to buy and sell their services freely, and thus avoid rigidities in the labour market.
Taxation	Minimum interference with the allocative mechanism through fiscal measures.
Land revenue	The ideal was the absorption of rent defined in Ricardian and Malthusian terms and the maintenance of the public sector without any 'real cost' to the society.
Economic development	Economic progress through individual enterprise, and provision of the appropriate institutional structure which among other things included a modicum of necessary public goods, a currency system, legal system and a police system.

provided by Classical political economy were found inadequate why did the subject continue to remain in high estimation among those involved in Indian administration?

Throughout the nineteenth century, but particularly in its second half, the more thoughtful among the policy makers began to show awareness of the folly of trying to translate English theories into Indian economic policies without any modification. While certain objectives were admirable in themselves, it was also realised that these could not be achieved by pursuing the policies suggested by Classical economic liberalism. It was becoming increasingly clear that the solutions offered by the Classical economists were for different problems in an entirely different set of circumstances. One can no doubt cite expressions of opinions by those connected with India even in the second half of the century, who proclaimed universal validity of economic doctrines, but they were few.[1] Apart from those who had great faith in the universal

---

[1] One writer suggested that, 'Its (political economy's) fundamental truths are as certain, and as immutable by man, as the laws of motion.' *Indian policy 1858*, p. 91. Malcolm Lewin of the Civil Service believed that 'the doctrines of Adam Smith, are more to be relied on, than the most obvious truths of religion and humanity'. *The Young India Party and Free Trade* (London, 1857), p. 13.

applicability of the principles of political economy, there were those who referred to the principles only to justify a given policy. Theory then provided, as we have seen very often, either a spurious façade to conceal the sectional interests of the mother country or to provide a convenient excuse for the shocking inefficiencies of the administration.[2]

By the middle of the century, many observers and participants in the economic life of the country had come to the conclusion that political economy was not adequate by itself to solve problems of economic policy. Professor H. Green of the Bombay Education Service thus told the students of the Literary and Scientific Society of Bombay: 'in applying your political economy to the cases which you observe in society, it is important to remember this; to bear in mind that other principles are frequently to be considered, and to make the necessary allowance for their action.'[3] Samuel Laing, who succeeded James Wilson to the finance membership, felt that, 'whoever would govern India well must be master of his theories, and not let theories master him; in other words, he must abstain from pushing principles, however good, to excess'.[4] Many arguments were advanced for this attitude towards political economy. One group of people affirmed that Indians were simply not ready for utilising political economy to the maximum advantage. Whereas the extreme view was that 'reasoning based on analogy, or the ethics of political economy simply, would not be accepted by the natives of India',[5] Sir Richard Temple propounded a more moderate version:

Now these considerations of political economy are just as applicable to India as to any other civilized country. It will hardly be denied that India *is* a civilized country. Although civilization, in a politico-economic sense, is not so diffused in India as in Europe ... still India has a fair proportion of civilization, has a large field for the exercise of political economy ... (but) inconsiderable relative to the vastness of the country.[6]

The view that English political economy 'assumes a condition of things that does not exist here' had a large measure of support.[7] It was also pointed out

---

[2] This led a pamphleteer to remark: 'Political economy is a very convenient thing in the hands of our statesmen when India is the victim. It is entirely ignored that a large percentage of the revenues of India is spent ... in utter defiance of the teachings of Adam Smith and John Stuart Mill,' *India: Before and After the Mutiny* (Edinburgh, 1886), p. 67.

[3] *Three Lectures on Political Economy* (Bombay, 1853), p. 30.

[4] *India and China, England's Mission in the East*, p. 38.

[5] G. W. Cline, *Remarks on State Paper Currency* (Calcutta, 1868), p. 13.

[6] Memorandum dated 19 June 1872 (Temple Papers, India Office Library).

[7] Editorial, *Indian Economist*, 21 September 1871, p. 28. There was of course no novelty in such opinions, because similar views had been expressed by some previously. See for Munro's views, Gleig, *Life of Munro*, Vol. III, p. 320; and *Alexander's East India and Colonial Magazine*, November 1838, vol. XVI, no. 96, p. 456.

that 'the pre-existing conditions can never, in reality exactly correspond with those on which the philosopher works in pursuit of his favourite theory' and hence 'there is probably no country in the world, and there probably never existed a country in which the pure maxim of political economy could be strictly carried into practice without the most dangerous consequences'.[8] A civil servant who had served a number of years in India wrote:

Between political economy as a science, and its application to the various social conditions of the human race, there is much the same relation as exists between pure and applied mathematics, one deals with subjects in the abstract, and the other with their actual and varying qualities.[9]

However, it was argued that the gulf between assumptions and reality was apt to become wide, especially because the political economist had a knowledge only of European economic experience which differed considerably from the capacities of Indians and the structure and operation of their economy. India was an agricultural country without a large stock of capital, and the English economic ideas assumed a situation where the economy was well developed in all sectors and had the capacity to accumulate capital. Apart from the nature of the economy, the attitudes of the Indian people were different from those of the British. The existence of such attitudes was given prominence by policy makers because, as we have seen, the individual entrepreneur is the hero of the Classical theory of economic policy. It was a mistake to assume that 'all men are, not merely potentially, but actually, alike, at all times, and in all places'.[10] English economic ideas treated 'only of the material Wealth of Nations' and not the social aspects which alone had immediate relevance in India. It was no doubt possible for the theorist to assume that men 'always strive to buy in the cheapest, and sell in the dearest market', because this is what happens usually; but, as pointed out by Emerson Dawson, 'the activity of races and nations in this respect exhibits remarkable differences'. Hence he said that just as friction and gravity prevent the perpetual motion of a body, the realities of social life prevent the ideal workings of the principles of political economy.[11] The more general a theory is, the more inapplicable it would be to particular circumstances, warned the *Indian Observer*:

If there is one thing more than another which it behoves officials, and especially Indian officials, to regard with suspicion, it is a symmetrical theory, and with increased suspicion in proportion to its symmetry. What have been all the great and acknowledged mistakes of the recent past but theories, whose captivating symmetry

[8] 'Social Science in India' *Calcutta Review*, vol. XLIV, no. LXXXVIII, 1866, p. 426.
[9] *A Lecture on the Material and Social Effects of English Rule* (Salisbury, 1878), p. 3.
[10] *Ibid.*
[11] Indopolite, *The Indian Land Question: A Timely Warning* (London, 1865), pp. 25, 36.

and logical completeness captivated men's intellects, as similar perfection of physical form steals away their hearts.[12]

Similar arguments were advanced by Sir Henry Maine to quash the proposal made by Dr Benjamin Jowett and enthusiastically recommended by Lord Northbrook to include political economy as one of the subjects to be taken by candidates for the Indian Civil Service examination.[13] Maine's answer centred on the fact that the precision one observed in political economy was acquired by a 'series of assumptions which are not by any means absolutely true of India'. One such assumption was that 'private or individual property exists as an institution, that its forms are perfectly distinct, and that its actual distribution has been determined by causes of so old a date that no inquiry into their propriety ought to be permitted'. Maine pointed out that this was not so in India, because individual property in India was still intertwined with common property, and everything was very imprecise. Hence his conclusion was that political economy, 'if studied by itself, is a source rather of confusion of mind than of clearness of thought in Indian officials'. He did not, however, object to the successful candidates being given instruction in political economy provided they were also asked to study the history of the land tenure system 'as established by the comparative method'.[14]

Economists had all along stressed the limited applicability of their theories and maintained that economics was but a mode of thinking. Nassau Senior, for instance, had emphasised the abstract nature of the principles of political economy by stressing the duty of economists to state general principles, but never to particularise about specific policies *qua* economists. John Stuart Mill, whose *Principles of Political Economy* headed the list of recommended texts for the candidates of the Indian civil service for many years, insisted that political economy was not a simple set of practical maxims. It was a science, an exposition of 'a theory of the manner in which causes produce effects'. The function of political economy was not to provide rules but to 'enable us to find the rules which ought to govern any state of circumstances with which we have to deal – circumstances which are never the same in any two cases'.[15] Even if the economist provides a policy, Mill said, 'there is almost always room for a modest doubt as to our practical con-

---

[12] *The Indian Observer*, 22 April 1871, p. 179.
[13] See B. Jowett to Lord Salisbury, 27 December 1874, *Parl. Papers*, Cmd. 1446, vol. 55 of Session 1876, pp. 285–8. Although this measure had little support from Indian civil servants, one supporter defended the proposal by claiming that political economy was already being studied by 'many students previous to the open examination, as a means of improving their style ... as a means of educating the mind to remember a long train of argument'. A. H. Haggard to the Secretary of Bengal Government, 12 August 1875, p. 340.
[14] *Ibid.*, Minute dated 12 November 1875, p. 507.
[15] *Hansard*, 3rd series, vol. CXC, p. 1525, 16 March 1868.

clusions'.[16] A leading disciple of Mill, Henry Fawcett, told Parliament that if the members took the abstract principles of political economy and applied them 'cut and dry' without considering the 'social and political circumstances of the case', they would be acting like pedants.[17]

Remarks of this nature helped critics of political economy absolve the principles, without affecting the validity of their criticisms of the specific applications. Referring to Senior's conception of economics, a writer in the *Calcutta Review* said, 'If this limited view of the science be correct; if the conclusions are not meant to be acted upon without continual reference to other considerations, then of course the science cannot be blamed.'[18] Caution was suggested against misusing the principles outside their time-horizon. Much of political economy was cast in terms of the long-run forces whereas the policy makers had immediate problems to solve. Viscount Cranborne (later Lord Salisbury) expressed this point clearly:

The doctrine of political economy had been worshipped as a sort of 'fetish' by officials who, because they believed that in the long run supply and demand would square themselves, seemed to have utterly forgotten that human life was short, and that men could not subsist without food beyond a few days. They mechanically left the laws of political economy to work themselves out while hundreds of thousands of human beings were perishing from famine.[19]

Thus economists and politicians, statesmen and journalists seemed to agree that the results of abstract theoretical speculations could not be utilised in policy formation without taking into account the circumstances of time and place.

It is of course true that no alternative existed to the use of political economy. A purely empirical method was simply not possible because sufficient statistics were not available, nor were the available data entirely reliable. Hence, in the words of Sir Louis Mallet; 'it is a far sounder course to start from a general principle, and qualify it as you go along by the thousand considerations which its application requires in the practical conduct of Government, than to discard it altogether, and deal separately with every set of facts which presents itself'. But if theory were completely to be set aside, the result would be 'to embark in a boundless sea of inquiry without chart or compass'.[20]

---

[16] *Unsettled Questions*, p. 156.

[17] *Hansard*, 3rd series vol. CCXXV, 10 July 1877.

[18] Vol. XLVI, no. XCI, 1867, p. 103.

[19] *Hansard*, 3rd series, vol. CLXXXIX, p. 809–10, 2 August 1867.

[20] Minute dated 12 April 1875, p. 21. *Financial Department Collections*, India Office Records, C/138. An anonymous author wrote in the *Calcutta Review*: 'whether political economy, meaning by the term the science as it exists and is taught in Europe, can fairly or advantageously be applied to Indian administration, we have some doubts, but that *a* science of political economy, which takes its data and forms its inferences from the state of society, we find here, ought to be so studied and applied, we are very certain'. Vol. XXXIX, no. LXXVII, 1864, p. 111.

Similarly a judge of the Calcutta High Court, C. L. Tupper, said that economic theory by itself was not to be blamed. It was a test of wise administration whether the officials and policy makers could utilise 'political economy,
not the abstract disquisitions of text writers illustrated by the experience of
another quarter of the globe, but applied political economy generalising
cautiously upon the best data which responsible investigation can provide'.[21]
Thus, as a result of such introspection concerning the nature and usefulness
of political economy, a consensus was said to have emerged which retained
the 'ideals' based on Classical economic liberalism, but many modifications
were effected in practice, and in some cases this happened to such an extent
that there was hardly any trace of the original ideal when the policy was
implemented.

What are the implications of this study for the wider issues of the economic
theory–policy nexus?

To begin with we need to make a distinction between the economist in
government and the role of economic ideas *per se*. As for the economist in
government, his influence will depend upon many considerations. Has he
got the necessary power and authority to formulate policies? Is he a mere
adviser or a functionary with full backing to lay down rules and guidelines?
Is there a proper climate of opinion in favour of utilising economic theories
in policy measures? Finally, has the economist in government got the will and
determination to push through his policies?

In spite of the most ideal conditions, a single economist's success is likely
to be a limited one because, even if possessed of considerable authority, he
must operate within a system. In so far as economic policies are concerned
he is in a better position because he possesses the expertise to understand the
usually tangled issues of policy and suggest solutions. But it is to be emphasised here that there is no such thing as pure 'economic policy',[22] and that
political issues enter the scene willy-nilly. The economist in government
(in principle) as an economist has only the function of identifying issues,
analysing problems and suggesting alternative solutions. Yet, as attested by
most economists who have acted as advisers, his role cannot remain so limited.
He inevitably assumes a political mantle and champions the solution he most
prefers. A distinguished modern practitioner of the art of economic advising
noted that in his experience the 'Economic adviser was no secluded oracle or
venerable sage, to be consulted at rare intervals. He was instead an ordinary
working member of the Department, drawing occasionally on his training

---

[21] *Notes on the Bengal Rent Bill* (Calcutta, 1882), pp. 11–12.
[22] See A. W. Coats, 'In defence of Heckscher' *Scandinavian Economic History Review*, vol. v,
no. 2, 1957.

in economic theory but far more commonly on experience.'[23] Professor Cairncross's experience was that the success of the economic adviser depends upon how large the political ramifications of the particular policy were. In his case, success was achieved in relatively minor issues such as fuel and export policies rather than in major policy measures such as devaluation of sterling.[24] This is the lot of economic advisers, including John Stuart Mill at the India office,[25] and they have to be satisfied with what they are able to do rather than worry about what they are unable to achieve.

The analysis of the role of economic ideas on the other hand, as we have seen in the previous chapters, is far more difficult because they have no temporal limits and can be pervasive.

Governments have to take decisions regarding what to do and where to do it. As Professor Raymond Bauer puts it, various labels are applied to decisions and actions depending in general upon the 'breadth of their implications'. There are 'routine actions' that are trivial and repetitive demanding little thought. Then there are 'tactical decisions' which need extended considerations. However, decisions that 'have the widest ramifications and the longest time perspective, and which generally require the most information and contemplation' are termed 'policies'.[26] The formulation of policies is essentially introspective. Hence economics, because it deals with the structures, mechanisms and operations of the economy in broad settings, is found useful. Economics can confer to the policy maker either a way of thinking and/or specific solutions to particular problems.

The question arises: how can we examine the influence of particular economic ideas in the complex process of policy making? The implied argument of this book is that the answer can be secured only through the framework of the broader problem of the mechanics of the transmission of ideas.

The influence of economic ideas and policies involves two distinct diffusion processes which may be called horizontal diffusion and vertical diffusion. The former is the spatial and temporal spread of an idea. The focus of attention here is not so much the development of ideas and theories, but how the idea once generated gains adherents in other regions, countries and times. If the horizontal diffusion refers to the mechanism of the transmission of ideas, vertical diffusion indicates the impact of an idea in a specific setting — in the present context the influence of the new idea from one scale to another

[23] Alec Cairncross, 'On being an Economic Adviser' *Scottish Journal of Political Economy*, no. 2, October 1955, p. 191.

[24] *Ibid.*

[25] *Autobiography* (ed. by Jack Stillinger: London, 1971), pp. 52–3.

[26] 'The Study of Policy Formation: An Introduction' in Raymond A. Bauer and Kenneth J. Gergen (eds.), *The Study of Policy Formation* (New York: 1968), pp. 1–2.

scale in the administrative hierarchy, e.g. from the economic adviser to the cabinet minister responsible for determining policy. In other words those processes necessary for an idea to get accepted widely within the various levels of an organisation. Both the horizontal diffusion and the vertical diffusion are closely related, as can be seen in the chart. The first stage in the process of transmission of an idea is a general movement that is part of the environment, whereas the second stage of the impact must of necessity take place within a specific context. While ideas themselves are impersonal, it is the individual economist or a group of economists who actually enable that idea to be put into practice. But for this to materialise they have to be part of an administrative system. Policy making is thus a social process involving the participation of many individuals who are the carriers of the ideas.

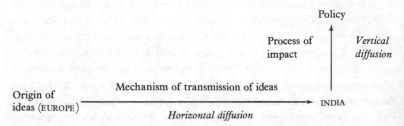

If new ideas are to replace the old, they have to act upon, push out and take the place of the obsolete modes of thinking at all levels of the hierarchy. But organisations — especially bureaucratic organisations — have in-built mechanisms to resist the intrusion of new ideas and modes of thinking. The routine drudgery of bureaucratic work precludes intellectual curiosity. Hence the typical administrator takes recourse to precedents which have no doubt been blessed by established opinions, but are irrelevant or unproductive in the changed contexts. The strength of this bureaucratic resistance will, however, be inversely proportional to the urgency of the economic problem that needs a solution, and the realisation of the inadequacy of the received doctrine. This cannot of course be precisely charted, because ideas do not always have an impact even if the conditions seem ideal for them. Bureaucracy is after all a social organism composed of individuals, and the impact of ideas on the individuals and their impact on the final outcome will be dependent on the strength of the processes of diffusion, and their resistances at various hierarchic levels.

SELECT BIBLIOGRAPHY

MANUSCRIPT SOURCES

Private papers of Sir Philip Francis, Sir Charles Wood, Lord Elgin, Sir John Lawrence, Lord Northbrook, Sir Richard Temple, Lord Lytton, Lord Cross and Lord George-Hamilton (India Office Library), Lord Ripon, Lord Lansdowne, Lord Liverpool, Sir Robert Peel and Lord Wellesley (British Museum), Lord Mayo and Sir James Fitzjames Stephen (Cambridge University Library), J. B. Smith (Central Library, Manchester). Lord Melville (John Rylands Library, Manchester), Lord Salisbury (Christ Church College, Oxford), and Lord Bentinck (Nottingham University Library archives).

OFFICIAL RECORDS

Charters & Treaties, Writer's Petitions, Home Miscellaneous Series, Despatches to Bengal, Bombay, Madras and India, Letters and Enclosures received from Bengal, Bombay, Madras and India, Revenue and Public Proceedings, India Financial Proceedings (India Office Library) and Papers relating to Individual Acts of Government of India (National Archives of India).

PARLIAMENTARY PAPERS

British Parliamentary Papers have been extensively used, and a complete list of those relating to India is to be found in, *Annotated Lists and General Index of Parliamentary Papers Relating to the East Indies Published during the years 1801 to 1907*, Parl. Papers, H.C. 89, vol. LXIV of Session 1909. House of Commons debates have also been extensively utilised.

PRINTED OFFICIAL PAPERS

Budget Speeches by Henry Dundas and Lord Castlereagh 1788–1805, (India Office Library).

Correspondence and Proceedings in the Negotiation for a Renewal of the East India Company's Charter (London: 1812).

Correspondence, debates in the Legislative Council and Minutes Relating to Direct Taxation in British India, 2 vols. (Calcutta: 1882).

Correspondence Relating to the Famine in Bengal and Bihar from October 1873 to May 31 1874 (Calcutta: 1874).

Directions for Revenue Officers in the Northwest Provinces of the Bengal Presidency Regarding the Settlement and Collection of the Land Revenue and the Other Duties (Calcutta: 1850).

East India Company, Selections of papers at the East India House Relating to Revenue, Police, and Civil Criminal Justice under the Company's Government in India, 4 vols. (London: 1820–1826).

East India Company, Regulations passed by the Governor-General in Council of Bengal, 3 vols. (London: 1828).

Papers Relating to the Passing of Act X of 1859, 2 vols. (Calcutta: 1859).

Land Revenue Policy of the Indian Government (Calcutta: 1902).

Madras, Government of, *First Report of the Commissioners Appointed to Enquire into and Report upon the System of Superintending and Executing Public Works in the Madras Presidency Submitted to the Rt. Hon. the Governor in Council of Fort. St. George* (Madras: 1856).

Minutes of Sir Henry Sumner Maine (India Office Library).

North Western Provinces, Government of, *Selections from the Revenue Records of Government; North Western Provinces,* vol. I (Calcutta: 1866). vol II (Allahabad: 1872), vol. III (Allahabad: 1873).

North Western Provinces, Government of, *Permanent and Temporary Settlements, North Western Provinces* (Allahabad: 1873).

Papers Connected with the Bombay Revenue and Settlement System (Calcutta: 1883).

Note on the Land Transfer and Agricultural indebtedness in India, (Calcutta: 1895).

Papers Relating to the Bengal Tenancy Act, 4 vols. (Calcutta: 1885).

Papers Relating to the Deccan Agriculturist's Relief Act During the Years 1875–1894 (Selection from the Records of Government of India, Home Department No. CCCXLII), 2 vols. (Calcutta: 1897).

Report of the Commissioners Appointed to Inquire into the Working of the Deccan Agriculturists' Relief Act, 1891–92 (Calcutta: 1892).

Report of the Famine in the Madras Presidency during 1896 and 1897 2 vols. (Madras: 1898).

Review of the Madras Famine 1876–78 (Madras: 1881).

Selections from Educational Records of the Government of India, 2 vols. (Delhi: 1960–63).

Selections from the Records of the Bombay Government, New Series, Volumes CVII and CL.

Selections from the Records of the Madras Government.
   1st Series, no. V (1854)
   2nd Series, nos. IX (1858), XII (1855) and XXII (1855)
   New Series, no. I (1906)

Selections from the Records of the Government of the Punjab, New Series, vol. XIII (1876).

Special Narratives of the Drought in Bengal and Bihar 1873–1874 (Together with Minutes by the Honourable Sir Richard Temple, Calcutta: 1874).

Trade, Tariffs, Customs (A Collection of Papers 1813–1894) (India Office Library).

CONTEMPORARY PERIODICALS

Alexander's East India and Colonial Magazine, Asiatic Journal, Asiatic Quarterly Review, Asiatic Researches, The *Bombay Quarterly Review,* The *Calcutta Review,* The *Economist, Edinburgh Review, Imperial and Asiatic Quarterly Review,* The

Indian Economist, Indian Observer, Journal of the East India Association, Journal of the Poona Sarvajanik Sabha, Journal of the Royal Asiatic Society of Great Britain and Ireland, Journal of the Royal Society of Arts, London Review, Madras Journal of Literature and Science, The *Nineteenth Century,* The *Pamphleteer,* The *Times, Westminster Review.*

CONTEMPORARY PUBLICATIONS

Agricultural and Administrative Reform in Bengal, by a Bengal Civilian (London: 1883).

Articles and Letters About the Indian Land Tax, Reprinted from the Bombay Saturday Review by I. P. H. (Bombay: 1866).

Articles on Indian Finance (Bombay: 1883).

Be just to India: Prevent Famine and Cherish Commerce by a Member of the Cotton Supply Association (Manchester: 1861).

The Bengal Rent Question (Calcutta: 1878).

The Bengal Tenancy Bill (London: 1884).

The British Jugernath, by G. L. M. (Calcutta: 1884).

A collection of papers connected with the question of a permanent settlement in the districts of N.W.P. as affected by Canal Irrigation (Allahabad: 1865).

Correspondence of the Honourable Court of Directors of the East India Company and of the Governor General in Council Respecting the Permanent Settlement of the Land Revenue (London: 1825).

A Demonstration of the Necessity and Advantages of a free trade to the East Indies and of a Termination of the Present Monopoly of the East India Company (London: 1807).

Direct Taxation for India: The Great Financial Blunder (Bombay: 1871).

An Essay on the Present State of the Bengal Money Market and a Projected Agency for the Honourable Company's Service by a Member of the Civil Service (Calcutta: 1825).

Examination of the Principles and Policies of the Government of British India, by a Gentleman in the Service of the East India Company. (London: 1829).

The Famine in Orissa, the Permanent settlement of the Land Revenue in India (London: 1867).

Free Commerce with India; a letter to the President of the Board of Trade with reference to his late Propositions in Parliament for the Improvement of the Colonial Mercantile Policy of Great Britain, by a Madras Civil Servant (London: 1825).

The Government of India as it has been, as it is and as it ought to be (London: 1858).

How to meet the Financial Difficulties of India, by A. C. B. (London: 1859).

India: Before and After the Mutiny, by an 'Indian Student' (Edinburgh: 1886).

The Indian Import Duties on Cotton Fabrics (Manchester: 1879).

Indian Policy: 1858 (London: 1858).

Indian Railways and Indian Finance (Bombay: 1869).

Indian Wheat Versus American Protection or the Influence on English Trade or American Protection of the Development of India (Calcutta: 1883).

An Inquiry into the Causes of the long Continued Stationary Condition of India and its Inhabitants with a brief Examination of the Leading Principles of two of the most approved Revenue Systems of British India, by a civil servant of the Honourable East India Company (London: 1830).

Ireland and Western India: A Parallel (London: 1868).

Irrigation in India in Connection with Indian Deficit, by a Member of the Bengal Civil Service (Calcutta: 1876).

Is India worth Keeping? By one who has seen and studied it (London: 1878).

A Lecture on the Material and Social Effects of English Rule in India, by An Anglo Indian of Fifty Years Service (Salisbury: 1878).

A Letter to the Chairman and Deputy-Chairman and Court of Directors of the East India Company on the Subject of Their College at Haileybury, by a Civilian (London: 1823).

Papers Relating to the Cultivation of Indigo in the Presidency of Bengal (Calcutta: 1860).

Railways in India: Their present state and prospects; Considered with Reference to the field they present for English Capital (London: 1855).

The Relations of Landlord and Tenant in India – A series of articles contributed to the Friend of India (Serampore: 1863).

Remarks on free trade to China (London: 1830).

Remarks on the Ryotwar System of Land Revenue as it Exists in the Presidency of Madras (Madras: 1853).

The Rent Question in Bengal, or Should Act X be Altered? by Agricola (Calcutta: 1865).

Usurers and Ryots, by an Indian civil servant (London: 1856).

What are they aiming at? A Letter to the People of England on Colonial and Indian Policy, by Medius (London: 1884).

ANDREW, Sir William Patrick, *Indian Railways and their Probable Results, by an old Indian Post-master* (London: 1884).

ARBUTHNOT, A. J. (Ed.), *Selections from the Minutes and Other Official Writings of Major General Sir Thomas Munro* (Madras: 1886).

BADEN-POWELL, B. H., *The Land Systems of British India*, 3 vols. (Oxford: 1892)

BARRINGTON, E. I., *The Servant of All, Pages from the Family, Social and Political Life of my Father, James Wilson*, 2 vols. (London: 1927)

BEAMES, John, *Memoirs of a Bengal Civilian* (London: 1961).

BELL, Evans and TYRRELL, Frederick, *Public Works and Public Service In India* (London: 1871).

BOURDILLON, James Dewar, *Brief Statement of the Principal Measures of Sir Charles Trevelyan's Administration at Madras* (Madras: 1860).

BRIGGS, John, *The Present Land Tax in India* (London: 1830).

BRUNYATE, J. B., *An Account of the Presidency Banks* (Calcutta: 1900).

BUCKLEY, Robert B., *The Irrigation Works of India and Their Financial Results* (London: 1880).

CAIRD, Sir James, *India, the Land and the People*, Third Edition (London: 1884).

CAMPBELL, Sir George, *India as it may be: An Outline of a Proposed Government and Policy* (London: 1853).

CAMPBELL, Sir George, *Memoirs of My Indian Career*, 2 vols. (London: 1894).

CAMPBELL, Sir George, *Our Finances* (Lucknow: 1859).

CARNEGY, Patrick, *Notes on the Indebtedness of the Agricultural Classes of India* (London: 1875).

CHAPMAN, John, *Cotton and Commerce of India* (London: 1851).

CHATTERTON, A. *Industrial Evolution in India* (Madras: 1912).

CHESNEY, George, *Indian Polity: A View of the System of Administration in India* (London: 1868).

CLARKE, Hyde *Colonization, Defence and Railways in our Indian Empire* (London: 1857).

COBDEN CLUB, *Systems of Land Tenure in Various Countries* (London: 1870).

CONGREVE, Richard, *India* (London : 1857).

CONNELL, A. K., *The Economic Revolution of India and the Public Works Policy* (London: 1883).

COOKE, C. N., *The Rise, Progress and Present Condition of Banking in India* (Calcutta: 1863).

CORNISH, W. R., *Influence of Famine on Growth of Population* (Madras: 1878).

COTTON, Sir Arthur T., *On Irrigation and Navigation in Connection with the Finances of India* (London: 1863).

COTTON, Sir Arthur T., *Proposed Additional Expenditure of 100 Millions on Indian Railways* (Paper read to the East India Association) (London: 1870).

COTTON, Henry John Stedman, *New India or India in Transition* (London: 1886).

CRAWFURD, John, *Sketch of the Commercial Resources and Monetary and Mercantile System of British India, with Suggestions for their Improvement by Means of Banking Establishments* (London: 1837).

CRAWFURD, John, *A View of the Present State and Future Prospects of the Free Trade and Colonization of India* (London: 1828).

CUNNINGHAM, H. S., *Notes on Some Disputed Points in Indian Fizance and Taxation* (London: 1880).

CURZON, Lord, *British Government in India*, 2 vols. (London: 1925)

DALYELL, R. A., *Memorandum on the Madras Famine* (Madras: 1866).

DANVERS, Frederick Charles and Others, *Memorials of old Haileybury College* (Westminster: 1894).

DANVERS, Juland, *Indian Railways: Their Past History, Present Condition, and Future Prospects* (London: 1877).

DAWSON, Emerson, *The Indian Land Question: A Timely Warning (Reprints from Times of India)*, by 'Indopolite' (London: 1865).

DILKE, Charles W., *Greater Britain*, 2 vols. (London: 1868).

DUNDAS, H., *Letters to the Chairman of the Court of Directors of the East India Company upon an Open Trade to India* (London: 1813).

DYKES, James William Ballantyne, *The Ryotwari Tenure* (Madras: 1858).

ETHERIDGE, A. T., *Report on Past Famines in Bombay Presidency* (n.p. 1868).

FIELD, C. D., *The Regulations of the Bengal Code* (Calcutta: 1875).

FIRMINGER, Reverend W. K. (Ed.), *Fifth Report from the Select Committee of the House of Commons on the Affairs of East India Company 1812*, 3 vols. (Calcutta: 1917–18).

GLEIG, George Robert, *Life of Sir Thomas Munro*, 3 vols. (London: 1830).

GRANT, Sir Alexander, *Some Observations on Educational Administration in India in a Letter to the Right Honourable Sir Stafford Northcote* (Edinburgh: 1868).

GREEN, H. *Three Lectures on Political Economy Delivered Before the Students' Literary and Scientific Society of Bombay* (Bombay: 1853).

HALSEY, W. S., *A Report on the Question of Temporary and Permanent Settlements, as Applied to the District of Cawnpore* (London: 1871).

HAMILTON, Lord George, *Parliamentary Reminiscences and Reflections* Vol. I (1868 to 1885), Vol. II (1886 to 1906) (London: 1917).

HASTINGS, Lord, *Summary of the Administration of the Indian Government 1813–23* (London: 1824).

HOLLINGBERRY, R. G., *The Zemindari Settlement of Bengal*, 2 Vols. (Calcutta: 1879).

HUGHSON, D., *The East India Question Fairly Elucidated by Considerations on the Expediency and Wisdom of Allowing the Outports to Infringe upon the Rights and Privileges of the Charter* (London: 1813).

HUNTER, W. W., *Bombay 1885–1900: A Study in Indian Administration* (London: 1892).

HUNTER, W. W., *The Uncertainties of Indian Finance* (Calcutta: 1869).

HUTTON, H. D., *Ancient Tenures and Modern Land Legislation in British India* (London: 1870).

IRWIN, H. C., *The Garden of India or Chapters on Oudh History and Affairs* (London: 1880).

KNIGHT, Robert, *The Indian Empire and Our Financial Relations Therewith: A Lecture Delivered at the London Indian Society on 25 May 1866* (London: 1866).

KNIGHT, Robert, *Fiscal Science in India: As Illustrated by the Income Tax* (Bombay: 1870).

LAW, Sir Algernon (Ed.), *India Under Lord Ellenborough March 1842 – June 1844 A Selection of Unpublished Papers and Secret Despatches* (London: 1926).

LESLIE-MELVILLE, W. H., *Remarks on the East India Bill* (London: 1833).

LOVE, Henry Davison, *Vestige of Old Madras 1640–1800*, 4 Vols. (London: 1913).

MACGEORGE, G. W., *Ways and Works in India* (London: 1894).

MACKENZIE, J. T., *The Trade and Commerce of India with an Appendix since added Containing a few Remarks on the Land Tenures*, (London: 1859).

MCCULLOCH, J. R., *A Descriptive and Statistical Account of the British Empire*, Second Edition, 2 Vols. (London: 1839).

MAINE, Henry Sumner, *Village Communities in the East and West* (London: 1871).

MALLET, Bernard, *Thomas George, Earl of Northbrook, G.C.S.I., A Memoir* (London: 1908).

MALTHUS, Thomas Robert. *A Letter to the Right Honourable Lord Grenville Occasioned by some Observations of his Lordship on the East India Company's Establishment for the Education of their Civil Servants* (London: 1813).

MASKELL, John, *The Circular Orders of the Board of Revenue from A.D. 1820 to 1850 Inclusive with Notes and References* (Madras: 1851).

MASKELL, John, *The Circular Orders of the Board of Revenue issued During the Years 1851, 1852, 1853* (Madras: 1854).

MILL, James, *History of British India*, 6 vols 2nd Edn, (London: 1820).

MILL, John Stuart, *Autobiography* (London: 1971 Reprint).

MILL, John Stuart, *Memorandum of the Improvements in the Administration of India During the last Thirty Years* (London: 1858).

O'DONNELL, Charles J., *The Black Pamphlet of Calcutta. The Famine of 1874*. By a Bengal Civilian (London: 1876).

PEACOCK, Sir Barnes, *Minutes of Sir Barnes Peacock* (Calcutta: 1901).

PHILLIPS, H. A. D., *A Blacker Pamphlet or An Attempt to Explain the Severity of the Late Famine and the Causes of the Poverty of the Madras Ryot* (Madras: 1878).

PRINSEP, Edward Augustus, *How to Make State Canals Without Borrowing: How to Raise Millions, and Remove the Income Tax: A Few Suggestions* (Lahore: 1870).

PRINSEP, Henry Thoby, *The India Question in 1853* (London: 1853).

PRINSEP, John, *Suggestions on Freedom of Commerce and Navigation more Especially with Reference to the East India Trade* (London: 1823).

RANADE, M. G., *Essays on Indian Economics* (Madras: 1906).

RICKARDS, Robert, *India or Facts Submitted to Illustrate the Character and Condition of the Native Inhabitants*, 2 Vols. (London: 1829–32).

RICKETTS, H., *A Few Last Words on the Rent Difficulties in Bengal* (London: 1864).

RICKETTS, H., *The Rent Difficulties in Bengal and How to Remedy Them?* (London: 1863).

ROBERTSON, Major Henry D., *Examination of the Principles and Policy of the Government of British India, Embracing a Particular Enquiry Concerning the Tenure of Lands; by a Gentleman in the Service of The East India Company* (London: 1829).

ROBERTSON, T. C., *Remarks on Several Recent Publications Regarding the Civil Government and Foreign Policy of British India* (London: 1829).

ROGERS, Alexander, *The Land Revenue of Bombay: A History of its Administration, Rise and Progress*, 2 Vols. (London: 1892).

ROSS, Charles (Ed.), *Correspondence of Charles, first Marquis of Cornwallis*, 3 Vols. (London: 1859).

ROYLE, J. F., *Essay on the Productive Resources of India* (London: 1840).

SHORE, F. J., *Notes on Indian Affairs*, 2 Vols. (London: 1837).

SKRINE, Francis Henry, *Life of Sir William Wilson Hunter* (London: 1901).

SLEEMAN, Colonel W. H., *Analysis and Review of the Peculiar Doctrines of the Ricardo, or New School of Political Economy* (Serampore: 1837).

SLEEMAN, Colonel W. H., *On Taxes, or Public Revenue, the Ultimate Incidence of their Payments, their Disbursement and the Seats of Their Ultimate Consumption. By an Officer in the Military or Civil Service of the Honourable East India Company* (London: 1829).

SLEEMAN, Colonel W. H., *Rambles and Recollections of an Indian Official*, 2 Vols. Ed. by V. A. Smith (London: 1893).

SMOLLETT, Patrick Boyle, *India: A Lecture* (Glasgow: 1863).

SPRY, H. H., *Modern India with Illustrations of the Resources and Capabilities of Hindusthan*, 2 Vols. (London: 1837).

STEUART, Sir James, *The Principles of Money Applied to the Present State of the Coin of Bengal* (London: 1772).

STRACHEY, Sir John, *India: Its Administration and Progress*, Fourth Edition (Revised by T. W. Holderness) (London: 1911).

TEMPLE, Sir Richard, *India in 1880* (London: 1881).

THOMPSON, George. *Six Lectures on the Condition, Resources and Prospects of British India and the Duties and Responsibilities of Great Britain to do Justice to that Vast Empire* (London: 1842).

THORBURN, S. S., *Musalmans and Money-lenders in the Punjab* (Edinburgh: 1886).

THORBURN, W. M., *The Great Game: A Plea for a British Imperial Policy by a British Subject* (London: 1875).

THORNTON, Edward, *India, Its State and Prospects* (London: 1835).

THORNTON, William T., *Indian Public Works and Cognate Indian Topics* (London: 1875).

TREVELYAN, C. E., *A Report on the Inland Customs and Town Duties of the Bengal Presidency* (Calcutta: 1835).

TUCKER, Henry St George, *Memorials of Indian Government* (London: 1853).

WEDDERBURN, W., *A Permanent Settlement for the Dekkhan* (Bombay: 1880).

WEST, Algernon, *Sir Charles Wood's Administration of Indian Affairs, 1859–1866* (London: 1867).

WEST, Sir Edward, *Emigration to British India*: *Profit, Investments for Joint Stock Companies* (London: 1857).

WEST, Raymond, *The Land and the Law in India. An Elementary Inquiry, and Some Practical Suggestions* (Bombay: 1873).

WHEATLEY, John, *Letter to the Right Honourable Charles Watkin William Wynn, President of the Board of Control, on the Latent Resources of India* (Calcutta: 1823).

WHINFIELD, E. H., *The Law of Landlord and Tenants as Administered in the Courts of the Bengal Presidency* (Calcutta: 1869).

WINGFIELD, Charles, *Observations on Land Tenure and Tenant Rights in India* (London: 1869).

YOUNG, Gavin, *An Essay on the Mercantile Theory of Wealth* (Calcutta: 1832).

YOUNG, Gavin, *An Inquiry into the Expediency of Applying the Principles of Colonial Policy to the Government of India* (London: 1822).

SECONDARY SOURCES

AMBEDKAR, B. R., *The Evolution of Provincial Finance in British India* (London: 1925).

AMBEDKAR, B. R. *The Problem of the Rupee*: *its Origin and its Solution* (London: 1923).

BALHATCHET, Kenneth, *Social Policy and Social Change in Western India 1817–1830* (London: 1957).

BANERJEA, Pramathanath, *A History of Indian Taxation* (London: 1930).

BANERJEE, A. C., *Indian Constitutional Documents 1757–1858*, 2nd edn, vol. I (Calcutta: 1948).

BANERJEE, Tarasankar, *Internal Market of India 1834–1900* (Calcutta: 1966).

BARRIER, G. N., *The Punjab Land Alienation Bill* (Durham, N. C.: 1966).

BEAGLEHOLE, T. H., *Thomas Munro and the Development of Administrative Policy in Madras 1792–1818* (Cambridge: 1966).

BEARCE, George Donham, *British Attitudes Towards India 1784–1858* (London: 1961).

BHATIA, B. M., *Famines in India and their Effect on Administration and Economic Policy 1850–1945* (Bombay: 1963).

BHATTACHARYYA, Sabyasachi, *Financial Foundations of the British Raj* (Simla: 1971).

BLACK, R. D. C., *Economic Thought and the Irish Question 1817–1870* (Cambridge: 1960).

BROWN, Lucy, *The Board of Trade*: *and the Free Trade Movement 1830–42* (Oxford: 1958).

CHANDRA, Bipan, *The Rise and Growth of Economic Nationalism in India*: *Economic Policies of Indian National Leadership 1880–1905* (New Delhi: 1966).

CHAUDHURI, K. N. (ed.), *The Economic Development of India Under the East India Company 1814–1858* (Cambridge: 1971).

CHOWDHURY, B., *The Growth of Commercial Agriculture in Bengal, 1757–1900* (Calcutta: 1964).

COATS, A. W. (Ed.), *The Classical Economists and Economic Policy* (London: 1971).

COYAJEE, J. C., *The Indian Currency System 1835–1926* (Madras: 1930).

DARLING, M. L., *Punjab Peasant in Prosperity and Debt* (Bombay: 1925).

DUTT, Romesh Chunder, *The Economic History of India*, 2 vols (Delhi: 1960).

FAY, C. R., *Imperial Economy and its Place in the Formation of Economic Doctrine 1600–1932* (Oxford: 1934).

FEAVER, George A., *From Status to Contract (A Biographical Study of Sir Henry Maine 1822–88)* (London: 1968).

FRYKENBERG, R. E. (Ed.), *Land Control and Social Structure in Indian History* (Madison: 1969).

GADGIL, D. R., *Industrial Evolution of India in Recent Times*, Fourth Edition (Bombay: 1942).

GOPAL, Sarvepalli, *British Policy in India 1858–1905* (Cambridge: 1966).

GRAMPP, William D., *The Manchester School of Economics* (Stanford: 1960).

GUHA, Ranajit, *A Rule of Property for Bengal: An Essay on the Idea of Permanent Settlement* (Paris: 1963).

GUPTA, S. C., *Agrarian Relations and Early British Rule in India* (Bombay: 1964).

HARLOW, Vincent T., *The Founding of the Second British Empire 1763–1793, 2 Vols.* (London: 1953, 1964).

HARNETTY, Peter, *Imperialism and Free Trade* (Manchester: 1972).

HUSAIN, Mohammed Imtiaj, *Land Revenue Policy in North-India 1801–1833* (Calcutta: 1967).

HUTCHISON, T. W., *'Positive' Economics and Policy Objectives* (London: 1964).

KLING, Blair, *The Blue Mutiny, The Indigo Disturbances in Bengal 1859–62* (Philadelphia: 1965).

KNORR, Klaus E., *A History of British Colonial Theories: 1570–1850* (Toronto: 1944).

KOEBNER, Richard and SCHMIDT, Helmut, *Imperialism: The Story and Significance of a Political Word 1840–1960* (Cambridge: 1964).

KUMAR, Ravinder, *Western India in the Nineteenth Century: A Study in Social History of the Maharashtra* (London: 1968).

MARSHALL, P. J. *Problems of Empire: Britain and India 1757–1813* (London: 1968).

MAYHEW, Arthur, *The Education of India. A Study of British Educational Policy in India 1835–1920* (London: 1926).

METCALF, Thomas R., *The Aftermath of Revolt in India, 1857–1870* (New Jersey: 1964).

MISRA, B. B., *The Administrative History of India 1834–1947* (London: 1969).

MISRA, B. B., *The Indian Middle Class: Their Growth in Modern Times* (London: 1961).

MOORE, R. J., *Sir Charles Wood's Indian Policy 1853–1866* (Manchester: 1966).

MUKHERJEE, Nilmani, *The Ryotwari System in Madras 1792–1827* (Calcutta: 1962).

NIYOGI, J. P., *Evolution of Indian Income Tax* (London: 1929).

PANIGRAHI, Devendra, *Charles Metcalfe in India: Ideas and Administration* (Delhi: 1968).

PHILIPS, C. J., *The East India Company 1784–1834* (Manchester: 1940).

PHILIPS, C. H. (ed.), *The Evolution of India and Pakistan 1858–1947 Select Documents* (London: 1962).

PLATT, D. C. M., *Finance, Trade, and Politics in British Foreign Policy 1815–1914* (Oxford: 1968).

RAJ, Jagdish, *Mutiny and British Land Policy in North India* (Bombay: 1966).

REDFORD, Arthur, *Manchester Merchants and Foreign Trade*, 2 vols. (Manchester: 1934, 1956).

ROBBINS, Lionel, *The Theory of Economic Policy in English Classical Political Economy* (London: 1953).

RUTHNASWAMY, M., *Some Influences that made the British Administrative System in India* (Madras: 1939).

SARADA RAJU, A., *Economic Conditions in the Madras Presidency 1800–1850* (Madras: 1941).

SCHLATTER, R., *Private Property: The History of an Idea* (London: 1951).

SEMMEL, Bernard, *The Rise of Free Trade Imperialism: Classical Political Economy, The Empire of Free Trade and Imperialism 1750–1850* (London: 1970).

SEN, Sunil Kumar, *Economic Policy and Development of India 1848–1926* (Calcutta: 1966).

SHAW, A. G. L. (ed.), *Great Britain and the Colonies 1815–1865* (London: 1969).

SILVER, Arthur, *Manchester Men and Indian Cotton 1847–72* (Manchester: 1965).

SINHA, N. C., *Studies in Indo-British Economy Hundred Years Ago* (Calcutta: 1946).

SINHA, N. K., *The Economic History of Bengal*, 3 vols. (Calcutta: 1956–62).

SRIVASTAVA, Hari Shankar, *The History of Indian Famines and Development of Famine Policy 1858–1918* (Delhi: 1968).

STOKES, Eric, *The English Utilitarians and India* (Oxford: 1959).

THOMAS, P. J., *Mercantilism and East India Trade* (London: 1926).

THORNER, Daniel, *Investment in Empire: British Railway and Steam-Shipping Enterprise in India 1825–1849* (Philadelphia: 1950).

THORNTON, A. P., *The Imperial Idea and its Enemies*, (London: 1959).

TRIPATHI, Amales, *Trade and Finance in the Bengal Presidency 1793–1833* (Bombay: 1956).

WILLIAMS, Judith Blow, *British Commercial Policy and Trade Expansion 1750–1850* (Oxford: 1972).

WINCH, D. N., *Classical Political Economy and Colonies* (London: 1965).

ZWEIG, Ferdinand, *Economic Ideas: A Study of Historial Perspectives* (New York: 1950).

INDEX